ALGERIA

EXPORT-IMPOR, TRADE AND BUSINESS DIRECTORY

STRATEGIC INFORMATION AND CONTACTS

International Business Publications, USA
Washington DC, USA - Algeria

ALGERIA

EXPORT-IMPOR, TRADE AND BUSINESS DIRECTORY

STRATEGIC INFORMATION AND CONTACTS

UPDATED ANNUALLY

We express our sincere appreciation to all government agencies and international organizations which provided information and other materials for this directory

Cover Design: **International Business Publications, USA**

2018 Edition Updated Reprint International Business Publications, USA
ISBN 1-4330-0082-2

For additional analytical, business and investment opportunities information, please contact Global Investment & Business Center, USA at (703) 370-8082. Fax: (703) 370-8083. E-mail: ibpusa3@gmail.com
Global Business and Investment Info Databank - www.ibpus.com

Printed in the USA

ALGERIA

EXPORT-IMPOR, TRADE AND BUSINESS DIRECTORY

STRATEGIC INFORMATION AND CONTACTS

TABLE OF CONTENTS

STRATEGIC AND DEVELOPMENT PROFILES

BASIC PROFILE

Capital and largest city	Algiers 36°42′N 3°13′E36.700°N 3.217°E
Official languages	Arabic
Other languages	• Berber language (constitutionally national) • French (business and education)
Ethnic groups	• 99% Arab-Berber • 1% European and others
Religion	Sunni Islam
Demonym	Algerian
Government	Unitary semi-presidential republic
- President	Abdelaziz Bouteflika
- Prime Minister	Abdelmalek Sellal
Legislature	Parliament
- Upper house	Council of the Nation
- Lower house	People's National Assembly
	Independence from France
- Recognized	3 July 1962
- Declared	5 July 1962
	Area
- Total	2,381,741 km^2 (10th) 919,595 sq mi
- Water (%)	negligible
	Population
- 2014 estimate	38,700,000 (34th)
- 2013 census	37,900,000
- Density	15.9/km^2 (208th) 37.9/sq mi
GDP (PPP)	2014 estimate
- Total	$302.476 billion
- Per capita	$7,816
GDP (nominal)	2014 estimate
- Total	$219.453 billion
- Per capita	$5,670
Gini (1995)	35.3 medium
HDI (2013)	0.717 high · 93rd
Currency	Algerian dinar (DZD)
Time zone	CET (UTC+01)

Drives on the	right
Calling code	+213
ISO 3166 code	DZ
Internet TLD	• .dz • .الجزائر

Algeria officially **People's Democratic Republic of Algeria**, is a country in North Africa on the Mediterranean coast. Its capital and most populous city is Algiers. With a total area of 2,381,741 square kilometres (919,595 sq mi), 90% of which is desert, Algeria is the tenth-largest country in the world, and the largest in Africa and on the Mediterranean. The country is bordered in the northeast by Tunisia, in the east by Libya, in the west by Morocco, in the southwest by Western Sahara, Mauritania, and Mali, in the southeast by Niger, and in the north by the Mediterranean Sea.

The territory of today's Algeria was the home of many prehistoric cultures, including Aterian and Capsian and the Proto-Berber cultures. Its area has known many empires and dynasties, including ancient Numidians, Phoenicians, Carthaginians, Romans, Vandals, Byzantines, Umayyads, Abbasids, Fatimids, Hammadids, Almoravids, Almohads, Ottomans and the French colonial empire. In recent decades, Algeria has experienced increased identity recognition demands, in response to which, Tamazight, the language of their 13,000 year old people, has been constitutionalized as a national language. Algeria is a semi-presidential republic consisting of 48 provinces and 1541 communes. With a population of 37.9 million, it is the 35th most populated country on Earth. Abdelaziz Bouteflika has been the President of Algeria since 1999 and has won four consecutive elections. However, according to the Democracy Index, Algeria is an authoritarian regime.

Algeria's economy is largely based on hydrocarbons, due to which manufacturing has suffered from Dutch disease. The country supplies large amounts of natural gas to Europe, and energy exports are the backbone of the economy. According to OPEC Algeria has the 17th largest reserves of oil in the world, and the second largest in Africa, while it has the 9th largest reserves of natural gas. Sonatrach, the national oil company, is the largest company in Africa.

Algeria has the second largest military in North Africa with the largest defence budget in Africa. Algeria has had a peaceful nuclear program since the 1990s. Algeria is a member of the African Union, the Arab League, OPEC, and the United Nations, and is a founding member of the Arab Maghreb Union.

Background:	After more than a century of rule by France, Algerians fought through much of the 1950s to achieve independence in 1962. Algeria's primary political party, the National Liberation Front (FLN), has dominated politics ever since. Many Algerians in the subsequent generation were not satisfied, however, and moved to counter the FLN's centrality in Algerian politics. The surprising first round success of the Islamic Salvation Front (FIS) in the December 1991 balloting spurred the Algerian army to intervene and postpone the second round of elections to prevent what the secular elite feared would be an extremist-led government from assuming power. The army began a crackdown on the FIS that spurred FIS supporters to begin attacking government targets. The government later allowed elections featuring pro-government and moderate religious-based parties, but did not appease the activists who progressively widened their attacks. The fighting escalated into an

	insurgency, which saw intense fighting between 1992-98 and which resulted in over 100,000 deaths - many attributed to indiscriminate massacres of villagers by extremists. The government gained the upper hand by the late-1990s and FIS's armed wing, the Islamic Salvation Army, disbanded in January 2000. However, small numbers of armed militants persist in confronting government forces and conducting ambushes and occasional attacks on villages. The army placed Abdelaziz BOUTEFLIKA in the presidency in 1999 in a fraudulent election but claimed neutrality in his 2004 landslide reelection victory. Longstanding problems continue to face BOUTEFLIKA in his second term, including the ethnic minority Berbers' ongoing autonomy campaign, large-scale unemployment, a shortage of housing, unreliable electrical and water supplies, government inefficiencies and corruption, and the continuing activities of extremist militants. The 2006 merger of the Salafist Group for Preaching and Combat (GSPC) with al-Qaida (followed by a change of name to al-Qaida in the Lands of the Islamic Maghreb) signaled an increase in bombings, including high-profile, mass-casualty suicide attacks targeted against the Algerian government and Western interests. Algeria must also diversify its petroleum-based economy, which has yielded a large cash reserve but which has not been used to redress Algeria's many social and infrastructure problems.

GEOGRAPHY

Location:	Northern Africa, bordering the Mediterranean Sea, between Morocco and Tunisia
Geographic coordinates:	28 00 N, 3 00 E
Map references:	Africa
Area:	total: 2,381,740 sq km land: 2,381,740 sq km water: 0 sq km
Area - comparative:	slightly less than 3.5 times the size of Texas
Land boundaries:	total: 6,343 km border countries: Libya 982 km, Mali 1,376 km, Mauritania 463 km, Morocco 1,559 km, Niger 956 km, Tunisia 965 km, Western Sahara 42 km
Coastline:	998 km
Maritime claims:	territorial sea: 12 nm exclusive fishing zone: 32-52 nm
Climate:	arid to semiarid; mild, wet winters with hot, dry summers along coast; drier with cold winters and hot summers on high plateau; sirocco is a hot, dust/sand-laden wind especially common in summer
Terrain:	mostly high plateau and desert; some mountains; narrow, discontinuous coastal plain
Elevation extremes:	lowest point: Chott Melrhir -40 m highest point: Tahat 3,003 m
Natural resources:	petroleum, natural gas, iron ore, phosphates, uranium, lead, zinc
Land use:	arable land: 3.17% permanent crops: 0.28% other: 96.55%
Irrigated land:	5,690 sq km
Total renewable water resources:	14.3 cu km
Freshwater withdrawal (domestic/industrial/agricultural):	total: 6.07 cu km/yr (22%/13%/65%) per capita: 185 cu m/yr

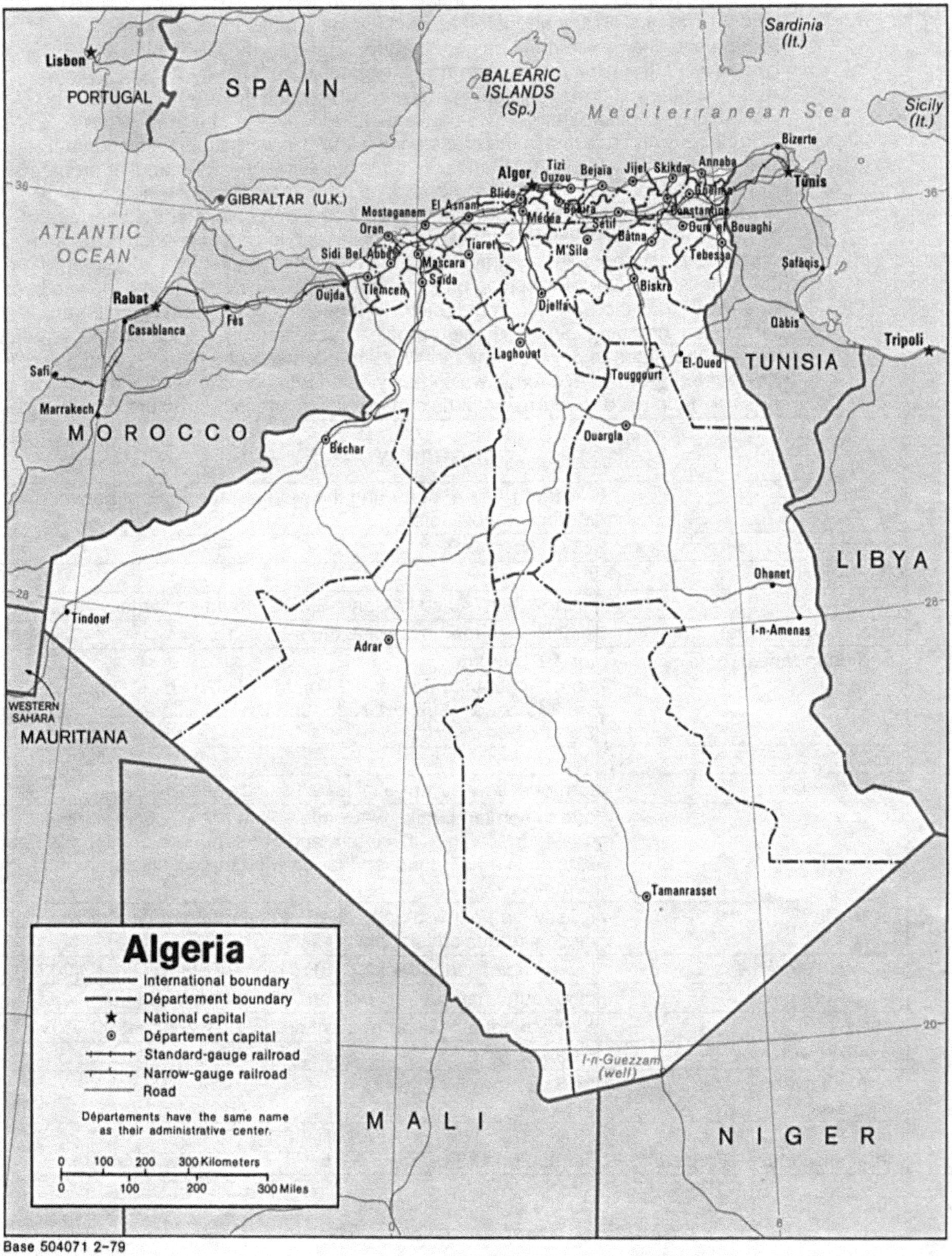
Algeria
International boundary
Département boundary
National capital
Département capital
Standard-gauge railroad
Narrow-gauge railroad
Road
Départements have the same name as their administrative center.
0 100 200 300 Kilometers
0 100 200 300 Miles
SPAIN
PORTUGAL
Lisbon
BALEARIC ISLANDS (Sp.)
Mediterranean Sea
Sardinia (It.)
Sicily (It.)
GIBRALTAR (U.K.)
ATLANTIC OCEAN
Rabat
Casablanca
Fès
Safi
Marrakech
MOROCCO
Oujda
Alger
Tizi Ouzou
Bejaïa
Jijel
Skikda
Annaba
Blida
El Asnam
Mostaganem
Oran
Médéa
Sétif
Constantine
Oum el Bouaghi
Bâtna
Tebessa
M'Sila
Tiaret
Sidi Bel Abbès
Mascara
Saïda
Tlemcen
Djelfa
Biskra
Laghouat
Touggourt
El-Oued
Ouargla
Béchar
Bizerte
Tunis
Safâqis
Qâbis
Tripoli
TUNISIA
LIBYA
Ohanet
I-n-Amenas
Tindouf
Adrar
WESTERN SAHARA
MAURITIANA
Tamanrasset
I-n-Guezzam (well)
MALI
NIGER
Base 504071 2-79

Natural hazards:	mountainous areas subject to severe earthquakes; mudslides and floods in rainy season
Environment - current issues:	soil erosion from overgrazing and other poor farming practices; desertification; dumping of raw sewage, petroleum refining wastes, and other industrial effluents is leading to the pollution of rivers and coastal waters; Mediterranean Sea, in particular, becoming polluted from oil wastes, soil erosion, and fertilizer runoff; inadequate supplies of potable water
Environment - international agreements:	party to: Biodiversity, Climate Change, Climate Change-Kyoto Protocol, Desertification, Endangered Species, Environmental Modification, Hazardous Wastes, Law of the Sea, Ozone Layer Protection, Ship Pollution, Wetlands signed, but not ratified: none of the selected agreements
Geography - note:	second-largest country in Africa (after Sudan)

PEOPLE

Population: 33,769,669

Age structure:
0-14 years: 26.3% (male 4,528,919/female 4,349,746)
15-64 years: 68.7% (male 11,699,701/female 11,509,619)
65 years and over: 5% (male 779,467/female 902,217)

Median age:
total: 26 years
male: 25.8 years
female: 26.2 years

Population growth rate: 1.209%

Birth rate: 17.03 births/1,000 population

Death rate: 4.62 deaths/1,000 population

Net migration rate: -0.31 migrant(s)/1,000 population

Sex ratio:
at birth: 1.05 male(s)/female
under 15 years: 1.04 male(s)/female
15-64 years: 1.02 male(s)/female
65 years and over: 0.86 male(s)/female
total population: 1.01 male(s)/female

Infant mortality rate:
total: 28.75 deaths/1,000 live births
male: 31.95 deaths/1,000 live births
female: 25.39 deaths/1,000 live births

Life expectancy at birth:
total population: 73.77 years
male: 72.13 years
female: 75.49 years

Total fertility rate: 1.82 children born/woman

HIV/AIDS - adult prevalence rate: 0.1%; note - no country specific models provided

HIV/AIDS - people living with HIV/AIDS: 9,100

HIV/AIDS - deaths: less than 500

Nationality: *noun:* Algerian(s)
adjective: Algerian

Ethnic groups: Arab-Berber 99%, European less than 1%
note: almost all Algerians are Berber in origin, not Arab; the minority who identify themselves as Berber live mostly in the mountainous region of Kabylie east of Algiers; the Berbers are also Muslim but identify with their Berber rather than Arab cultural heritage; Berbers have long agitated, sometimes violently, for autonomy; the government is unlikely to grant autonomy but has offered to begin sponsoring teaching Berber language in schools

Religions: Sunni Muslim (state religion) 99%, Christian and Jewish 1%

Languages: Arabic (official), French, Berber dialects

Literacy: *definition:* age 15 and over can read and write
total population: 69.9%
male: 79.6%
female: 60.1%

GOVERNMENT

Country name:

conventional long form: People's Democratic Republic of Algeria
conventional short form: Algeria
local long form: Al Jumhuriyah al Jaza'iriyah ad Dimuqratiyah ash Sha'biyah
local short form: Al Jaza'ir

Government type:

republic

Capital:

name: Algiers
geographic coordinates: 36 45 N, 3 03 E
time difference: UTC+1 (6 hours ahead of Washington, DC, during Standard Time)

Administrative divisions:

48 provinces (wilayas, singular - wilaya); Adrar, Ain Defla, Ain Temouchent, Alger, Annaba, Batna, Bechar, Bejaia, Biskra, Blida, Bordj Bou Arreridj, Bouira, Boumerdes, Chlef, Constantine, Djelfa, El Bayadh, El Oued, El Tarf, Ghardaia, Guelma, Illizi, Jijel, Khenchela, Laghouat, Mascara, Medea, Mila, Mostaganem, M'Sila, Naama, Oran, Ouargla, Oum el Bouaghi, Relizane, Saida, Setif, Sidi Bel Abbes, Skikda, Souk Ahras, Tamanrasset, Tebessa, Tiaret, Tindouf, Tipaza, Tissemsilt, Tizi Ouzou, Tlemcen

Independence:

5 July 1962 (from France)

National holiday:

Revolution Day, 1 November (1954)

Constitution:

adopted 8 September 1963; amended several times, last in 2008 (2013)

Legal system:

mixed legal system of French civil law and Islamic law; judicial review of legislative acts in ad hoc Constitutional Council composed of various public officials including several Supreme Court justices

International law organization participation:

has not submitted an ICJ jurisdiction declaration; non-party state to the ICCt

Suffrage:

18 years of age; universal

Executive branch:

chief of state: President Abdelaziz BOUTEFLIKA (since 28 April 1999)

head of government: Prime Minister Ahmed OUYAHIA (since 16 August 2017)
cabinet: Cabinet of Ministers appointed by the president

elections/appointments: president directly elected by absolute majority popular vote in two rounds if needed for a 5-year term (2-term limit reinstated by constitutional amendment in February 2016); election last held on 17 April 2014 (next to be held in April 2019); prime minister nominated by the president from the majority party in Parliament
election results: Abdelaziz BOUTEFLIKA reelected president for a fourth term; percent of vote - Abdelaziz BOUTEFLIKA (FLN) 81.5%, Ali BENFLIS (FLN) 12.2%, Abdelaziz BELAID (Future Front) 3.4%, other 2.9%

Legislative branch:
description: bicameral Parliament consists of the Council of the Nation (upper house with 144 seats; one-third of members appointed by the president, two-thirds indirectly elected by simple majority vote by an electoral college composed of local council members; members serve 6-year terms with one-half of the membership renewed every 3 years) and the National People's Assembly (lower house with 462 seats including 8 seats for Algerians living abroad); members directly elected in multi-seat constituencies by proportional representation vote to serve 5-year terms)
elections: Council of the Nation - last held on 29 December 2015 (next to be held in December 2018); National People's Assembly - last held on 4 May 2017 (next to be held in 2022)

election results: Council of the Nation - percent of vote by party - NA; seats by party - NA; National People's Assembly - percent of vote by party - NA; seats by party - FLN 164, RND 97, MSP-FC 33, TAJ 19, Ennahda-FJD 15, FFS 14, El Mostakbel 14, MPA 13, PT 11, RCD 9, ANR 8, MEN 4, other 33, independent 28

Judicial branch:
highest court(s): Supreme Court or Cour Supreme (consists of 150 judges organized into 4 divisions: civil and commercial; social security and labor; criminal; and administrative; Constitutional Council (consists of 12 members including the court chairman and deputy chairman); note - Algeria's judicial system does not include sharia courts
judge selection and term of office: Supreme Court judges appointed by the High Council of Magistracy, an administrative body presided over by the president of the republic, and includes the republic vice-president and several members; judges appointed for life; Constitutional Council members - 4 appointed by the president of the republic, 2 each by the 2 houses of Parliament, 2 by the Supreme Court, and 2 by the Council of State; Council president and members appointed for single 6-year terms with half the membership renewed every 3 years
subordinate courts: appellate or wilaya courts; first instance or daira tribunals

Political parties and leaders:
Algerian National Front or FNA [Moussa TOUATI]
Algerian Popular Movement or MPA [Amara BENYOUNES]
Algerian Rally or RA [Ali ZAGHDOUD]
Algeria's Hope Rally or TAJ [Amar GHOUL]
Dignity or El Karama [Mohamed BENHAMOU]
Ennour El Djazairi Party (Algerian Radiance Party) or PED [Badreddine BELBAZ]
Front for Change or FC [Abdelmadjid MENASRA]
Front for Justice and Development or El Adala [Abdallah DJABALLAH]
Future Front or El Mostakbel [Abdelaziz BELAID]
Green Algeria Alliance or AAV [Bouguerra SOLTANI] (includes Islah, Ennahda Movement, and MSP)
Islamic Renaissance Movement or Ennahda Movement [Mohamed DOUIBI]
Justice and Development Front or FJD
Movement of National Understanding or MEN
Movement for National Reform or Islah [Djilali GHOUINI]
Movement of Society for Peace or MSP [Abderrazak MOKRI]
National Democratic Rally (Rassemblement National Democratique) or RND [Ahmed OUYAHIA]
National Front for Social Justice or FNJS [Khaled BOUNEDJEMA]
National Liberation Front or FLN [Djamel OULD ABBES]
National Party for Solidarity and Development or PNSD [Dalila YALAQUI]
National Reform Movement or Islah [Djahid YOUNSI]
National Republican Alliance or ANR [Redha MALEK]
New Dawn Party or PFJ [Tahar BENBAIBECHE]
New Generation or Jil Jadid [Soufiane DJILALI]
Oath of 1954 or Ahd 54 [Ali Fawzi REBAINE]
Party of Justice and Liberty [Mohammed SAID]
Rally for Culture and Democracy or RCD [Mohcine BELABBAS]
Rally for Hope in Algeria or TAJ
Socialist Forces Front or FFS [Mustafa BOUCHACHI]
Union of Democratic and Social Forces or UFDS [Noureddine BAHBOUH]
Vanguard of Freedoms [Ali BENFLIS]
Youth Party or PJ [Hamana BOUCHARMA]
Workers Party or PT [Louisa HANOUNE]

note: a law banning political parties based on religion was enacted in March 1997

Political pressure groups and leaders:
Algerian League for the Defense of Human Rights or LADDH [Noureddine BENISSAD]
SOS Disparus [Nacera DUTOUR]
Youth Action Rally or RAJ

International organization participation:
ABEDA, AfDB, AFESD, AMF, AMU, AU, BIS, CAEU, CD, FAO, G-15, G-24, G-77, IAEA, IBRD, ICAO, ICC (national committees), ICRM, IDA, IDB, IFAD, IFC, IFRCS, IHO, ILO, IMF, IMO, IMSO, Interpol, IOC, IOM, IPU, ISO, ITSO, ITU, ITUC (NGOs), LAS, MIGA, MONUSCO, NAM, OAPEC, OAS (observer), OIC, OPCW, OPEC, OSCE (partner), UN, UNCTAD, UNESCO, UNHCR, UNIDO, UNITAR, UNWTO, UPU, WCO, WHO, WIPO, WMO, WTO (observer)

Diplomatic representation in the US:
chief of mission: Ambassador Madjid BOUGUERRA (since 23 February 2015)
chancery: 2118 Kalorama Road NW, Washington, DC 20008
telephone: [1] (202) 265-2800
FAX: [1] (202) 986-5906
consulate(s) general: New York

Diplomatic representation from the US:
chief of mission: Ambassador John P. DESROCHER (since 5 September 2017)
embassy: 05 Chemin Cheikh Bachir, El Ibrahimi, El-Biar 16030 Algieria
mailing address: B. P. 408, Alger-Gare, 16030 Algiers
telephone: [213] (0) 770-08-2000
FAX: [213] (0) 770-08-2064

Flag description:

two equal vertical bands of green (hoist side) and white; a red, five-pointed star within a red crescent centered over the two-color boundary; the colors represent Islam (green), purity and peace (white), and liberty (red); the crescent and star are also Islamic symbols, but the crescent is more closed than those of other Muslim countries because the Algerians believe the long crescent horns bring happiness

National symbol(s):

star and crescent; fennec fox

National anthem:

name: "Kassaman" (We Pledge)
lyrics/music: Mufdi ZAKARIAH/Mohamed FAWZI
note: adopted 1962; ZAKARIAH wrote "Kassaman" as a poem while imprisoned in Algiers by French colonial forces

ECONOMY

Algeria's economy remains dominated by the state, a legacy of the country's socialist post-independence development model. In recent years the Algerian Government has halted the privatization of state-owned industries and imposed restrictions on imports and foreign involvement in its economy.

Hydrocarbons have long been the backbone of the economy, accounting for roughly 30% of GDP, 60% of budget revenues, and nearly 95% of export earnings. Algeria has the 10th-largest reserves of natural gas in the world and is the sixth-largest gas exporter. It ranks 16th in oil reserves. Hydrocarbon exports enabled Algeria to maintain macroeconomic stability and amass large foreign currency reserves while oil prices were high. In addition, Algeria's external debt is extremely low at about 2% of GDP. However, Algeria has struggled to develop non-hydrocarbon industries because of heavy regulation and an emphasis on state-driven growth. Declining oil prices since 2014 have reduced the government's ability to use state-driven growth to distribute rents and fund generous public subsidies. Algeria's foreign exchange reserves have declined by more than 40% since late 2013 and its oil stabilization fund has decreased from about $75 billion at the end of 2013 to about $7 billion in 2017, which is the statutory minimum.

Algiers has strengthened protectionist measures since 2015 to limit its import bill and encourage domestic production of non-oil and gas industries. Since 2015, the government has imposed additional regulatory requirements on access to foreign exchange for imports and import quotas for specific products, such as cars, to limit their importation. Meanwhile, Algeria has not increased non-hydrocarbon exports, and hydrocarbon exports have declined because of field depletion and increased domestic demand.

With declining revenues caused by falling oil prices, the government has been under pressure to reduce spending. A wave of economic protests in February and March 2011 prompted Algiers to offer more than $23 billion in public grants and retroactive salary and benefit increases, moves which continue to weigh on public finances. In 2016, the government increased taxes on electricity and fuel, resulting in a modest increase in gasoline prices, and in 2017 raised by 2% the value-added tax on nearly all products, but has refrained from directly reducing subsidies, particularly for education, healthcare, and housing programs.

Long-term economic challenges include diversifying the economy away from its reliance on hydrocarbon exports, bolstering the private sector, attracting foreign investment, and providing adequate jobs for younger Algerians.

GDP (purchasing power parity):

$629.3 billion (2017 est.)
$620.2 billion (2016 est.)
$600.4 billion (2015 est.)
note: data are in 2017 dollars
country comparison to the world: 37

GDP (official exchange rate):
$175.5 billion (2017 est.)

GDP - real growth rate:
1.5% (2017 est.)
3.3% (2016 est.)
3.7% (2015 est.)
country comparison to the world: 173

GDP - per capita (PPP):
$15,100 (2017 est.)
$15,200 (2016 est.)
$15,000 (2015 est.)
note: data are in 2017 dollars
country comparison to the world: 110

Gross national saving:
34.9% of GDP (2017 est.)
37.2% of GDP (2016 est.)
36.3% of GDP (2015 est.)
country comparison to the world: 13

GDP - composition, by end use:
household consumption: 42.7%
government consumption: 21.4%
investment in fixed capital: 42.7%
investment in inventories: 7.6%
exports of goods and services: 21%
imports of goods and services: -35.5% (2017 est.)

GDP - composition, by sector of origin:
agriculture: 13.2%
industry: 36.1%
services: 50.7% (2017 est.)

Agriculture - products:
wheat, barley, oats, grapes, olives, citrus, fruits; sheep, cattle
Industries:
petroleum, natural gas, light industries, mining, electrical, petrochemical, food processing

Industrial production growth rate:
0.9% (2017 est.)
country comparison to the world: 172

Labor force:
11.82 million (2017 est.)
country comparison to the world: 51

Labor force - by occupation:
agriculture: 30.9%
industry: 30.9%
services: 58.4% (2011 est.) (2011 est.)

Unemployment rate:
11.7% (2017 est.)
10.5% (2016 est.)
country comparison to the world: 153

Population below poverty line:
23%

Household income or consumption by percentage share:
lowest 10%: 2.8%

highest 10%: 26.8% (1995 est.)

Distribution of family income - Gini index:
35.3 (1995 est.)
country comparison to the world: 96

Budget:
revenues: $52.08 billion
expenditures: $70.74 billion (2017 est.)

Taxes and other revenues:
29.7% of GDP (2017 est.)
country comparison to the world: 84

Budget surplus (+) or deficit (-):
-10.6% of GDP (2017 est.)
country comparison to the world: 210

Public debt:
19.9% of GDP (2017 est.)
18% of GDP (2016 est.)
note: data cover central government debt, as well as debt issued by subnational entities and intra-governmental debt
country comparison to the world: 188

Fiscal year:
calendar year
Inflation rate (consumer prices):
5.5% (2017 est.)
6.4% (2016 est.)
country comparison to the world: 177

Central bank discount rate:
4% (31 December 2010 est.)
4% (31 December 2009 est.)
country comparison to the world: 98

Commercial bank prime lending rate:
8% (31 December 2017 est.)
8% (31 December 2016 est.)
country comparison to the world: 111

Stock of narrow money:
$86.45 billion (31 December 2017 est.)
$85.11 billion (31 December 2016 est.)
country comparison to the world: 43

Stock of broad money:
$126.5 billion (31 December 2017 est.)
$125 billion (31 December 2016 est.)
country comparison to the world: 54

Stock of domestic credit:
$105.8 billion (31 December 2017 est.)

$86.53 billion (31 December 2016 est.)
country comparison to the world: 56

Current account balance:
$-22.87 billion (2017 est.)
$-26.31 billion (2016 est.)
country comparison to the world: 194

Exports:
$33.15 billion (2017 est.)
$29.06 billion (2016 est.)
country comparison to the world: 60

Exports - commodities:
petroleum, natural gas, and petroleum products 97%

Exports - partners:
Italy 17.4%, Spain 12.9%, US 12.9%, France 11.4%, Brazil 5.4%, Netherlands 4.9%, Turkey 4.5%, Canada 4.3% (2016)

Imports:
$49.99 billion (2017 est.)
$49.43 billion (2016 est.)
country comparison to the world: 50

Imports - commodities:
capital goods, foodstuffs, consumer goods

Imports - partners:
China 17.8%, France 10.1%, Italy 9.8%, Spain 7.6%, Germany 6.4%, US 4.9%, Turkey 4.1% (2016)

Reserves of foreign exchange and gold:
$97.67 billion (31 December 2017 est.)
$114.7 billion (31 December 2016 est.)
country comparison to the world: 26

Debt - external:
$8.163 billion (31 December 2017 est.)
$5.088 billion (31 December 2016 est.)
country comparison to the world: 122

Stock of direct foreign investment - at home:
$26.24 billion (31 December 2017 est.)
$25.74 billion (31 December 2016 est.)
country comparison to the world: 72

Stock of direct foreign investment - abroad:
$2.123 billion (31 December 2017 est.)
$2.025 billion (31 December 2016 est.)
country comparison to the world: 81

Exchange rates:
Algerian dinars (DZD) per US dollar -

108.9 (2017 est.)
109.44 (2016 est.)
109.44 (2015 est.)
100.69 (2014 est.)
80.58 (2013 est.)

ENERGY

Electricity - production:

46.25 billion kWh
country comparison to the world: 54

Electricity - consumption:

33.68 billion kWh
country comparison to the world: 59

Electricity - exports:

803 million kWh
country comparison to the world: 62

Electricity - imports:

736 million kWh
country comparison to the world: 67

Electricity - installed generating capacity:

11.33 million kW
country comparison to the world: 52

Electricity - from fossil fuels:

97.5% of total installed capacity
country comparison to the world: 61

Electricity - from nuclear fuels:

0% of total installed capacity (2010 est.)
country comparison to the world: 35

Electricity - from hydroelectric plants:

2.5% of total installed capacity
country comparison to the world: 134

Electricity - from other renewable sources:

0% of total installed capacity
country comparison to the world: 149

Crude oil - production:

1.875 million bbl/day
country comparison to the world: 15

Crude oil - exports:

1.097 million bbl/day
country comparison to the world: 16

Crude oil - imports:

6,400 bbl/day
country comparison to the world: 79

Crude oil - proved reserves:

12.2 billion bbl
country comparison to the world: 16

Refined petroleum products - production:

571,400 bbl/day
country comparison to the world: 29

Refined petroleum products - consumption:

316,400 bbl/day
country comparison to the world: 40

Refined petroleum products - exports:

471,900 bbl/day
country comparison to the world: 14

Refined petroleum products - imports:

17,270 bbl/day
country comparison to the world: 110

Natural gas - production:

82.76 billion cu m
country comparison to the world: 10

Natural gas - consumption:

28.82 billion cu m
country comparison to the world: 29

Natural gas - exports:

52.02 billion cu m
country comparison to the world: 7

Natural gas - imports:

0 cu m
country comparison to the world: 151

Natural gas - proved reserves:

4.504 trillion cu m
country comparison to the world: 10

Carbon dioxide emissions from consumption of energy:

117.2 million Mt

COMMUNICATIONS

Telephones - main lines in use:

3.2 million
country comparison to the world: 49

Telephones - mobile cellular:

37.692 million
country comparison to the world: 32

Telephone system:

general assessment: privatization of Algeria's telecommunications sector began in 2000; three mobile cellular licenses have been issued and, in 2005, a consortium led by Egypt's Orascom Telecom won a 15-year license to build and operate a fixed-line network in Algeria; the license will allow Orascom to develop high-speed data and other specialized services and contribute to meeting the large unfulfilled demand for basic residential telephony; Internet broadband services began in 2003
domestic: a limited network of fixed lines with a teledensity of less than 10 telephones per 100 persons has been offset by the rapid increase in mobile-cellular subscribership; in 2011, mobile-cellular teledensity was roughly 100 telephones per 100 persons
international: country code - 213; landing point for the SEA-ME-WE-4 fiber-optic submarine cable system that provides links to Europe, the Middle East, and Asia; microwave radio relay to Italy, France, Spain, Morocco, and Tunisia; coaxial cable to Morocco and Tunisia; participant in Medarabtel; satellite earth stations - 51 (Intelsat, Intersputnik, and Arabsat)

Broadcast media:

state-run Radio-Television Algerienne operates the broadcast media and carries programming in Arabic, Berber dialects, and French; use of satellite dishes is widespread, providing easy access to European and Arab satellite stations; state-run radio operates several national networks and roughly 40 regional radio stations

Internet country code:

.dz

Internet hosts:

676
country comparison to the world: 178

Internet users:

4.7 million
country comparison to the world: 49

TRANSPORTATION

Airports:

157
country comparison to the world: 36

Airports - with paved runways:

total: 64
over 3,047 m: 12
2,438 to 3,047 m: 29
1,524 to 2,437 m: 17
914 to 1,523 m: 5
under 914 m: 1 (2013)

Airports - with unpaved runways:

total: 93
2,438 to 3,047 m: 2
1,524 to 2,437 m: 18
914 to 1,523 m: 39
under 914 m:
34 (2013)

Heliports:

3

Pipelines:

condensate 2,600 km; gas 16,415 km; liquid petroleum gas 3,447 km; oil 7,036 km; refined products 144 km

Railways:

total: 3,973 km
country comparison to the world: 45
standard gauge: 2,888 km 1.435-m gauge (283 km electrified)
narrow gauge: 1,085 km 1.055-m gauge (2008)

Roadways:

total: 113,655 km
country comparison to the world: 42
paved: 87,605 km (includes 645 km of expressways)
unpaved: 26,050 km

Merchant marine:

total: 38
country comparison to the world: 77
by type: bulk carrier 6, cargo 8, chemical tanker 3, liquefied gas 11, passenger/cargo 3, petroleum tanker 4, roll on/roll off 3
foreign-owned: 15 (UK, 15) (2010)

Ports and terminals:

major seaport(s): Algiers, Annaba, Arzew, Bejaia, Djendjene, Jijel, Mostaganem, Oran, Skikda
LNG terminal(s) (export): Bethioua, Skikida

TERRORIZM

Terrorist groups - home based:
al-Qa'ida in the Islamic Maghreb (AQIM):
aim(s): replace the Algerian Government with one ruled by Sharia; establish a regional Islamic caliphate across all of North and West Africa
area(s) of operation: leadership headquartered in Algeria; operates in Tunisia, Libya, and northern Mali
note(s): al-Qa□ida's affiliate in North Africa; Tunisia-based branch known as the Uqbah bin Nafi Battalion; Mali-based cadre merged with allies to form JNIM in March 2017, which pledged allegiance to AQIM and al-Qa□ida
Islamic State of Iraq and ash-Sham (ISIS)-Algeria:
aims(s): replace the Algerian Government with an Islamic state and implement ISIS's strict interpretation of Sharia
area(s) of operation: maintains an operational and recruitment presence mostly in the northeast
note(s): formerly known as Jund al-Khilafa - Algeria (JAK-A) (April 2018)
Terrorist groups - foreign based:
HAMAS:

aim(s): fundraising and diplomatic outreach in Algeria
area(s) of operation: small contingent of officials, probably in Algiers (April 2018)

MILITARY

Military branches:

People's National Army (Armee Nationale Populaire, ANP), Land Forces (Forces Terrestres, FT), Navy of the Republic of Algeria (Marine de la Republique Algerienne, MRA), Air Force (Al-Quwwat al-Jawwiya al-Jaza'eriya, QJJ), Territorial Air Defense Force (2009)

Military service age and obligation:

17 is the legal minimum age for voluntary military service; 19-30 years of age for compulsory service; conscript service obligation is 18 months (6 months basic training, 12 months civil projects)

Manpower available for military service:

males age 16-49: 10,273,129
females age 16-49: 10,114,552

Manpower fit for military service:

males age 16-49: 8,622,897
females age 16-49: 8,626,222

Manpower reaching militarily significant age annually:

male: 342,895
female: 330,098

Military expenditures:

4.48% of GDP
country comparison to the world: 7
4.36% of GDP (2011)
4.48% of GDP (2010)

TRANSNATIONAL ISSUES

Disputes - international:

Algeria and many other states reject Moroccan administration of Western Sahara; the Polisario Front, exiled in Algeria, represents the Sahrawi Arab Democratic Republic; Algeria's border with Morocco remains an irritant to bilateral relations, each nation accusing the other of harboring militants and arms smuggling; dormant disputes include Libyan claims of about 32,000 sq km still reflected on its maps of southeastern Algeria and the National Liberation Front's (FLN) assertions of a claim to Chirac Pastures in southeastern Morocco

Refugees and internally displaced persons:

refugees (country of origin): 90,000 (Western Saharan Sahrawi, mostly living in Algerian-sponsored camps in the southwestern Algerian town of Tindouf); 1,500 (Mali) (2013)
IDPs: undetermined (civil war during 1990s)

Trafficking in persons:

current situation: Algeria is a transit and, to a lesser extent, a destination and source country for women, and, to a lesser extent, men subjected to forced labor and sex trafficking; criminal networks, which sometimes extend to sub-Saharan Africa and to Europe, are involved in both human smuggling and trafficking; sub-Saharan adults enter Algeria voluntarily but illegally, often with the aid of smugglers, for onward travel to Europe, but some of the women are forced into prostitution; some Algerian women are also forced into prostitution; some sub-Saharan men, mostly from Mali, are forced into domestic servitude

tier rating: Tier 3 - Algeria does not fully comply with the minimum standards for the elimination of trafficking and is not making significant efforts to do so; the government has not held any perpetrators of sex trafficking or forced labor accountable with jail time; some trafficking victims are treated as illegal migrants and are subject to arrest, detention, and deportation because authorities continue to confuse human trafficking and smuggling; the government has not developed or employed systematic procedures for identifying trafficking victims and referring them for protective services; no public awareness campaigns are conducted and no plan of action was developed to complement Algeria's anti-trafficking law

IMPORTANT INFORMATION FOR UNDERSTANDING ALGERIA

PROFILE

OFFICIAL NAME: People's Democratic Republic of Algeria

LOCATION

Location: Northern Africa, bordering the Mediterranean Sea, between Morocco and Tunisia.
Area: *Total*--2,381,740 sq. km. *Land*--2,381,740 sq. km.; *water*--0 sq. km. More than 3 times the size of Texas.
Cities: *Capital*--Algiers.
Terrain: Mostly high plateau and desert; some mountains; narrow, discontinuous coastal plain. Mountainous areas subject to severe earthquakes; mud slides.
Climate: Arid to semiarid; mild, wet winters with hot, dry summers along coast; drier with cold winters and hot summers on high plateau; sirocco is a hot, dust/sand-laden wind especially common in summer.
Land use: *Arable land*--3%; *permanent crops*--0%, *permanent pastures*--13%; *forests and woodland*--2%.

GEOGRAPHY

Algeria, the second-largest state in Africa, has a Mediterranean coastline of about 998 kilometers (620 mi.). The Tellian and Saharan Atlas Mountain ranges cross the country from east to west, dividing it into three zones. Between the northern zone, Tellian Atlas, and the Mediterranean is a narrow, fertile coastal plain--the Tell (Arabic for hill)--with a moderate climate year round and rainfall adequate for agriculture. A high plateau region, averaging 914 meters (3,000 ft.) above sea level, with limited rainfall and great rocky plains and desert, lies between the two mountain ranges. It is generally barren except for scattered clumps of trees and intermittent bush and pasture land. The third and largest zone, south of the Saharan Atlas range of mountains, is mostly desert. About 80% of the country is desert, steppes, wasteland, and mountains.

Algeria's weather is irregular from year to year. In the north, the summers are usually hot with little rainfall. Winter rains begin in the north in October. Frost and snow are rare, except on the highest slopes of the Tellian Atlas Mountains. Dust and sandstorms occur most frequently between February and May.

Soil erosion from overgrazing and other poor farming practices; desertification; dumping of raw sewage, petroleum refining wastes, and other industrial effluents is leading to the pollution of rivers and coastal waters; the Mediterranean Sea, in particular, is becoming polluted from oil wastes, soil erosion, and fertilizer runoff; there are inadequate supplies of potable water.

ADMINISTRATIVE STRUCTURE

THE 48 WILAYAS OF ALGERIA			
01-Adrar	13 -Tlemcen	25 -Constantine	37 -Tindouf
02 -Chlef	14 -Tiaret	26 -Medea	38 -Tissemsilt
03 -Laghouat	15 -Tizi-Ouzou	27 -Mostaganem	39 -El Oued
04 -Oum El Bouaghi	16 - Alger*	28 -M'sila	40 -Khenchela
05 -Batna	17 - jelfa	29 -Mascara	41 -Souk Ahras
06 -Bejaia	18- Jijel	30 -Ourgla	42 -Tipaza
07 -Biskra	19 -Setif	31- Oran	43 -Mila
08 -Bechar	20 -Saida	32 -El Bayadh	44 -Ain Defla
09 -Blida	21 -Skikda	33 -Ilizi	45 -Naama
10 -Bouira	22 -Sidi Bel Abbes	34 -Bordj Bou Arreridj	46 -Ain Temouchent
11 -Tamanrasset	23 -Annaba	35 -Boumerdes	47 -ghardaia
12 -Tebessa	24 -Guelma	36 -ELTarf	48 -Relizane

PEOPLE

Nationality: *Noun*--Algerian(s); *adjective*--Algerian.
Population: 31,736,053.
Annual growth rate : 1.71%. *Birth rate*--22.76 births/1,000, population; *death rate*--5.22 deaths/1,000 population.
Ethnic groups: Arab-Berber 99%, European less than 1%.
Religions: Sunni Muslim (state religion) 99%, Christian and Jewish 1%.
Languages: Arabic (official), French, Berber dialects.
Education: *Literacy* (definition--age 15 and over can read and write)--total population, 61.6%; male 73.9%, female 49% Health : *Infant mortality rate*--40.56 deaths/1,000 live births. *Life expectancy at birth*--total population, 69.95 years; male 68.6 years, female 71.34 years.
Work force : 9.1 million. *Government*--29%; *construction and public works*--15%; *industry*--11%; *other*--20%.

Ninety-one percent of the Algerian population lives along the Mediterranean coast on 12% of the country's total land mass. Forty-five percent of the population are urban, and urbanization continues, despite government efforts to discourage migration to the cities. About 1.5 million nomads and semi-settled bedouin still live in the Saharan area. According to 1986 data, 45% of the population is under age 15.

Nearly all Algerians are Muslim, of Arab, Berber, or mixed Arab-Berber stock. A mostly foreign Roman Catholic community of about 45,000 exists, as do very small Protestant and Jewish communities. As of January 2002, there were about 600 American citizens in the country, the majority of whom live and work in the oil/gas fields of the south.

Algeria's educational system has grown dramatically since 1962; in the last 12 years, attendance has doubled to more than 5 million students. Education is free and compulsory to age 16. Despite government allocation of substantial educational resources, population pressures and a serious shortage of teachers have severely strained the system, as has terrorism attacks against the educational infrastructure during the 1990s. Modest numbers of Algerian students study abroad, primarily in Europe and Canada. In 2000, the government launched a major review of the country's educational system.

Housing and medicine continue to be pressing problems in Algeria. Failing infrastructure and the continued influx of people from rural to urban areas has overtaxed both systems. According to the UNDP, Algeria has one of the world's highest per housing unit occupancy rates for housing, and government officials have publicly stated that the country has an immediate shortfall of 1.5 million housing units.

HISTORY

Since the 5th century B.C., the indigenous tribes of northern Africa (identified by the Romans as "Berbers") have been pushed back from the coast by successive waves of Phoenician, Roman, Vandal, Byzantine, Arab, Turkish, and, finally, French invaders. The greatest cultural impact came from the Arab invasions of the 8th and 11th centuries A.D., which brought Islam and the Arabic language. The effects of the most recent (French) occupation--French language and European inspired socialism--are still pervasive.

North African boundaries have shifted during various stages of the conquests. The borders of modern Algeria were created by the French, whose colonization began 1830. To benefit French colonists, most of whom were farmers and businessmen, northern Algeria was eventually organized into overseas departments of France, with representatives in the French National Assembly. France controlled the entire country, but the traditional Muslim population in the rural areas remained separated from the modern economic infrastructure of the European community.

Indigenous Algerians began their revolt on November 1, 1954, to gain rights denied them under French rule. The revolution, launched by a small group of nationalists who called themselves the National Liberation Front (FLN), was a guerrilla war in which both sides used terrorist tactics. Eventually, protracted negotiations led to a cease-fire signed by France and the FLN on March 18, 1962, at Evian, France. The Evian accords also provided for continuing economic, financial, technical, and cultural relations, along with interim administrative arrangements until a referendum on self-determination could be held.

The referendum was held in Algeria on July 1, 1962, and France declared Algeria independent on July 3. On September 8, 1963, a constitution was adopted by referendum, and later that month, Ahmed Ben Bella was formally elected president. On June 19, 1965, President Ben Bella was replaced in a bloodless coup by a Council of the Revolution headed by Minister of Defense Col. Houari Boumediene who was elected president of the republic on December 10, 1976. He died 5 years later.

Following nomination by an FLN Party Congress, Col. Chadli Bendjedid was elected President in 1979 and re-elected in 1984 and 1988. A new constitution was adopted in 1989 that allowed the formation of political associations other than the FLN. It also removed the armed forces, which had run the government since the days of Boumediene, from a designated role in the operation of the government. Among the scores of parties that sprang up under the new constitution, the militant Islamic Salvation Front (FIS) was the most successful, winning more than 50% of all votes cast in municipal elections in June 1990 as well as in first stage of national legislative elections held in December 1991.

Faced with the real possibility of a sweeping FIS victory, the government canceled the second stage of elections in January 1992. This action, coupled with political uncertainty and economic turmoil, led to a violent reaction on the part of the Islamists. A campaign of terror in the country, including assassinations, bombings, and massacres, commenced. Charging the FIS with supporting or encouraging such actions, Bendjedid declared a national state of emergency, resigned, and appointed a five-member High Council of State (HCS) to run the government. The HCS officially dissolved and outlawed the FIS in 1992 and began a series of arrests and trials of FIS members that reportedly resulted in over 50,000 members being jailed.

Despite efforts to restore the political process, violence and terrorism characterized the Algeria landscape during the 1990s. In 1994, Lamine Zeroual was appointed Head of State for a 3-year term. During this period, the Armed Islamic Group (GIA) launched terrorist campaigns against government figures and institutions to protest the banning of the Islamist parties. A breakaway GIA group--the Salafist Group for Preaching and Call (GSPC)--also undertook terrorist activity in the country. Govenrment officials estimate that more than 100,000 Algerians died during this period.

Zeroual called for presidential elections in 1995, though some parties objected to holding elections that excluded the FIS. Zeroual was elected president with 75% of the vote. By 1997, in an attempt to bring political stability to the nation, the Rassemblement National Democratique (RND) party was formed by a more progressive group of FLN members. Zeroual announced that presidential elections would be held in early 1999, nearly 2 years ahead of the scheduled time.

Algerians went to the polls in April 1999, following a campaign in which seven candidates qualified for election. On the eve of the election, all candidates except Abdelaziz Bouteflika pulled out amid charges of widespread electoral fraud. Bouteflika, the candidate who appeared to enjoy the backing of the military, as well as FLN and RND party regulars, won with an official vote count of 70% of all votes cast. He was inaugurated on April 27, 1999 for a 5-year term.

President Bouteflika's agenda focused initially on restoring security and stability to the country. Following his inauguration, he proposed an official amnesty for those who fought against the government during the 1990s unless they had engaged in "blood crimes," such as rape or murder. This "Civil Concord" policy was widely approved in a nationwide referendum in September 2000. Government officials estimate that 85% of those fighting the regime during the 1990s have accepted the amnesty offer and have been reintegrated into Algerian society. Bouteflika also has launched national commissions to study education and judicial reform, as well as restructuring of the state bureaucracy. His government has set ambitious targets for economic reform and attracting foreign investment.

Three years into Bouteflika's mandate, the security situation in Algeria has improved markedly. However, terrorism has not been totally eliminated, and terrorist incidents still occur, particularly in remote or isolated areas of the country. An estimated 100-120 Algerians are killed monthly, down from a high of 1,200 or more in the mid-1990s. In 2001, Berber activists in the Kabyle region of the country, reacting to the death of a youth in gendarme custody, unleashed a resistance campaign against what they saw as government repression. Strikes and demonstrations in the Kabyle region have become commonplace as a result and some have spread to the capital. Chief among Berber demands is recognition of Amagizh (Berber) as a national language, restitution for death of Kabylies killed or wounded in demonstrations, and some type of autonomy for the region. Representatives of major Kabylie factions are currently in discussions with the government on this matter. In November 2001, devastating floods hit Algeria, killing more than 800 people, mostly in Algiers. The floods caused an estimated $350 million in damages. Algeria is planning for a new round of legislative elections in Spring 2002.

GOVERNMENT

GOVERNMENT

Type: Republic.
Independence: July 5, 1962 (from France).
Constitution: November 19, 1976, effective November 22, 1976; revised November 3, 1988, February 23, 1989, and November 28, 1996. NOTE: Referendum approving the revisions of November 28, 1996 was signed into law December 7, 1996.
Branches: Legal system based on French and Islamic law; judicial review of legislative acts in ad hoc Constitutional Council composed of various public officials, including several Supreme Court justices; has not accepted compulsory ICJ jurisdiction.
Administrative divisions: 48 provinces (wilayet; singular, wilaya). Suffrage: 18 years of age; universal.
Flag: Two equal vertical bands of green (hoist side) and white; a red, five-pointed star within a red crescent centered over the two-color boundary; the crescent, star, and color green are traditional symbols of Islam (the state religion).
National holiday: Revolution Day, November 1, 1954.

Under the 1976 Constitution (as modified 1979, and amended in 1988, 1989, and 1996) Algeria is a multi-party state. All parties must be approved by the Ministry of the Interior. To date, Algeria has had more than 40 legal political parties. According to the Constitution, no political association may be formed if it is "based on differences in religion, language, race gender or region." The head of state is the President of the republic, who is elected to a 5-year term, renewable once. Algeria has universal suffrage. The President is the head of the Council of Ministers and of the High Security Council. He appoints the Prime Minister who also is the head of government. The Prime Minister appoints the Council of Ministers.

The Algerian parliament is bicameral, consisting of a lower chamber, the National People's Assembly (APN), with 380 members and an upper chamber, the Council of Nation, with 144 members. The APN is elected every 5 years. The next round of legislative elections are scheduled to take place in 2002. Two-thirds of the Council of the Nation are elected by regional and municipal authorities; the rest are appointed by the President. The Council of the Nation serves a 6-year term with one-half of the seats up for election or reappointment every 3 years. Either the President or one of the parliamentary chambers may initiate legislation. Legislation must be brought before both chambers before it becomes law. Sessions of the APN are televised.

Algeria is divided into 48 wilaya (state or province) headed by walis (governors) who report to the Minister of Interior. Each wilaya is further divided into communes. The wilayas and communes are each governed by an elected assembly.

PRINCIPAL GOVERNMENT OFFICIALS

President and Minister of National Defense--Abdelaziz Bouteflika
Prime Minister--Ahmed Ouyahia

Incumbent	Office	Website
Ahmed Ouyahia	Prime Minister	Prime Minister's website http://www.premier-ministre.gov.dz/
Noureddine Zerhouni	Deputy Prime Minister	
Abdelaziz Belkhadem	Minister of State, Personal Representative of the Head of	

	State	
Abdelmalek Guenaizia	Minister Delegate to the Minister of National Defence	
Dahou Ould Kablia	Minister of Interior and Local Government	
Mourad Medelci	Minister of Foreign Affairs	www.mae.dz
Tayeb Belaiz	Minister of Justice and Keeper of the Seals	www.mjustice.dz
Karim Djoudi	Minister of Finance	www.mf.gov.dz
Youcef Yousfi	Minister of Energy and Mines	www.mem-algeria.org
Abdelmalek Sellal	Minister of Water Resources	www.mre.dz
Abdelhamid Tenmar	Minister of Forecasting and Statistics	
Bouabdallah Ghlamallah	Minister of Religious Affairs and Waqf	www.marw.dz
Mohamed Cherif Abbes	Minister of Mojahedin	www.m-moudjahidine.dz
Cherif Rahmani	Aménagerment Minister of Planning and Environment	
Amar Tou	Minister of Transport	www.ministere-transports.gov.dz
Boubekeur Benbouzid	Minister of National Education	www.m-education.gov.dz
Rachid Benaissa	Minister of Agriculture and Rural Development	www.minagri.dz
Amar Ghoul	Minister of Public Works	www.mtp.gov.dz
Said Barkat	Minister of National Solidarity and Family	www.massn.gov.dz
Khalida Toumi	Minister of Culture	www.m-culture.gov.dz
Mustapha Benbada	Minister of Trade	www.mincommerce.gov.dz
Rachid Harraoubia	Minister of Higher Education and Scientific Research	www.mesrs.dz
Mahmoud Khedr	Minister of Relations with Parliament	www.mcrp.gov.dz
El Hadi Khaldi	Minister of Professional Education and Training	www.mfep.gov.dz
Noureddine Moussa	Minister of Housing and Urban Development	
Tayeb Louh	Minister of Labour, Employment and Social Security	www.mtess.gov.dz
Djamel Ould Abbes	Minister of Health, Population and Hospital Reform	
Smail Mimoune	Minister of Tourism and Handicrafts	www.mta.gov.dz
Hachemi Djiar	Minister of Youth and Sports	www.mjs.dz
Mohamed Benmeradi	Minister of Industry, Small and medium enterprise and	

	investment promotion	
Moussa Benhamadi	Minister of Post and Communication Technology and Information	www.mptic.dz
Abdellah Khenafou	Minister of Fisheries and Marine Resources	www.mpeche.gov.dz
Nacer Mehal	Communications Minister	www.ministerecommunication.gov.dz
Abdelkader Messahel	Minister Delegate to the Minister of Foreign Affairs with special responsibility for African and Maghreb Affairs	
Saadia Nouara Jaafari	Minister Delegate to the Minister of National Solidarity and Family, for the Family and the Status of Women	
Souad Bendjaballah	Minister Delegate to the Minister of Higher Education and Scientific Research, responsible for scientific research	
Ali Boukrami	Secretary of State to the Minister of Forecasting and Statistics, in charge of statistics	
Halim Benatallah	Secretary of State to the Minister of Foreign Affairs, in charge of the national community abroad	
Ahmed Noui	Secretary General of Government	

Ministers Delegate
Minister Delegate in Charge of Maghrebian and African Affairs--Messahel, Abdelkader
Minister Delegate in Charge of the Family and Women's Affairs--Djaafar, Nouara Saadia
Minister Delegate in Charge of Financial Reform--Djoudi, Karim
Minister Delegate in Charge of Local Collectives--Kablia, Daho Ould
Minister Delegate in Charge of National Community Abroad--Messadi, Sakina
Minister Delegate in Charge of Rural Development--Benaissa, Rachid
Minister Delegate in Charge of Scientific Research--Bendjaballah, Souad
Minister Delegate in Charge of Town Planning & Environment--Boukerzaza, Abderrachid
Minister Delegate in Charge of Participation & Investment Promotion--Hamlaoui, Yahia
Secretary General of the Government--Noui, Ahmed
Speaker of the National People's Assembly (Lower House)--Saidani, Amar
Speaker of the Council of Nations (Upper House)--Bensalah, Abdelkader
Governor, Central Bank--Laksaci, Mohamed

Ambassador to the United States--vacant
Permanent Representative to the UN, New York--Baali, Abdallah

POLITICAL CONDITIONS

A decade of terrorist violence in Algiera has resulted in more than 100,000 deaths since 1991. Although the security situation in the country has improved, addressing the underlying issues which brought about the political turmoil of the 1990s remain the government's major task. In keeping with its amended Constitution, the Algerian Government espouses participatory democracy and free-market competition. The government has stated that it will continue to open the political process and encourage the creation of political institutions. More than 40 political parties, representing a wide segment of the population, are currently active in Algerian national politics. Legislative elections are planned for Spring 2002. President Bouteflika has pledged to restructure the state as part of his overall reform efforts. However, no specifics are yet available as to how such reforms would affect political structures and the political process itself.

Algeria has more than 30 daily newspapers published in French and Arabic, with a total publication run of more than 1.5 million copies. Although relatively free to write as they choose, in 2001, the government amended the penal code provisions relating to defamation and slander, a step widely viewed as an effort to rein in the press. Government monopoly of newsprint and advertising is seen as another means to influence the press, although it has permitted newspapers to create their own printing distribution networks.

Population growth and associated problems--unemployment and underemployment, inability of social services to keep pace with rapid urban migration, inadequate industrial management and productivity, a decaying infrastructure--continue to plague Algerian society. Increases in the production and prices of oil and gas over the past decade have led to a budgetary surplus of close to $20 billion. The government began an economic reform program in 1993 which focuses on macroeconomic stability and structural reform. These reforms are aimed at liberalizing the economy, making Algeria competitive in the global market, and meeting the needs of the Algerian people.

DEFENSE

Algeria armed forces, known collectively as the Popular National Army (ANP), total 119,000 members, with some 100,000 reservists. The army is under the control of the president, who also is minister of National Defense. Defense expenditures accounted for some $1.9 billion or 1.5% of GDP. Two years of national military service is compulsory for males.

Algeria is a leading military power in the region and has its force oriented toward its western (Morocco) and eastern (Libya) borders. Its primary military supplier has been the former Soviet Union, which has sold various types of sophisticated equipment under military trade agreements, and China. Algeria has attempted, in recent years, to diversify its sources of military material. Military forces are supplemented by a 45,000-member gendarmerie or rural police force under the control of the president and 30,000-member Sureté National or Metropolitan police force under the Ministry of the Interior.

FOREIGN RELATIONS

Algeria has traditionally practiced an activist foreign policy and in the 1960s and 1970s was noted for its support of Third World policies and independence movements. Algerian diplomacy was instrumental in obtaining the release of U.S. hostages from Iran in 1980. Since his inauguration, President Bouteflika worked to restore Algeria's international reputation, traveling extensively throughout the world. In July 2001, he became the first Algerian President to visit the White House in 16 years. He has made official visits to France, South Africa, Italy, Spain, Germany, China, Japan, and Russia, among others, since his inauguration.

Algeria has taken the lead in working on issues related to the African Continent. Host of the OAU Conference in 2000, Algeria also was key in bringing Ethiopia and Eritrea to the peace table in 2000. It has worked closely with its African neighbors to establish the New African Partnership. Algeria has taken a lead in reviving the Union of the Arab Maghreb with its regional neighbors.

Since 1976, Algeria has supported the Polisario, a group claiming to represent the population of Western Sahara. Contending that Sahwari have a right to self determination under the UN Charter, Algeria has provided the Polisario with material, financial, and political support and sanctuary in southwestern Algeria around Tindouf. UN involvement in the Western Sahara includes MINURSO, a peacekeeping force, and UNHCR, for refugee assistance and resettlement. Active diplomatic efforts to resolve the dispute under the auspices of the Special Representative of the Secretary General are on-going. Although the land border between Morocco and Algeria was closed in the wake of a terrorist attack, the two have worked at improving relations. Algeria has friendly relations with its other neighbors in the Mahgreb, Tunisia and Libya, and with its Sub-Saharan neighbors, Mali and Niger. It closely monitors developments in the Middle East and has been strong proponent of the rights of the Palestinian people, calling publicly called for an end to violence in the Occupied Territories.

Algeria has diplomatic relations with more than 100 foreign countries, and over 90 countries maintain diplomatic representation in Algiers.

U.S.-ALGERIAN RELATIONS

In July 2001, President Bouteflika became the first Algerian President to visit the White House since 1985. This visit, followed by a second meeting in November 2001, is indicative of the growing relationship between the United States and Algeria. The United States and Algeria worked closely on the 2000 peace accords between Ethiopia and Eritrea, and the United States consult closely on key international and regional issues. The pace and scope of senior-level visits has accelerated: after a hiatus of more than a decade, three Cabinet-level officials visited Algeria in 2000-01. Since the September 11, 2001 terrorist attacks in the United States, contacts in key areas of mutual concern, including law enforcement and counter-terrorism cooperation, have intensified. Algeria has publicly condemned the terrorist attacks on the United States and has been strongly supportive of the international war against terrorism.

The U.S.-Algerian economic relationship is deepening and broadening. U.S. direct investment in Algeria totals $4.5 billion, most of which in the petroleum sector, which U.S. companies dominate. American companies also are active in the banking and finance, services, pharmaceuticals, medical facilities, telecommunications, aviation, and information technology sectors. An American Chamber of Commerce was established in 2002, consisting of 40 members. Algeria is the United States' fifth-largest market in the Middle East/North African region. Exports to Algeria from the United States rose by more than 150% in 2001. Algeria exports $3 billion of petroleum products and LNG to the United States, primarily to New England.

In July 2001, the United States and Algeria signed a Trade and Investment Framework Agreement which establishes common principles on which the economic relationship is founded. The Eximbank has an active guarantee program in Algeria; current exposure is more than $1.9 billion, primarily for petroleum projects and aircraft acquisition. Within the framework of the U.S.-North African Economic Partnership (USNAEP), the United States provides about $1.2 million in technical assistance to Algeria. This program supports and encourages Algeria's economic reform program and includes support for privatization, implementation of intellectual property protection, WTO accession negotiations, and improving the investment climate. In addition, the U.S. Department of Agriculture has provided Algeria with a GSM 102 program valued at $50 million for the purchase of U.S. agricultural products.

The United States has a small ($200,000 per year) International Military Education and Training (IMET) Program for training Algerian military personnel in the United States. Contacts between the Algerian and U.S. militaries have accelerated in the past 2 years: Algeria has hosted U.S. Naval ship visits and has begun a series of joint Naval exercises. Staff exchanges between the two sides are frequent ,and Algeria has hosted senior U.S. military officials.

The United States has a modest exchange program in Algeria, which includes Humphrey and Fulbright Educational grants. In 2001, Algeria was the recipient of a grant under a new U.S. program, the Ambassadors' Fund for Cultural Preservation. That fund made a grant of $15,000 for the protection of Roman mosaics at an antiquities site at Cherchell.

The official U.S. presence in Algeria remains limited, due in large part to reductions in staff during the mid-1990s in response to a deteriorating security environment. During the past 2 years, the embassy has moved toward more normal operations and now provides most embassy services to the American and Algerian community.

PRINCIPAL U.S. OFFICIALS

chief of mission: Ambassador John P. DESROCHER (since 5 September 2017)

Deputy Chief of Mission--Thomas F. Daughton
Political/Economic Chief--Mark Schapiro
Economic/Commercial Officer--Jeffrey Mazur
Foreign Commercial Service Officer (resident in Casablanca)--Rick Ortiz
Foreign Agriculture Service Officer (resident in Rabat)--Mike Fay
Consular Officer--Joshua Fischell
Management Officer--Kristi Morton-Lahmar
Public Affairs Officer--Rafik Mansour
Defense Attaché--Col. Steven Drago, USAF
Office of Defense Cooperation--Lt. Col. James D'Amour, USAF
Regional Security Officer--Melissa Foynes

The U.S. embassy is located at 4 Chemin Cheich Bachir Brahimi, Algiers; Tel. 213 (21) 691255; Fax: 213 (21) 693979.

ECONOMY

Currency	Algerian dinar (DZD)
Trade organisations	OPEC, GECF, WTO and others
	Statistics
GDP	$522.6 billion
GDP rank	46th (nominal) / 34th (PPP)
GDP growth	3.3%
GDP per capita	$13,788 PPP
GDP by sector	agriculture: 8.4%; industry: 61.1%; services: 31.5%
Inflation (CPI)	3.9%
Population below poverty line	23%
Gini coefficient	35.3
Labour force	11.31 million
Labour force by occupation	agriculture: 14%; industry: 13.4%; construction and public works: 10%; trade: 14.6%; government: 32%; other: 16%
Unemployment	9.8%

Main industries	petroleum, natural gas, light industries, mining, electrical, petrochemical, food processing, steel
Ease-of-doing-business rank	148th
	External
Exports	$76.84 billion (2012 est.)
Export goods	petroleum, natural gas, electronics and petroleum products 97%
Main export partners	United States 16.1% Spain 13.9% Canada 10.4% Netherlands 8.4% France 8.0% Brazil 5.6% United Kingdom 5.1%
Imports	$48.27 billion
Import goods	capital goods, foodstuffs, consumer goods
Main import partners	France 17.2% China 11.5% Spain 9.4% Italy 9.1% Germany 4.6%
FDI stock	$17.34 billion
Gross external debt	$5.413 billion
	Public finances
Public debt	8.5% of GDP
Revenues	$79.32 billion
Expenses	$84.29 billion
Foreign reserves	$190.5 billion

In 2012, the Algerian economy grew by 2.5%, up slightly from 2.4% in 2011. Excluding hydrocarbons, growth has been estimated at 5.8% (up from 5.7% in 2011). Inflation is increasing and is estimated at 8.9% (up from 4.49% in 2011). Despite the financial authorities' good performance, thanks to modernisation reforms, the budget deficit widened to 3.3% of GDP in 2012 (as against 1.3% in 2011) due to the continuation of the expansionary fiscal policy initiated in 2011 to meet strong social demands in terms of purchasing power, jobs and housing. The oil and gas sector is the country's main source of revenues, having generated about 70% of total budget receipts. The economy is projected to grow by 3.2% in 2013 and by 4.0% in 2014. The country's external position remained comfortable in 2012, with a trade surplus of about USD 27.18 billion.

The current-account surplus is estimated at 8.2% of GDP and official foreign-exchange reserves have been estimated at USD 190.7 billion at end-December 2012, or the equivalent of more than three years of imports of non-factor goods and services. Oil and gas export earnings made up more than 97% of total exports. Algeria has enormous possibilities to boost its economic growth, including huge foreign-exchange reserves derived from oil and gas. A development strategy targeting stronger, sustained growth would create more jobs, especially for young people, and alleviate the housing shortage the country is facing. The national strategic option is therefore to revitalise the process intended to diversify the economy starting with the non-oil sector while deepening the reforms needed for the structural transformation of the economy

Algeria is classified as an upper middle income country by the World Bank. Algeria's currency is the dinar (DZD). The economy remains dominated by the state, a legacy of the country's socialist post-independence development model. In recent years, the Algerian government has halted the privatization of state-owned industries and imposed restrictions on imports and foreign involvement in its economy.

Algeria has struggled to develop industries outside hydrocarbons in part because of high costs and an inert state bureaucracy. The government's efforts to diversify the economy by attracting foreign and domestic investment outside the energy sector have done little to reduce high youth unemployment rates or to address housing shortages. The country is facing a number of short-term and medium-term problems, including the need to diversify the economy, strengthen political, economic and financial reforms, improve the business climate and reduce inequalities amongst regions.

A wave of economic protests in February and March 2011 prompted the Algerian government to offer more than $23 billion in public grants and retroactive salary and benefit increases. Public spending has increased by 27% annually during the past 5 years. The 2010–14 public-investment programme will cost US$286 billion, 40% of which will go to human development

The Algerian economy grew by 2.6% in 2011, driven by public spending, in particular in the construction and public-works sector, and by growing internal demand. If hydrocarbons are excluded, growth has been estimated at 4.8%. Growth of 3% is expected in 2012, rising to 4.2% in 2013. The rate of inflation was 4% and the budget deficit 3% of GDP. The current-account surplus is estimated at 9.3% of GDP and at the end of December 2011, official reserves were put at US$182 billion. Inflation, the lowest in the region, has remained stable at 4% on average between 2003 and 2007.

In 2011 Algeria announced a budgetary surplus of $26.9 billion, 62% increase in comparison to 2010 surplus. In general, the country exported $73 billion worth of commodities while it imported $46 billion.

Thanks to strong hydrocarbon revenues, Algeria has a cushion of $173 billion in foreign currency reserves and a large hydrocarbon stabilization fund. In addition, Algeria's external debt is extremely low at about 2% of GDP. The economy remains very dependent on hydrocarbon wealth, and, despite high foreign exchange reserves (US$178 billion, equivalent to three years of imports), current expenditure growth makes Algeria's budget more vulnerable to the risk of prolonged lower hydrocarbon revenues.

In 2011, the agricultural sector and services recorded growth of 10% and 5.3%, respectively. About 14% of the labor force are employed in the agricultural sector. Fiscal policy in 2011 remained expansionist and made it possible to maintain the pace of public investment and to contain the strong demand for jobs and housing. Algeria has not joined the WTO, despite several years of negotiations.

In March 2006, Russia agreed to erase $4.74 billion of Algeria's Soviet-era debt during a visit by Russian President Vladimir Putin to the country, the first by a Russian leader in half a century. In return, Algerian President Abdelaziz Bouteflika agreed to buy $7.5 billion worth of combat planes, air-defense systems and other arms from Russia, according to the head of Russia's state arms exporter Rosoboronexport.

The hydrocarbons sector is the backbone of the Algerian economy, accounting for roughly 60% of budget revenues, 30% of GDP, and over 95% of export earnings. Algeria has the fifth-largest reserves of natural gas in the world and is the second-largest gas exporter; it ranks 14th for oil reserves. Its key oil and gas customers are Italy, Spain, France, and the United States. U.S.

companies have played a major role in developing Algeria's oil and gas sector; of the $4 billion in U.S. investment in Algeria, the vast bulk is in the petroleum sector.

Faced with declining oil revenues and high-debt interest payments at the beginning of the decade, Algeria implemented a stringent macroeconomic stabilization program and rescheduled its Paris Club debt in the mid-1990s. The macroeconomic program has been particularly successful, reducing inflation to approximately 1% and narrowing the budget deficit. Algeria's economy has grown at about 4% annually since 1999. The country's foreign debt has fallen from a high of $28 billion in 1999 to its current level of $24 billion. The spike in oil prices in 1999-2000 and the government's tight fiscal policy, as well as a large increase in the trade surplus and the near tripling of foreign exchange reserves has helped the country's finances. However, an ongoing drought, the after effects of the November 10, 2001 floods and an uncertain oil market make prospects for 2002-03 more problematic. The government pledges to continue its efforts to diversify the economy by attracting foreign and domestic investment outside the energy sector. However, it has thus far had little success in reducing high unemployment, officially estimated at 30% and improving living standards.

President Bouteflika has announced sweeping economic reforms, which, if implemented, will significantly restructure the economy. Priority areas are banking reform, improving the investment environment, and reducing government bureaucracy. The government has announced plans to sell off state enterprises: sales of a national cement factory and steel plant have been completed and other industries are up for offer. In 2001, Algeria signed an Association Agreement with the European Union; it has started accession negotiations for entry into the World Trade Organization.

TRAVEL AND BUSINESS INFORMATION

The U.S. Department of State's Consular Information Program provides Consular Information Sheets, Travel Warnings, and Public Announcements.

Consular Information Sheets exist for all countries and include information on entry requirements, currency regulations, health conditions, areas of instability, crime and security, political disturbances, and the addresses of the U.S. posts in the country. **Travel Warnings** are issued when the State Department recommends that Americans avoid travel to a certain country.

Public Announcements are issued as a means to disseminate information quickly about terrorist threats and other relatively short-term conditions overseas which pose significant risks to the security of American travelers. Free copies of this information are available by calling the Bureau of Consular Affairs at 202-647-5225 or via the fax-on-demand system: 202-647-3000. Consular Information Sheets and Travel Warnings also are available on the Consular Affairs Internet home page: http://travel.state.gov. Consular Affairs Tips for Travelers publication series, which contain information on obtaining passports and planning a safe trip abroad are on the internet and hard copies can be purchased from the Superintendent of Documents, U.S. Government Printing Office, telephone: 202-512-1800; fax 202-512-2250.

Emergency information concerning Americans traveling abroad may be obtained from the Office of Overseas Citizens Services at (202) 647-5225. For after-hours emergencies, Sundays and holidays, call 202-647-4000.

Passport information can be obtained by calling the National Passport Information Center's automated system ($.35 per minute) or live operators 8 a.m. to 8 p.m. (EST) Monday-Friday ($1.05 per minute). The number is 1-900-225-5674 (TDD: 1-900-225-7778). Major credit card users (for a flat rate of $4.95) may call 1-888-362-8668 (TDD: 1-888-498-3648). It also is available on the internet.

Travelers can check the latest health information with the U.S. Centers for Disease Control and Prevention in Atlanta, Georgia. A hotline at 877-FYI-TRIP (877-394-8747) and a web site at http://www.cdc.gov/travel/index.htm give the most recent health advisories, immunization recommendations or requirements, and advice on food and drinking water safety for regions and countries. A booklet entitled Health Information for International Travel (HHS publication number CDC-95-8280) is available from the U.S. Government Printing Office, Washington, DC 20402, tel. (202) 512-1800.

Information on travel conditions, visa requirements, currency and customs regulations, legal holidays, and other items of interest to travelers also may be obtained before your departure from a country's embassy and/or consulates in the U.S. (for this country, see "Principal Government Officials" listing in this publication).

U.S. citizens who are long-term visitors or traveling in dangerous areas are encouraged to register at the U.S. embassy upon arrival in a country (see "Principal U.S. Embassy Officials" listing in this publication). This may help family members contact you in case of an emergency.

ECONOMIC, BUSINESS AND LEGAL INFORMATION AND STRATEGIC OPPORTUNITIES

POLITICAL ENVIRONMENT

Algeria is an authoritarian regime, according to the Democracy Index 2010. The Freedom of the Press 2009 report gives it rating "Not Free".

Elected politicians are considered to have relatively little sway over Algeria. Instead, a group of unelected civilian and military "décideurs", known as "le pouvoir" ("the power"), actually rule the country, even deciding who should be president. The most powerful man may be Mohamed Mediène, head of the military intelligence.[60] In recent years, many of these generals have died or retired. After the death of General Larbi Belkheir, Bouteflika put loyalists in key posts, notably at Sonatrach, and secured constitutional amendments that make him re-electable indefinitely.

The head of state is the president of Algeria, who is elected for a five-year term. The president was formerly limited to two five-year terms, but a constitutional amendment passed by the Parliament on 11 November 2008 removed this limitation.[62] Algeria has universal suffrage at 18 years of age.[63] The President is the head of the army, the Council of Ministers the High Security Council. He appoints the Prime Minister who is also the head of government.

The Algerian parliament is bicameral; the lower house, the People's National Assembly, has 462 members who are directly elected for five-year terms, while the upper house, the Council of the Nation, has 144 members serving six-year terms, of which 96 members are chosen by local assemblies and 48 are appointed by the president.[65] According to the constitution, no political association may be formed if it is "based on differences in religion, language, race, gender, profession or region". In addition, political campaigns must be exempt from the aforementioned subjects.

Parliamentary elections were last held in May 2012, and were judged to be largely free by international monitors, though local groups alleged fraud and irregularities.[65] In the elections, the FLN won 221 seats, the military-backed National Rally for Democracy won 70, and the Islamist Green Algeria Alliance won 47

Political System Algeria has a popularly-elected president since November 1995. National legislative elections were held in June 1997. Most of Algeria's political parties fielded candidates. Some foreign and domestic observers who monitored the elections noted irregularities. Most Algerians nevertheless believe that the elections represented a modest step toward a more representative democracy. The two legal Islamist parties comprise a large parliamentary minority group and members of one of the parties are ministers of a coalition government. Municipal elections are scheduled for October 1997. A constitution approved in late 1996 will permit the installation of a second legislative chamber (a Senate) shortly after the municipal elections.

Security Environment The cancellation of parliamentary elections in January 1992 was one of the causes of the violence that Algeria is experiencing. Since then, armed Islamist groups have been targeting not only the security services but also civilians from all walks of life including journalists, intellectuals, government officials.

The victims have also included old men and women, and children. As many as 60,000 Algerians may have died of violence during the last five years. About 120 foreigners have been murdered since December 1993. Seven French monks were decapitated south of Algiers in April 1996.

About six months later an Eastern European national, a former military attache who had become a businessmen, had his throat slit in a park in Algiers. The group thought responsible for those murders has threatened specifically the Algerians and foreigners working in the hydrocarbons sector. Although violence has receded since 1994-1995, terrorists carried out bloody attacks against civilians throughout the past year.

RELATIONS WITH THE UNITED STATES

Algeria is an important trading partner of the United States in the Middle East/North Africa region. Algeria remained the fifth largest export market for U.S. products in the Arab World in 1996. U.S. exports totalled $632 or $911 million depending on whether statistics from the U.S. Census Bureau or the Algerian Customs Service are cited. The first figure represents a decline of 18.5 percent relative to that of 1995. The fall was due to weaker demand for agricultural commodities and intermediate goods, the latter reflecting widespread insolvency in Algeria's industrial sector. U.S. imports from Algeria rose to $2.3 billion in 1996. Natural gas and other energy products accounted for nearly all of these imports. In late spring of 1997 the U.S. Export-Import Bank guaranteed a $150 million loan to Algeria for projects in the energy sector.

The United States supports Algeria's economic reform program within the IMF and the World Bank. The U.S. Government believes that a successful economic reform program that improves general living standards is essential for long-term stability and social peace in Algeria. An end to terrorist violence, which remains an impediment to broad-based investment in the economy, would facilitate the reform process. Due to terrorism, the Department of State advises Americans not to travel to Algeria. Those who do are urged to have substantial armed protection while there. The United States welcomes Algeria's participation in multilateral regional discussions, such as those on the creation of a Middle East/North Africa Development Bank and at the Sharm al-Sheikh anti-terrorism summit, under the aegis of the Middle East peace process. The United States welcomes Algerian commercial and cultural exchange visitors to the United States.

RELATIONS WITH EU

POLITICAL BACKGROUND

President Bouteflika's programme is based on the return to peace in the country and restoring Algeria's image internationally. The *civil concord* law allowed members of armed groups who gave themselves up to benefit from amnesties under certain conditions. This option was meant to last for a 6-month period ending January 13, 2001, but in practice is still open.

In spite of the reintegration into Algerian society of Islamists who laid down their arms and the relative calm seen at the end of 1999 and beginning of 2000, violence and terrorist actions have flared up again, especially outside the cities. On the domestic political scene, the government in November 2000 refused to recognise Wafa, the new Islamist grouping led by Mr Taleb Ibrahimi.On the international scene, Algeria condemned the terrorist attacks of September 11 against the United States and has offered co-operation in the fight against international terrorist networks.

Riots broke out in the Kabylie region in April 2001 following the murder of a young student held in police custody. There have been many demonstrations since then, both in the Kabylie region and in other parts of the country, including Algiers. These have been put down violently. The President set up a national commission of inquiry and made public its report. The report implicated the national gendarmerie in the violence. On October 3, 2001, the President declared

Berber an official national language, announced compensation for the victims of violence, as well as the launch of legal proceedings against those responsible in the security forces.

In the area of fundamental freedoms and human rights, there are still concerns about the application of the law on civil concord, about torture, and about 4800 "disappeared" people. The written media is reasonably free as can be seen in the open nature of the political debate in the media. However, civil society was extremely concerned about an amendment to the penal code on the defamation of state institutions.

A government reshuffle on May 31, 2001 saw ministerial changes in the area of the economic reform programme. In April 2001, the government announced a major new programme to relaunch the economy over the 2001-2004 period. The pace of economic reform has been rather slow with the privatisation of public companies, in particular, still to be announced. However, three presidential decrees in August 2001, on privatisation, investments, and on customs duties could boost the reform process.

In foreign policy, Algeria works on the regional aspects of the Euro-Mediterranean Partnership. It also supports other regional integration activities like the Arab Maghreb Union, but the pace of progress in this area is influenced by the conflict in the Western Sahara and by relations with neighbouring Morocco. On the African scene, Algeria played an important mediating role in the Ethiopian/Eritrean conflict during its chairmanship of the Organisation of African Unity (OAU) in 2000.

Until the entry into force of the EU/Algeria Association Agreement, political dialogue takes place on an ad hoc basis, through twice-yearly meetings at ministerial level. The last meeting, in the Troika format, took place on December 5, 2001. The EU has also issued statements on the political situation in Algeria, the last on the situation in the Kabylie region, in June 2001 at the Göteborg European Council.

TRADE LINKS

Trade links between the EU and Algeria are good. The Union takes 62.7% of Algeria's exports and supplies 58% of its imports. The trade balance is in Algeria's favour (EUR 11,250 million in 2000). The Algerian economy is largely dependent on hydrocarbons (oil and gas), which make up 97% of exports, contribute 30% of GDP, and fund 65% of the State budget. Agriculture is marginal, while the non-hydrocarbons industrial sector contributes just 7% to GDP in spite of a massive restructuring and privatisation programme.

Thanks to two foreign debt reschedulings in 1994-1995, and with the help of IMF, the World Bank and the EU, Algeria has started an important economic reform programme and a withdrawal of the State from the economy. The main social and economic challenges facing the country are the privatisation programme, strengthening the non-hydrocarbon industrial sector and the regulatory framework, restructuring the financial services sector, job creation (with the official unemployment rate standing at 29.8%), and building and repairing housing (Algeria has one of the highest occupancy rates per housing unit in the world).

COMMUNITY AID

FINANCIAL PROTOCOLS

The political and security situation in the country has made financial co-operation between the EU and Algeria difficult, and has led to long delays in the implementation of this co-operation.

Channelled through four Financial Protocols, Community funds to the country amounted to EUR 949 million between 1978 and 1996. This was made up of EUR 309 million from the Community and EUR 640 million from the European Investment Bank. These funds are 66% committed, while the payment rate stands at 47%.

Projects have been funded in the following sectors: social and economic infrastructure (60%), water management (11%), agriculture and fisheries (9%), energy sector (7%), and scientific co-operation.

MEDA

Financial co-operation is being reorientated in light of the Association Agreement. Priorities for the future aim to contribute to the transition towards a market economy, develop the private sector, and strengthen the socio-economic and social balance in the country.

EUR 164 million of Meda funds were committed in the 1996-1999 period. Programmes committed in this period were:

- Structural adjustment facility: (EUR 125 million, EUR 30 million of which came from Meda), committed in 1996. Partial disbursement of the second tranche should take place soon.
- Promoting small- and medium-sized enterprises (EUR 57 million). This project has been operational since October 2000.
- Support for industrial restructuring and privatisation (EUR 38 million). This project has been operational since June 2001.
- Modernising the financial services sector (EUR 23 million). Financing convention signed in 2000, project has been operational since September 2000.
- Interest-rate subsidy on EIB loan for projects in the area of industrial waste clean-up operations (EUR 10.75 million).
- Project to support Algerian development organisations (EUR 5 million), committed at the end of 1999, and aiming to support 50-60 NGOs and development organisations.

EUR 90 million has been committed since 2000 for four new programmes. They are:

- Support for telecoms and postal services reform (EUR 17 million)
- Support for journalists and the Algerian media (EUR 5 million)
- Support to modernise the police force (EUR 8 million)
- Reform of professional training (EUR 60 million, end 2001).

In December 2001, the Med Committee gave its green light to the new National Indicative Programme for the 2002-2004 period. The programme gives even greater focus on the Association Agreement and will work in four main areas:

- Support for economic reforms and to strengthen market economy institutions
- Developing infrastructure
- Developing human resources
- State of law and good governance.

The European Investment Bank (EIB) has granted loans worth EUR 620 million since 1996. Sectors covered are energy, transport, water resources management, and the environment.

EC/ALGERIA AGREEMENTS

Financial co-operation is based on the 1979 Co-operation Agreement between the EC and Algeria, which was followed up by four Financial Protocols, then by the Barcelona Declaration and the MEDA regulation.

Negotiations on an Association Agreement ended in December 2001, and the Agreement was initialled by the two parties on December 19. The main elements of the agreement are:

- Political dialogue and regular economic dialogue;
- Gradual establishment of free trade area, in line with WTO rules;
- Clauses on freedom of establishment, liberalisation of services, free movement of capital and the application of Community rules on competition;
- Clauses in the area of justice and home affairs;
- Strengthening economic co-operation;
- Setting up social and cultural co-operation;
- Financial co-operation;
- Setting up an Association Council and Association Committee with decision-taking powers.

BILATERAL INVESTMENT AGREEMENTS

On July 13, 2001, the U.S. and Algeria signed a Trade and Investment Framework agreement (TIFA) to create a forum for involved discussion. The first TIFA Council meeting was held in Algiers April 8, 2001, and the second in Washington D.C December 2-3, 2004.

The discussions could eventually lead to a Bilateral Investment Treaty (BIT) and a Free Trade Agreement.

In December 2001, Algeria and the EU concluded negotiations on the Association Agreement that was ratified by the Algerian Senate on March 31, 2005 and took effect September 1 2005. The Association Agreement will commit both sides to further liberalization of bilateral trade and is intended to make Algerian businesses and consumers benefit from the development of trade and investment ties. (http://europa.eu.int/comm/external_relations/algeria/docs/index.htm[1]) The Agreement provides for the gradual removal of import duties on EU industrial products over twelve years, and removes duties immediately on 2,000 other products. The Agreement will lay an important foundation for economic liberalization in Algeria. It also provides for an exchange of concessions regarding trade in services. On December 12, 2002 a joint declaration of cooperation was signed among the members of the European Free Trade Association (EFTA, http://www.efta.int/[2]) with the European Union providing for expanded and liberalized trade with EFTA members Iceland, Liechtenstein, Norway and Switzerland.

Algeria has signed bilateral investment agreements for the protection and promotion of investments with the following countries in the indicated years: Belgium/Luxembourg (1991), Italy (1991), France (1993), Romania (1994), Spain (1994), China (1996), Germany (1996), Jordan (1996), Mali (1996), Vietnam (1996), Egypt (1997), Bulgaria (1998), Mozambique (1998), Niger (1998), Turkey (1998), Denmark (1999), Yemen (1999), Czech Republic , Greece , and Malaysia . There is no bilateral investment treaty between Algeria and the United States. Prospects for a U.S.-Algeria BIT were discussed at the December 2004 TIFA meetings and received periodic mention throughout 2005.

Algeria has also signed bilateral treaties to prevent double taxation with the following nations: United Kingdom (1981), France (1982), Tunisia (1985), Libyan Arab Jamahirya (1988), Morocco

(1990), Belgium (1991), Italy (1991), Romania (1994), Turkey (1994), Syrian Arab Republic (1997), Bulgaria (1998), Canada (1999), Mali (1999), Vietnam (1999), Bahrain , Oman , Poland , Ethiopia (2002), Lebanon (2002), Spain (2002), and Yemen (2002). There is no double taxation treaty between Algeria and the United States.

In 1990, Algeria signed both investment protection and double taxation agreements with the Arab Maghreb Union (UMA) countries (Libya, Morocco, Mauritania and Tunisia).

ECONOMY

Prior to independence in 1962 Algeria's economy had been dominated by agriculture for a millennium and was known as 'the breadbasket of the Roman empire'. However, with rising oil revenues throughout the 1960s and 1970s, the government embarked on a major program of industrialization which has transformed the economy, making Algeria one of the wealthiest nations in Africa. Fuelled by oil revenues, Algeria's economy grew dramatically throughout this period.

Declining oil prices during the 1980s drastically reduced economic growth of the now oil-dependent country. Annual per capita income fell from $2,360 in 1988 to $1,541 in 1992. As a socialist country, Algeria's entire oil industry is controlled by the state.

Although agriculture no longer dominates the economy it remains an important sector. During the first half of the 1990s the national budget registered expenditures of $14.6 billion as against revenues of $14.4 billion annually.

AGRICULTURE

Prior to independence Algeria provided 93% of its agricultural requirements. Today, the country must import over 60% of its cereal requirements. By the late 1980s agriculture only contributed 15% of Algeria's Gross Domestic Product.

Cereals including wheat, barley, oats, maize, and sorghum, comprise the country's main agricultural crops. Vegetables are also important: crops include beans, lentils, potatoes, peas, cucumbers, tomatoes, onions, carrots, melons, artichokes, sunflowers, sugar beets and tobacco. Grapes and a variety of citrus fruits including oranges, mandarins, lemons, grapefruit and clemencies are also grown. Exports include olives, figs, dates, wine and tobacco.

The agricultural sector has suffered from lack of effective government support. The government favored industry until agricultural output became a critical issue, but by the time there was administrative will to address the problem, financial resources had fallen as a result of declining oil revenues.

TRADE AND INDUSTRY

Algeria's main exports are natural gas, petroleum, iron ore, vegetables, tobacco, phosphates, fruit, cork and leather hides. Principal imports are machinery, textiles, sugar, cereals, iron and steel, coal and gasoline.

Almost two-thirds of all Algeria's export trade is with European Union countries, with the United States and Japan taking much of the remainder. Annual exports during the early 1990s amounted to about $11.6 billion, mostly in the form of petroleum, natural gas and lubricants, while imports totaled about $8.2 billion.

The sale of natural gas and petroleum provided Algeria with 87% of its foreign exchange earnings during 1992. Petroleum and natural gas industries generated 38.1% of the government's income and contributed about 17.7% of the country's Gross Domestic Product. However, with only 9,200 million barrels of proven reserves, Algeria's petroleum will be depleted within 21 years and the government has emphasized the exploitation of its natural gas reserves which, as of 1993, were 3,600 million cubic meters and estimated to last for 71 years.

Algeria has developed a petrochemical and refining industry based in Arzew, Bijaya and Skikda but thus far these projects have been costly and inefficient and have yet to contribute to the economy in a significant way.

The mining industry contributes 17% to Algeria's Gross Domestic Product. Mineral production includes mercury, iron ore, phosphates, zinc, silver, gypsum, and barite. The manufacturing industry contributes 14% to the GDP and includes construction materials (cement, bricks, structural steel), steel production, automobile manufacturing and consumer goods manufacturing.

The centrally controlled Algerian government has a large service sector encompassing industries like water supply, sewage, telecommunications and transport. Much of Algeria's financial resources have been channeled toward non-commercial projects and to finance a bloated socialist military and civilian bureaucracy. The services industry sector comprises 36% of the GDP.

ALGERIAN ECONOMY: IMF EVALUATION

Over the past four years, Algeria has implemented a comprehensive program of economic adjustment and structural reform, supported by a stand-by arrangement and subsequently, since May 1995, by an extended arrangement that expired on May 21, 1998. In addition to Fund resources, Algeria's program was supported by other multilateral and bilateral donors including the Arab Monetary Fund and the World Bank, and by debt relief from Paris and London club creditors. The objectives of the program included achieving macroeconomic stabilization and assisting Algeria in a process of reforms aimed at reinvigorating growth by creating a market-based and private sector-led economy integrated with the rest of the world.

Under the Fund-supported programs, Algeria was successful in restoring macroeconomic balances: inflation was lowered to 5 percent and international reserves exceeded nine months of imports at the beginning of 1998. At the same time, backed by a broad consensus between government, labor, and the private sector, a large number of reforms were implemented to dismantle the existing centrally planned system, open up the economy, and establish market mechanisms, including the liberalization of all prices and the elimination of generalized food subsidies. Moreover, the state started to withdraw from production activities, and a large number of local public enterprises have been closed or privatized. However, progress in privatizing the large public enterprises (EPEs) has been slow. This significant change in Algeria's economic direction was achieved against a backdrop of civil unrest that muted the supply response to economic reforms.

In 1997, despite the robust performance of the hydrocarbon sector, real GDP growth slowed to 1.2 percent after two consecutive years of growth at 4 percent. Agricultural output fell in the wake of a severe drought, and industrial production continued to decline due to the ongoing restructuring process in the public sector and low foreign and domestic investment. These developments put further strain on the labor market as unemployment remained high at around 28 percent. Meanwhile, tight fiscal and monetary policies, coupled with a relatively high level of oil prices, led to a strengthening of public finances and the external position. Indeed, the authorities, as in 1996, saved most of the oil windfall. As a result, the budget surplus reached 2.4 percent of GDP while the external current account showed a surplus equivalent to 7.3 percent of GDP, contributing to a further accumulation of international reserves. Economic reforms focused on restructuring public enterprises. More than half of the small local public enterprises were liquidated or privatized, while the public sector withdrew almost completely from distribution and importing activities. In addition, in the second half of 1997 Algeria accepted the obligations of the Fund's Article VIII and established the full convertibility of the dinar for current account transactions.

For 1998, while economic growth is likely to rebound, financial balances are expected to deteriorate due to the sharp decline in oil prices. Agricultural output should rebound in response to more favorable weather conditions and industrial production is projected to recover. Moreover, despite cuts in output to support international oil prices, hydrocarbon production is estimated to grow by about 6 percent. Nonetheless, with lower oil prices, the budget balance was projected to deteriorate. To preserve the gains obtained on the stabilization front, the authorities have taken measures to compensate for lower than expected budgetary receipts and to deal with needed additional capital expenditure on infrastructure that had been previously postponed. As a result, the outcome for 1998, on the basis of present policies, would be a budget deficit limited to 1.9 percent of GDP. As far as the external accounts are concerned, and despite lower export receipts and a projected import recovery, only a small current account deficit is expected for the year. Despite the end of external debt rescheduling as of June 1998, international reserves would decline only slightly in 1998. Structural reforms are expected to focus on the privatization of the 250 EPEs that comprise the government's program for 1998–99, and legislation is expected to clarify private ownership rights over agricultural land. Privatization of large public enterprises should help consolidate financial sector reforms, in particular the development of the stock exchange that was opened at the beginning of 1998. Meanwhile steps to increase private participation in and modernize the operations of banks, notably the payments system, should enhance their efficiency. Efforts will continue to establish an adequate institutional and legal framework to protect property rights and to reform the public housing sector.

Although recent discoveries have boosted prospects for hydrocarbon production, Algeria's medium-term economic prospects are clouded by the risk of low oil export prices. Therefore, creating an environment conducive to increased private sector investment and growth in thenonhydrocarbon sector is essential for employment creation and a sustained improvement in living standards.

EXECUTIVE BOARD ASSESSMENT

Executive Directors commended the authorities for their steadfast implementation, under very difficult circumstances, of an ambitious program of macroeconomic adjustment and structural reform supported by the Extended Arrangement. They noted that over the past four years, tight macroeconomic management, favorable oil prices, and the timely implementation of a comprehensive program of structural reforms had resulted in the substantial deceleration in inflation, a strengthening of the fiscal and external position of Algeria, and further progress toward a market-oriented economy.

However, Directors expressed concern about the sluggish economic growth in 1997 in the nonhydrocarbon sector and the resulting further tensions in the labor market, and about the potential impact on the budget and the external position of the recent fall in oil prices. In that connection, they emphasized the need to maintain a tight stance of fiscal and monetary policies to preserve the stabilization gains of recent years and to accelerate structural reforms to achieve the ambitious growth and employment objectives outlined in the government's medium-term program.

Executive Directors praised the authorities' determination to save the windfall from higher oil prices in 1996 and 1997 which, coupled with firm expenditure restraint, had led to fiscal and external current account surpluses. They underscored that those prudent policies would make Algeria better prepared to weather the current external oil price shock.

Directors recognized the unavoidable deterioration in the budgetary and external position, owing to the recent fall in oil prices. They therefore supported the authorities' revised fiscal plan for 1998. However, they emphasized the need for the authorities to be ready to take supplementary spending and revenue measures in the event of a further deterioration in oil prices, so as to contain the internal and external imbalances that might emerge. Over the medium term and in order to reduce the budget's heavy dependence on hydrocarbon revenues, Directors also emphasized the importance of further broadening the tax base through reform of the value-added tax and reducing tax and customs exemptions. They also recommended that the authorities contain public sector wages and pursue the reform of the civil service so as to allow adequate budgetary allocation for priority expenditure in key social sectors.

Directors endorsed the authorities' intention to pursue a prudent monetary policy geared toward keeping inflation low and strengthening external reserves, while providing adequate financing to the private sector. They welcomed the authorities' intention to conduct monetary policy mainly through open market operations.

Directors recognized the difficult political and social context that had slowed to a certain extent the current structural reform process. Nevertheless, they underscored the need to deepen and accelerate structural reforms, in particular the privatization of public enterprises, land, financialintermediaries, and housing. Those reforms would help to promote private sector participation in the economy. In that regard, Directors welcomed the progress made in dismantling and privatizing local public enterprises and the courageous measures aimed at restructuring all public enterprises, while noting that those actions had resulted in numerous liquidations and widespread labor retrenchment. They were concerned about delays in privatizing the 250 public enterprises announced in September 1997, and especially the large ones, and urged the authorities to move swiftly in that area. They stressed that a rapid implementation of the program would help boost confidence and signal the government's commitment to reform. Directors also underscored the beneficial role that the law on privatization of agricultural land could have in promoting investment in the agriculture sector, and urged the authorities to act promptly to adopt that legislation.

Directors welcomed the measures taken in recent years to strengthen the financial position of banks. They encouraged the authorities to speed up the auditing process of state-owned banks in order to proceed rapidly with their privatization and to preserve a sound financial system, as a key element for improved resource allocation and economic development. In that regard, Directors stressed the need to strengthen banking supervision. Directors welcomed the steps taken to deepen financial markets, including the establishment of a stock market and the associated regulatory institutions for its operations. Those developments should help promote investment, especially foreign direct investment, and encourage savings.

Directors emphasized the need to preserve an adequate social safety net, which would also help to maintain the social consensus in support of economic reforms. In particular, they emphasized the need to maintain the financial viability of the unemployment insurance scheme, which had come under pressure in the wake of higher unemployment following the restructuring of the industrial public sector. In addition, Directors urged the authorities to take rapidly the required steps to restore the financial soundness of the pension system. Also, Directors underscored the critical role of the housing sector for employment creation, promoting private-sector-based growth and alleviating urgent social needs. While Directors welcomed the creation of new financial institutions, they urged the authorities to pursue the needed reforms in that sector.

Directors welcomed the strengthening of the external accounts, with the official foreign exchange reserves reaching almost a year of imports at end-March 1998. They underscored, however, that the medium-term balance of payments prospects are now less favorable than at the time of the last review under the Extended Arrangement, because of the much lower prevailing oil prices, while alternative sources of external financing remain scarce as Algeria has yet to regain full access to foreign financing on appropriate terms. These developments illustrate the vulnerability of Algeria's external position and underscore the need to develop nonhydrocarbon exports. Directors stressed the need for an exchange rate policy in line with the economic fundamentals so as to avoid a real effective appreciation of the dinar on a sustained basis, in order to support the diversification of the economy and increased openness without undermining the inflation objective. They welcomed the steps taken to open the economy and commended the authorities for the removal of all restrictions on the convertibility of the dinar for current transactions. Directors encouraged the authorities to undertake furthernonpreferential tariff reductions to increase competition, improve resource allocation, lay the basis for export development, and pursue the opening of the economy.

Directors observed that major challenges remain to be addressed in order to ensure the transformation of Algeria into a full market economy. They hoped that the continued close cooperation with the Fund, including further technical assistance, would contribute to the transition process. In that context, some Directors indicated that the Fund should remain open to a request from the authorities for a more intensive policy dialogue.

Public Information Notices (PINs) are issued, at the request of a member country, following the conclusion of the Article IV consultation for countries seeking to make known the views of the IMF to the public. This action is intended to strengthen IMF surveillance over the economic policies of member countries by increasing the transparency of the IMF's assessment of these policies.

[1]Under Article IV of the IMF's Articles of Agreement, the IMF holds bilateral discussions with members, usually every year. A staff team visits the country, collects economic and financial information, and discusses with officials the country's economic developments and policies. On return to headquarters, the staff prepares a report, which forms the basis for discussion by the Executive Board. At the conclusion of the discussion, the Managing Director, as Chairman of the Board, summarizes the views of directors, and this summary is transmitted to the country's authorities. In this PIN, the main features of the Board's discussion are described.

ALGERIA MINING INDUSTRY - STRATEGIC INFORMATION AND OPPORTUNITIES

Algeria has major deposits of phosphates and iron ore, as well as smaller deposits of coal, lead and zinc. All of these are mined as well as some mercury and copper. Mining and beneficiation operations in Algeria are owned and operated by the government.

A bonanza of high-grade gold has been found in the Hoggar desert hills of southern Algeria. Five vast geological provinces, each about 600 km long, have been identified. Exploration drilling at two deposits have produced yields graded at 25,1 g/t and 16,49 g/t. In South Africa's declining gold industry, 6,4 g/t is considered good. The Algerians are looking for foreign companies with expertise to come in and do some exploration, increase the reserves and actually start mining.

The industry is regulated by the
Ministry of Mines and Industry,
4 rue Ahmad Bey,
Immeuble le Colisee, Algiers.
The telephone number is +213 (0)2 60-1326.

LARGEST COMPANIES

ENTREPRISE NATIONALE DU FER ET DU PHOSPHATE

General Information

Organization Type:	Company
Registered in:	Algeria
Nick name/Abbrev.:	FERPHOS
Business Sector(s):	Mining & Quarrying Chemical & Fertilizer Mineral Mining

SOCIETÉ NATIONALE DE RECHERCHES ET D'EXPLOITATION MINIERES

General Information

Organization Type:	Parastatal
Registered in:	Algeria
Nick name/Abbrev.:	SONAREM
Business Sector(s):	Mining & Quarrying Mining Industry

ALGERIA CHEMICAL INDUSTRY

Algeria's's chemical and plastics industries have been developed using the hydrocarbon feedstock from its well-developed oil industry. The country's aim is to produce an integrated, broad-based petrochemical industry to reduce Algeria's dependence on imports and increase the volume of petrochemicals and fertilizers available for export. The Algerian chemicals industry is one of the largest in Africa and contributes substantially to the country's economy.

The Algerian chemical industry is dominated by Sonatrach, the Algerian national oil company which is responsible for the management of the country's oil and associated industries. This includes an important role in the chemicals where its chemicals subsidiary, Entreprise Nationale d'Industrie Petrochimique (ENIP) is active. Through its subsidiary activities Sonatrach owns petrochemical facilities and fertilizer plants.

- **Petrochemicals**
- **Fertilizers**
- **Other chemicals**

PETROCHEMICALS

The Algerian chemicals industry is based in three centres which include Skikda, Arzew and Annaba. These sites are industrial and refining centres which include the Arzew refinery and the Skikda refinery. The refinery at Skikda has an aromatics complex which supplies the following products:

Product	Capacity (1,000 year/year)
Benezene	90
Toluene	5
Xylenes	245
Paraxylenes	40
Linear alkyl benzene	50

ENIP, has a large petrochemical complex at Skikda which is geared towards the production of polymers and plastics. The range of products produced at Skikda includes:

- ethylene (120 ktpa)
- chlorine (35 ktpa) & caustic soda
- hydrochloric acid (10 ktpa)
- Vinyl chloride monomer (VCM) (40 ktpa)
- Polyvinyl chloride (PVC) (35 ktpa)
- LDPE (48 ktpa)
- HDPE (130 ktpa)

ENIP has been progressing the expansion of its ethane cracking capacity at Skikda from 120 thousand year/year to 220 thousand year/year. Other developments at Skikda include a petrochemicals plant with a capacity of 30 thousand year/year orthoxylene, 71 thousand year/year paraxylene and 25 thousand year/year phthalic anhydride. Another development includes a 130 thousand tonne/year polyethylene plant joint venture between Repsol Quimica (Madrid) and ENIP.

The petrochemical centre at Arzew produces petrochemicals including fertilizers. Apart from fertilizer components and finished products, Arzew is the source of methanol and associated products. The range of products and capacities are as follows:

- Methanol (100-115 thousand year/year)
- Phenol resin (6 thousand year/year)
- melamine resins (0.5 thousand year/year)
- Urea resins (0.8 thousand year/year)

An expansion of the methanol capacity at Arzew through the establishment of a new 660 thousand tonne/year plant has been subject of agreements between Sonatrach and Itochu Corporation. Reservations have been the price of the gas feedstock. An objective has been to use one-third of the output in a downstream methyl tert-butyl ether plant planned by Sonatrach, Ecofuel, and Total and the remainder would be exported

Expansion and devlopment projects at Arzew include a $1.45-billion petrochemical complex with a 500 thousand tonne/year ethane cracker, and downstream units for; 110 thousand year/year of linear low-density polyethylene (LDPE); 90 thousand year/year of high-density (HDPE); 20 thousand year/year of polypropylene; and 40 thousand year/year of vinyl acetate monomer. Also in development is a 10 thousand tonne/year polyester resins complex which would use imported feedstocks.

FERTILIZERS

Algeria produces both nitrogenous and phosphate fertilizers mainly for the domestic market. Local fertilizer production can meet most of the domestic demand which is over 600 thousand tones per year. Algeria tends to be stronger in nitrogenous fertilizers than in the phosphate products. Nitrogenous fertilizers are produced at a plant in Arzew using natural gas as feedstock. The plant has a capacity of 800 thousand tones per year.

There is a second fertilizer complex at Annaba. This site produces 550 ktpa ammonium phosphate, sulphuric acid (495 ktpa), phosphoric acid (165 ktpa) and diammonium phosphate (330 ktpa). Sodium tripolyphosphate (STPP) (40 ktpa) produced at Annaba is supplied to the Société Nationale des Industries Chimiques (SNIC) for detergent manufacture.

OTHER CHEMICALS

Other recent chemical projects include a helium and nitrogen plant which is a joint venture between Sonatrach, Air Products & Chemicals Inc (USA) and L'Air Liquide (France). It is situated in the natural gas liquefaction complex at Béthious, near Arzew and has a liquid helium capacity of 16 million m^3/a and liquid and gaseous nitrogen capacity of 33 ktpa respectively. Liquid helium from this plant and from Oran are to be exported to Europe. Air Products and Chemicals has built a distribution center in Rognac, near Marseilles in France for supply of bulk helium to Europe.

Algeria has plans to develop the manufacture of pharmaceuticals by means of joint ventures with various international partners. Plans include the construction of a plant near Algiers to manufacture a range of drugs, a joint venture between Novo-Nordisk Pharmaceuticals (Denmark) and Enterprise Nationale d'Approvisionnement en Produits Pharmaceutiques. Other joint ventures, with Pfizer (USA) and Rhône-Poulenc Rohrer (France) are also in the pipeline. The principal trade union in the chemical industry is Secteur Energie et Pétrochimie, which is affiliated to Union Générale des Travailleurs Algériens (UGTA).

ALGERIA: OIL INDUSTRY AND OPPORTUNTIES

The first exploration of hydrocarbons in Algeria goes back to the ends of 1890's, in the Chellif bassin but it was only in 1948 that the first discovery was made at Oued Guetirini, in the north of the country at 150 km of Algiers.

In the fifties, exploration works where extended to the Sahara, where many oil and naturel gas discoveries were made, drastically changing the knowledge of Algerian underground ressources.Algeria has a sedimentary surface of over one and half million km2, the exploration of which is far from being completed. On the 24th of Februayr 1971, President Houari Boumedienne announced the nationalisation of hydrocarbons that were previously owned by foreign companies. About 25 years ago, a decisive impetus was given to the development of oil and gas deposits, the construction of production and transformation facilities as well as transport and exploration infrastructures.

From 1986, adapting to the evolution trend of the world economy, Algeria provided its self with an attractive legislation, and it was made more offensive in 1991 it made possible the opening of the national mining domain to international investments, in association with the national company Sonatrach.

The hydrocarbon industry is key to the Algerian economy earning it $8.6 billion in 1994 or 95% of its foreign exchange revenue. Based on an oil price of $16.5/barrel for its crude, the Algerian government forecasts oil and gas revenues of $10.4 billion in 1996. Its current proven hydrocarbon **reserves** are estimated to be 4.2 thousand million tons of oil equivalent of which 1.2 thousand million tonnes are of crude oil (9.2 thousand million barrels) and 3.6 trillion cubic meters (tcm) or 128 tcf of natural gas. This represents 0.9% of the world's crude oil reserves and 2.6% of the world's natural gas reserves. At current production levels, its reserve-to-production ratio is 20.9 years for crude oil and 72 years for natural gas.

Algeria's **crude oil production** has risen from 49.5 million tonnes (1,135,000 barrels) in 1984 to reach 55.7 million tonnes (1,300,000 barrels) in 1994, representing 1.7% of the world's crude oil production. Its natural gas production was 28.3 million tons of oil equivalent (mtoe) in 1984, rising to 45.3 mtoe in 1994, or 2.4% of the world's total natural gas output. Gas production is expected to rise significantly and exports are projected to reach 60 bcm in 1997. Crude oil production is projected to rise by a further 65,000 barrels per day.

The major **oil fields** in Algeria were discovered in 1956 and production began on a commercial scale in 1958 with Algeria's output in 1959 totalling 1.2 million tonnes. There are currently about 34 major producing oil fields. The main fields are located in the east central region of the country at Hassi Messaoud in central Algeria, and around Ain Amenas near the Libyan frontier. Recently a cluster of new fields with commercial potential have been discovered at Hassi Berkine, east of Hassi Messaoud towards Algeria's border with Tunisia.

A four-year struggle between Islamist militants and the Algerian security forces shows little sign of receding and there signs that it is now spreading to include local oil workers who up to now have not been drawn into the struggle. Despite the political unrest which creates difficult conditions for foreign companies to operate in Algeria, 12 new exploration and production sharing agreements have been signed by foreign oil companies, and between $300 and $400 million has been invested in the country's oil industry since 1992. The total area of acreage under exploration is in the order of 90,000 square kilometres.

Current exploration activity is mainly conducted by the national oil company, Sonatrach since after 1970, all foreign oil company interests were nationalised and Sonatrach gained responsibility for all of Algeria's hydrocarbon production. However, owing to declining reserves and the need to attract investment in its hydrocarbon industry, Algeria has been revising its oil fiscal terms.

In 1991 a new hydrocarbons law was passed which allowed foreign companies to participate in existing oil fields in order to improve recovery rates and so increase output, and exploration and production-sharing agreements in gas fields were permitted for the first time.

Foreign companies which have entered the Algerian upstream industry include Total, Cepsa, Agip which has recently become the first foreign company to start producing in Algeria, Repsol, and Anadarko (partly owned by Sonatrach) which recently together with its partners, Lasmo and Maersk, discovered a major commercial field in the Hassi Berkine region. More recent entrants to the Algerian upstream scene are Mobil, Arco, Petro-Canada and the Argentinian oil company, Pluspetrol, which operates 2 permits in the Ghadames basin in the southeast region of Algeria in which the Hungarian company, MOL, has a 50% farm-in stake.

Anadarko (50%), the operator, Lasmo (25%) and Maersk Oil (25%) report total gross discovered oil and condensate reserves on Ghadames Basin Blocks 208, 211, 245 and 404 as 2 billion barrels. Since 1989, Anadarko has drilled 28 wells on the acreage, of which 19 have been classified exploratory and the remainder as appraisals. Eleven of the wells resulted in discoveries. The partners are progressing the Hassi Berkine (HBN), Hassi Berkine South (HBNS) and Qoubba (QBA) projects on block 404. HBNS production is scheduled to begin in early 1998 at about 60,000 BOPD. Production from all three fields will exceed 300,000 bpd by 2000.

Production from Cepsa's Rhourde el Khrouf field in Rhourde Yacoub block 406A, which began production in June 1996, is to be increased from under 7000 b/d to some 20,000 b/d, following development consent allowing the exploitation of all 10 wells at the field.

Arco (75%) and TPAO (25%) have found oil in the Hassi Bir Rekaiz block in the Ghadames basin. During 1997 Anadarko (Rhourde Berkine I), Sonatrach (Djebel I) and BHP (Sif Fatima) have made discoveries in Algeria.

Sonatrach and its partners will spend some $19.3 billion on oil and gas projects between 1997 and 2001. Petronas is involved in exploration in two onshore blocks with partners

Algerian oil fields generally produce light crude oils with a low sulphur content. The principal crudes are Sahara Blend and Zarzaitine. **Exports** of crude oil and refined products from Algeria total over 1,2 million bpd, 18% of which is in the form of crude oil, 24% condensates, 25% gas and 19% refined products. The bulk of Algeria's exports of crude oil go to Western Europe (80%) with about 10% going to markets in the USA.

Algeria is particularly rich in condensates and **natural gas** and the government has instituted a strategy of investing in facilities for exploiting these resources. The country has now become one of the world's leading exporters of condensates with exports of some 400,000 bpd. While Algeria's crude oil constitutes 30% of the country's recoverable hydrocarbon reserves, its natural gas constitutes 70% and it ranks eighth in the world in terms of gas reserves. Output of natural gas in Algeria is in the order of 33 bcm and this is expected to increase significantly in the next few years to 60 bcm by 1998. Apart from encouraging foreign oil companies to develop Algeria's gas fields, the government is also promoting the use of natural gas in the domestic market especially in the industrial sector where plants can easily be converted from fuel oil to gas.

The major natural gas fields are located at Hassi R'Mel, in central Algeria, 400 km south of Algiers. Other gas fields are found at Alrar, along the Libyan frontier, at Rhourde Nouss, south of Hassi Messaoud, and at In Salah south west of Ain Amenas where BP is to develop a major gas field following its signing of a $3.5 billion partnership agreement in December 1995. The agreement, which BP expects to last for 20 to 30 years, entails BP bearing 65% of the costs in return for a third of the profits. Production at a rate of 10 bcm per year is expected to start in 2002. The agreement also includes the setting up of a joint marketing company to sell gas in Europe. Following the BP agreement, it has also been announced that Exxon is negotiating with Algeria on a similar natural gas deal close to the BP site.

Other significant companies involved in exploiting Algeria's gas and condensate resources are BHP Petroleum and Total, which signed an agreement in 1991 to develop condensate and LPG reserves at the Hamra field, 250 km from Hassi Messaoud. Japanese companies, notably Mitsubishi, JGC and Itochu, as well as Sofregaz, Bechtel and MW Kellog are involved in the rehabilitation of the gas infrastructure.

Algeria ranks as the second largest exporter of **LPG** in the world with an output of over 6 million tonnes in 1995 and its aim is to boost output to 8 million tons/year by the end of 1997. To this end, the LPG facilities at its Arzew refinery are being upgraded and the capacity of the LPG pipeline between Hassi R'Mel and Arzew is to be increased to 9 million tons/year. Sonatrach's LPG marketing strategy is to target isolated regions that have no natural gas to compete with LPG. So far it has signed agreements with among others the Dominican Republic, Cyprus and the Canary Islands.

The prospective nature of the Algerian minning domain which extends over more then 1.5 million Km^2 is acknowledged and confirmed by recent discoveries. But there is still a large part that is under exploited, only half the domain has been intensively exploited up to the present day.

Many other Algerian companies(Oil services, Refining, Petrochemical, Enginneering, Project and construction) highly competent and experienced linked to the oil industry also belong to this sector.

ALGERIA LARGEST OIL & GAS COMPANIES

SONATRACH (ENTREPRISE NATIONALE SONATRACH)

Nature of Business

Enterprise Nationale Sonatrech, founded in 1963, is the national oil company of Algeria. It is responsible for the management of the country's oil industry which encompasses organization of Algerian exploration, production, transport, refining, processing, marketing and distribution of oil, gas and related products. Included in this portfolio is management of exploration bidding rounds for oil and gas. Sonotrach also has an important role in the chemicals industry of Algeria, owning fertilizer plants and petrochemical facilities.

Sonatrach is structured as a holding company with five major operating subsidiaries which encompass: Exploration, production and marketing of oil, gas and chemicals Management of the Algerian oil refineries Transport, including pipeline operation and maintenance Gas liquefaction and operation of the Arzew and skilda LNG and LPG plants International operations, including management of foreign investments and overseas sales offices Sonatrach has begun an 18 billion US dollar, 5 year investment plan which includes a 25 year oil recovery enhancement project with Arco.

General Information

Organization Type:	Company
Registered in:	Algeria
Nick name/Abbrev.:	Sonatrach
Business Sector(s):	Oil And Gas Industry Exploration & Production

Directors/Managers

Director General: Mr NCE Zouioueche (Nazim)

Chairperson: Mr A Attar (Abdeknadhud)

CONTACT INFORMATION

Sonatrach (Entreprise Nationale Sonatrach)

Tel: +213 (0)2 663300

Office Address: 80 Ave Ahmed Ghermoul
Algiers
Algeria

AFRICA OPERATIONS

TOTAL has extensive assets in Africa encompassing both upstream and downstream investments. TOTAL has business activities in at least 38 African countries and its trademark is present in 32 of these. The company distributes six million tones of petroleum products in Africa annually and it employs 3,800 employees. It's upstream activities are centered in Algeria, Angola, Cameroon, Gabon and Tunisia.

TOTAL is one of the largest oil marketers in Africa, operating 2,300 service stations in 32 African countries and boasting an overall market share of roughly 15%. TOTAL's largest affiliate in Africa is that in South Africa which has an extensive marketing network as well as refining, lubricant base oil and blending assets. Through the South African operation, the company is also active in neighboring countries by means of subsidiary companies which include TOTAL Namibia, TOTAL Botswana, TOTAL Lesotho, and TOTAL Swaziland.

TOTAL Cote d'Ivoire operates no less than 95 stations in the country, including 35 former Esso stations acquired two years ago (along with the stations in Senegal), giving it a 20.8% share of the road network market. In addition, TOTAL Cote d'Ivoire holds a 10.1% stake in SIR, where it acts as technical assistant, and 15% in Sifal (lubes). TOTAL has over the past two years been the upgrading the standards of some 700 of its stations across Africa at a reported cost of Ffr800 million.

Refining is carried out in Africa through its 34% share in Natref Refinery in South Africa and through various equity shares in smaller units located in the Ivory Coast (Abidjan). Cameroon (Limbe), Gabon (Port Gentil), and Senegal (Dakar).

ARZEW REFINERY

The oil refinery at Arzew, Algeria, is a topping and reforming refinery with a nameplate distillation capacity of 3,000 ktonnes per annum (60,000 bpd). It was built by a consortium of Japanese contractors and completed in 1973. It processes Saharan crude piped to it along the Haoud El Hamra/Arzew pipeline. Half of its output is consumed locally with the remainder being exported. The refinery is owned by the Algerian national oil company, Sonatrach.

Following the country's expansion of its gas exports, the Arzew refinery is undergoing a major rehabilitation of its GL1-Z and GL2-Z gas liquefaction plant. Contractors are Bechtel and the Japanese companies, IHI and Itochu, who have been awarded contracts to install new equipment and expand existing facilities.

REFINERY UNITS

The refinery has the following main production units (capacities in barrels per day):

Refinery Units	Capacity (bpd)
Crude unit	60,000
Vacuum unit	5,500
Catalytic reformer	11,600
Catalytic hydrotreater	11,000
Lubes production	2,400
Asphalt production	2,400

CONTACT DETAILS

Postal Address: P O Box 37, Arzew, Algeria

Street Address: Emir Abdel Kader St, Arzew, Algeria

SONATRACH AN INTERNATIONAL PETROLEUM GROUP

A far-reaching scope

Sonatrach is the Algerian oil and gas company. According to the Petroleum Intelligence Weekly, it is ranked as the twelveth company in the world.

It is the first oil company in the Mediterranean, the fourth world largest exporter of natural gas and the second one for LPG.

A leading role

Upon its creation in december 1963, Sonatrach role was, essentially, to contribute in the national development of Algeria. It was mostly targeted to generate external payment means, but also to meet the existing and future hydrocarbons requirements of Algeria.

An impressive growth

For purposes of maximizing the long term value of the Algerian hydrocarbons resources, Sonatrach undertook a tremendous development of activities.
Production has been multiplied by four since 1970 and is expected to be twice as much by 2007.

Significant assets

- A highly qualified human potential.
- A very competitive and attractive law on hydrocarbons.
- An important reserve base.
- Sedimentary basins with a high potential and still largely under-explored.
- An expertise of thirty years operations in field exploitation and development.

- A great experience in gas industry.
- A privileged geo-economic situation, neighbouring the important European Union market and open to the remainder of the world.
- A most positive partnership track record.

Exports

Given the privileged geo-economic situation of Algeria, Sonatrach has developed a strong commercial relationship with Western Europe and the United States and is particularly interested in the Mediterranean countries and the Maghreb.

(In millions of toe)

Product	1995	1996	1997	1998	1999	2000
Crude oil	15.42	18.17	17.35	19,3	19,3	21,4
NGL (condensate)	17.44	18.16	17.85	17,3	17,1	17,7
Refined products	14.64	13.91	15.81	14,1	14,9	14,9
Natural gas	18.58	20.08	22.88	26,4	32,1	32,9
Liquefied natural gas	17.59	19.63	24.07	24,5	26,0	26,6
Liquefied petroleum gas	4.03	4.52	5.82	6,8	7,8	8,5
Total	87.70	94.47	103.78	108,3	117,2	122,1

The important exploration efforts of Sonatrach have resulted in 30 important discoveries in the last few years in 1994 and 1995, 15 discoveries were made, followed by 10 others in 1996.

Algeria was ranked as one of the most important oil discovering country. 5,680 billion barrels of oil, 200 million barrels of condensate and 71 billion m3 of natural gas represent the total of what has been discovered in the last few years.

Sonatrach is present in the production and the exploration of deposits with more than 3.9 million barrels of oil equivalent / day. The production of crude oil is forecast to exceed 60 million tonnes by the beginning of the next century, exceeding by far the maximum achieved in 1978 which was 54 million tonnes

.Sonatrach produces liquid and gaseous hydrocarbons on 75 fields and nearly. It 200 wells, it also exploits more than a hundred plants and facilities such as crude oil separation centers, natural gas processing and recovry plants, LP.G extraction units, compression gas and water injection units as well as crude oil refining plants.Sonatrach has an important transport network composed of 11 ags pipelines and 14 oil pipelines reaching a total lengh of nearly 13 000 Km.

The transport capacity of Sonatrach has increased thanks to the entry into service of new infrastructures among which are those particulary designed for exports such as the G.M.E and the doubling of the TRANSMED which links the gas deposits of the Algerian Sahara to the countries of southern Europe.

Sonatrach owns four LNG plants with a total annual capacity of 30.5 billion m^3 natural gas. Concerning LPG, Sonatrach has two separation plants (butane and propane) totaling an annual capacity of 4.6 million tonnes. Thanks to its priveliged geographic position with respect to the great consuming markets, Sonatrach has developed its marketing actions towards Western Europe and the United States with a particular attention to the Mediterranean and Maghrebine countries.Consolidating its position on the international markets, Sonatrach managed to penetrate new ones in western and central Europe and Asia. In order to meet a growing demand in energy, Algeria with Sonatrach envisage export growth and diversification.

Présidé par Monsieur **Chakib KHELIL**, Président Directeur Général, le Comité Exécutif est Composé des membres suivants :

Monsieur **Abdelmalek ZITOUNI**	Secrétaire Général
Monsieur **Djamel Eddine KHENE**	Vice-Président Amont (AMT)
Monsieur **Abdelhamid ZERGUINE**	Vice-Président Transport: par Canalisations (TRC)
Monsieur **Bachir ACHOUR**	Vice-Président Aval (AVL)
Monsieur **Ali HACHED**	Vice-Président Commercialisation (COM)
Monsieur **Abdelhafid FEGHOULI**	Directeur Général Adjoint Ressources Humaines et Communication (RHC)
Melle **Fatma-Zohra BENOUGHLIS**	Directrice Exécutive Stratégie, Planification et Economie (SPE)
Monsieur **Ahmed MOSTEFAOUI**	Directeur Exécutif Finances (FIN)
Monsieur **Mohamed SENHADJI**	Directeur Exécutif Activités Centrales (ACT)
Monsieur **Rabah Nadir ALLOUANI**	Directeur Central Santé, S écurité et environnement (HSE)

SCHEMA ORGANISATIONNEL ET FONCTIONNEL DE LA MACROSTRUCTURE SONATRACH
11 Juin 2002

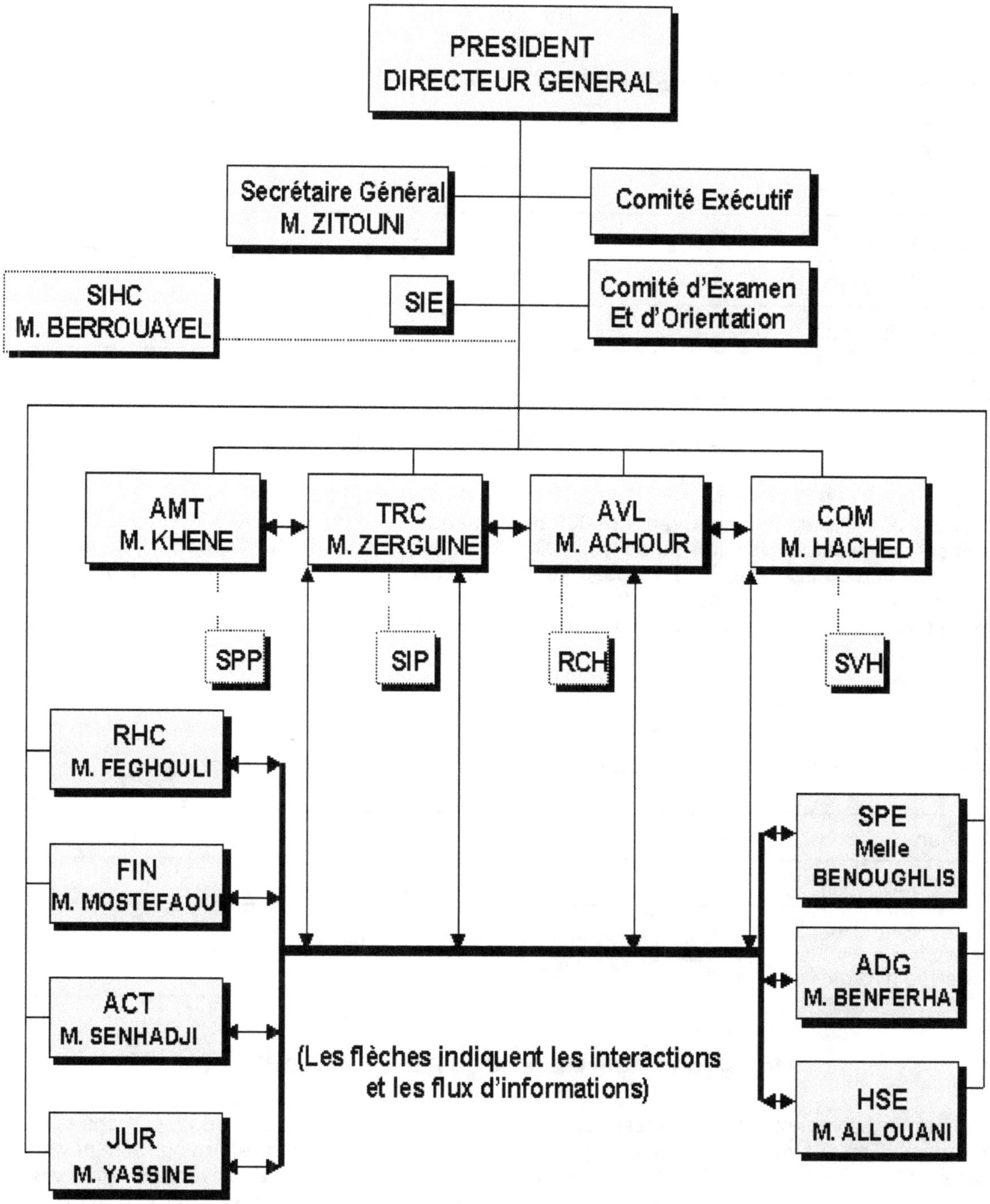

ALGERIA SKIKDA REFINERY

The oil refinery at Skikda, Algeria, built by Snamprogetti and which became fully operational in 1981, is the country's largest being capable of processing 15 million tons of Saharan crude and 300,000 tons of imported reduced crude annually. The refinery is supplied with Saharan crude by the Haoud El Hamra/Skikda pipeline and with imported crude from the oil terminal at Skikda. The refinery is owned by the Algerian state oil company, Sonatrach

REFINERY UNITS

The refinery has the following main production units (capacities in barrels per day):

Refinery Units	Capacity (bpd)
Crude unit	320,000
Vacuum unit	9,000
Catalytic reformer	30,000
Isomerisation unit	1,900
Asphalt unit	2,900

ALGERIA EL DJAZAIR REFINERY (ALGIERS)

The El Djazair Refinery at Maison Carree, Algiers, Algeria, came on stram in 1964 with an initial capacity of 1,400 ktonnes per year (28,000 bpd) but has been progressively increased to its present nameplate distillation capacity of 3,000 ktonnes per annum (60,000 bpd). The refinery processes crude from the Hassi Massaoud oilfields piped to it along the Haoud El Hamra/Algiers pipeline. The refinery's output is distributed to the central part of Algeria for local consumption except for naphtha which is exported. The refinery is owned by the Algerian national oil company, Sonatrach.

REFINERY UNITS

The refinery has the following main production units (capacities in barrels per day):

Refinery Units	Capacity (bpd)
Crude unit	60,000
Catalytic reformer	15,000
Catalytic hydrotreater	15,000

ALGERIA HASSI MESSAOUD REFINERY COMPLEX

The refinery complex at Hassi Messaoud in the middle of the oilfields of Algeria, comprises 2 refineries. The first refinery, originally opened in 1962, is a topping and reforming refinery with a nameplate distillation capacity of 1,700 ktonnes per annum (30,000 bpd). A second refinery with a capacity of 1,200 ktonnes per annum came on stream in 1979 and supplies a large part of southern Algeria.. The refinery complex is owned by the Algerian national oil company, Sonatrach.

PRODUCT RANGE

The product spread of the Hassi Messaoud Refinery complex includes :

- Gas oil
- Gasoline (premium and regular grades)
- Paraffin
- Krosene
- Butane

GOVERNMENT AND BUSINESS CONTACTS

STRATEGIC GOVERNMENT AND BUSINESS CONTACTS

NATIONAL AGENCY FOR INVESTMENT DEVELOPMENT (ANDI)

Accompanying investment is a key objective of government.

ANDI - National Agency for Investment Development - was created in 2001 to meet this objective.

Under the control and direction of the Minister of Investment Promotion, ANDI carries out its missions in seven major areas:

Information: welcome and inform investors.
Facilitation: identify constraints to the realization of investments and propose organizational and regulatory measures to address them.
Investment promotion: promote the general investment environment in Algeria, improve and strengthen the brand image of Algeria abroad.
Support: advise and assist investors with other administrations in the implementation of their projects.
Participation in the management of economic land: to inform investors about the availability of land and the management of the property portfolio.
Management advantages: verify eligibility for benefits reported investments contribute to the identification of projects of particular interest to the national economy and participate in the negotiation of benefits to be granted to these projects.
Action: Ensure an observation service, statistics and listening on the status of registered projects.
As for institutional redeployment occurred in October 2006, the mission of the ANDI were strengthened in the facilitation, promotion, information and assistance. However, its related benefits management missions have been reduced.

Who to contact?

Branch ANDI:

Address: 27, rue Mohamed Hussein-Dey Merbouche (Headquarters CNAT) ALGER Tel: 213 (0) 21 77 32 62/213 (0) 21 77 32 63 Fax: 213 (0) 21 77 32 57 Email: information @ andi . dz
-
PSCs decentralized (GUD) ANDI

GUD are the privileged interlocutors of investors.

Through them, ANDI helps the investor to form his company and start the project.

The coordinates of GUD are available on the website of the ANDI: click on the home page:

http://www.andi.dz/ or directly on:

http://www.andi.dz/contact/Contact.htm

To view their location and the territories they cover, click: http://www.andi.dz/gu/gud.htm

The main steps to launch an investment project are given by: http://www.andi.dz/guide/guide.htm

To learn more about ANDI, see Executive Decree No. 06-356 of 9 October 2006 on the responsibilities, organization and functioning of the National Agency for Investment Development.

AGENCE NATIONALE DU DÉVELOPPEMENT ET DE L'INVESTISSEMENT (ANDI)

Adresse: 27 rue Mohamed Merbouche Hussein Dey - (Siège du CNAT) Alger
Tel: 213 (0)21 77 32 62 - 021 77 32 63
Fax: 213 (0)21 77 32 57
E-mail :information@ANDI.dz
site web: http://www.andi.dz

La Direction Générale :	Tél. : 213 (0) 21 77 32 62 et 63 Fax : 213 (0) 21 77 32 57 Email:information@andi.dz
Monsieur DAOUD Abderahmane Directeur Guichet Unique d'Alger	27, Rue Mohamed MERBOUCHE Hussein-Dey (siège du CNAT) Tél. : 213 (0) 21 77 32 62 et 63 Fax : 213 (0) 21 77 32 57 gualger@andi.dz
Guichet Unique d'Oran	11, Rue KHIAT Salah Hai El Ghoualem Secteur Communal d'El Hamri Oran Tél. : 213 (0) 41 34 25 05 Fax : 213 (0) 41 34 24 33 guoran@andi.dz
Monsieur BRANKI Salim Directeur Guichet Unique de Annaba	Locaux de l'Agence Foncière Boulevard Benboulaid Annaba Tél. : 213 (0) 38 86 36 93 Fax : 213 (0) 38 86 36 97 guannaba@andi.dz
Monsieur MEGA Mohamed Directeur Guichet Unique de Ouargla	Rue Chenine Kaddour Ouargla Tél./Fax : 213 (0) 29 76 55 72 guouargla@andi.dz
Madame MOKRAOUI Hassiba Directeur Guichet Unique de Blida	Place du 1er Novembre Rue Ayach Abdellah Blida Tél. : 213 (0) 25 40 81 78 Fax : 213 (0) 25 40 85 81 gublida@andi.dz

Monsieur LAOURARI Hacene
Directeur Guichet Unique de Constantine
Cité administrative Ali MENDJELI nouvelle ville Constantine

Tel : 213 (0) 31 95 73 32
Fax : 213 (0) 31 95 73 33 guconstantine@andi.dz

Monsieur **ABDELLAHI** Abderahmane
Responsable du Guichet Unique d'Adrar
Siège de la Wilaya d'Adrar
Tel : 213 (0) 49 96 05 70
Fax : 213 (0) 49 96 05 95
guadrar@andi.dz

Monsieur **HADJADJ** Omar
Responsable du Guichet Unique de Sétif
Rue du 17 Octobre 1961 Sétif
Tel : 213 (0) 36 84 18 58
Fax : 213 (0) 36 84 19 59
gusetif@andi.dz

Monsieur **BELARBI** Mohamed El-Amine
Responsable du Guichet Unique de Tlemcen
Boulevard de la Soummam BP 428 Imama Tlemcen
Tel : 213 (0) 43 20 22 83
Fax : 213 (0) 43 20 22 79
gutlemcen@andi.dz

Centre Algérien de Contrôle de la Qualité et de l'Emballage (CACQE)
Adresse: Route nationale n°5 Bab Ezzouar Alger Algérie
Tel :+213 (0)21 24.31.65
Fax : +213 (0)21 24.30.11

Société Algériennes des Foires et Exposition (SAFEX)
Adresse: Palais des Expositions - Pins maritimes Alger Algérie
Tel : +213 (0)21 21.01.23 / 21.01.35 à 42
Fax : +213 (0)21 21.05.40 / 21.06.30
E.mail: safex@wissal.dz
site web:http://www.safex.com.dz

Agence Nationale de Soutien A l'Emploi des Jeunes (ANSEJ)
Adresse: 8,Rue Arezki Benbouzid El-Annasers - Alger
Tel: +213 (0)21 67.82.61 / 67.82.38 / 67.82.39
Fax: +213 (0)21 67.75.74 / 67.75.87

OFFICE ALGÉRIEN DE PROMOTION DU COMMERCE EXTÉRIEUR (PROMEX)

Adresse: Route nationale n°5 Mohammadia Alger Algérie
Tel : +213 (0)21 52.20.82 /12.10
Fax : +213 (0)21 52.11.26
E.mail: promex@wissal.dz
site web:http://www.promex.com.dz

CONTACTS	Address	Téléphone	Fax
Adrar	Cite Aissat Idir,BP N°108.W.adrar	(049) 96.06.91	(049) 96.06.91
Chlef	**CIA Des fonctionnaires BLOC C N°03 ET 04.BP N°100.**	(027) 77.27.21	(027) 77.43.10
Laghouat	Cité Maamourah BP N° 1224	(029) 93.30.22	(029) 93.30.22
Oum El Bouaghi	**CITE AMEL EXTENTION BP N° 33.**	(032) 42.85.60	(032) 42.85.62
Batna	CITE L'ABORATOIR 18 LOGEMENTS BP N°58 allées Ben Boulaid.	(033) 86.22.78	(033) 86.85.20
Bejaia	**BD KRIM Belkacem promotion SOMACOB Zone industrielle**	(034) 21.57.57	(034) 21.57.57

	IHADDADEN ,BT D1.BP N°212 LIBERTE Bejaia.		
Biskra	CITE DES 100 VILLAS CADRES ZHUN OUEST.N°126 EL_AMEL .	(033) 74.58.22	(033) 74.38.22
Bechar	Cité Djihani la Berga, N°419 RP ,Bechar.	(049) 81.85.70	(049) 81.02.46
Blida	Cité 142 logts Bt C4, Bab-Djazair W.de Blida.	(025) 41.18.71	(025) 41.03.76
Bouira	CITE 250 LOGTS COMMUNE DE BUIRA N°45.	(026)94.45.47.	(025) 94.45.39
Tamanrasset	**RUE 5 JUILLET SERSOUF.N°1942.**	(029) 34.40.82	(029) 34.24.49
Tebessa	BP N°276 Bd Houari Boumediène Tebessa.	(037) 48.22.88	(037) 48.41.11
Tlemcen	FIN BOULEVARD PRINCIPAL KIFFANE .BP N°389.	(043) 20.26.50	(043) 20.74.15
Tiaret	ROUTE AIN GUESMA HAI EL BADR.BP N°79.	(046) 42.68.60	(046) 42.77.14
Tizi Ouzou	CITE 104 LOGTS EPLF BT B5 NOUVELLE VILLE .CASE 006 POSTE ANNANE.	(026)21.88.49.	(026) 21.88.49
Alger (Laarbi Ben M'hidi)	40/42 Rue Laarbi Ben M'hidi Alger.30 ,rue capitaine mennani.	(021) 73.80.51	(021) 73.80.51
Alger (Mennani)	30, Rue Capitaine Mennani, Alger.	(021) 66.32.17	(021) 66.02.38
Djelfa	Cité Bendjermain Boulevard 08.N°3302 AIN EAHIH.Djelfa.	(027) 87.65.59	(027) 87.65.59
Jijel	VILLAGE MOUSSA 24 LOGTS EPLF BLOC N°03.BP N°204/1er Novembre.	(034) 47.34.66	(034) 49.89.42
Setif	**15 Avenue 08 Mai 1945 Sétif BP N°454.**	(036) 93.57.45	(036)93.05.05.
Saida	Rue Zighout Youcef,N°187 RP ,Saida.	(048) 51.31.08	(048) 51.33.10
Skikda	Avenue 'Arsenal, BP N°216.	(038) 75.90.16	(038)75.66.18.
Sidi Bel Abbes	Avenue Abbane Ramdane,N° 162/85 AA ,SIDI-YACINE.	(048) 56.86.45	(048) 56.96.78
Annaba	**Place Belouizdad ,Chambre de Commerce BP N°174 RP.**	(038) 80.30.57	(038)80.30.57.
Guelma	**Cité Ben Souilah Bloc 05 ,N°05.BP N°326**	(037) 26.49.63	(037)26.13.46.
Constantine	rue du 26 Novembre BP N° 13 RP.	(031)92.67.60.	(031)92.69.36.
Médéa	Rue du 19 Mars 1962 BP N° 73 Médéa.	(025)58.99.47.	(025) 58.25.32
Mostaganem	01,Rue Belahouel belahouel .N°21	(045) 21.14.58	(045) 21.14.58
M'sila	BD Colonel Amirouche, Route de BBA ,BP N°195 RP.	(035) 55.16.78	(035) 55.98.16
Mascara	Rue Hassi el Ghella,N°670 à BABA ALI .	(045) 80.17.21.	(045) 81.22.92
Ouargla	Avenue de le république Souk El Hadjr Ouargla BP N°448.	(029) 71.38.12	(029) 71.50.62.
Oran	118, RUE MOHAMED BOUDIAF EX RUE DE MOSTAGHANEM BP N°1527 ORAN.	(041) 50.34.87	(041) 41.38.61
El Bayed	Rue Djelaila Cheikh El-Bayadh.N°172RP	(049) 71.46.75	(049) 71.86.80
Illizi	ZHUN ILLIZI BPN°142 ILLIZI.	(029) 42.17.28	(029) 42.23.55.

Bourdj B Arreridj	Lot Benziouche Route Bir Snab W.B.B.Arreridj BP 373.	(035) 68.38.33	(035) 68.57.55
Boumerdes	CITÉ 1406 LOGTS BT 30B N° 07 BOUMERDES.	(024) 81.72.96	(024) 81.72.96
El Tarf	Rue Mahrech Boudjemaa BP N°70 PTT Commune Bouteldja W.el Taref.	(038) 60.92.01	(038) 60.95.89
Tindouf	CITE 83 LOGTS EL_ KASSABI ,BP N°438 ,TINDOUF.	(049) 92.39.17	(049) 92.16.18
Tissemsilt	Cité 100 Logts,route de tiaret BP 164 Bloc 1 ,BP N°164, Tissemssilt.	(046) 47.76.09	(046) 47.85.01
El Oued	Cité erimel BP 128 El-oued.	(032) 24.92.91	(032) 24.84.13
Khenchela	Cite du 1er Mai Khenchla. BP N°NR186.	(032) 31.78.43	(032) 32.28.40
Souk Ahras	Lotissement Behidji Mansour cite 1700 logts. BP N°304 Souk-Ahras.	(037) 32.69.33	(037) 32.63.11.
Tipaza	CHEMIN DE LA WILAYA BP N°37 Tipaza.	(024) 47.00.23	(024) 47.00.23
Mila	CITE 500 LOGTS BT E ENSEMBLE II ,BPN° 155 .	(031) 57.78.49	(031) 57.78.49
Ain Defla	Bloc A N°01 CITE 231 LOGEMENTS EPLF BP N°144 martyrs.	(027) 60.16.00	(027) 60.33.45
Nâama	Cité Administrative,N°22, Naâma.	(049) 79.64.54	(049) 79.61.28
Ain Temouchent	Cité Omar Ibn El Khatab, Ain-Témouchent. BP N°171.	(043) 60.13.90	(043) 60.22.75
Ghardaia	Rue Didouche Mourad,Bouhraoua BP N°44.C.T.R.	(029) 88.59.02	(029) 88.59.02
Relizane	Rue des Figuiers N° 431, Relizane.	(046) 92.44.91	(046) 92.94.83

Centre National de l'Informatique et des Statistiques (CNIS)
Adresse:17, Rue Mourabi Tounes Alger Algérie
Tel: +213 (0)21 71.56.00
Fax: +213 (0)21 71.56.40
E.mail: statistique@douanes-cnis.dz
site web:http:// www.douanes-cnis.dz

Direction Générale des Douanes
Adresse: Rue Docteur Saâdane Alger Algérie
Tel: +213 (0)21 72.59.59 / 72.60.00
Fax: +213 (0)21 72.59.75
site web:http://www.douane.gov.dz
Compagnie Algérienne d'Assurance et de Garantie des Exportations (CAGEX)

Adresse:10, Route Natioanle Dély Ibrahim BP 116 Algérie
Tel: +213 (0)21 91.00.49 / 91.00.51
Fax: +213 (0)21 91.00.44 à 45
E.mail : cagex@wissal.dz / cagex@cerist.dz
site web:http://www.cagex.com.dz
Ministère du Commerce

Adresse:46, Boulevard Mohamed V Alger Algérie
Tel: +213 (0)21 63.12.24
Fax: +213 (0)21 64.32.44/45

Institut Algérien de Normalisation (IANOR)

Adresse:5, Rue Abou Hamou Moussa BP104 RP Alger Algérie
Tel: +213 (0)21 63.96.38 / 42.92.12
Fax: +213 (0)21 42.03.96
Ministère des Finances

Adresse: Cité Malki Ben Aknoun Alger Algérie
Tel: +213 (0)21 59.51.51 / 59.52.52
Fax: +213 (0)21 59.53.53 / 59.54.54
Office National des Statistiques (ONS)

Adresse:8 & 10 Rue des moussebilines Alger Algérie
Tel: +213 (0)21 63.99.74 à 76
Fax: +213 (0)21 63.79.55
E.mail: ons@onsieg.ons.dz
site web: http://www.ons.dz
Centre National du Registre de Commerce (CNRC)

Adresse: Route Nationale n°24 BP. 18
Tel: +213 (0)21 20.55.38 / 20.37.53
Fax: +213 (0)21 20.37.53 / 20.19.71
site web: http://www.cnrc.org.dz

Site de la chambre nationale des notaires

Tel : (021)63.53.45/48
Fax : (021)63.53.46
E.mail :president@c-notaires.dz
amana@c-notaires.dz
revue@c-notaires.dz

site web: http://www.c-notaires.dz

ALGERIAN MINISTRIES

Ministry of Finance
Palais du Gouvernement
Algiers, Algeria
Phone: (213-2) 732340
Fax: (213-2) 735472

Ministry of Commerce
Palais du Gouvernement
Algiers, Algeria
Phone: 732340
Fax: 733091

Ministry of Industry and Restructuring
Immeuble le Colisée
Algiers, Algeria
Phone: 592440
Fax: 604584

Ministry of Small and Medium Industry
Immeuble le Colisée
Algiers, Algeria
Phone: 592232
Fax: 592658

Ministry of Energy and Mines
80 avenue Ghermoul
Algiers, Algeria
Phone: 673300
Fax:

Ministry of Equipment
Ex-Grand Séminaire
Kouba
Algiers, Algeria
Phone: 689503

Ministry of Post and Telecommunications
4 boulevard Krim Belkacem
Algiers, Algeria
Phone: 711220
Fax: 711771

Ministry of Transport
119 rue Didouche Mourad
Algiers, Algeria
Phone: 747506
Fax: 656637

Ministry of Agriculture
4 rue des Quatre Canons
Algiers, Algeria
Phone: 711712
Fax: 612542

Investment Promotion Agency
APSI
(Agence de Promotion, de Soutien
et de Suivi des Investissements)
Boulevard du 11 décembre 1960
El Biar
Algiers, Algeria
Phone: 924269
Fax: 924647

CUSTOMS OFFICE

Direction Générale des Douanes
Avenue du Dr. Saadane
Algiers, Algeria

Phone: 711616
Fax: 746974

CNIS
(Centre National de l'Informatique et des Statistiques)
Avenue du 1er novembre
Algiers, Algeria
Phone: 715600
Fax: 715640

COMMERCIAL BANKS

BADR (Banque de l'Agriculture et du Développement Rural)
17 boulevard Colonel Amirouche
Algiers, Algeria
Phone: 746117
Fax: 615551

Al Baraka (Algerian-Saudi bank)
12 boulevard Colonel Amirouche
Algiers, Algeria
Phone: 745627
Fax: 745629

BDL (Banque du Développement Local)
5 rue Gaci Amar
Staoueli
Tipaza, Algeria
Phone: 392850
Fax: 392351

BEA (Banque Extérieure d'Algérie)
11 boulevard Colonel Amirouche
Algiers, Algeria
Phone: 605241
Fax: 602253

BNA (Banque Nationale d'Algérie)
8 boulevard Che Guevara
Algiers, Algeria
Phone: 713540
Fax: 713623

CPA (Crédit Populaire d'Algérie)
Boulevard Colonel Amirouche
Algiers, Algeria
Phone: 740528
Fax: 641179

Union Bank (private bank)
5 bis chemin Macklay
El Biar

Algiers, Algeria
Phone: 914552
Fax: 914548

LARGE PUBLIC SECTOR ENTERPRISES

Sonatrach (hydrocarbons)
10 rue du Sahara
Hydra
Algiers, Algeria
Phone: 607000
Fax: 601949

Sonelgaz (electric power and natural gas)
2 boulevard Krim Belkacem
Algiers, Algeria
Phone: 644555
Fax: 611314

ENIP (petrochemicals)
Zone Industrielle
BP 215, Skikda
Skikda, Algeria
Phone: (8) 958862
Fax: (8) 756146

SIDER (steel)
Chaiba, Commune Sidi Amar
BP 342, Annaba
Annaba, Algeria
Phone: (8) 851011
Fax: (8) 838957

SNVI (industrial vehicles)
BP 153, Rouiba
Boumerdes, Algeria
Phone: 851970
Fax: 857345

CHAMBER OF COMMERCE

CACI
(Chambre Algérienne de Commerce et d'Industrie)
Ali Habour, President
Mohamed Chami, Director General
Palais Consulaire
Place des Martyrs
Algiers, Algeria
Phone: 574444
Fax: 577025

PRIVATE SECTOR EMPLOYERS ASSOCIATIONS

ACE
(Association des Chefs d'Entreprise)
Mohand Amokrane Haddadi, President
Route d'Ouled Fayet
Cheraga
Algiers, Algeria
Phone: 365154
Fax: 365155

CAP
(Confédération Algérienne du Patronat)
Lamine Titah, President
Hotel Aurassi
Niveau C, Bureau 7
Algiers, Algeria
Phone: 647030
Fax: 647020

CGOEA
(Confédération Générale des Opérateurs
Economiques Algériens)
Habib Yousfi, President
27 rue Ferhat Abdelkader
Staouéli
Tipaza, Algeria
Phone: 392145
Fax: 392146

CNPA
(Confédération Nationale du Patronat Algérien)
Noureddine Nait-Abdelaziz, Acting President
39 rue Rahmoune Dekkar
El Biar
Algiers, Algeria
Phone: 922495
Fax: 922498

U.S. EMBASSY TRADE PERSONNEL

U.S. Embassy Algiers
Joseph Philippe Grégoire
Economic-Commercial Officer/Consul
Kamel Achab, Commercial Assistant
Karima Yadi, Economic Assistant
Anise Moussa, Agricultural Assistant
BP 408, Alger-Gare
16000 Algiers, Algeria or
Amembassy Algiers
Department of State
Washington, D.C. 20521-6030
Phone: [213-2] 693973
Fax: [213-2] 693979

U.S. Consulate General Casablanca
Albert Nahas, Senior Commercial Officer
8, blvd Moulay Youssef
Casablanca, Morocco
Phone: [212-2] 264550
Fax: [212-2] 220259

U.S. Embassy Rabat
Quintin Gray, Agricultural Attache
2 avenue de Marrakech
Rabat, Morocco
Phone: [212-7] 762265
Fax: [212-7] 765661

WASHINGTON-BASED COUNTRY CONTACTS

U.S. Department of Commerce
David Guglielmi
Algeria Desk Officer
Washington, D.C. 20230
Phone: (202) 482-1860
Fax: (202) 482-0878

MDBO, Multilateral Development Bank Operations
Janet Thomas, Acting Director
14th and Constitution, NW
Washington, D.C. 20007
Phone: (202) 482-3399
Fax: (202) 482-5179

TPCC, The Trade Promotion Coordinating Committee
TPCC Trade Information Center
Phone: 1-800-USA-TRADE

U.S. Department of State
Cynthia Kiersicht, Room 5250
Algeria Desk Officer
Washington, D.C. 20520
Phone: (202) 647-4680
Fax: (202) 736-4458

U.S.-BASED MULTIPLIERS

ExIm, Export-Import Bank
Hala El Mohandes
Project Officer
811 Vermont Ave, NW
Washington, D.C. 20571
Phone: (202) 566-8945
Fax: (202) 566-7524

TDA, U.S. Trade and Development Agency
John Richter, Regional Director
Nathan Younge, Country Manager
Africa and Middle East Region
SA-16, Room 309
Washington, D.C. 20523-1602
Phone: (703) 875-4357
Fax: (703) 875-4009

OPIC, Overseas Private Investment Corporation
James Williams, Insurance Officer
1100 New York Ave, NW
Washington, D.C. 20527
Phone: (202) 336-8575
Fax: (202) 408-5142

U.S. Department of Agriculture
Foreign Agricultural Service
Trade Assistance and Promotion Office
Phone: (202) 720-7420

ALGERIA CONSULATES GENERAL

FRANCE		
Lille 120, rue Solferino 59800 Tel: 20 54 56 & 30 Fax : 20.42.01.30	Lyon 7, rue Vauban 69006 Tel: 04.72.83.95.50 Fax : 04.782.83.85.62	Marseille 363 rue Paradis 13272 Cedex 08 Tel: 04.91.13.99.50 Fax : 04.91.37.13.73
Paris 48, rue Bouret 75019 Tel: 33.153.72.07.07 Fax : 33.145.02.14.12 & 33.153.72.07	Strasbourg 101, route de Shirmeck BP 445 -67200 Cedex 02 Tel: 03.88.30.17.51 Fax : 03.88.30.17.53	
GERMANY	**SAUDI ARABIA**	**BELGIUM**
Berlin Gorscstrasse 45-446 13187 Pankow Tel: (49-30) 48.16.17.0 Fax: ((49-30) 48.631 38 & 37	Djeddah Hai El Bawadi P.O. Box 8132 Tel : (009662) 6985034 Fax: (009662) 6985038	Bruxelles 30-32 rue de Lausanne 1060 Tel: (02) 537 8133 & 537 8241 Fax: (02) 537 9732
MOROCCO	**SWITZERLAND**	**TUNISIA**
Casablanca 159 Bd Moulay Idriss 1er Tel: (222) 80.41.76 & 77 Fax : 81.92.35	Geneva 308 bis Route de Lausanne 1293 Bellevue Tel: (4122) 774.19.19 & 774 19.09 Fax : 774 19.06	Tunis 83 avenue Jugurtha Tel: (218 21) 44 40 025 Fax : 44. 47 042

LIBYA		
Tripoli 12, rue de Kairouan Tel: 846.740 7 287 139 Fax : 790. 852		

LARGEST NEWSPAPERS

Al Chaab
1 Avenue Pasteur, Place Audin -Alger-
Tel: (02) 73 90 73, 73 95 15 Fax: (02) 73 94 94

An nasr
zone industrielle 24 fevrier -Constantine-
Tel: (04) 93 68 19
Fax: (04) 69 15 59

El djemhouria
6 rue Bensnoussi Hamida -Oran-
Tel: (06) 39 16 41; 39 06 42; 39 06 43
Fax: (06) 39 34 61

El Massa
Maison de la presse Abdelkader Safir, Kouba -Alger-
Tel: (02) 59 52 11; 59 63 33
Fax: (02) 59 64 57

El Moudjahid
20 rue de la Liberté -Alger-
Tel: (02) 73 70 30
Fax: (02) 73 90 43

L'Authentique
1 rue Bachir Attar, Place du 1er Mai -Alger-
Tel: (02) 65 80 03; 65 69 00
Fax: (02) 65 68 97

Le Matin
1 rue bachir attar,place du 1er mai -Alger-
Tel: (02) 66 07 08; 65 97 09
Fax: (02) 66 20 97

La tribune
1 rue Bachir Attar, Place du 1er Mai -Alger-
Tel: (02) 65 94 38; 65 94 39
Fax: (02) 65 82 59
El Watan
1 rue Bachir Attar, Place du 1er mai -Alger-
Tel: (02) 66 26 41; 66 26 42; 66 26 44
Fax: (02) 65 02 27
E_mail: elwatan@ist.cerist.dz

BANKS AND FINANCIAL INSTITUONS

ASSOCIATION OF BANKS AND INSTITUTIONS FINANCIAL "ABEF"

Headquarters: 3 Roman Way Val d'Hydra, Algiers
Telephone: 021 91 55 77
Fax: 021 91 55 60

THE BANKS

COMMERCIAL BANKS

BANK OUTSIDE OF ALGERIA "BEA"
Registered office: 48 Rue des Frères Bouadou,
Bir Mourad Rais - Algiers
Telephone: 021 56 25 70

Fax: 021 56 30 50/56 51 54
CEO: Mr. Loukal

NATIONAL BANK OF ALGERIA "BNA"
Registered Office: 8, Boulevard Ernesto Che Guevara, Algiers
Phone: 021 43 99 98
Fax: 021 43 94 94
Chairman and CEO: Benbouzid

BANK FOR AGRICULTURE AND RURAL DEVELOPMENT "BADR"
Head Office: 17, Boulevard Colonel Amir, Algiers
Telephone: 021 64 26 70-63 38 78
Fax: 021 63 51 46 / 64 34 44
Chairman and CEO: Mr. DJEBAR

BANK OF DEVELOPMENT LOCAL "BDL"
Registered office: 5, rue Gaci Amar Staoueli Algiers
Telephone: 021 39 34 89-39 52 15
Fax: 021 39 37 57
Chairman and CEO: Mr. Bachtarzi

POPULAR VOTE OF ALGERIA "CPA"
Registered Office: 2, Boulevard Colonel Amir, Algiers
Telephone: 021 63 57 12
Fax: 021 63 56 98 / 63 58 83
CEO: Mr. Djellab

CASE OF SAVINGS AND INSURANCE "CNEP BANK"
Registered Office: Lot # 2 Garidi, Kouba - Alger
Telephone: 021 28 47 38-28 47 67
Fax: 021 28 47 35
CEO: Mr. BESSA

AL BARAKA BANK ALGERIA
Headquarters: Hai Bouteldja Houidef, Villa No. 1 Bypass South,
Ben Aknoun - Algiers
Phone: 021 91 64 50-55 - 55 35 00
Fax: 021 91 64 57 and 58
General Manager: Mr. H SIDDIK AFID

ARAB BANKING CORPORATION ALGERIA "ABC"
Registered office: 54 Avenue des Trois Frères Bouadou
(ex ravine wild woman) Bir Mourad Rais, Algiers
Telephone: 021 54 03 LD 45/54 Jan. 83/54 15 15/54 15 34 /
54 14 37/54 16 00
Fax: 021 54 16 04

NAT I XIS BANK
Head Office: 62, Chemin Drareni, Hydra, Algiers
Telephone: 023 92 41 23 and 36
021 48 01 01/48 02 02/48 03 03
Fax: 023 92 41 51/43 43
CEO: Mr. Mouffok

GENERAL COMPANY ALGERIA
Headquarters: 16105 Karma El Residence Gue de Constantine
Algiers- BP: 55 Bir Khadem
Phone: 021 45 13 70
Fax: 021 45 13 75
CEO: Gerald LACAZE

ALGERIA CITYBANK NA
(Branch Bank)
Head Office: 7, Rue Larbi Allik, Hydra, Algiers
Telephone: 021 54 78 20-021 54 81 21
Fax: 021 54 81 85
Chairman and CEO: Mr. Kamel DRISS

ARAB BANK PLC ALGERIA
(bank branch)
Headquarters: Boulevard Benyoucef Benkhedda,
Sidi Yahia # 46 - Algiers
Telephone: 021 48 49 26-48 00 02-48 00 03
Fax: 021 48 00 01 / LD: 021 60 49 86
CEO: Mr. BOHLI

BNP PARIBAS EL DJAZAIR
Head Office: 10, Rue Abou Nouas, Hydra - Alger
Telephone: 021 60 39 42-60 39 29
Fax: 021 60 72 19 / LD: 021 48 05 75
CEO: Mr. Depuch

TRUST BANK ALGERIA
Head Office: 70, Chemin Larbi Allik, Hydra - Alger - BP 772
Phone: 021 54 97 55

Fax: 021 54 97 50
Chief Executive Officer: Mr. Taleb REDHA SLIMANE

GULF BANK ALGERIA
Headquarters: Haouche Road Chéraga,
BP 26a Delly Ibrahim - Algiers
Telephone: 021 91 00 31 to 91 August 76
Fax: 021 91 02 64/91 74 10
Chief Executive Officer: Mr. Louhab

THE HOUSING BANK FOR TRADE ANDFINANCE -ALGERIA
Head Office: 16, Ahmed Ouaked, PO Box 103, Postal Code No. 16320 Delly Ibrahim - Algiers
Telephone: 021 91 80 11/91 87 57
Fax: 021 91 88 78
Chief Executive Officer: Mr. MAHMOUD

Fransabank EL-DJAZAIR
Headquarters: 45 B. Lot Petite Provence,
Sidi Yahia - Hydra - Alger
Telephone: 021 48 December 96 / 48 27 48
Fax: 021 48 December 43
CEO: Mr. JOSEPH Dakak

AGRICULTURAL CREDIT CORPORATE
AND INVESTMENT BANK - ALGERIA

Registered Office: Tower Business Center, Maritime Pine,
Mohammedia - Algiers
Phone: 021 89 13 00
Fax: 021 89 November 99
Chief Executive Officer: Mr. DUCHMANN

AL SALAM BANK - ALGERIA - SPA
Headquarters: 233? Rue Ahmed Brahim Ouaked Dély - Algiers
Phone: 021 91 September 83
Fax: 021 91 April 25
Chief Executive Officer: Mr. IBRAHIM fenik

ALGERIA HSBC (bank branch)
Headquarters: Business Center, maritime pines
El Mohammedia - Algiers
Phone: 021 89 40 00/89 40 05
Fax: 021 89 40 04
Chief Executive Officer: Mr. R. SEKAK

FINANCIAL INSTITUTIONS

II.1 FINANCIAL INSTITUTIONS A GENERAL PURPOSE

NATIONAL FARM MUTUAL FUND "CNMA"
Registered office: 24 Boulevard Victor Hugo, Algiers

Telephone: 021 74 99 06
Fax: 021 73 July 31 - 74 99 07

FINANCIAL investment company, PARTICIPATION AND INVESTMENT - SPA - (Sofinance - SPA)
Headquarters: Avenue Mohamed Belkacemi
(Building Agenor) El Anassers - Algiers
Telephone: 021 47 66 00-03
Fax: 021 47 66 30
Chief Executive Officer: Mr. Mansoor

COMPANY REFINANCING hypotécaire "SRH"
Registered Office: 3, Central Business
Said Hamdine - Algiers
Phone: 021 56 47 99
Fax: 021 56 44 36
CEO: Mr. Abdelkader BELTAS

ARAB LEASING CORPORATION (COMPANYOF CREDIT LEASE)
Headquarters - Rue Ahmed Ouaked Dely Ibrahim - Algiers
Phone: 021 91 77 63-91 77 67
Fax: 021 91 76 72
Chief Executive Officer: Mr. Kamel azira

Cetelem ALGERIA
Headquarters - 92, Chemin Mohamed Gacem,
El Mouradia Algiers
Phone: 021 27 54 36/49
Fax: 021 27 February 45
Chief Executive Officer: Mr. GROS BERTRAND
DG Phone: 021 27 August 97

Maghreb Leasing Algeria
Headquarters - 31, Avenue Mohamed Belkacemi
The Annassers - Algiers
Phone: 021 77 17 79-77 17 81
Fax: 021 77 17 82
Chief Executive Officer: Mr. ABDELKAFI

NATIONAL SOCIETY LEASING - SPA
Headquarters - November 1st Avenue
Zéralda - Algiers Phone: 021 32 89 53-32 91 03Fax: 021 32 89 55 Chief Executive Officer: Mr.Mohammed KRIM

Ijar LEASING ALGERIA - SPA
Headquarters:
elephone:
Fax:
Director:

EL DJAZAIR Ijar - SPA
Headquarters:

elephone:
Fax:
Director:

II.2 FINANCIAL INSTITUTIONS A SPECIFIC PURPOSE

ALGERIA DEVELOPMENT BANK "BAD "
Registered office: 21 Boulevard Zighout Youcef, Algiers
Telephone: 021 73 99 04-73 76 38
Agency Birkhadem: Lot Mont Froid Zenka, Birkhadem
LD Phone 021 55 41 09-55 22 89-99
Fax: 021 55 55 20
Chief Executive Officer: Mr. ALLILET

LIAISON OFFICES

BRITISH ARAB COMMERCIAL BANK
Headquarters - 12, Chemin Abdelkader Gadouche, Hydra
Phone: 021 69 July 20
Fax: 021 60 19 61
Representative: Mr. HALTALI

UNION BANK OF ARAB AND FRENCH
Headquarters - 72 Avenue Ahmed Ghermoul Algiers
Phone: 021 46 40 61-01
Fax: 021 47 38 13-88
Representative: Mr. BOUHARAOUA

INDUSTRIAL AND COMMERCIAL CREDIT
Headquarters - 36, rue Brothers Benali (eg Parmentier)
Hydra - Alger -
Telephone: 021 60 15 55/56
Fax: 021 69 27 74
Representative: MA MOSTEFAOUI

AGRICULTURAL CREDIT INDOSUEZ
Headquarters - 43, Chemin Parmentier, Hydra, Alger
Phone: 021 60 77 99
Fax: 021 60 April 71
Manager: John Lorenz Ehrentrant

TUNIS INTERNATIONAL BANK
Headquarters - Road Macklay Sidi Merzouk
(CIP ISSU WB Villa # 17 Ben Aknoun)
Phone: 021 91 69 42
Fax: 021 91 41 08
Representative: Mr. BAGHDADI

FORTIS BANK
Headquarters - 01, rue Assus Sacred Heart
- Algiers -
Telephone: 021 71 62 09
Fax: 021 71 62 14
Representative: Mr. Yacine YAKER

BANCO SABADEL
Subdivision Piette, 1 Rue No. 10 Paradou
- Algiers -
Telephone: 021 60 16 January
Fax: 021 48 14 96
Representative: Ms. Hassiba Bestandji

IMPORTANT TRADE AND EXPORT CONTACTS

GOVERNMENT AND TRADE SUPPORTING ORGANIZATIONS

ALGERIA ORGANIZATIONS

Bank of Algeria / Banque D'Algerie
www.bank-of-algeria.dz
The Bank of Algeria is the national bank of the People's Democratic Republic of Algeria. Created in December 1962, the Bank of Algeria sets the operational guidelines and norms for all banks operating in Algeria including accounting standards, reserve requirements, and the usage of funds.

Embassy of Algeria in Washington, DC
www.algeria-us.org
Located in the heart of the US Capitol, the Embassy of Algeria is the official post of the People's Democratic Republic of Algeria in Washington, DC. The website provides news on Algeria, cultural highlights, economic opportunities, visas and consular services, information on the political system, and speeches on the history of Algeria. The Honorable Ambassador Abdallah Baali is the Algerian Ambassador to the United States.

Ministry of Commerce / Ministere du Commerce
www.cnrc.org.dz (French)
The Ministry of Commerce of the Peoples Democratic Republic of Algeria hosts the National Commerce Register as well as the National Chamber of Commerce. The Ministry of Commerce centralizes and distributes information and statistics on businesses operating in Algeria, and economic conditions and opportunities. The Ministry of Commerce is the site for registration of businesses operating in Algeria and promotes the development of commerce in Algeria.

Ministry of Energy and Mining / Ministere de l'Energie et des Mines
www.mem-algeria.org (English)
www.mem-algeria.org/fr (French)
The Ministry of Energy and Mines of Algeria develops the legislative, regulatory and institutional mechanisms intended to attract investment and further develop foreign investments, both direct and through partnerships, in the hydrocarbon, energy and mining sectors, including activities such as those downstream of hydrocarbons and the production of renewable energies. The Honorable Minister Chakib Khelil is the Algerian Minister of Energy & Mines.

Ministry of Education / Ministere de l'Education National
www.meducation.edu.dz

Ministry of Foreign Affairs / Ministere des Affaires Etrangeres
www.mae.dz
The Ministry of Foreign Affairs is the centralized diplomatic agency coordinating with all Algerian ambassadors and diplomats serving throughout the world. The Ministry also coordinates visits of foreigners to Algeria and manages visa procedures.

Ministry of Health / Ministere de la Sante
www.sante.dz

Ministry of Housing / Ministere de l'Habitat et de l'Urbanisme
www.mhu.gov.dz

Ministry of Justice / Ministere de la Justice
www.mjustice.dz

Ministry of New Technologies, Post and Telecommunications
www.postelecom.dz

Ministry of Work and Social Security / Ministere du Travail et de la Securite Sociale
www.mtss.gov.dz

Ministry of Participation and the Promotion of Investment / Ministere de la Particpation et la Promotion de l'Investissment
www.mppi.dz

Ministry of Small and Medium Sized Enterprises and Artisans /Ministere des PME et de L'Artisanat
www.pmeart-dz.org/fr
The Ministry of Small and Medium Sized Enterprises and Artisans promotes local opportunities for investments in small to medium sized enterprises to national and international investors. The Ministry works to ameliorate the operating environment for thee firms as well as develop the richness of Algerian handicrafts. The Ministry also encourages entrepreneurship through the development of new enterprises.

Ministry of Water Ressources / Ministere des Ressources en Eaux
www.mre.gov.dz

National Business Registery / Centre National de Registre Du Commerce
www.cnrc.org.dz/ (French)
Founded in 1963, the role of the National Business Registry is to maintian records of all active comapnies in Algeria, to provide informative updates on the commercial implications of governemnt legislation, and to create statistical reviews on ecnomic players and trends.

National Company of Fairs and Exhibits / Societe Algerienne de Foires et Exportations
www.safex.com.dz

National Customs Agency of Algeria
www.douanes-cnis.dz/

National Office of Statistics / Office National des Statistiques
www.ons.dz (English)
www.ons.dz (French)
The National Office of Statistics attends to the precise compilation and regular diffusion of information adapted to socio-economic agents' needs. It assures the regular reliability of data, statistical analysis and economic studies necessary to generate socio-economic policy. The National Office of Statistics releases information in pursuance of the statistical national program, indexes, indicators of the national economy as well as the nation's accounts.

National Office of Wine Culture / Office National de Commercialisation des Produits Viti-vinicoles
www.oncv-groupe.com
An agent of the Ministry of Agriculture, the ONCV of Algeria has partnered with numerous foreign investors to develop the wine industry of Algeria. The first bottles of Algerian wine were exported to the United States in the 1980's.

National Popular Assembly / Assemble Nationale Popularie
www.apn-dz.org

National Taxation Administration / Direction National des Impots
www.impots-dz.org

University of Algiers
www.univ-alger.dz (French)
www.univ-alger.dz/ang (English)
Founded in 1909 the University of Algiers remains one of the most respected educational institutions in Algeria.

Presidency of the Republic of Algeria / El Mouradia
www.elmouradia.dz

Supreme Court of Algeria / Le Cour Supreme
www.coursupreme-dz.org

UNITED STATES TRADE ORGANIZATIONS

Bilateral US-Arab Chamber of Commerce
www.bilateralchamber.org
The Bilateral US-Arab Chamber of Commerce is a not-for-profit 501(c) 6 international network of business leadership headquartered in Houston, Texas (USA). The Bilateral Chamber was founded in 1997 by Aida Araissi, who works with its exclusive membership network of CEOs to establish strategic connections between the United States and Middle East/North Africa (MENA) for the purpose of fostering economic growth, educational advancement and social progress in both regions.

Export-Import Bank of the United States (EXIM Bank)
www.exim.gov
The Export-Import Bank of the United States supports the financing of US goods and services, turning export opportunities into real transactions, maintaining and creating more US jobs. The EXIM Bank assumes credit and country risks the private sectro is unable or unwilling to accept.

United States International Trade Administration (ITA)
www.ita.doc.gov
The United States International Trade Administration is the trade promotion agency of the US Department of Commerce. The ITA promoted US exports of manufactured goods, nonagricultural commodities and services.

Office of the US Trade Representative (USTR)
www.ustr.gov
The Office of the US Trade Representative (USTR) is responsible for developing and coordinating US international trade, commodity and direct investment policy, and overseeing negotiations with other countries including the negotiations for bilateral free trade agreements.

Overseas Private Investment Corporation (OPIC)
www.opic.gov
The Overseas Private Investment Corporation (OPIC) was established as a development agency of the US Government in 1971. OPIC helps US businesses invest overseas, fosters economic development in new and emerging markets, complements the private sector in managing the risks associated with foreign direct investment, and supports US foreign policy.

US BUREAU OF ECONOMIC ANALYSIS
www.bea.gov
The US Bureau of Economic Analysis provides the most comprehansive statistical picture available of the US economy.

US Department of Agriculture
www.ustda.gov
The US Department of Agriculture is a research leader in everything from human nutrition to new crop technologies that allow us to grow more food using less water and pesicides. The USDA helps ensure open markets for US agricultural products. The US Department maintains a liason office at the US Embassy in Algiers.

US Department of Commerce
www.doc.gov
The Honorable Secretary Carlos Guttierez is the 35th Secretary of the US Department of Commerce, the voice of business in government. Secretary Gutierrez is a core member of President Bush's economic team, advising the President on many issues, including pro-growth and job creating economic policies, international trade, business concerns, and energy policy. The US Department of Commerce maintains a liason office at the US Embassy in Algiers.

US Department of State
www.state.gov
The US Department of State is part of the Executive Branch of the US Government. The Department of State advances US objectives and interests in shaping a freer, more secure and more prosperous world through its primary role in developing and implementing the President's foreign policy. In additon to supporting the foreign affairs activites of the US Department of Commerce and USAID, the US Department of State provides and array of important services to US citizens and to foreigners seeking to visit or immigrate to the United States.

US Embassy in Algiers
www.algiers.usembassy.gov
Situated in the heart of the capitol city of Algeria, the US Embassy in Algiers is the official representative of the US Government. This website provides information about embassy services, bilateral relations, and consular affairs including visas for travel to the United States. The US Ambassador to Algeria is the Honorable Ambassador Henry Ensher.

US Energy Information Administraion
www.eia.doe.gov
The Energy Information Administration of the United States (EIA), created by Congress in 1977, is a statistical agency of the US Department of Energy. The EIA provides policy-independent data, forecasts, and analyses to promote sound policy making, efficient markets and public understanding regarding energy and its interaction with the economy and the environment.

US Patent and Trademark Office
www.uspto.gov
An agency of the US Department of Commerce, the US Patenet and Trademark Office provides patenet and trademark protection to inventors and businesses for their inventions and corporate and product identificaion. Through preservation, classificaion and dissemination of patent information, the USPTO encourages innovation and the scientific and technical advancement of US industry.

US Trade and Development Agency
www.ustda.gov
As a core priority, the USTDA facilitates development in emerging markets by promoting US

partnerships in high priority overseas projects. Teh USTDA responds to the development priorities of public and private sector project sponsors in host countries. The USTDA offers a wide range of opportunities for US firms to apply their products, technology and expertise in the pursuit of important development objectives. To date, these opportunities have been connected with more than US$21billion in US exports. The USTDA supports the development of a fair and open trading environment.

World Trade Center of Chicago
www.wtcil.org
The World Trade Illinois (WTI) is "Your Trusted Partner in World Trade". A not for profit organization providing vital international trade services to WTIL members. Headquartered in Schaumburg, Illinois with ten satellite offices located around the State of Illinois, World Trade Illinois is a bridge between member organizations and World Markets. World Trade Illinois (WTI) is proud to announce securing the Chicago Option from World Trade Center Association as of October 10, 2010.

LARGEST EXPORTERS

LIVESTOCK, LIFTING PRODUCTS AND AGRICULTURAL PRODUCTS E

BRIMED IMPORT EXPORT Lot 140 Alioua Fodil Ché raga ALGER	0770 33 62 19 0661 33 62 19	021 36 20 69		Fresh truffles
AGRO CONSULTING INTERNATIONAL 194, Rue Boujemâa Khellil Oued El Achour Roumane 16403 ALGER	021 February 30 08 021 30 83 39 021 30 81 66 021 30 81 65	021 30 83 66	www.aci-algerie.com info@aci-algerie.com	Peas
B-TRANS Sarl City Djbel Chilia Bt 01 Ain Taya ALGER	0550 47 July 50	023 96 16 32	lachter@live.fr	Dates
CETRADE Epe Spa 48, Rue Boudjemâa Meghani Hussein Dey ALGER				Potato
CITY INDUSTRY Sarl Abdi quoted Mouloud Villa No. 05 Khraicia ALGER			city-industrie@hotmail.com	Chicken feet
FMP AGRI Eurl City El Merdja, Lot	021 85 14 14	021 85 14 15	fmpagri@hotmail.com	Peas

No. G 25 Rouiba 16012 ALGER				
GOLDEN SEED Sarl City Saliba No. 24 ZI Oued Smar 16270 ALGER	021 20 71 49	021 20 71 29		Locust bean seeds
FX PRO LIMITED Eurl Street Fonar Bt 02 Sidi M'hamed ALGER				Dates, Soft Drinks, Fruit Juices

KINKEL TRADING Eurl City Sonelgaz Cage No. 02 Ford L 308 Constantine ALGER	021 73 35 65	021 73 35 65		Dates
MANAR chamal IFRIQUIA IMPORT EXPORT City Château Rouge, Rue 06 Loc NR 16 Eucalyptus ALGER	0770 73 32 24		manar-algerie2011@hotmail.fr	Chicken feet
SALAM M'ZAB EXPORT Eurl City Bt 384 07 # 56 Re GHAIA ALGER	0664 September 11 14			Truffles
LADAOURA Eurl City Diar El Afia # 20 Bourouba ALGER	July 35 0550 08 0550 15 38 43	021 30 61 81		Truffles
RED DRAGON Sarl Villa Lot No. 08 of satde Birkhadem ALGER	February 95 0771 02 021 40 51 96	021 40 51 96	dragonrouge06@yahoo.fr	Fresh truffles
TRADING BEL Sarl Lot 09 Alioua Fodil Ché raga ALGER	021 36 78 66	021 36 78 71	sarl_trading@hotmail.fr	Truffles
FRUIT STORE EXPORT (ESF) 13 Allotment Khoja No. 01 kouba ALGER				Truffles

WAFRA DATES Sarl City November 1, 1954 Villa No. 08 Baba Hassen ALGER	November 99 0662 41 021 35 Sept. 94	021 35 September 94	wafadattes@yahoo.fr	Dates
KAMALAH TRADE Sarl Hai Ouled Maamar Heuraoua ALGER	0772 15 96 42			Chicken feet
MALAKANI IMPORT & EXPORT Quarter 1200 Bt B 08 Ekama Al Jamila Al Bab Ezzouar ALGER	0977 December 23 14 0551 33 70 77 0664 40 44 80		m.malakani @ yahoo.com	Chicken feet
PERFECT INTERNATIONAL GROUP Sarl City Garidi 1, 216 Housing, Tower No. 03, Etage54, Kouba ALGER	0661 66 95 85 021 28 48 40	021 28 48 40	perfectgroup2009@hotmail.com	Chicken feet
SELECT DATES Sarl 22 Route des Dunes Ché raga ALGER	021 38 35 69	021 38 35 69	selectdattesalger@yahoo.fr	Dates
Sabetta Sarl Oued City Eddeheb II, Bt # 24 ANNABA	038 84 14 July 0661 32 54 14	038 84 July 14		Wild onions, Snails
AGRO FOOD "AMRIDJ" Eurl Ighzer Amokrane Ouzellagene BEJAIA	0661 53 November 73	021 54 81 01	agro-amridj@yahoo.fr	Dates
BELKHICHENE Snc BEJAIA	026 95 May 21	034 31 40 91	snc_ebf@yahoo.fr	Poultry products
Frulact ALGERIA Spa BEJAIA	034 35 71 66	034 35 71 03		Pre paration strawberry
AGRONIMA Sarl Tolga BISKRA	0661 35 17 22	033 78 79 08		Dates
	033 74 70	033 74 70		Dates

BIO-OASIS Area of Activity OUMECHE BISKRA	90	90		Dates
BISCOFRUITS Sarl Area é equipment 38 BISKRA	033 75 98 21 033 75 98 22	033 75 96 17 033 75 96 58	www.duna-dattes.com.dz biscofruits@yhaoo.fr	Dates, paste dates
CHENNOUFI Salah 09, Rue Ben Aissa AMEUR - TOLGA BISKRA	033 78 77 35 0661 54 94 96	033 78 84 98	chenoufi-salah@yahoo.com	Dates
DATOL Eurl 122 Avenue SI EL HAOUES - TOLGA BISKRA	0770 61 57 16 033 78 75 75	033 78 69 03	datol@hotmail.com	Dates
KERBAA ABDELKRIM property RW No. 03 Lichana Tolga BISKRA	2 May 02 0560 033 75 51 21	033 75 51 21	kerbaa@yahoo.fr	Dates
ECODATTE Area é equipment BISKRA	033 75 95 80 033 75 98 74	033 75 95 05		Dates
EL MOUKHTAR.Co Lot Benghana No. 3 BISKRA	033 74 63 24 0661 62 August 40	033 74 63 24 033 74 63 27 021 35 14 96	www.dattes-moukhtar.com elmoukhtarco@hotmail.com	Dates, Fruit Juice
Haddoud Salim Ets Area of Activity TOLGA BISKRA	033 78 61 54 033 78 85 40	033 78 61 53	haddou_s@yahoo.fr	Dates
PHENIX Sarl Droh, Common Chetma BISKRA	0661 59 84 04 0661 59 84 05	033 74 41 28	sarlphenixdattes@yahoo.fr	Dates, paste dates
SUDACO Epe Spa Avenue de la Gare - BP 64 RP	033 74 57 59	033 74 17 27	sudaco2002@yahoo.fr	Dates
DANA DATES Area of Activity s Oumache BISKRA			www.dana-dattes.com	Dates

MALIK Ets Area é equipment Biskra Biskra	95	95		
NOUR DATES Sarl Street 1 November Foughala BISKRA				Dates
BiOasis Sarl Area of Activity s Oumache BISKRA				Dates
HAMZA DATES Eurl 103 Area é equipment BISKRA	033 75 99 69	033 75 99 87		Dates
SOUTH DATES Eurl Rue Mohamed Tahar Athmani Tolga BISKRA	033 78 53 72	033 78 53 72	suddatte@hotmail.fr	Dates
ALIM AGROFOOD Sarl 56, Rue Amrane Hifnawi Doucen BISKRA	0797 09 79 29 0774 36 30 71		alim-agrofood@rambler.ru	Dates
EL BISKRIA MARKETING AGRICULTURAL PRODUCTS Area é equipment BP 457-07000 BISKRA	033 75 98 52	033 75 97 59	bicpag@yahoo.fr	Dates
ABCA Eurl Street BENDALI Bey - Beni Mered BP 74 BLIDA	025 42 00 01	025 42 March 17	abca-dz@yahoo.fr	Locust bean seeds are crushed
INTERNATIONAL BUSINESS CONNECTIONS Eurl 02, Rue Bouaageb - Boufarik BLIDA	0661 56 34 72	021 39 November 28	connexions@qc.aira.com	Dates, Truffles
FRUITS TASSILI Eurl City Logts 206 Bt S 21 ° 04 Ouled Yaich BLIDA	0661 77 17 17	025 40 17 44	fruitassili@hotmail.fr	Truffles
	0668 41 00	030 23 78		Hey lix

EL KHALIL Sarl 164 City Fodhil Didouche Mourad CONSTANTINE	81	49		snail, wild onions
KHELAF PASTA Eurl 164 City Fodhil [illegible] [illegible] Yasmine DIDOUCHE CONSTANTINE	0550 87 83 70	031 90 51 47		Wild onions
SOCOFEL Sarl ZAM Ali Mendjeli City El Khroub CONSTANTINE	0661 36 January 73	031 90 99 56		Dates
DHAOUIA Sarl BP 407 Route de Touggourt EL WADI	032 21 73 09 032 21 85 45	032 21 52 07 032 21 89 27	www.daouia.yahoo.fr.gd utpa_sea_daouia@yahoo.fr.gd	Dates
SOUF DATES BP 27 TEKSEBT - El Oued	032 21 85 45 032 21 84 45	032 21 84 45		Dates
UTPA Daouia Sarl Road Touggourt EL WADI	032 21 89 44 032 21 98 92	032 21 89 27 032 21 98 91	utpa_sea_daouia@yahoo.fr	Dates
LMSADFA MOHAMED El Oued El Hamraia				Dates
Baya ROSE Sarl BP 85 Zelfana GHARDAIA	029 86 August 31	029 86 35 18 029 86 32 56		Dates
AGRO CONSULTING MERCHELA Sarl Capt. El Fedjoudj GUELMA	037 23 63 27 037 23 63 32		sarlacna@yahoo.fr	Agricultural products
SOLTANI FAOUZI Eurl Capt. of Bouchegouf GUELMA	0770 44 34 76 037 22 78 10		m.faouzisoltani @ yahoo.fr	Snail

Eurl El Bahri area Tanafdour El Milia JIJEL	41 031 57 64 92	92		onions
AGRO FOOD GIS Sarl City of Gardens - Sig MASCARA	045 84 84 75 040 46 56 89	045 84 84 75		Wild onions
ALLOUACHE EXPORT Eurl City Senaoua Sup MILA	0771 97 16 17 031 57 95 39	031 57 95 39	allouacheexport@live.com	Wild onions
CHELGHOUMI EXPORT Sarl Subdivision Ben Boulaid Chelghoum Laid MILA	0772 44 00 84			Snail
Soudi Smaine EXPORT Sarl Street El Qods Zeghaia MILA	0772 16 36 84 031 55 42 03	031 55 42 03	sydsmn09@gmail.com	Chestnut, snail, wild onions
LA VIDA IMPORT-EXPORT Eurl Cited 05 July 1962 Bt 78 # 29 MOSTAGANEM	045 21 Jan. 64	045 21 Jan. 64		Fresh truffles
FNQ IMPORT EXPORT MOSTAGANEM Sarl 484 ENTR2 Djebli Med Beavers MOSTAGANEM	045 33 November 82			Potato
Metidji Spa Area of Activity Salamander MOSTAGANEM	045 30 80 80	045 30 81 81	contact@groupe-metidji.com	Ce re ales
BIODATTES - ALGERIA 01, Rue des Frères MISSOURI ORAN	040 22 27 00	040 22 27 00 041 34 66 52	www.biodattes.com contact@biodattes.com	Organic dates
	0772 92 95	041 39 39	d.bouabdellah @ caramail.com	Snail living

EL badjo EXPORT 33, Boulevard Emir Abdelkader - Misserghin ORAN	05	72	djouher@nomade.fr	Snail living
EL badjo EXPORT / ESMA Benabderrahmane 33, Boulevard Emir Abdelkader - Misserghin ORAN / Lot 26 Lot 154 Hai Khemisti Bir El Djir ORAN	05 / 0570 49 14 54 0795 17 68 14 040 21 30 59	72 / 041 42 15 40	djouher@nomade.fr	Dates
Bousetta MOHAMED 12 November 1954 1st Avenue SETIF	0779 40 00 02 036 93 52 70	036 93 52 70		Bitter almonds are de cortiqué
BOUKELLAL MOHAMED TAHAR Ets 02, Rue Bel Air entered e 02 NR 12 SETIF			boukellal@yandex.ru	Dates
ALARGAN INTERNATIONAL Sarl 24, Rue Sidi Bel Abbes Boukhanifis	0550 60 31 69	048 65 21 28	r.fibre @ hotmail.com	Apricot kernel bitter
RUSICADIA Eurl City Larbi Ben M'hidi # 18 GTP SKIKDA	038 75 Jan. 56	038 75 March 22	rusicadia-export@hotmail.fr	Alfa
AKBAOUI Khatari TAMANRASSET	0661 48 80 96			Dates
BIOSOL IMPORT EXPORT City Fatima Zohra TEBESSA	0553 September 31 11 037 49 27 36	037 49 27 51		Wild onions
AGRICULTURAL SELMANI Has Imghor Mechatrasse 15000 Tizi Ouzou	0552 54 71 70	026 21 75 10	selmaniagricole@yahoo.fr	Lé vegetables

AMOKRANE City Kabilya Bt No. 02 to No. 25 btp 15001 Tizi Ouzou	70	10		vegetables
BOUBLENZA Sarl Lot 09 D ZI Remchi TLEMCEN	043 23 61 51 043 27 38 90	043 27 38 92 043 23 61 52	www.sarl_boublenza.com contact@sarl-boublenza.com sarl_boublenza@hotmail.com	Carob powder, carob crushed, flour carob pulp, seeds, carob flour olive pits
DEPOTLALLA Sarl Rue Colonel Lotfi No. 192 Maghnia TLEMCEN	0770 60 November 38	043 30 36 20	dehaoui2008@yahoo.fr	Wild onions
SUPER TASTE 45 Lot A and B Oujlida TLEMCEN	0557 21 36 86	043 21 December 72		Dates

AGRO-INDUSTRIAL PRODUCTS

FOOD BEAUTIFUL Sarl Rue des Roses, Villa No. 44 - Mohammadia ALGER	021 82 07 91 021 82 July 92 July 94 82 021	July 90 021 82 021 82 October 18	www.labellealgerie.com rebia@labellealgerie.com	Lé dry vegetables, roasted ground coffee relied, Soybean Oil, Couscous, Margarine, Soap
ALJUS Sarl Route Ouled Fayet Ché raga ALGER	021 36 44 48 021 37 17 17	021 36 44 48		Juice
FLAVORS OF ALGERIA Eurl 66 Road MEFTAH, ZI Oued Smar ALGER	021 51 58 50 021 51 53 17	021 51 35 77	www.aromedalgerie.com aromealg@yahoo.fr commercial@aromedalgerie.com	Aromatic emulsions
ATLAS BOTTLING CORPORATION Sarl ZI Rouiba RN # 5 ALGER	021 81 34 33 021 81 39 29 021 81 17 55	021 81 34 33 021 81 31 23	www.abcpepsi.com abc@abcpepsi.com	Soft drinks
	021 30 90	021 30 91	www.groupebimo.com	Cocoa butter, cocoa

COCOA BIMO Sarl 6 A, Brick Road - ALGIERS Ali Baba	90 021 30 91 91	27 021 30 98 01	bimoindustrie@yahoo.fr	mass, cocoa powder, Cocoa Cake
[illegible] Sarl [illegible] [illegible] Birtouta ALGER	[illegible]21 40 81 [illegible]21 30 91 [illegible]21 40 81 34	[illegible] [illegible]8 01 021 40 81 39	bimoindustrie@yahoo.fr	[illegible] cocoa powder, Cocoa Cake
DJENAH RABAH City Merbouni Bougara BLIDA			djenahexpo@gmail.com	Pre-cooked frozen food s s
Fruital COCA COLA Sarl RN # 5, ZI Rouiba ALGER	October 59 021 81 021 81 25 42 021 81 71 01 021 81 15 60	021 81 71 02 81 34 79 021 021 81 October 44	saidothmani@yahoo.fr	Soft drinks
HAMMOUD BOUALEM & Cie Ets 201, Rue Hassiba Ben Bouali - ALGIERS Belouizdad	021 67 Aug. 20 021 67 47 40	021 67 Aug. 20 021 67 59 04	www.hamoud-boualem.com hbexportation@gmail.com	Soda
LABOREF Sarl Street A, No. 12A Area of Activity Dunes - Che raga ALGER	021 35 42 94 021 35 42 68 021 38 13 96 021 38 13 97	021 38 13 90 021 35 41 09	www.laboref-dz.com commercial@laboref-dz.com	Im liorants bread, food Weapons powder, liquid food flavorings, savory aromas s, Emulsions for sodas, Ge lifiant, essential oils are distilled
MAROUANI BEVERAGES GROUP ZI Reghaia, Route de la Gare - Re GHAIA ALGER	021 84 84 84 021 84 03 50	021 84 88 48	amaatoug@mgbroyal.com	Soda
MILLS SAHELIAN Sarl Area Parks and Seats - ALGIERS Zeralada	021 32 96 27	021 32 96 34		Couscous Pasta
NCA ROUIBA Spa ZI Rouiba, National Road No. 5 ALGER	021 81 November 51	021 81 22 93 021 50 70 88	www.Rouiba.com.dz nca@Rouiba.com.dz b-mohamed@Rouiba.com.dz	Nectar drinks are fruity, fruit juices, fruit juice milk

NEW BISCUIT OF CHERCHELL 13, Rue Mouloud BELHOUCHET Hussein Dey ALGER	021 77 77 33 021 77 77 11 021 77 77 22	021 23 18 37	export@nbc.dz	Biscuits filled with cocoa s
NOVIDIS FOOD IMPORT - EXPORT City Zerhouni Mokhtar, Bt 9, No. 55 - Mohammadia ALGER	021 20 25 63 020 40 01 42	021 20 25 58 021 20 25 63		Olive oil, juice cocktail, orange juice
ONCV Spa 112, Quai Sud ALGER	021 73 82 59 021 73 82 60 021 73 72 75 021 73 72 79	021 73 69 40 021 73 72 97	www.oncv-groupe.com dg@oncv-groupe.com	Wine bottles, wine in bulk
PASTA SPIGA D'ORO Sarl 47 Briquetterie Road - ALGIERS Baba Ali	021 30 97 44 024 46 49 36	024 46 49 37 021 30 92 41	intpasta@yahoo.fr	Pasta
Promasidor DJAZAIR Sarl ZI Rouiba, Channel C, No. 11 ALGER	021 81 16 78 021 81 26 74 021 81 18 74	021 81 18 99 024 81 18 59	www.promasidor-dz.com office@promasidor-dz.com	Beverages are flavored powder, instant powdered chocolate, custard, instant milk powder, liquid milk UHT
RECYCLOIL Sarl Baha 03 Lot 04 El Mohammadia ALGER	021 20 34 11 021 20 34 44	021 20 44 75	contact@recycloil-dz.com	Oil vee gen tale used e
Snta Spa 40, Rue HOCINE Noureddine - ALGIERS Belouizdad	021 65 56 54 021 65 06 05	66 021 25 February 021 65 41 80	www.snta-dz.com directoire@snta-dz.com	Matches, sticks filter, Cigars, Cigarettes, Cigarillos, chewing tobacco, pipe tobacco, snuff
SOBCO Sarl Co operative El Mabnia No. 30 - ALGIERS Birkhadem	021 56 21 15	021 56 24 60	palmary.palmary @ yahoo.fr	Sandwich cookies
MOKADEM AL DISTRIBUTION Sarl 04, Rue des bois Hydra ALGIERS	021 28 28 51	021 68 94 82		Semolina, couscous

BFCI Eurl 75 Allotment of Bryère Bouzaréah ALGER	021 79 June 59	021 79 June 59		Soft drinks
SMEN BEAUTIFUL Hai El Hamma 02 # 23 Ben Talha Baraki ALGER	021 82 07 91 021 82 07 94	021 82 90 57		Ve gen pure fat tale (smen vee tal gen)
COMPANY PRODUCTS SUGAR (SPS) Spa BP 131 Route de Ain Staouali Bé nian ALGER	021 30 34 11 021 30 34 59	021 30 20 62	spss@assila.net	Confectionery
EL Harrat Eurl Lot 03 Riviera Beach and Sea extension Algiers Bordj El Kiffan ALGER	0772 44 84 48			Flower honey
KAYA FOOD Sarl Co operative El Mebnia Birkhadem # 29 ALGER	021 56 21 15	021 56 24 60	palmary.export @ yahoo.com	Chocolate
BISCUIT BIMO Sarl 06 A, Road brickworks Ali Baba ALGER	021 30 90 90 021 30 91 91	021 30 91 27 021 30 98 01	www.groupebimo.com bimoindustrie@yahoo.fr	Milk cake
LANKAM Sarl 95 C Place Fairouz Hammamet Bath Romanian ALGER	0771 18 61 84	021 62 15 99		Honey, water flowers, Water undermined eral
CATO Epic 05, Rue Ferhat Boussad ALGER	021 23 73 13			Feed barley bulk
INTERNATIONAL FOOD BUSINESS (IBF) Sarl Allotment No. 176 City Zonka Birkhadem ALGER		021 79 June 59		Soft drinks
SOHHEX EXPORT	021 60 62	021 60 62	sohhex@gmail.com	Soft drinks

Sarl AEK Wahrani El Oued Romane # 66 ALGER	95	95		
TAIBA FOOD COMPANY Sarl Lot 344 Section 07 ZI Rouiba ALGER	021 81 Aug. 18 021 81 October 94	021 81 15 27	ramymail10@gmail.com	Juice
PAP ALGERIA EXPORT TRADING Sarl City Logts Bt 297 06 No. 02 Birtouta ALGER	021 44 17 40	021 44 17 40	pap_trading@yahoo.fr	Harissa, vinegar, drinks are lyophilized, Infusion mint, verbena
CARTHAGO DISTRIBUTION Commune of Sidi Ammar ZI Mabaoudja ANNABA	030 81 76 49	030 81 76 50	carthago.dis @ gmail.com	Soft drinks
MAHBOUBA Sarl ZI Berrahal 23100 ANNABA	038 80 71 74 038 80 71 75	038 80 71 76	www.mahbouba.com info@mahbouba.com	Pasta
N'gaous PRESERVED Spa ZI BP 07 05600 N'gaous BATNA	033 88 72 83 033 88 70 75	033 88 73 75		Waters are fruity, Jams
CEVITAL Spa New Quay, Port of Be-BP jaia 334 BEJAIA	034 22 July 48 034 20 20 00	034 22 June 96	www.cevital.com rabia.merar @ cevital.com hafid.auochiche @ cevital.com	Acid oil, water undermined speaking, Edible oils, fruit juices, margarine, Mé tired refinery, white crystallized sugar
COGB BEAUTIFUL Spa ZI - Route des Aures - BP 406 BEJAIA	034 21 26 84	034 20 24 38 034 22 30 65	cogblabelle@yahoo.fr	E oil refined, HOUSEHOLD soap, glycerol rine codex, Fats
IBRAHIM et Fils Sarl"" IFRI Ighzer Amokrane BEJAIA	034 35 10 17 034 35 12 66	034 35 December 32	www.ifri-dz.com ifri@ifri-dz.com sce.export @ ifri-dz.com	Eral water undermined fruity e, Water undermined eral gassed ified e, Water mined natural speaking, Soda
IFRI OLIVE	0661 93 94 05	034 35 December		Olive oil

Ighzer Amokrane BEJAIA	94 05 034 35 November 17	12		
DAIRY SOUMMAM National Highway No. 26 TAHARACHT - Akbou BEJAIA	034 35 95 91 034 35 95 93	034 35 96 92	www.laiteriesoummam.com laiterie@laiteriesoummam.com	Fruit compote, cream dessert, fresh cheese, fermented milk
SABI OLIVE Town of El Flaye BEJAIA	034 29 42 60 034 29 39 96	034 29 39 96		Olive oil
SOUMMAM GRANNY BEJAIA	034 35 85 17	034 35 97 59		Flour
SET Toudja Sarl BEJAIA	034 20 20 45	034 20 20 44	set.toudja @ gmail.com	Low fruit drinks
FRUICADE Sarl BEJAIA	030 40 00 00	030 42 83 02	is-fruica@hotmail.com	Soda
GUEDILA MINERAL WATER Ntionale Route 87 Djemorah BISKRA	033 70 44 72		www.guedila.com	Eral waters undermined
SIM INDUSTRIAL GROUP Spa ZI of An Romana - BP 51a 032/0 Mouzaia BLIDA	025 38 11 06 025 38 11 14 025 38 11 04 025 38 11 02	025 38 11 05 025 38 11 09 025 38 11 95	www.groupesim.com fa.ezzraimi @ groupesim.com	Semolina, couscous, Water undermined speaking, Pasta
SOPI Sarl Lot No. 13, Road Boufarik - Guerouaou BLIDA	025 49 01 73 025 49 01 74	025 49 Jan. 75		Pasta
SOSEMIE Eurl City Ben Aissa - Beni Mered CP 09130 BLIDA	025 42 08 92 025 42 08 93 025 42 01 18 025 42 02 55	025 42 02 55 025 42 05 90 025 42 08 93	sosemie@yahoo.fr	Pasta
	025 41 70	025 41 28	www.trefle-dz.com	Drinks are milk,

CLOVER DAIRY Sarl ZI website Ben 01 Boulaid BLIDA	80 025 41 28 86 025 36 00 57	83 025 41 28 88 025 36 00 57	www.trefle-dz.com	cream dessert, UHT Milk, Fresh Cheese, Whey (Leben), flavored yogurt, fruit yogurt
[illegible]	[illegible]	[illegible]	www.vitajus.com vitajus@vitajus.com	[illegible] (Leben), flavored yogurt, fruit yogurt
SIM AQUA Spa BP 75 Route de Hatatba Mouzaia BLIDA	025 39 21 73 025 39 21 75	020 59 24 61	contact@groupesim.com	Eral waters undermined soft and natural, tomato paste, tomato sauce, juice concentrate
DAIRY BENI TAMOU Spa Street fre res Zerdi Beni Tamou BLIDA	025 42 83 42	025 42 82 01		Pasteurized milk
DFIE Sarl 61, Rue de Palestine BLIDA	0661 58 80 78	025 39 30 13 021 32 13 78		Waters are fruity, Apricot Nectar, Orange Drink
INDUSTRIAL GROUP GOUMIDI Spa Site No. 38 ZI Ouled Yaich 09200 BLIDA	025 43 78 98 025 43 80 22	025 43 79 57	www.goumidigroupe.com contactgig@goumidigroupe.com okidsgoumidi@yahoo.fr	Milk and riveted s, e Puré potato, chocolate powder
APEXAL Sarl 115 Bd of Palestine and 24 Lot Said Abid 09000 BLIDA				Fruity waters are
BISCOSTAR Sarl 21 ZI Route M'sila Bordj Bou Arreridj	035 68 03 54 035 68 02 91	035 68 April 13	biscostar@yahoo.fr	Biscuits filled s, Cookies, Ge noises
FALCO Sarl ZI n ° 06 A 4 Bordj Bou Arreridj 34000	035 68 68 88	035 67 67 65	falcodz2000@yahoo.fr	Chocolate Candy
ISO-9 INTERNATIONAL Sarl November 1st Avenue - BP 10 Isser BOUMERDES	024 88 14 09 024 88 14 67	024 88 19 15	www.isserdelice.com iso_9international@yahoo.fr	Cookies, shortbread cookies filled s s, Cookies, Ge noises

DAHMANI Hai Ouled Moussa Mouliha BOUMERDES	91 021 82 07 94	57		
ENASEL Spa Rhumel ZI - BP 18 B Couidat CONSTANTINE	031 66 47 38 031 66 43 39	031 66 48 85 031 66 48 84 031 66 47 38	www.enasel.com dg@enasel.com exportations@enasel.com	Salt die neigement, food salt, bath salt, salt conservation, EM dical Salt, Salt for dishwasher, Pellets of salt, baking soda
GVC Boulmerka Sarl 27 ZI Palma CONSTANTINE	031 66 49 04	031 66 May 00	contact@feder.fr boulmerkat@yahoo.fr	Vinegars, flavorings
MEXICALI Sarl ZI Mourad DIDOUCHE CONSTANTINE	031 90 76 00 031 90 56 64	031 90 75 83	www.mexicali-dz.com contact@mexicali-dz.com	Semolina, couscous
GENERAL TRADE AND SERVICES Sarl 10 Avenue Bourefrouf Slimane CONSTANTINE				Semolina
SO.AL.TU.BI Sarl 2 K ZI Mourad Didouche CNE BP 54 CONSTANTIN E	031 90 83 83	031 90 84 84	saaltubi@yahoo.fr	Biscuits
SEL EL HAMRAIA El Oued El Hamraia				Industrial salt
EL GOLEA Area of Activity BP 418 El Golea GHARDAIA	029 81 38 61 029 81 35 85	029 81 47 67		Soft drinks, waters undermined eral
ETS SEBAA Sarl BP 3456 Fek Hammouda Beriane GHARDAIA	0661 80 66 63	029 84 37 68		Pasta
	037 23 83	037 23 83		Tomato paste, red

CAB Sarl BOUATI Mahmoud GUELMA	02 037 23 83 00 037 23 65 65 037 23 62 42	02	cabsami@yahoo.fr mbguelma@yahoo.fr cab@amorbenamor.com	pepper concentrate, apricot jam, mayonnaise, cooked dishes s, Pizza Sauce, Pasta
ALGERIA CREAM Sarl Bir El Djir ORAN	041 27 32 85 041 27 32 83 041 56 43 41 041 56 43 40	041 27 32 82 041 56 43 38	contact@algeriecreme.com	[illegible], cheese bar, Cheese portions
WEST IMPORT Sarl Liaison Office Hai Chouhada ex.Beavers Villa # 66 ORAN	045 81 February 59	045 81 March 24		Mé tired of sugarcane
WALGOM Sarl Activity Zone El Ksab Misserghine BP 33 ORAN	041 49 September 96	041 49 August 32	walgom@hotmail.com	Gum base
ACID OLMED AEK Sarl Level I Commercial Center El Anik ORAN	041 39 00 43	041 39 72 63	sarlolmed@yahoo.fr	Olive oil
RAMOUL NACER RN 43 Talamous SKIKDA	0771 62 20 77			Olive oil
MAMI Spa BP 595 19000 SETIF, ZEA # 27 SETIF	036 83 37 51 036 83 34 28	036 93 60 84	www.groupe-mami.com info@groupe-mami.com	Soft drinks are
ORIENTAL lemonade SARMOUK Sarl ZEA # 18 SETIF	036 83 76 86	036 83 44 64	www.losarmouk.com	Flavored soft drinks and juices are
SBC SETIF Sarl ZI Lot No. 101 SETIF	036 93 89 09 036 92 66	036 91 59 17	sarlsbc@gmail.com	Soft drinks , fruit waters are

	66 036 92 66 67			
EL BARAKA Sarl ZI n ° 15 BP 222 Bis SETIF	036 91 73 73 036 91 69 45	036 93 73 20	moulins.guezzout @ yahoo.fr	Flour, semolina, couscous, pasta
JUICE BEAUTY Sarl ZAC 06 th Tranche SETIF	021 82 07 91 021 82 07 94	021 82 October 18		Juice
ALLEN AISSA TAMANRASSET	029 34 98 18 0667 60 83 90			Eral waters undermined
INTRACE Lot No. 76 ZI BP 220 Bou Ismail TIPAZA	024 46 49 35 024 46 49 36	024 46 26 60		Flour
ATLAS TOBACCO Spa Road Stadium Fouka City TIPAZA	020 53 36 16	024 51 October 01		Tobacco
BISCUIT MAGHREB Sarl Draa El Mizan road Boghni Tizi Ouzou	026 28 38 10	026 28 41 27		Biscuits
THE MODERN MILLS MOHAMMEDI MOHAMED Tizi Ouzou Tizi 15480 Ghenif	0770 24 88 74	026 20 60 45		Olive oil

FISHERY PRODUCTS

MUSKATEN Sarl 19, Bois des Cars I - DELY BRAHIM ALGER	021 43 81 52 021 71 21 50	021 43 81 52 021 71 21 50	www.muskaten.net muskaten@yahoo.fr	Octopus, Fish, Fish, Frozen s, ornamental fish
COUNTER FISHING SARL 45, Avenue de l'ALN ANNABA	0773 47 10 90 014 09 77 48	014 September 77 48		Fresh fish
Birem MED KARIM 73 City Valmascort ANNABA	038 86 57 51	038 86 57 50		Frozen shrimp are

FINTA FISHING Sarl 69 Rue Brahim MOKHTARI City Seybouse ANNABA	0770 93 37 15			Frozen shrimp are
Gouraya GOLF BEJAIA	034 23 95 51	034 23 91 45	gourayathon@gmail.com	Canned tuna
LA CALLE FRESH FISH Freedom Square El Kala EL TARF	038 66 35 02 0661 58 00 98	038 66 17 70		Octopus, Bream, Lotte, scorpionfish, Saupe, Sar
EL DJEMBARIE Eurl Port seat Boudis JIJEL	0770 00 66 91			Seafood
Crustal Eurl Sayad MOSTAGANEM	045 27 December 38	045 27 December 08	eurlcrustal@hotmail.fr	Products frozen sea s
ARIPICOPECHE Eurl 06 Ilot No. 03 ORAN	0661 October 67 66		aripicopeche@hotmail.fr	Pisces
KHALDI MOHAMED Ets Ilot 11 No 02 Hai Khmisti Bir El Djir ORAN	0770 31 41 19			Pisces
ORAN FISHING Sarl 69 Coop operative Errabie Dawn ORAN	0550 95 16 66 0661 21 68 68		oranpeche@yahoo.fr	Pisces
AGROMAR 10. Rue Abdelkader MECHERI ORAN	0770 30 87 23 041 46 52 27	041 45 55 74	agromar_a@hotmail.com	Fish, Seafood, Octopi
ALFISH Sarl Co operative of 20 Aot 55. No. 22 - ORAN Canastel	0770 28 58 79 041 39 83 14	041 53 46 22 041 39 83 14		Octopus, gray shrimp, prawn
HAAL Sarl ZI Hassi Ameur, Block 44 - BP 261 Hassi Bounif ORAN	0555 00 45 55 041 52 53 86 040 22 91 11	040 22 91 10 041 52 53 92 041 27 51 53	sarlhaal@yahoo.fr	Canned tuna in oil
Excimer Sarl 10. Rue Beau Sé day Ain El Turck ORAN	0771 69 23 47 040 20 25 17		sarleximmer60@yahoo.fr	Shrimp

RAFEXPORT Sarl 27, Rue Chakib Areslane ORAN	0772 50 32 80	041 34 98 63	rafex_port@yahoo.fr	Pisces
RAJA FOOD INDUSTRY Sarl ZI n ° 03 Senia Oran	041 51 35 041 08 51 49 29	041 51 49 29	rajafooddz@yahoo.fr	Canned tuna in oil
ZAMA EXPORT Sarl 27, Rue Chakib Areslane ORAN	0661 20 37 64	041 35 58 05	zamamariscos@yahoo.fr	Pisces
KARAM FISH Sarl 35, Eastern Suburbs Tizirinz Cherchel TIPAZA				Red shrimp

MINING PRODUCTS

FIRST FIRINDAR Sarl 14, Rue AMIR Abdelkader El Hajar ANNABA	038 89 December 12	038 89 December 12		White marble block
SOMIPHOS / FERPHOS Group 08, Rue SOUAHI Madani ANNABA	038 84 48 12	038 84 81 43	www.ferphos.com dg@somiphos.ferphos.com	Phosphate rock, phosphate Dusty re s
AZROAVERKAN BEJAIA	034 21 37 72	034 21 37 72	sarl.azzro @ yahoo.fr	Pallet stones
Facing with marble DERIVATIVES AND THE ROCK "Kaoula FERHAT" CONSTANTINE	031 93 75 86	031 92 54 94		Marble
SOALKA BP 113-18300 El Milia JIJEL	030 49 44 03	030 49 43 93		Kaolin
MEGA MARBLE Sarl South subdivision No. 114-01 MILA	0552 21 79 18		mega.marbre @ yahoo.fr	White marble
	043 31 65	043 31 40	bental13300@yahoo.fr	Bentonite

Bental GROUP ENOF BP 67 Rue GHARROBEN Maghnia TLEMCEN	88	78	bental13300@yahoo.fr	Bentonite
ENAMARBRE GROUP BP 278 Bridge Saf Saf SKIKDA	088 75 64 10 038 70 68 71	088 75 64 09 038 70 68 71	www.enamarbre.dz enamarbre@hotmail.com	Marble
SNMC Sahi 12 F Agadir TLEMCEN	043 20 74 32	043 26 43 17		Marble blocks, stones

É PRODUCTS NERGE TICKS AND TROCHIMIQUES PE PRODUCTS

HAMADI ZM EXPORT City 1200 Logts Bt C D residence Bahdja El Bab Ezzouar ALGER	021 24 62 20	021 24 62 20		Industrial oil used e
COMPANY ALGERIA ELECTRICITY AND GAS "SONELGAZ" 02, Boulevard Krim BELKACEM ALGER	021 72 31 00	021 72 26 90		Energy é electric
COGIZ Spa BP 114 31230 ORAN Ain El Bia	041 48 01 65 041 48 02 86	041 48 February 86	cogiz_benrahalboumediene@yahoo.fr	Helium gas
ASTRA OIL Eurl Lot 170 No. 103 Chehairia Ain El Bya ORAN	0661 55 March 55			Hydraulic oil h e uilë used industrial

CHEMICALS, COSMETICS TICKS, PHARMACEUTICAL AND VETERINARIANS TEE VEE

Aboulkacem Ets 01 SKOTO - Bab El Oued ALGER	021 96 52 75 021 96 58 19	021 96 61 00 021 96 53 04	www.habba-sawda.com	Black seed oil, soap made from honey, soap with nigella oil olive oil soap with nigella oil, shampoo base
ARGILEV 08, Rue Haouche Habki Zounka 16105 ALGER Birkhadem	021 55 21 78 0661 62 86 90	021 40 59 60	info@argilevtn.com	Cosmetic products and natural tick: Clay mask oils, natural clay mask, shampoo clay, black soap, pumice, Alum, k'hol
ARMEDIC Sarl 03, Rue de l'Industrie KOUBA ALGER				Measuring Spoon
HUILERIE MECQA Sarl Hai Douzi 3, Lot # 104 - Bab Ezzouar ALGER	021 20 40 97 0551 01 93 03	021 20 40 97	huilemiracle@yahoo.fr	Cumin oil, Oil habbatou sawda, Habbatou sawda, Olive Oil, Siwak, k'hole, black soap, shampoo habbatou sawda Herbal Tea, Honey Soap
IMC "MEDICAL INDUSTRIES CHIRUGICALES" ZI Route A - Rouiba ALGER	021 81 19 05 021 81 19 06 021 81 30 67 021 81 30 68	021 81 32 73 021 81 27 14	www.imc-dz.com export@imc-dz.com	Fistula needles, cartridges bicarbonate, sodium chloride, filter dialysis, dialysis lines, Infusion, Pockets glucose, insulin syringes, disposable syringes, Transfusion
LABORATORIES MERINAL SARL Way U30 ZI - Oued S'mar ALGER	021 51 32 22 021 51 32 24	021 51 32 77 021 51 32 78	www.merinal.com labs_merinal@hotmail.com	Pharmaceuticals for human use
LABORATORIOS HISPALAB Sarl Subdivision Sonelgaz, No. 41 - Ford of Constantine Algiers	021 83 82 82 021 83 90 90	021 83 00 84	contact@groupepalc.com contact@groupepad.com	Aero rosol
LINDE GAS ALGERIA (Ex-ENGI) 23 Avenue of the NLA - Hussein Dey ALGER	021 49 75 81	021 49 75 81	naziha-bouamama@linde.com	Acetone acetylene, carbon dioxide, liquid argon, liquid nitrogen, pure and meth diapered Gas, Hydrogen, Liquid Oxygen, Nitrous Oxide

SAIDAL Epe Spa 01, Rue Yahia Layachi, Brush - Hussein Dey ALGER	021 77 74 40 021 77 74 21	021 77 74 22	www.saidalgroup.dz tasdir_saidal@yahoo.fr	Pharmaceuticals
SANDOZ Spa ZI CW 118 BP 74 M Oued S'mar ALGER	021 51 31 43 021 51 67 31	021 51 31 43 021 51 67 31		Mé medication to use human
SCENTS Eurl Cooperative El Yasmine, lot 89, No. 23, Jolie View - Kouba ALGER	021 28 73 13	021 28 73 13	eurl.senteurs @ gmail.com	Rose essential oil
SPLENDID Eurl Road School Grand Che raga ALGER	021 38 11 73 021 38 28 42 021 38 28 43	021 38 11 74 021 38 28 41	groupe_splendid@yahoo.fr	Depilatory cream, toothpaste, scented, Eau de Toilette, Hair Gel, Perfume
Tabiri Sarl The subdivision Rosiers C Lot No. 51 El Hamiz ALGER	020 38 62 59	021 87 73 68	tabiri_tz@yahoo.fr	Candles EM ste
HYGIMED Spa 06 Boulevard Khemisti Algiers ALGIERS	021 64 28 99	021 64 Jan. 28	www.hygimed-dz.com contact@hygimed-dz.com	Roll hydrophobic
HENKEL ALGERIA 22 Rue Ahmed Ouaked 03 Del Wood Descartes Ibrahim 16320 ALGER	021 91 86 07 021 91 86 07 021 91 86 09	021 91 86 22		De detergents
CEVA LAVAL Spa ZA El Boutène Rahmania BP 76 16301 Cp Mhalema ALGER	021 October 00 October 00 18 17 021 021 19 October 00	021 15 October 00		Products tee vee veterinarians
	020 24 73	021 94 75	www.hygindust.com	De detergents

HGININDUST Sarl 11 Rue De cember 1960 Section 08 Ilot # 100 Ouled Chebel ALGER	01 020 24 73 02 021 94 75 95	95 021 56 43 08 021 31 April 41	hygindust@yahoo.fr contact@hygindust.com	De detergents
[illegible] Sarl 11 Rue De cember [illegible] [illegible] [illegible] ALGER	[illegible] 53 53 [illegible] 24 73 [illegible] 20 35 [illegible] 94 75 [illegible] 62 December 81 021 35 52 07	[illegible] 56 [illegible] [illegible] 31 April 41	[illegible] [illegible]	Insecticides and disinfectants die
El Ferdous EURL Lot Essalah (ex-Charbonier) No 162 ALGER Birkhadem				Cumin oil, Shampoo, Cream Argan Vaseline, L deodorant
CONCORDAL Spa 19, Rue Menad Arab Sources (formerly Marcello Fabri) Bir Mourad Rais Algiers	021 44 72 61 021 54 43 93	021 44 72 62	sarlconcordal@hotmail.com	Paints, Glue & Riverside s Sanitary Products
ALGERIA DISTRIBUTION COMPANY PRODUCT PROLECTRO (SADPP) Sarl Co operative Properties Zhun Aissat Mustapha # 19 Re GHAIA ALGER	0772 March 21 26	021 85 Jan. 12	gamvert@hotmail.fr	Frying oil (reaction mix oil vee gen tale inedible for technical or industrial uses)
FERTIAL Epe Spa Route des Salines, BP 3088 Annaba	038 53 93 17 038 53 93 10 038 53 93 14	038 53 93 42	fertial@fertial-dz.com	Ammonia and liquid bulk
LINDE GAS ALGERIA Spa Bridge Mouth ZI BP 82 El Hajar ANNABA	030 81 59 05 038 89 December 22	030 81 59 05 038 89 December 22		Acetone acetylene

Spa BP 193, Tower Business Chaiba - Sidi Amar ANNABA	25 030 82 24 24	00 038 87 14 52	contact@hydrosid.com	crystallized
SDI Sarl Seybouse City, Street Melouah Med Salah ANNABA	038 35 95 11 030 81 04 68	038 53 91 61		Lacquer thinner and paint thinner organic
KIMIAL Spa Route des Salines BP 204 El Bouni ANNABA	038 53 94 12 038 03 08 26	038 53 94 07	www.kimial.com infokimial@kimial.com	Sodium tripolyphosphate
PROFERT Sarl Rue de Lille rear port Bé jaia 06000 BEJAIA	034 22 99 61	034 20 20 90	www.profert-dz.com profert@profert-dz.com	Fertilizer: NPK, MGO, TRACE ELEMENTS
VENUS LABORATORIES SAPECO Sarl 80, Rue du 17 September 1956 - Ouled Yaich BLIDA	025 43 85 85 025 43 80 80	025 43 71 71 025 43 78 78	www.labovenus.dz contact@labovenus.dz k.moula @ labovenus.dz	Cosmetic products ticks: anti-wrinkle cream, Crème de pigmenting, Moisturizer, body odor De, Screen solar total, Slimming Gel, Gel for hair care line men care lines BE BE s, Shampoos
ZIPHEE.BIO Sarl Bouderbala Bouira 10016 BOUIRA	026 90 51 83 0661 89 74 04	026 90 54 11	zipheebio@yahoo.fr zipheebio@hotmail.com zipheebio1@gmail.com	Essential oil pistachio, wild carrot essential oil / lemon / grapefruit
SOCOTHYD Epe Spa Isser BOUMERDES	024 88 20 81 024 88 19 81	024 88 21 43 024 88 20 81	www.socothyd.com contact@socothyd.com	Cotton wool, personal hygiene products, Band e plastered Products, gas, compresses
ALGERIAN ANIMAL HEALTH PRODUCT 07, Rue Benmaâti Abdelouahab CONSTANTINE	031 66 77 88 031 66 06 80 031 66 06 83 031 66 06 81	031 67 57 57 031 66 June 84	www.aahp-dz.com aahplabo@yahoo.fr	Products tee vee veterinarians
Wouroud Perfumes ZI Kouinine 39450 EL WADI	032 20 15 25 032 20 15 26	032 20 15 60 032 21 60 60	www.wouroud.com wouroud@wouroud.com	Fragrant, Eau de Toilette, Fragrance, are fragrant pouches, Soap
LABORATORY	038 69 20	038 86 14	hygienova@yahoo.fr	Soap

HYGIENOVA Lot 67 ZAC BP 28 B BEN Me HIDI EL TARF	58 038 69 20 59	92	hygiena@yahoo.fr	
N'FIDSA AMAR Lots # 37 Boudaroua Capt. Oued Fragha Bouchegouf GUELMA	0770 44 62 21 024 44 62 21		etsnfidsa@yahoo.fr	Paint, varnishes, printing ink
Cartañá MOSTA Sarl ZI Souk El-Sayad Lil Ouled Bachir 27235 MOSTAGANEM	045 33 13 63	045 33 13 64	sarlcaftana@hotmail.com	De fragrant cosmetic products ticks
ADWAN CHEMICALS COMPANY ALGERIA Spa Fornaka ZI n ° 2 & 3 MOSTAGANEM	040 45 68 69 040 45 55 55 040 45 67 67	040 45 55 55 040 45 68 75 040 45 67 67	bailiche@adwanchem.com kouidri@adwanchem.com	Silica Flour
KAPACHIM ALGERIA Sarl Block 65 lot 129 Hassi Ameur ZI ORAN	0661 25 87 51		kap393@ccioranie.com	Sulfonic acid
SMPCA ZI Senia Oran	041 58 15 15	041 58 15 14	smpca_oran@yahoo.fr	Aluminium sulphate
Larbes ABBES Eurl K'sar Sbahi OUM EL bouaghi Back to top	032 40 51 01			Candied Walnut
Plastic products, rubber and glass products				
Michelin ALGERIA Spa Road Birkhadem - ALGIERS Bachdjarah	021 86 81 99 021 58 22 40	021 89 14 70 021 26 84 00		Tires
TECHNICAL	021 81 39	021 81 23	www.sgt-Pet.com	Caps, PET Pre Forms

SOCIETE GENERALE Spa Route B ZI - Rouiba ALGER	49 021 81 15 42	83	sgt-algerie@sgt-pet.com	
TECMECA Sarl Oued Smar ZI - BP 53 M ALGER	0661 52 70 62 021 51 36 66	021 28 26 22	www.tecmecasarl.com www.tecmeca.biz info@tecmecasarl.com info@tecmeca.biz	Floor Squeegees, Cleaning Products, Broom handles, Dustpans
ALPHA PET 16 Channel C ZI Re GHAIA ALGER	021 81 72 50	021 81 66 80		Plastic caps
TNMS Eurl Lot Alioua Fodil Amara 02, Villa No. 325 Che raga ALGER	021 36 44 44 021 36 30 September 021 37 41 13 021 37 41 14	021 36 20 96	eurltnms@yahoo.com	Plastic bottles
USAS TURKEY Sarl City Kames No. 48 Dar El Beida ALGER	021 82 74 85	021 82 74 87		Recyclable plastic bottles
PLASTINATTE Sarl / OGI ZI Meboudja - Sidi Amar - El Hajar ANNABA	038 52 32 37 038 88 81 46	038 52 32 36 038 88 81 45	plastinatte-ogi@yahoo.fr	Polypropylene mats, woven polypropylene bags s
FLAT capsules ZI City KECHIDA BATNA	033 92 33 17	033 92 33 16	capsuplast@yahoo.fr	Plastic film
ALL PLASTIC Sarl ZAC Taharacht - Akbou BEJAIA	034 35 32 21 034 35 32 20 034 35 32 41	034 35 90 42	www.allplast.com info@allplast.com contact @ Allplast-algerie.com	Band polystyrene, polypropylene tray
GENERAL PLASTIC Sarl Area of Activity Taharacht - Akbou 06200 BEJAIA	034 35 98 00 034 35 98 03	034 35 98 03 034 35 98 34 034 35 98 25	gp@generalplast-dz.com	Preforms
STB TOLGA EL-	033 78 70	033 78 65	www.el-baraka.com	Plastic bags, Styrofoam

BARAKA Sarl Area of Activity # 68 - BP 14 Tolga BISKRA	01 033 78 87 54	69	manaa-99@yahoo.fr	Trays
MEDITERRANEAN FLOAT GLASS (MFG) 29 Route Meftah - The arbaa BLIDA	021 44 86 67 021 44 86 04	021 44 85 55 021 44 85 80	mfg@cevital.com	Flat glass
PLASTICS PROCESSING COMPANY MITIDJA (SMTP) Sarl Route Cimemitère Europé in Ouled Yaich 09100 BLIDA	025 43 78 80 025 43 78 59	025 43 78 59 025 43 14 26	www.smtp-dz.com aggoun_smtp@yahoo.fr	Plastic film
PETROCHIMCO Sarl Hai Garidi Rue Ouled November 1st Hadaj BOUMERDES	0661 92 91 17	024 87 71 62		Canisters
THERMOPLAST Sarl ZI Bordj Menail BOUMERDES	024 88 84 84 024 88 84 85	024 88 84 86		S printed plastic pots
GALION ALGERIA Spa Section 06, Block of properties ty # 284 Hammadi BOUMERDES	020 79 05 63 020 79 05 64 021 56 20 60	021 56 20 60		Pot lids
COGITELA Area Indutrielle Didouche Mourad CNE BP 54 CONSTANTIN E	031 90 89 08	031 90 89 05	contact@cogiela.com	Polyester films EM tallisé
SMART TRADE COMPANY Sarl City Promotional Zianides Bt 03 No. 3R2 New Town	0561 27 98 23	031 66 74 84		Used tires s, s rubber granulate

MENDJLI Ali El Khroub CONSTANTINE				
COMAVER Sarl BP 25 - ZI Garet Ettam - Bounoura GHARDAIA	029 87 32 86 029 87 33 60 029 87 31 86	029 87 32 66 029 87 31 70	comaverdz@yahoo.fr	Articles HOUSEHOLD glass portholes é lighting, window to Verrines
SAVER Sarl BP 25 ZI Garet Ettaam - Bounoura GHARDAIA	029 87 33 60 029 87 32 86 029 87 31 86	029 87 32 66 029 87 31 70	saver_dz@yahoo.fr	Articles HOUSEHOLD glass tiles glass building, glass windows, lighting
AFRICAVER Epe / Spa Salah Taher ZI BP 06 18200 JIJEL	034 44 72 75	034 44 April 24	afv@wissal.dz	Multi-laminated glass
POLYMA Sarl ZI - Tizi MASCARA	045 85 89 89 045 85 89 88	045 85 89 86	polyma-1@hotmail.com	Round pots with lids iml (vital) 250 GRS, round pots with lids iml (meadow) 250 GRS
JOKTAL Sarl AGHBEL ZI - BP # 7 - Oued Tlelat ORAN	041 43 71 44 041 43 66 00	041 43 75 46	www.joktal.com info@joktal.com	Plastic packaging
STAR PLASTIC Sarl Lot 140 ZI n ° 2 Es-Senia Oran	041 58 37 36	041 51 49 11	smain@etoileplastique.com	Buckets and plastic bowls
SBOA 31 Operations Sidi Brahim - Oued Tlelat ORAN	041 43 67 00 041 43 67 04	041 43 66 57		Glass bottles, plastic bottles
TRANSREP Sarl 08, Rue Mohamed BAKI, Saint-Eugène ORAN	041 28 21 46 041 28 21 47	041 28 21 45	sarltransrep@yahoo.fr	Handles of pots, tableware EM lamin
RIFA PLAST Sarl Route Sidi Chahmi Nedjma Ex-Chtebo ORAN	041 49 46 65		rifaplast14525@ccioranie.com	Plastic products
		041 29 93	alver@ccioranie.com	Glass bottles

ALVER Spa Avenue des Martyrs of the Re volution BP 33 Es-Senia Oran		62	alver@ccioranie.com	Glass bottles
SPOA Spa 22 Avenue Khiali Ben Salem ORAN	041 41 68 70	62	spoa1418@ccioranie.com	Plastic
CROSS INDUSTRY Sarl 369 Coop operative Properties Ennour Ilot 384 Bir El Djir ORAN	0778 50 41 87		cross.industry @ gmail.com	Plastic
Khadim Ali Bd Med Khemisti 48340 El H'madna RELIZANE	046 97 34 56	046 97 34 56		Plastic bags
AGRO-FILM PACKAGING Sarl Activity Zone, Lot No. 07 SETIF	036 93 09 09 036 93 09 10	036 93 84 68 036 91 61 79	www.agro-film.com contact@agro-film.com	Agricultural film, Film complex food or detergents dice Film é stretchable film pouch milk, polypropylene film, Shrink Film
CHIALI PROIPLAST ZI SETIF	036 91 February 08	036 93 60 06	info@groupe-chiali.com	PVC windows
ENPC-SOFIPLAST ZI - BP 107 SETIF	036 91 01 66 036 93 59 40 036 91 01 65	036 93 59 40 036 93 00 80	sofiplast2008@yahoo.fr	Plastic film, plastic Mail
GLASSWARE OF EASTERN Sarl BP 467 - ZI Souk AHRAS	037 35 18 54 037 35 12 12 037 35 17 17	037 35 19 19	www.verest-dz.com verest@verest-dz.com	Glass ashtrays, Dishes, Glasses, Glasses tea

MECHANICAL PROCESSING OF POLYMERS (ATMP) BP 13 15010 Anane Tizi Ouzou Tizi Ouzou	97 020 60 03 57	18		

CHAIRED RURGIQUES PRODUCTS AND METH METALLIC

BAG Spa Road Baraki - Gue de Constantine ALGER	021 83 94 09 021 83 94 12	021 83 93 61	bagspal@hotmail.com	Gas cylinders, fire extinguishers, LPG tanks Ré
STAR FILTER Eurl 07, Rue Mohamed BELKACEM, Belle Vue - El Harrach ALGER	0661 52 47 39 021 21 41 21	021 21 45 43	www.starfiltre.com contact@starfiltre.com	Created pines stainless wire wound hydraulic drilling stainless tubes for hydraulic drilling extensions
CRE POWER INDUSTRY Eurl OB 21 Wood Riadh El Feth arcades El Madania ALGER	021 66 50 93	021 66 50 93		Lead ingots
COMET MEDICAL ZI les Zouines Baba Al ALGER	021 30 96 37 021 30 95 00	021 30 95 95	www.cometmed.com	Mate rial EM dical
MEFTAH MOHAMED Ets Co operative El Houda Bi-touta ALGER	0662 75 42 10	021 86 75 80		Aluminum ingots
Baticim Spa ZI Route de Oued Smar Meftah BP 88 ALGER	021 51 56 51 021 51 56 53	021 51 56 50		EM galvanized metallic frame e
MCI BAKIR MOSTEFA Hai Sidi Saadi # 22 Beni Messous ALGER	0550 16 93 80 021 85 61 21	021 85 61 21	www.mci-dz/net www.zincalgeria.com bakirmoste@mci-dz.net	Zinc oxide
ARCELOR MITTAL	038 87 15	038 87		Pig iron, cold rolled

STEEL Spa BP 2055 SIDI AMAR - El Hajar ANNABA	81 038 87 18 30	18 30 038 87 17 72 038 87 17 32		dice are hot coils are rated, galvanized coils are
MANSOURI METABOX Sarl ZI El Kalitoussa Lot 10 Berrahal BP A26 ANNABA	038 86 35 34	038 86 40 07		Covers standard tinplate
ORFEE Spa Route Agricultural Village Aomar - Bordj Menaiel BOUMERDES	024 88 50 77 024 88 50 76	024 86 67 63 024 88 50 78	www.bcr-spa.com orfee@wissal.dz orfee_spa@yahoo.fr	Cutlery stainless steel tableware silver stainless steel kitchen sinks, stainless steel dishes, silver dishes, pottery, stainless steel, silver Pottery, Bowls in stainless steel, silver Terrines
ETS Boumaraf & CIE Sarl ZI Kharouba Boudouaou BOUMERDES	021 50 18 96 024 85 13 88	024 85 13 88		Copper billet, Industrial Gas Hose
Vallena Sarl ZI 35400 Boudouaou BOUMERDES	024 84 29 96	024 84 30 74		Aluminum discs
MNER Eurl CONSTANTINE	031 63 49 53	03163 49 53		Zinc mattes
EL Ste NOUHOUD Hai Ennour EL WADI	029 67 42 90			Iron
TA-ALU Sarl Neighborhood Takbou me a 26000 MEDEA	025 58 97 02	025 58 97 02	www.ta-alu.com.dz contact@ta-alu.com.dz	Whiteboards steel
POVAL Epe Spa Unit valves Berrouaghia BP 425 26200 ZI Berrouaghia MEDEA	025 57 92 24	025 57 83 03		Pumps and valves
	0555 02			Lead

OYA METAL Sarl ZI n ° 04 Chelghoum Laid MILA	34 16 0550 02 34 17 0555 02 34 18 0555 02 34 22 0770 51 62 97			Lead
ALGAL PLUS Sarl ZI M'sila BP 702 28000 M'sila M'sila	035 55 18 6	035 55 18 88	www.algalplus.com info@algalplus.com	S profile raw aluminum
MARK ENVIRONMENT Sarl 05, Rue Menudie Re residence Panorama City Small ORAN	041 35 97 36 041 35 69 84	041 35 97 36 041 35 69 81	sarl-repere@hotmail.com	Aluminum ingots
FERB Eurl 31, Cité El Kssab ZI Messerghine ORAN	041 35 97 36	041 35 97 36		Aluminum
ORSIM / BCR Group Avenue Larbi Ben Mhidi - BP 68/69 - Oued Rhiou RELIZANE	046 97 82 69 046 97 82 66 046 97 68 43	046 97 70 46 046 97 70 63	www.bcr-spa.com orsim@wissal.dz	Screw slide se curity
SOGEX Omane Sarl BP 339 Ain El Bia Bethioua ORAN	041 37 70 87	041 37 70 82		Turbine gas
ADTPA EURL City 128 logts BTF # 8 15425 Boghni Tizi Ouzou	026 28 46 10 026 28 46 15 020 66 57 15	026 28 46 20	adtpa@hotmail.com	Tie wire for construction and public works, baling wire for agriculture
SOTREFIT ZI Zâaroura TIARET	046 42 28 40	046 42 28 38		Baling wire
TALEB DJAFFAR PRPILAINE Ets	0661 66 July 86		propilaine@yahoo.fr	EM fibers METALLIC

Area POTS # 29 Tizi Ouzou				
ALZINC Spa Lighthouse Road, PO Box 456 - Ghazaouet TLEMCEN	043 32 33 30 043 32 31 90	043 32 42 93 043 32 33 06	www.metanof.com alzinc@yahoo.com	EM zinc metal, sulfuric acid, copper, zinc ferrite, Zinc Lozenges, Zamac acid, zinc dross

FERROUS AND NON-FERROUS WASTE

Hachoud MED EL AMINE 19 City 44300 Salem El Attaf AIN DEFLA	0550 58 37 46	041 27 63 41	hhnihad@yahoo.fr	Ferrous waste
ALTRASID Eurl Beautiful estate co operative Re residence City Housing 1200, Bt A, No. 2 - BAB EZZOUAR ALGER	021 24 33 86 021 24 59 99	021 24 59 99	altrasid@yahoo.fr	Scrap
HUANGHE HYDROLOGY Haouche Beglem New Town, Section 03, Lot No. 11 Dar El Beida ALGER	021 91 84 65	021 91 84 65		Lead ingots
MAPEX Eurl Lot D Villa No. 03 El Achour Algiers	021 30 85 42	021 30 85 42	mapex.alg @ gmail.com	Waste plastic die
MODERN RECUP Sarl 36, Rue Souidani Boudjemâa Ché raga ALGER	0770 41 53 23 021 37 42 83	021 37 42 83		Waste plastic die
KAROUI Khaoula Plain City West 1172 Logts ANNABA	0550 99 October 19	038 84 August 00		Waste plastic die
SAS RECYCLING 65 ZI Alalligne the 1st installment - EL Bouni ANNABA	038 83 16 80 038 83 31 57	038 83 16 78 038 83 16 43		Lead ingots
FLEA AND METALS	0661 32			Ash zinc smelter,

Eurl Area of Activity Ain Berda BP 03 Annaba	June 36			Chet copper, brass foundry Ash
REAL SIMCO Sarl 23000 17 Avenue El Qods ANNABA	0661 75 96 63 0661 75 96 64 038 80 50 27	038 80 50 27		Waste iron die
SAYAD METAL Eurl BEJAIA				Waste scrap die
EXP UNITED Sarl 11, City of Roses - BENI MERAD BLIDA	025 42 09 09 0770 96 13 94	025 42 September 46	www.expunited.com expunited@expunited.com	Ferrous waste
MKHT Sarl 06 City Brakni 180 Logts Bt C BLIDA	025 31 15 41	025 39 24 78		Waste scrap all die from
METALU FERS Sarl Haouche Ben Zahra Lot 698 No 12 Beni Tamou BLIDA	025 41 Jan. 21	025 41 20 95		Waste die and break aluminum die
CEZAL Sarl ZI Ouled Brahim - Hamadi BOUMERDES	021 50 76 08 024 81 12 March	021 50 76 28		Aluminum ingots
NADMETAL Sarl Melha City, Ouled Moussa BOUMERDES	0661 21 71 36 020 79 86 08	020 79 86 08		Scrap
LAI-METALS City Ben Hamza No. 04 GPE Hammadi BOUMERDES	19 August 0770 82	021 86 75 08		Waste die feraille
K-METAL Eurl Ben Amar Hai Hammadi BOUMERDES	0550 33 52 16	021 50 48 49		De ferrous waste and breakage iron
RECIBAT Sarl Bo 170 Activity Zone Soudane Beriane GHARDAIA	029 84 41 02 029 84 38 66	029 84 53 36 029 84 38 66		Lead, Battery
	021 77 20	021 77 15	ercdz@hotmail.com	Are sheared scrap,

ERC Spa 12 A, Captain Street Aziouz Mouzaoui Hussein Dey ALGER	15 021 77 20 15 021 77 15 46 021 77 20 34	46 021 77 20 34	ercdz@hotmail.com	ferrous waste, waste of non-ferrous
METAL G BOUMEDJEL Housing Plan 30 S 20 N 79 MILA [illegible]	[illegible] 66 [illegible] 55 36 26 [illegible]	[illegible]	yarametalg@yahoo.fr postagem@yahoo.fr	Aluminum ingot, Copper, Batteries empty [illegible]
Sarl MEDIA DISC 05, Rue de la Paix ORAN	041 39 46 60 041 45 46 47 0554 50 72 44	041 45 41 20	media1461@ccioranie.com	Waste plastics
CORPORATE RECOVERY WEST Spa 01, Rue Mohamed Latreche ORAN	041 39 34 27	041 39 53 96		Scrap
REBERE OF envoronnement Sarl 350 Logts Glacier Block 17 05 e Tagus ORAN	041 35 97 36		rebe1527@ccioranie.com	Die steel waste
AMINE WAFA Eurl Headquarters No. 02 Lot No. 136 Hassi Sidi Labiod Chahmi ORAN				Aluminum ingot
Bekam Sarl Hai Ibn Roched City Daybreak Block No. 09 ORAN				Waste scrap all die from
RMRE IMPORT EXPORT Eurl Ghabel Touazet 190 fraction No. 01 Oued Tlelat ORAN				Waste scrap die
ASTRADE RECOVERY OF METALS EXPORT Eurl Hai Ibn Roched Djamila Street and Rue 20 Aot Local No. 03 ORAN				Waste iron die from any

KNLC Activity Zone El Kerma Section 02 Ilot 180 El Kerma ORAN	March 86	March 87		any
KOUCHAM SALAH AYRON Sarl Activity Zone El Kerma Section 02 Ilot 180 El Kerma ORAN	March 86	March 87		Waste iron die from any
EL Guedra Sarl Zone Pot, Lot No. 44 Hamadi Krouma SKIKDA	038 93 15 03 030 92 36 46 030 92 36 49	038 93 74 61 038 93 15 03		Brass
UDS INDUSTRY Sarl ZI Bousmail, No. 192 TIPAZA	024 46 27 50 024 46 73 07	024 46 73 07	uds_industrie@hotmail.com	Chet waste batteries are acid free, ferrous waste
KERKOUMETAL Eurl Road Chaig Chaiba TIPAZA	0662 39 December 59	021 77 94 63		Waste aluminum die
ALTECH ALUMINIUM Sarl ZI No. 147 Plot No. 08 Kole has TIPAZA	0770 44 44 17 021 50 55 24	021 50 55 24		Aluminum ingots

EQUIPMENT, MATÉ RIEL AND PRODUCTS INDUSTRY MECHANICAL ME

PMA TRADING Epe Spa 16, Rue ARAB Si Ahmed - ALGIERS Birkhadem	021 55 27 57 021 55 27 54 021 55 27 56	021 55 25 81	www.pmat-dz.com info@pmat-dz.com	Plows, spreaders fertilizers, mowers, harrows, Combine harvesters, planters, harvesters potatoes, Pick-up balers, Seeders, Tractors
SODEXIN Sarl Ihedadhene City, Street Tekamera, Bt A1; prom immob SOMACOB,	034 21 33 11	034 21 33 10	sarlsodexin@hotmail.fr	Automotive spare parts (p oulies)

BEJAIA				
GARNIFLEX 43, Rue De cember 11 Ben Boulaid BLIDA	025 40 36 01	025 40 21 25	garniflex2005@yahoo.fr	Automotive spare parts
SFMO Moussaoui Sarl BP 82 Hallouya - Soumaa BLIDA	025 47 35 83 025 47 35 84 025 39 94 66	025 47 35 85 025 39 94 73	www.sfmotools.com info@sfmotools.com	Cutting shears iron bé tone metal cutting shears, Shears are combined, Poinonneuse lever, Trononneuses
IRRI INDUSTRIES Eurl Ahmed Hamouda Street Lot 140 No 22 El Affroune BLIDA	025 38 83 51	025 38 83 56	irri.industrie @ yahoo.fr	Agricultural equipment
Cofrem Sarl ZI No. 14 Ben Badis El Khroub CONSTANTINE	031 95 41 74	031 95 41 73	www.cofrem-dz.com cofrem25@yahoo.fr	Brake linings and brake pads, construction and automotive painting
COMPANY OF AGRICULTURAL TRACTORS "Etrag" BP 74 El Oued Hamimime Khroub CONSTANTINE	031 95 52 09 031 95 54 12	031 95 53 25		Box
ENMTP ZI Ain Smara 25140 CONSTANTINE	031 97 38 30 031 97 38 45	031 97 38 71		Spare parts for compactors, Bé tonnière, Dumper, spreader
SOMEMI Sarl Taher ZI BP 195 18200 Jijel JIJEL	034 44 55 52 043 44 68 00	034 44 50 20		Aluminum rings, mechanical parts EM
SOMAFAM Sarl 60, Rue Alla Ahmed Choupot ORAN	0661 20 71 27 041 34 02 65 041 58 82 20	041 58 77 25	www.somafam.com contact@somafam.com	Spur gear steel
Orxy PLAST Allotment No. 199 November 1 Ain M'lila OUM EL bouaghi	0663 30 60 09	032 44 91 25		Automotive spare parts
	048 56 78	048 56 84	info@akhenteur.com	Automotive components

KCA KHENTEUR Spa BP 135 RP ZI Sidi Bel Abbes	25	32	info@akhenteur.com	Automotive components
KCA KHENTEUR Spa BP 135 RP ZI Sidi Bel Abbes	25	32		

EQUIPMENT AND ELECTRICAL ITEMS É, É ELECTRONIC

BMS AS ELBI Sarl Street HAMIDI Said - ALGIERS Birkhadem	021 55 51 05 021 35 47 20	021 55 51 06 021 35 33 34	www.bmselectric.com info@bmselectric.com	Switch, thread cutter, sockets, Power strip, Electric Drive é, é electrical sockets
DACE Sarl 175 Farm Pons - Kcuba ALGER	0555 05 26 43 021 28 59 66 021 28 52 22	021 28 51 93	www.dace.dz dace@dace.dz	EM mixer beater
EDIEL EL ACHOUR EL ACHOUR - BP n ° 03 Draria ALGER	021 30 February 69 April 30 35 021 021 30 February 70	021 April 30 34 January 30 30 021 021 30 February 62	www.ediel.net ediel_dg@ediel.net	Electric distribution station é, é electrical low voltage equipment, electrical equipment é medium voltage
EL Sewedy CABLES ALGERIA ZI AIN DEFLA	027 59 15 83 027 59 15 86 027 59 15 87	027 59 15 85		É electric cables
Spa EIS (Electronic Industry Service) Village Bridja - BP 32 16101 Sidi Fredj Staoueli ALGER	021 39 20 87 021 39 38 94	021 39 December 64	eis_algerie@yahoo.fr	Empty battery cabinets
SOCOMIB Sarl 39, Rue Tahar Adlane Creek ALGER	021 67 36 40			Industrial Machinery: Filling, Welder
Essalem	021 24	021 24 41		Washing

ELECTRONICS Lot No. 34 Area of Activity El Alia Bab Ezzouar ALGER	42 38 021 24 42 39	31 021 24 43 32	www.essalem-electronics.com consommateur@essalem-electronics.com	machines
HB TECHNOLOGIES ZI ISLAND 69 Rouiba 16012 ALGER	021 81 54 04 021 85 52 83	021 85 56 38	www.hb-technologies.com.dz	Cards with magnetic strip tick HI.co
ELECTRIC MONO Road Snta Baba Hassen ALGER	021 35 50 64	021 35 33 34	www.monoelectric.com contact@monoelectric.com	Switches, Sockets, Cable, Socket, Cup current extension
Raylan Eurl Zac Min Lot No. 05 El Bouni 23000 ANNABA	038 88 82 76	038 88 82 77	raylandz@gmail.com	Semi automatic washing machines
Amimer ENERGY BP 98 - Seddouk BEJAIA	034 32 38 72 034 32 31 48 034 32 31 49	034 32 31 35	www.amimer.com contact@amimer.com	Groups é lectrogènes, Plants electric é Groups welding motor pumps, voltage regulators Re é electric
ELECTROMEL Sarl Village Ibourassen, RN No. 12 - Oued Ghir BEJAIA	030 43 35 95 030 41 57 15 030 43 35 94	030 43 35 95	www.electromel.net contact@electromel.net info@electromel.net	Lamps é é economy of energy
ENI.CA-Epe BISKRA Spa ZI de Biskra - BP 131 07000 RP BISKRA	033 75 43 21 033 75 43 22	033 74 15 19	info@enicab.dz	É electric cables low voltage electric cables é domestic electrical high voltage cables é, PVC Compound, wooden reels
PRO'DISTRIBUTEUR BP 61F exchanger Boufarik North BLIDA	025 47 35 83 025 47 35 84	025 47 35 85	www.pro-dist.com info@pro-dist.com	Machine saw, copy milling
Ababou ELECTRONICS Sarl BP 506, Route Nationale # 5 - Ashir El Bordj Bou Arreridj	035 68 48 84 035 67 43 01	035 68 48 58	www.groupe-ababou.com www.cristor dz.com- info @ groupe-ababou.com	Digital satellite receivers re AMERICAS, Re frige operators, air conditioners, you the sights
CONDOR	035 67	035 67 68	www.condor.dz	Digital satellite

ELECTRONICS Area of activity s Road M'sila Bordj Bou Arreridj	68 30	48	info@condor.dz	receivers re AMERICAS, Re frige operators, air conditioners, washing machines, you the LCD viewfinders
ATTIA ELECTRONICS Sarl Rue Souk El Houari Boumediene Fellah Bordj Bou Arreridj	035 68 96 96	035 68 97 24	attiael@yahoo.fr administration@attiaelectronics.com	Water heater
Alemo BP 570 El Oued Hamimine Khroub CONSTANTINE	031 95 51 88	031 95 54 51	alemodg@yahoo.fr	Machine tools
ECRC Company Sarl Air Conditioning Avenue Aouati Mostefa CONSTANTINE	031 92 73 73	031 92 95 55	contact@ecrc-dz.com	AHU air
SOFACC Sarl BP 170, Hai Bassa - Beriane GHARDAIA	029 84 62 95 029 84 41 02	029 84 53 36	www.bergan-energy.com info@bergan-energy.com	Batteries
Technosat 220 City Belghanem GHARDAIA	029 86 48 29	029 86 48 30		Satellite Dishes
BYA ELECTRONIC 46 47 Area of Activity AIN EL BIA BP 393 ARZEW ORAN	040 20 30 61 040 20 30 62	041 47 47 19 040 20 30 55	www.bya-electonic.com bya@ccioranie.com contact @ bya-electonic.com	Satellite dishes, appliances é lectromé agers, e electronic equipment, LCD TV
ENPEC 04 th KM El Hassi, BP 88 Route de Constantine SETIF	036 93 67 11 036 93 67 12 036 62 51 45	036 93 72 82 036 62 51 45 036 62 51 49		Products higher electro-chemistry
SENSUS METERING SYSTEMS Spa Road Batna El Eulma SETIF	036 86 32 43 036 87 29 63	036 87 62 25	aissa.chouder @ sensus.com	Counters

ENIE SBA BP 101 Route de Mascara ZI Sidi Bel Abbes	048 56 February 05	048 56 50 66	eniedcfc@yahoo.fr	TV, LCD
ALGIERS LIGHT Sarl 04 Rue de la Mairie BP 04 Fouka TIPAZA	024 58 21 17	024 48 68 82	algerlumiere@gmail.com	É electrical box, full plates for cabinet
ENIEM BP 605 RP Tizi Ouzou	026 20 02 15 026 20 04 23 026 20 03 09 026 22 50 77	026 20 04 54 026 22 51 34 026 22 54 90 026 20 01 83	www.eniem.com.dz commercial@eniem.com.dz	Leave lators, Refrigerators
SITEL Spa ZI Chetouane TLEMCEN	043 27 14 66	043 27 20 93	contact@sitel.dz	É electronic products

MATÉ CONSTRUCTION MATERIALS AND CERAMIC CE

AFITEX ALGERIA Spa City of Beaver Villa No. 150 Bordj El Kiffan ALGER	021 21 19 59	021 21 19 59	www.afitexalgerie.com contact@afitexalgerie.com	Ge osynthetique
AZZARO AVERKANE Sarl BEJAIA	034 21 37 72	034 21 37 72	sarl.azzaro @ yahoo.fr	Tiling
Kanaan IMPORT-EXPORT Eurl City Logts Bt 80 S No. 04 Bordj Bou Arreridj	035 65 October 21	035 65 17 26		Marble blocks
GHARDAIA PLASTER Sarl Garat Taam ZI GHARDAIA				Cement
PETER ALGERIA Spa Road belkheir GUELMA	037 26 29 74 037 26 42 15		eteralgerie@yahoo.com	Ce ceramic sanitary

CERAMIC SOCIETY HEALTH Constantine ZI BP 109 El Milia JIJEL	034 42 80 30 034 42 95 88	034 42 62 03	scselmilia@yahoo.com	Ce ceramic
CEMENT WHITE ALGERIEN Spa 01, Boulevard de l'Indie pendence Sig MASCARA	045 84 88 98	045 84 87 31	paul.rousselot @ dz.lafarge.com	White cement
CERAMIC UNI Sarl ZI Oued Othmania BP 63 Route Chelghoum Laid MILA	031 53 08 84 031 53 08 85 031 53 08 86	031 53 August 79	info@uniceramic.net	Ce ceramic tiles
KNAUF PLATRES Fleurus Spa Benferha Oran BP 02 Boufatis ORAN	0661 21 28 91 041 50 10 50 041 52 10 51	041 52 12 26 041 52 14 62	knauf1466@ccioranie.com	Plasterboard
SAFCER Sarl ZI n ° 15 - BP 90 SETIF	036 93 81 81 036 93 86 33 036 93 65 00	036 93 March 03	safcer@homail.com	Wall covering and flooring
HADDAD CERAMIC Sarl ZI El Eulma SETIF	036 87 67 67 036 87 68 68 036 87 69 69	036 87 65 65 036 87 65 64	elhib_dz@hotmail.com	Ce ceramic tiles
MARBLE COMPANY SKIKDA (SOMASK) Eurl BP 130 Skikda Skikda	030 92 60 73	030 92 60 73		Marble blocks
CERAMIC SEAHORSE Sarl Road Chaiba - Bou Ismail TIPAZA	024 46 46 74	024 46 28 86 024 46 48 42	www.cerhippocampe.com cerhippocampe@cerhippocampe.com	Ce ceramic tiles
	040 90	040 90	www.groupeco-dz.com	Sets bathroom

CERAMIG Spa BP 235 - 13400 Ghazaouet TLEMCEN	07 86 040 90 00 05 040 90 07 72	07 75 040 92 72 93 043 32 43 99	ceramig_ghz@yahoo.fr	ceramic sanitary ce

CERAMIG Spa BP 235 - 13400 Ghazaouet TLEMCEN	07 86 040 90 00 05 040 90 07 72	07 75 040 92 72 93 043 32 43 99	ceramig_ghz@yahoo.fr	ceramic sanitary ce

CORK AND ARTICLES OF WOOD

EBLA Sarl BP 71 - ZI de Gue de Constantine ALGER	021 83 91 59 020 29 80 12 020 29 80 14	021 83 91 61	www.ets.benslim.com ets.benslim @ hotmail.com @ ets.benslim caramail.com	Blocks natural cork stoppers re agglomeration, natural cork stoppers, Carob crushed, discs of natural cork, carob pods, seeds, carob plates agglomerated cork insulation re black expanded, cork agglomerated re Boudins
SIAL Sarl Rue Mohamed-Salah MELOUAH - City Seybouse ANNABA	038 84 August 11	038 84 18 78		Cork, cork washers, cork agglomerated panels D, cork soles
TISSENTACHE Spa BEJAIA	021 53 17 51 020 48 49 90 020 48 49 91	021 53 23 32		Cork
EL WIAM KABYLIE Sarl Village BELGHIMOUZ Ancer JIJEL	034 41 34 87	034 41 August 31 034 41 Jan. 31	wpk.dz @ hotmail.com	Tubes cork, Corks
NET FORCE Eurl 190 City Bekira 3 rd Tranche CONSTANTINE	0550 April 19 05	031 94 17 49		Granulated cork
BELKOUICEM LOTFI ZI Salah JIJEL		034 44 52 72	eurleb@yahoo.fr	Cork

Corks ALGERIA Sarl 34, Zone Pot - El Haddada JIJEL	030 47 November 81	034 47 34 00	sarlbouchonneriealgerie@hotmail.com bouchonneriealgeriesarl@yahoo.fr	Granulated cork
BOULFELFEL Ets Machta El Kherba Achkfa JIJEL				Cork
JIJEL LIEGE SEAL Epe Spa BP 88 Route de Bé jaia JIJEL	034 47 19 40 034 49 54 52	034 49 76 76	www.jle.com.dz jle@jle.com.dz	Re agglomerated cork balls black foam
SIBL Sarl ZI Ouled Salah Taher BP A47 RP JIJEL	034 44 52 03	034 44 51 85	siblliege@yahoo.fr	Insulation boards cork granules
TAREXIM Eurl 09 B Street BOUCHEFRA Safia City Mustapha JIJEL 18000	034 47 40 48 0550 93 November 22	034 47 40 48	tarexim@gmail.com	Discs of natural cork
RISE Sarl # 67 City Rabta JIJEL	034 47 22 43	034 47 22 43		Stoppers and cork gaskets
BEJIA FEIRA CORK (CFB) Eurl Machta Boualayag Taher JIJEL	0550 September 8, 21		bejaiafeiracork@gmail.fr	Natural cork
ZAHRA Eurl Beni Ahmed Kaous JIJEL	0771 August 37 01	034 47 63 34		Granulated cork
FELLOURI A.EL OUAHAB City 486 Logts Lamuija El Milia JIJEL				Stoppers and cork gaskets
GELLILE NACERA Road Tanadfour El Milia JIJEL	034 42 94 01			Stoppers and cork gaskets
NBB Sarl Storage area El Hadada City # 19 JIJEL	034 49 76 60	034 49 76 60		Stoppers and cork gaskets

SIFOUR SALAH Oued Bourmel JIJEL	0661 51 16 82			Cork
COLLO CORK Sarl Bin El Ouiden, BP 6M Collo Skikda	038 71 64 40	038 71 64 40		Corks
Teleza LIEGE Epe Road Teleza BP 84 Collo Skikda	038 71 68 02	038 71 67 47		Agglomerated cork insulation re
BUSINESS TRANSFORMATION OF CORK YOUSFI Taguercift - Freha 15346 Tizi Ouzou	0772 75 December 98 026 34 May 30	026 34 24 44		Stoppers and cork gaskets, cork granules

PAPER AND CARDBOARD

MARSA.DILA LOT Alioua Fodil Amara No. 139 Che raga ALGER	021 36 43 69	021 36 86 79	marssadila@yahoo.fr	Waste paper de
AL MADAR FOR PAPER Route Lyce e Abdelmoumène - Rouiba ALGER	021 81 49 80	021 81 49 78	almadar_alg@yahoo.com	Waste paper de
Clariant Nort Sarl 17, Boulevard AMMANI Belkacem Hydra ALGIERS	0550 65 38 35 0550 32 33 37		sarl_clariant@hotmail.fr	Alve ole
KAME & Co. Sarl Rue Ibn Choubène No. 01 Rouiba ALGER	0550 65 38 35 0550 32 33 37	021 50 70 77	sarl_kame-co@hotmail.fr	Alve ole
CLASVIT Sarl ZI BP 59 Oued Smar ALGER	021 51 62 94 021 51 37 65 021 51 37 66	021 51 60 29	www.clasvit.com clasvit@hotmail.com clas@clasvit.com	Office supplies, hanging folders, Shirts é elastic flap cardboard
GIPEC Spa Route de la Gare - Ali Baba ALGER	021 26 88 63 021 30 98 84 021 30 92 91	021 26 88 92 021 30 91 94 021 30 96 38	www.gipec.dz gipecur@hotmail.com marketing_gipec@yahoo.fr	Papers re cupé ration bags Kraft paper, packing paper, solid board boxes

Subsidiary of Papirec GIPEC Lakhdaria area - Park Talha BP 133 El Harrach ALGER	021 26 88 93	021 26 88 92	www.gipec-dz.com gipecucr@hotmail.com	Wastepaper
PLATINUM Sarl Lot # 14, Zone Activity Zeralda ALGER	021 32 63 41 021 32 63 42	021 32 64 51 021 32 51 21	www.platinium.dz info@platinium.dz	Complex PET / hot melt coated paper printed
WAFA FAILE Sarl 132 ZI Amara - BP 18 Ché raga ALGER	020 34 14 46 020 34 14 47 021 37 19 69	021 37 19 69 021 37 17 43	wafa_soft@yahoo.fr	Paper towels, Film é stretchable, handkerchiefs box, Tissues, Foil, Paper hygienic lunch, napkins paper
HYGIENE CAN Spa City Logts 468 Bt 22 B Gue de Constantine ALGER	81 021 31 October 021 81 21 July 81 21 86 021	0 21 81 12 63		BE BE layers
FADERCO HYGIENE Sarl ZI les Ecalyptus Lot # 22 The Road arbaa ALGER	June 30 021 50 021 50 34 67	021 50 14 67		Techniques hygienic towels, cotton stalks
CARIO IMPORT Eurl City Logts 1010 Bt 02 Local No. 04 Lot 21 Hai El Badr Bachedjerah ALGER	0661 34 72 78		eurlcarioimportation@yahoo.fr	Old paper
ONYKRAB Spa 02, Rue de la Station Re GHAIA ALGER	021 85 94 95	021 85 96 78	onykrahocine@yahoo.fr	valve bags in 2 folds
DAF CELLUOSE Sarl Activity Zone El Bouni BP 202 Annaba	038 52 52 59	038 52 52 81 038 52 52 59		Waste die cardboard waste Dice White Paper
ECO-NADAF RECUP Area of Activity Allaleik El Bouni ANNABA	030 87 86 61	030 87 86 61		Waste paper de
GENERAL PACKAGING Sarl ZAC Taharacht - Akbou 06200 BEJAIA	034 35 68 60 034 35 68 61	034 35 90 43	contact@generale-emballage.com	TN cardboard, waste cardboard dice, cardboard plates

HAYAT DHC ALGERIA Sarl RN 29 Activity Zone Bouinan BLIDA	025 39 42 21	025 39 43 39		BE BE layers
Embag Spa ZI Route M'sila - BP 60 Bordj Bou Arreridj	035 68 59 46 035 68 91 54	035 67 26 92 035 68 53 47	www.embag.dz embagbba@yahoo.fr	Kraft paper bags, boxes boxboard
CENCELLA INDUSTRY Sarl Area of Activity Mhidi BEN EL TARF	038 69 30 31 030 87 55 05	038 69 30 25		BE BE layers
NACHITA Eurl City Daira Mustapha Ben M'hidi Cp 36220 EL TARF	038 69 30 31 038 30 87 55	038 69 30 25		Techniques hygienic towels
RECUP OR National Highway No. 04 crossbow Oued Tlelat ORAN	041 32 97 40	041 32 97 40		Waste paper de
SAM Sarl 15, Rue Jean Marie Larbiaire ORAN	041 33 54 63	041 33 19 98	sam@kouadria.com	Waste paper de
GMC Sarl Frikat Draa El Mizan Tizi Ouzou	026 38 61 52 026 38 61 75	026 38 61 52		Notepad and E ments
TONIC PACKAGING ZI Bou Ismail TIPAZA	024 46 17 22 024 46 41 40 024 46 41 43	024 46 August 13	info@tonic-emballage.com	Packaging
SOFATHY Sarl 02, Rue Abdelkader Senouci TLEMCEN	043 27 60 42 043 27 60 43	043 27 32 12	sofathy-sarl@gmail.com sofathy@gmail.com	Paper, napkins, paper towels hygienic techniques, Couches BE BE, hygienic paper lunch

GRAPHIC ARTS EDITION

OK GRAPHICS 69, Lot La Bruyère Bridge Carnot - ALGIERS Bouzareah	021 79 24 34	021 79 August 01	www.ok-graphics.com contact@ok-graphics.com	RPNs, Puzzles, Paper Bags, Bags fabrics, Mousepad
WHITE HOUSE	0777 46 72	020 38 17		Books

ALGERIA Sarl 03 Caves City, Street 54 Villa No. 16 B El Harrach BP 153 ALGER	91 0555 25 36 96 020 38 17 97	97		
Chemloul SAMIR Eurl 28 Rue des Frères BOUZIDI Tizi Ouzou				Cookbooks

LEATHER PRODUCTS, HIDES AND SKINS

BOULANDJAS Sarl 151, Rue de Hussein Dey Algiers Tripoli	021 23 38 70 021 23 38 76 021 77 36 65	021 77 46 44	www.blj-dz.com info@blj-dz.com	Shoes se curity
FULL LEATHER FLOWERS Sarl ZI Route B - Rouiba ALGER	0661 51 93 84 021 81 45 82 021 81 45 80 021 81 45 02	021 81 88 18	www.cpf-dz.com sarlcuirspleinsfleurs@yahoo.fr	Sheep skins wet blue, semi-finished leather
TMTA Sarl Lots 138/139, Zone Activity - BP 233 Dar El Beida ALGER	0770 90 41 21 0770 82 61 11 0661 52 19 33 021 75 33 23	021 83 56 13		Wet blue sheep skins, finished leather, skins of bovine, bovine skin leather furniture, leather bovine leather hides, skins bovine leather upholstery and belt
TANNERIE MEGISSERIE MITIDJA ZI Rouiba ALGER	021 81 18 00 021 81 57 50	021 81 18 00 021 81 57 50	zcheboub@hotmail.com	Finished leather, semi-finished leather, wet blue leather
TANNERIE MEGISSERIE TAMEG ROUIBA Spa Nle ZI Route No. 05 Rouiba ALGER	021 81 32 55	021 81 70 01		Leather
MEGA BATNA ZI City KECHIDA BATNA	033 92 22 92 033 92 13 93	033 92 22 94	megabatna@yahoo.fr	Semi-finished semi-finished goat leather, sheep leather
TANNERIE	0550 47	034 32	sarltannerie@live.fr	Raw hides are salted

MEGISSERIE KABYLIE Sarl Halba Seddouk 06011 BEJAIA	66 17 034 32 38 66	38 66		beef
TANNERIE MEGISSERIE KHENIFAR 3 Km Road Constantine El Milia BP 261 El Milia JIJEL	034 42 63 63 034 42 99 90	034 42 61 25	khenifar-cuir@caramail.com khenifar.cuir @ gmail.com	Leather
Nabu LEATHER Sarl ZI M'sila	035 55 71 71 035 55 72 72	035 55 97 39	sarl-nabou@yahoo.fr	Leather
DISTRICUIR Sarl 01, Rue Abderrahmane BENALI ORAN	0661 20 23 44 041 39 93 22 041 39 19 66	041 39 97 40 041 39 08 82	districuir@hotmail.com	Sheepskins
GSPC Avenue des Martyrs of the Re volution ORAN	0771 25 75 58 041 34 29 10 041 34 29 07	041 34 19 42	smcp@algeriecom.com smcp@ccioranie.com	Sheepskins are tanned
MARINE TEC Sarl Cité Grande Terre Bt H Block 01 Porte101 ORAN	046 92 67 51	046 92 67 95	marine_tec_2006@yahoo.fr	Salted bovine hides s waste Dice crusts beef
TANNERIE AIN Fakroun Sarl OUM EL bouaghi	032 41 73 07	032 41 73 07		Cowhide

TEXTILE AND CLOTHING ARTICLES

ALCOVEL ZI, RN # 26 - BP # 63 Akbou BEJAIA	034 34 73 19 034 34 73 69	034 34 73 18 034 34 73 28	www.alcovel.com info@alcovel.com	Fabrics, yarn s, Linen, Velvet fine ribs, Velvet large ribs, medium Velvet coast
LADY RELEASE Eurl BEJAIA	034 21 87 97	034 21 87 97		Firefighting gear
WEAVING AND FINISHING TIFIB BISKRA ZI BP 130 BISKRA	033 75 41 68	033 75 41 65	tifibiskra@hotmail.com	Textile

SOBITEX Sarl 69 Touates Ouled Yaich BLIDA	025 43 82 65	025 43 82 64		Tablecloth, placemat
SAIM TEXTILES Sarl 49 ZI - Bordj Bou Arreridj	035 67 67 67 035 60 26 26	035 68 52 88	saimblanket@yahoo.fr	Covers are printed
CHIRIFI BIO Eurl Site the valley e Lot No. 05 Office 01 BOUMERDES	024 81 53 82	024 81 53 82	bioplus-dz@yahoo.fr	Surgical mask, protective suit, shoe cover nonwoven, Charlotte, Camisole, Hood disposable
LACE SAHARA Sarl ZI Guerrara GHARDAIA	029 85 34 70	029 85 32 50		Textile
INOTIS Sarl ZI Es-Senia - BP 62 A ORAN	041 58 25 50 041 58 25 84	041 51 31 95	www.inotis.com inotis1412@ccioranie.com contact@inotis.com	Hydrophilic nonwoven, nonwoven Wirewound s es
TAPIDOR Sarl Vicinal path No. 01 - Hassiane Ettoual ORAN	041 52 81 82 041 52 81 83	041 54 18 05 041 52 81 02	www.tapidor.net contact@tapidor.net amelounes@tapidor.net	Carpet, upholstery
MAKING CLOTHING "TOUAREG" Sarl Tizi Rached Bouatelli 15550 Tizi Ouzou	026 21 38 51 026 31 40 40 026 31 38 38	026 31 30 29	touareg5@hotmail.com	Man together in 100% cotton canvas

HANDICRAFTS

AGENOR Avenue Mohamed BELKACEMI - El Madania ALGER	021 67 77 13 021 67 77 11 021 67 77 14	021 67 77 11 021 77 71 53	www.agenor.dz	Gold bullion, platinum bullion, gold and silver Findings, aurocyanide, Jewels, traditional silver jewelry, silver solder, gold chloride, analytical nitrate, silver nitrate
WORKSHOP OF CERAMIC ART BELAZZOUG 98, Krim Belkacem Boulevard ALGER	021 74 87 24	021 74 October 12		Ce ceramic articles
CERAMIC ART	021 77 50	021 77 50		Ce ceramic articles

MOHAND BELKACEM KNOW 06, Rue Ali MEDDOUCHE - HUSSEIN DEY ALGER	41	41		
CORAL JEWELRY Sarl Lot 02 Ben Socna Hadadi # 62 Che raga ALGER	021 36 88 57	021 36 88 57	www.corail-bijoux.com contact@corail-bijoux.com	Coral jewelery
AMINE Bernaoui IMPORT-EXPORT Eurl 22, Rue Mohamed Ayachi Belouizdad ALGER				Jarre, Boots, Candle, Plates, Glasses, Vases, Rugs
Bekkaï Rafika City BOUANANI # 19 Sebdou TLEMCEN	043 34 53 62	049 76 18 67	kdj_h100@hotmail.com	Traditional clothes

MULTIPLE TRADE AND IMPORT-EXPORT

EL RAKINA Sarl ADRAR				Eral waters undermined
LEMSDFA Hamdi Taouriret tamest Fenoughli ADRAR				Mattresses, industrial salt, Dates
REBIKA IMPORT-EXPORT Eurl 84 City 60 Logts Bt 04 El Amria AIN TEMOUCHENT	0551 00 July 38	043 66 March 83		Candy, Chocolate, Dates, Dried Fruits
AGRO GRAS INVEST (AGI) 38a Djenane BENDANOUN - Kouba ALGER	021 23 November 11	021 47 79 45	agidz@hotmail.com	Waste paper die (cartons, newspapers and magazines), fresh fruit and vegetables
CIT Sarl Logis Lot # 31 Kouba ALGER	021 68 83 85	021 68 83 35		Soft drinks, Harissa
EXPLATEAU Sarl	0550 October 24 35			Soft drinks, fruit juices, Flan, Biscuits

9A Coop rative El Yasmine Khraicia ALGER	24 35 0559 41 47 46			
FINANCE ONE Eurl 182, Rue Beni Idir Aissat Messous ALGER	020 39 52 69	021 28 90 79		Semolina
FRUIDEX 10, Rue Mouloud Belhouchet Hussein Dey ALGER	021 23 44 63	021 77 February 79		Eral natural waters undermined
KIKEL TRADING Eurl City Sonelgaz 02 Lot 308 Gue de Constantine ALGER	021 73 35 65	021 73 35 65		Industrial salt, Lemonade, Juice, Dates, undermined eral Water, Oil, Biscuits
SEGHAIRI MOHAMED YAZID (SMYCIE.EG) Coop Iommb El Bouchera Bt 01 Local # 24 B EL Mohammadia El Harrach 16211 ALGER	021 53 69 66	021 53 69 66	smy_export@yahoo.fr	Dates, Couscous, Drinks
ALGERIA OTHERWISE Sarl Subdivision 70 Logts 47 Kaouche Ché raga ALGER	0663 29 01 50 0555 02 10 76	021 37 19 36		Handicrafts: Curb silver Chain box, hook earrings, Brooches, Chains coral
AOUDIA Bouzid EXPORT Eurl 38 Rue Hocine Beladjel ALGER	0550 70 23 80 0550 October 83 30 021 68 14 87	021 68 14 87	aoudia-export@hotmail.com	Soft drinks
PRO-EXPORT Eurl City Logts Bt 602 24 No. 03 B Ché raga ALGER	021 38 53 85 0551 78 16 26	021 38 55 55		BE BE layers, techniques hygienic towels, detergents
SERAVIC Eurl 15 Rue Kramdi Local No. 01 Kouba ALGER	026 27 36 79	021 44 56 73		hatching eggs
LAZAAR Layachi	021 70 91	021 70 91		Biscuits, Industrial

IMPORT-EXPORT 144 Avenue Hamid Kebladj Rais Hmidou ALGER	95	95		Salt, Oil, Soft Drinks, Mattresses é sponges, Dates
SIDAY FOOD Eurl City Larouci Hamoud 184 Local 01 Khraicia 16143 ALGER	021 35 16 14	021 35 16 15		Green Olive, Pepper, Couscous, Vanilla, Semolina, Frik, Café
Mena FAST Eurl Street Boumaaraf Boukal 03 Batna BATNA	0661 83 32 33	033 81 20 73	fouad.boudouh @ caramail.com	Pasta, Couscous
El ABBACHERIF RASHID (ABR) No. 06 Taklait Ihddaden BEJAIA	0661 77 81 32		abbacherif_rachid@yahoo.fr	Flour, soft drinks, cookies Oil
Ladli SAID BEJAIA	0770 37 54 77	034 22 April 27		Pasta, semolina, flour bag, cement bag, crude salt
IRIS Deriche Eurl 04 Frantz FANON BOUMERDES	024 91 34 50	024 91 34 49	eurlirsderiche@yahoo.fr	Grass synth tick
Mokhbi Eurl 38 Salah DERRADJI City - El Khroub CONSTANTINE	031 57 57 28 0770 83 06 38	031 57 57 28		Wild onions
Rafif Eurl CONSTANTINE	031 92 49 72	031 92 49 72		Apricots
KEHEL BRAHIM EXPORT 07 Mila Street City Bouyahia	0771 83 June 38	031 57 57 28		Wild onions
Daadi EXPORT Hai Ouled Ahmed El Oued				Pasta
OULED EL Bekkaï ABDERRAHMANE El Oued El Hamraia				Industrial salt
BELLI IMPORT-EXPORT Eurl BP 237 47000 CTR GHARDAIA	029 89 00 90	029 89 00 93	belli.importexport @ gmail.com	Food

Ouled Sidi Cheikh Ste SERVICE Avenue Colonel Amir El Menia GHARDAIA	029 81 December 25	029 81 December 26	steouledsidchikh@yahoo.fr	Bitumen é tench ity, Ge geotextile, Lemonade, Water undermined eral natural
UGLY IMPORT-EXPORT Eurl BP 3220 El Ateuf GHARDAIA				Pasta
MESSAITFA CHIKH Chaabet Afari DAYA GHARDAIA				Industrial salt
CHELGOUM UGLY City Hadj Messaoud GHARDAIA				Industrial salt
BEN DEB UGLY City Hassi Nour Zelfana GHARDAIA				Industrial salt
PKJ IMPORT EXPORT Sarl Hai El Wafa Logts 510 Block 33 No. 05 Akid Lotfi ORAN	041 28 62 83			S cleaned dice onions cut frozen s s
TIDJDIT IMPORT Sarl City St Geroge ORAN	0770 68 18 95	043 33 October 67	simohammed@yahoo.fr	Gen eral food born
TOP AGRO Eurl Subdivision 83 Yahia Cherif City Cdt # 267 Senia Oran	0770 59 60 99			Wild onions
YOUCEF Rafik Eurl City Hashemi 3 rd tranche H 245 SETIF	036 84 88 43 0661 73 00 43	036 84 88 43		Food
SUICO BP 141 Ramdane Djamel SKIKDA	038 92 15 22	038 75 55 66		Fruity waters are
Rabei BILEL Sarl City Chott Ain Beida SIDI ABDELKADER OUARGLA	0560 45 57 43	037 44 77 80		Mattresses, industrial salt
	0662 18			Mattress

REKADI OUIAHET TAMANRASSET	62 62			Mattress
[illegible] (overprinted: REKADI OUIAHET) TAMANRASSET	[illegible] 70 18 56			Mattresses, plastic rolls, Plaster
MANSOURI Mahedi City Centre TAMANRASSET	0661 64 90 12	029 34 43 44		Soap, Wheelbarrows, Mattresses, Re frige operators
ALLANE AISSA TAMANRASSET	0667 60 83 90 0550 46 89 68			Eral water undermined
DERMECHAKI AHMED TAMANRASSET	0661 64 93 55			Mattress
EL Khier ETS TAMANRASSET	0561 36 80 10			Plaster
OULED Bekkaï EL BADI Communal market GuezzamTAMANRASSET	0665 June 42 48			Industrial salt
BELIT Sarl Rue Pasteur ABI-AYAD Abdelkrim TLEMCEN	043 20 34 77	043 20 35 15	sarlbelit@yahoo.fr	Bedding, sleeping Articles
SAFFEC Eurl 06, Rue Abdelkrim Zerrouki TLEMCEN	043 28 62 10	043 28 51 03		Cotton

SELECTED EXPORTERS BY INDUSTRY

FOOD PRODUCTS

PRODUITS	COMPAGNIE	CONTACT
Biscuits, Minoterie & Produits céréaliers	ERIAD Alger	Tel : (213-2) 52 24 40. Fax ; (213-2) 52 51 46
Conserverie	Ezdihar	Tel : (213-8) 86 35 34. Fax : (213-8) 86 40 07.
Conserverie	El Bousten	Tel : (213-8) 86 83 79. Fax : (213-8) 86 83 84.

Boissons, Jus	EMAL-GBA	Tel : (213-2) 23 18 15. Fax ; (213-2) 23 15 61.
Conserves, Jus	ENAJUC	Tel : (213-3) 41 78 91. Fax : (213-8) 41 74 91.
Boissons	ETS. Ibrahim& Fils Ifri	Tel : (213-5) 35 10 19. Fax : (213-5) 35 72 37.
Conserves	ETS. Zenati	Tel : (213-2) 35 31 85. Fax ; (213-2) 35 31 87.
Conserverie	NCA	Tel : (213-2) 85 21 50. Fax : (213-2) 85 22 93.
Conserves	Co- Imex	Tel : (213-6) 39 60 79 . Fax : (213-6) 39 60 79.
Vins	ONCV	Tel : (213-2) 63 09 40. Fax ; (213-2) 73 82 61.
Sel	ENASEL	Tel : (213-4) 68 70 87. Fax : (213-4) 66 48 84.
Dattes	CAID	Tel : (213-4) 74 15 23. Fax : (213-4) 74 11 77.
Dattes	SOCODAT	Tel : (213-4) 74 15 23 . Fax ; (213-4) 74 09 35.
Dattes	ECODATTES	Tel : (213-4) 74 01 48 Fax : (213-4) 74 01 48.
Dattes	SUDACO	Tel : (213-4) 74 57 59. Fax ; (213-4) 74 57 59.
Dattes	SID	Tel : (213-4) 74 08 59. Fax ; (213-4) 74 15 06.
Dattes	DRAPAL	Tel : (213-4) 93 85 15 . Fax : (213-4) 93 99 02.
Dattes	BEIDA EXPORT	Tel : (213-2) 50 80 74 . Fax : (213-2) 50 80 74
Dattes	ETS Nour El Islam	Tel : (213-2) 86 79 91 Fax ; (213-2) 86 79 91.
Dattes	ETS TROUDI	Tel : (213-4) 75 54 39. Fax : (213-4) 75 54 39.

FISHING

Poissons, Crustacés	CORDIAL	Tel : (213-6) 36 57 10. Fax : (213-6) 36 57 10.
Poissons, Crustacés	Comptoir El Hana	Tel : (213-8) 86 88 43. Fax : (213-8) 86 88 43.
Poissons, Crustacés	ETS Bouziane	Tel : (213-8) 86 14 39. Fax ; (213-8) 86 14 39.
Corail	Algerian Trans- Corail	Tel : (213-8) 84 11 26. Fax ; (213-8)87 11 26.
Corail	Méditerranée Corail	Tel : (213-2) 79 69 54 . Fax : (213-2) 79 63 90.

BREEDING

Bétail	ONAB	Tel : (213-2) 58 91 15. Fax : (213-2) 58 62 19

CHEMICAL AND PETROCHEMICAL

Peintures	ENAP	Tel : (213-3) 90 11 44. Fax ; (213-3) 90 10 93.
Colles	BELCOL	Tel : (213-2) 51 64 10 Fax : (213-2) 76 72 14.
Produits Chimiques & Pétrochimiques	DIPROCHIM	Tel : (213-2) 59 59 40. Fax : (213-2) 59 65 12.
Produits Chimiques & Pétrochimiques	ENIP	Tel : (213-8) 86 14 39. Fax ; (213-8) 75 61 46.
Engrais & Fertilisants	ASMIDAL	Tel : (213-8) 84 11 26. Fax ; (213-8) 84 61 22.
Détergents & Produits d'entretien	ENAD	Tel : (213-3) 96 59 29 . Fax : (213-3)96 63 25.
Détergents & Produits d'entretien	PROCHIMAL	Tel : (213-2) 58 91 15. Fax : (213-2)46 29 36.
Produits Pharmaceutiques	ARMEDIC	Tel : (213-2)23 27 73 . Fax ; (213-2) 23 44 54.
Produits Pharmaceutiques	SAIDAL	Tel : (213-2) 53 89 69. Fax : (213-2) 50 52 68.
Produits Pharmaceutiques	SOCOTHYD	Tel : (213-2) 36 57 10. Fax : (213-2)88 45 13.
Produits Pharmaceutiques	ENPC	Tel : (213-5) 91 02 08 . Fax ; (213-5) 93 05 65.
Huile Végétale & Corps gras	CEVITAL	Tel : (213-2) 59 43 84 Fax ; (213-2) 59 43 84.
Huile Végétale & Corps gras	ENCG	Tel : (213-2) 74 47 28 Fax : (213-2) 74 44 21.
Produits Oléicoles	ORECPO	Tel : (213-3) 83 21 76 Fax : (213-3) 92 00 88
Produits Oléicoles	ORPO	Tel : (213-6) 34 06 36 Fax ; (213-6) 34 84 32.
Produits Oléicoles	SOA	Tel : (213-3) 93 69 16 Fax : (213-3) 93 69 16.

ELECTRICAL AND ELECTRONICS EQUIPMENT

Câbles électriques & grenaille	ENICA- Biskra	Tel : (213-4) 74 18 66 Fax ; (213-4) 74 15 19
Fils électriques	SPICI-Decolletage	Tel : (213-2) 55 58 64 Fax : (213-2) 55 58 64.
Électroménager	ENIEM	Tel : (213-3) 21 87 45 Fax : (213-3) 21 87 44
Téléviseurs, chaînes HIFI, Magnétoscopes	ENIE	Tel : (213-7) 56 88 44 Fax ; (213-7) 56 54 32.

LEATHER GOODS, LEATHER & FOOTWEAR

Chaussures	El Manar	Tel : (213-3) 39 39 83 Fax : (213-3) 39 39 83.
Maroquinerie, cuir et chaussures	EMAC	Tel : (213-6) 34 77 55. Fax ; (213-6) 84 01 97.
Maroquinerie, cuir et chaussures	DISTRICH	Tel : (213-2) 77 66 42 Fax : (213-2) 23 42 51.
Chaussures	SAFA Footwear	Tel : (213-5) 47 28 09 Fax : (213-5) 47 28 09
Chaussures	MACVIL	Tel : (213-2) 21 10 36 Fax ; (213-2) 21 10 36.
Chaussures	MA. HI.RA	Tel : (213-7) 40 71 97 Fax : (213-7) 40 71 97.
Peaux tannées et Cuir	ENIPEC	Tel : (213-5) 46 48 25 Fax : (213-5) 47 28 09.

CONSTRUCTION MATERIALS

Marbre	ENAMARBRE	Tel : (213-8) 75 64 08 Fax ; (213-8) 75 43 64.
Céramique	Modern-céramique	Tel : (213-2) 36 28 65 Fax : (213-2) 37 59 80.
Céramique	Milevienne & céramique	Tel : (213-4)93 80 82 Fax ; (213-4) 93 80 82.
Liége	ROUIKHA	Tel : (213-2) 71 01 64 Fax : (213-2) 71 01 64.
Liége	COLLOCORK	Tel : (213-8) 91 57 28 Fax : (213-8) 91 57 28
Liége	ENL	Tel : (213-8) 86 40 39 Fax ; (213-8) 86 55 87.
Liége	SIBL	Tel : (213-5) 47 29 46 Fax : (213-5) 47 29 46.
Liége	ETS Benchemam	Tel : (213-5) 46 00 73 Fax : (213-5) 46 00 73.
Liége	ETS Zaimeche	Tel : (213-5) 43 66 66 Fax : (213-5) 43 66 66
Verre	LUMIVERRE	Tel : (213-3) 41 60 14 Fax ; (213-3) 41 60 18.
Verre	AFRICAVER	Tel : (213-5) 45 92 75 Fax : (213-5) 45 92 75.

MECHANICAL

Matériel agricole et machines outils	ENMTP	Tel : (213-4) 97 11 11 Fax : (213-4) 97 25 55.
Matériel agricole et machines outils	ENPMO	Tel : (213-4) 96 26 01 Fax : (213-4) 96 25 72.
Matériel agricole et machines outils	PMA	Tel : (213-2) 55 39 68 Fax : (213-2) 55 25 51.
Matériel agricole et machines outils	MAGI	Tel : (213-2) 85 16 59 Fax : (213-2) 85 16 59

Compteurs, électricité	AMC	Tel : (213-2) 73 26 50 Fax ; (213-2) 73 26 50.
Cycles, Motocycles	CYCMA	Tel : (213-5) 26 15 90 Fax : (213-8) 26 60 90.
Camions &Véhicules industriels	SNVI	Tel : (213-2) 8523 39 Fax : (213-2) 85 21 33.
Matériel ferroviaires	FERROVIAL	Tel : (213-8) 85 77 41 Fax ; (213-8) 85 23 98
Filtres a air	SAFI	Tel : (213-4) 85 64 02 Fax : (213-4) 86 55 40.
Pompes &motopompes	POVAL	Tel : (213-2) 53 31 79 Fax : (213-2) 85 10 40
Boulonnerie & visserie	BCR	Tel : (213-5) 85 44 45 Fax ; (213-5) 91 80 60

SIDERURGIE & METALLURGIE

Chaudières à vapeur & à eau chaude	ECFERAL	Tel : (213-2) 76 43 95 Fax : (213-2) 52 19 58.
Réservoirs & Chaudières	ENCC	Tel : (213-6) 91 34 08 Fax : (213-6) 33 48 73.
Mobilier Métallique	SOMEX	Tel : (213-2) 86 87 56 Fax : (213-2) 86 76 48.
Zinc Electrolytique	METANOF	Tel : (213-7) 20 13 61 Fax : (213-7) 20 16 89
Zinc Electrolytique	PROSIDER	Tel : (213-8) 84 47 01 Fax ; (213-8) 84 47 01
Fonte en gueuse	COMERSID	Tel : (213-2) 60 12 10 Fax : (213-2) 60 12 10.
Fonte en gueuse	ALFASID	Tel : (213-8) 87 18 99 Fax : (213-8) 87 18 99.
Fonte en gueuse	SIDER	Tel : (213-8) 87 28 22 Fax : (213-8) 87 29 12.
Tubes, Profiles et Rayonnages	ANABIB	Tel : (213-3) 85 10 73 Fax : (213-3) 85 10 71
Tubes, Profiles et Rayonnages	PROFILOR	Tel : (213-2) 50 77 16 Fax ; (213-2) 50 86 08

MINES & ENERGIE

Produits Miniers (kaolin, mercure)	ENOF	Tel : (213-2) 52 52 40 Fax : (213-2) 52 23 74.
Produits Miniers (kaolin, mercure)	FERPHOS	Tel : (213-8) 47 24 03 Fax : (213-8) 87 18 99.

REGIONAL DIRECTORATES AND DEPARTMENTS OF COMMERCE

REGIONAL DIRECTORATE OF COMMERCE BATNA

(wilaya code 05)

- Regional Direction of Trade Batna Bechar	www.drcbatna.dz
- Direction of Trade of the Wilaya of Batna	www.dcwbatna.dz
- Direction of Trade of the Wilaya of Biskra	www.dcommerce-biskra.dz
- Direction of Trade of the Wilaya of Oum El Bouaghi	www.dcwoumelbouaghi.dz
- Direction of Trade of the Wilaya of Tébessa	www.dcwtebessa.dz
- Direction of Trade of the Wilaya of Constantine	www.dcwconstantine.gov.dz
- Direction of Trade of the Wilaya of Khenchela	www.dcwkhenchela.dz

REGIONAL DIRECTORATE OF COMMERCE BECHAR

(wilaya code 08)

- Regional Direction of Trade Bechar	www.drc-bechar.dz
- Direction of Trade of the Wilaya of Bechar	www.dcwbechar.dz
- Direction of Trade of the Wilaya of Nâama	www.dcw-naama.dz
- Direction of Trade of the wilaya of Adrar	www.dcwadrar.dz
- Direction of Trade of the Wilaya of Tindouf	www.dcwtindouf.dz
- Direction of Trade of the Wilaya of Elbayadh	www.dcwelbayadh.dz

REGIONAL DIRECTORATE OF COMMERCE BLIDA

(wilaya code 09)

- Regional Direction of Trade Blida	www.drcblida.dz
- Direction of Trade of the Wilaya of Blida	www.dcwblida.dz
- Direction of Trade of the Wilaya of Djelfa	www.dcwdjelfa.dz
- Direction of Trade of the Wilaya of Bouira	www.dcwbouira.dz
- Direction of Trade of the Wilaya of Tizi Ouzou	www.dcwtiziouzou.dz
- Direction of Trade of the Wilaya of Ain Defla	www.dcwaindefla.dz
- Direction of Trade of the wilaya of Medea	www.dcwmedea.dz

REGIONAL DIRECTORATE OF COMMERCE OF ALGIERS

(wilaya code 16)

- Regional Direction of Trade Algiers	www.drcalger.dz
- Direction of Trade of the wilaya of Algiers	www.dcwalger.dz
- Direction of Trade Tipaza	www.dcwtipaza.dz
- Direction of Trade Boumerdes	www.dcwboumerdes.dz

REGIONAL DIRECTORATE OF TRADE SETIF

(wilaya code 19)

- Regional Direction of Trade Setif	http://www.drc-setif.dz
- Direction of Trade of the wilaya of Setif	http://www.dcwsetif.dz
- Direction of Trade of the wilaya of Bejaia	http://www.dcwbejaia.dz
- Direction of Trade of the wilayaof Jijel	http://www.dcwjijel.dz
- Direction of Trade of the wilaya of Mila	http://www.dcwmila.dz
- Direction of Trade wilaya M'sila	htt p :/ / www.dcommerce-msila.dz
- Direction of Trade Bordj Bouarreridj	http://www.dcommercebba.gov.dz

REGIONAL DIRECTORATE OF COMMERCE SAIDA

(wilaya code 20)

- Regional Direction of Trade Saida	www.drc-saida.dz
- Direction of Trade of the Wilaya Saida	www.dcw-saida.dz
- Direction of Trade of the Wilaya of Tiaret	www.dcw-tiaret.dz
- Direction of Trade of the Wilaya Relizane	www.dcw-relizane.dz
- Direction of Trade of the Wilaya de Chlef	www.dcw-chlef.dz
- Direction of Trade of the Wilaya of Tissemsilt	www.dcwtissemsilt.dz
- Direction of Trade Mascara	http://www.dcmascara.gov.dz

REGIONAL DIRECTORATE OF COMMERCE ANNABA

(wilaya code 23)

- Regional Directorate of Trade of Annaba	http://www.drc-annaba.dz
- Direction of Trade Souk Ahras	http://www. dc wsoukahras . gov.dz
- Direction of Trade Guelma	http://www.dcwguelma.gov.dz
- Direction of Trade of the Wilaya of Skikda	http://www.dcommerce-skikda.dz

REGIONAL DIRECTORATE OF COMMERCE OUARGLA

(wilaya code 30)

- Regional Directorate of Trade of Ouargla	http://www.drcouargla.dz
- Direction of Trade of the Wilaya of Ouargla	http://www.dcommerce-ouargla.dz
- Directorate of Trade of the Wilaya of Ghardaia	http://www.dcwghardaia.dz
- Directorate of Trade of the Wilaya of Laghouat	http://www. dclaghouat . gov.dz
- Directorate of Trade of the Wilaya of Tamanrasset	http://www.dcwtamanrasset . dz
- Direction of Trade of the Wilaya Illizi	http://www. dcwillizi . dz
- Direction of Trade of the wilaya of Eloued	http:// www.dcommerce-eloued.dz

REGIONAL DIRECTORATE OF TRADE ORAN

(wilaya code 31)

- Regional Direction of Trade Oran	www.drcoran.dz
- Direction of Trade of the Wilaya of Oran	www.dcworan.dz
- Direction of Trade of the Wilaya of Tlemcen	www.dcwtlemcen.dz
- Direction of Trade of the Wilaya of Sidi Bel Abbes	www.dcwsidibelabbes.dz
- Direction of Trade of the Wilaya of Ain Timouchent	www.dcwaintemouchent.dz
- Direction of Trade of the Wilaya of Mostaganem	http://www.dcw-mostaganem.dz/

CHANBERS OF COMMERCE

CHAMBER OF COMMERCE AND INDUSTRY OF THE SAHEL

Tel: (024) 91 12 36/81 76 25 Fax: (024) 91 12 36/81 92 37
Address: Boulevard Abane Ramdane.Bp 33M Boumerdes Algeria
General information about the company Nature of business:
Service Branches and group: Ministry of Trade Regime:
EPIC Date updated: 07-01-2014 Source of Information: informed by the institution Contact (s) Name / Surname: Boudjelti Belaid - Gender: Male - Function: Speaker Name / Name: Ahmed Khadraoui - Function: Director

CHAMBER OF COMMERCE AND INDUSTRY SAF SAF

Tel: (038) 75 24 26 Fax: (038) 75 24 26 Address: 12, rue Mohammed Nafir Skikda Algeria Address 2 General information about the company Nature of business: Service and Subsidiaries Group: Ministry of Trade Regime: EPIC Last updated: 07-01-2014 Source of Information: informed by the institution Contact (s) Name / Surname: Hamani Kamel - Gender: Male - Function: President - Email: Info.cciskikda @ yahoo.fr Name / Name: Moussa El Mechemaa - Gender: Male - Function: Director

CHAMBER OF COMMERCE AND INDUSTRY OF BENI HAROUN

Tel: (031) 57 68 44/57 68 46 Fax: (031) 57 68 45/53 04 33
Address: City Boutout. 240 bp Mila Algeria
General information about the company Nature of business: Service and Subsidiaries Group: Ministry of Trade Regime: EPIC Date updated: 07-01-2014 Source of Information: informed by the institution Contact (s) Name / Surname: Benhacine Abdennacer - Gender: Male - Function: Speaker Name / Surname: Taiba Abdelouaheb - Gender: Male - Function: Director

CHAMBER OF COMMERCE AND INDUSTRY ZACCAR

Tel: (027) 60 21 25 Fax: (027) 60 21 25
Address: 142 City housing Ain Defla Algeria
General information about the company Nature of business: Service and Subsidiaries Group: Ministry of Trade Regime: EPIC Date Update: 07-01-2014 Source of Information: informed by the institution Contact (s) Name / Surname: Abbas Belkacem - Gender: Male - Function: Speaker Name / Surname: Selman Cherif - Gender: Male - Function : Director

CHAMBER OF COMMERCE AND INDUSTRY MEZGHENNA

Tel: (021) 73 80 00 Fax: (021) 73 99 16
Address: 7 Place Port Said.Alger Algiers Algeria
General information about the company Nature of business: Service and Subsidiaries Group: Ministry of Trade Regime : EPIC Date updated: 24-09-2013 Source of Information: informed by the institution Contact (s) Name / Surname: Korichi Mustapha - Gender: Male - Function: Speaker Name / Surname: Ammor Shaaban - Title: man - Function: Director - Email: contact@cci-mezhghena.dz Name / Surname: Korichi Mustapha - Gender: Male - Position: President

CHAMBER OF COMMERCE AND INDUSTRY M'ZI

Tel: (029) 93 21 90/90 32 48 Fax: (029) 90 68 90
Address: 38 City logements.RN 1.Bp No 3309 Laghouat Algeria
General information about the company Nature of business: Service and Subsidiaries Group: Ministry of Trade Regime: EPIC Date updated: 07-01-2014 Source of Information: informed by the institution Contact (s) Name / Surname: Djoubar Belkhir - Gender: Male - Function: President Name / Surname: Taouti Bashir - Gender: Male - Function: Director

CHAMBER OF COMMERCE AND INDUSTRY TIKJDA

Tel: (026) 93 81 81/93 44 39 Fax: (026) 93 81 81/93 44 98 Address: 130 Bt No. 7.Cité housing Bouira Algeria Address 2 General information about the company Nature of business: Service and Subsidiaries Group: Ministry of Trade Regime: EPIC Date updated: 07-01-2014 Source of Information: informed by the institution Contact (s) Name / Surname: Banouh Hamdan - Gender: Male - Function: President - Email: hbanouh@yahoo.fr Name / Surname: Ahmed Samir Abdelmalek - Gender: Male - Function: Director

CHAMBER OF COMMERCE AND INDUSTRY SAOURA

Tel: (040) 85 45 75 Fax: (049) 80 17 20
Address: Rue Colonel Lotfi ville.68 housing, No. 58 20.Bp Bechar Algeria
General information about the company Nature of business: Service Branches and group: Ministry of Trade Regime: EPIC Date updated: 07-01-2014 Source of Information: informed by

the institution Contact (s) Name / Surname: Hammadi Othman - Gender: Male - Function: Speaker Name / Name: Mustapha Benabadelmoulla - Gender: Male - Function: Director

CHAMBER OF COMMERCE AND INDUSTRY OF BENI CHOUGRANE

Tel: (045) 81 62 63 Fax: (045) 81 62 53
Address: 13, rue November 1 1954.Bp 302 Mascara Algerie
General information about the company Nature of business: Service and Subsidiaries Group: Ministry Trade Regime: EPIC Date updated: 07-01-2014 Source of Information: informed by the company Contact (s) Name / Surname: Bousbia Mustapha - Gender: Male - Function: Speaker Name / Surname: Benkhalifa Bouziane - Gender: Male - Function: Director - Tel: 0661 95 39 53.

CHAMBER OF COMMERCE AND INDUSTRY OF EL BIBANE

Tel: (035) 68 75 86/67 48 66 Fax: (035) 68 91 67/68 13 66/67 48 66
Address: Former headquarters of the Wilaya Bordj Bou Arreridj 34000 Algerie
General information about the company Nature Company: Service Number: 07 Subsidiaries and Group: Ministry of Commerce Trade register: 34/00-0463651B08 start date of activity: 07/01/2008 Regime: EPIC NIS: 000834010006760 NIF: 000834019019051 taxation Article: 34012107267 Last updated: 07-01-2014 Source of Information: informed by the institution Contact (s) Name / Surname: Amara Najeeb - Gender: Male - Function: Speaker Name / Surname: Haid Abdelkader - Gender: Male - Function: Director

CHAMBER OF COMMERCE AND INDUSTRY NEMEMCHAS

Tel: (037) 49 39 67 Fax: (037) 49 37 02
Address: Rue de Constantine Tebessa Algeria
General information about the company Nature of business: Service and Subsidiaries Group: Ministry of Trade Regime: EPIC Date Update: 07-01-2014 Source of Information: informed by the institution Contact (s) Name / Surname: Guerboussi Saad - Gender: Male - Function: Speaker Name / Surname: Benaicha Ibrahim - Gender: Male - Function: Director - Tel: 0661 36 80 60.

NATIONAL REAL ESTATE DEVELOPMENT COMPANY

Tel: (021) 60 16 09/60 16 49 Fax: (021) 60 16 87
Address: Route de Sidi Rais Yahia.Said Hamdine.Bir Mourad Alger Algerie
General information about the company Nature Company: Service Social Capital (DA) 1000000000 Legal form: SPA Regime: EPE
Source of Information: informed by the company (SALON BATIMATEC) Contact (s) Name / Surname: El Hadj Meriem - Gender: Female

IMPORTANT INDUSTRIAL AND BUSINESS CONTACTS

Firms and companies interested in doing business in Algeria or seeking information should contact:

US-Algeria Business Council
2121 Crystal Drive, Suite 104A
Arlington, VA 22202
Tel. 703 271 6300
Fax 703 271 0600

Dr. Ismael Chikhoune
President and CEO
chikhoune@us-algeria.org

Ms. Elisabeth Lord Stuart
Operations Director
stuart@us-algeria.org

USABC EventsRSVP
rsvp@us-algeria.org

PROMEX: The Algerian Board for the Promotion of External Trade at:
Phone: (213 21) 52 20 82
Fax numbers:(213 21) 52 11 26
(213 21) 52 12 10
(213 21) 52 15 71
(213 21) 52 28 03
E-mail: promex@ist.cerist.dz

CACI: The Algerian Chamber of Commerce and Industry:
Palais consulaire 06, Boulevard Amilcar Cabral 16003 Alger BP 100 Algerie.
Phone numbers: (213 21) 96 77 77
(213 21) 96 66 66
(213 21) 96 50 50
Fax : (213 21) 96 70 70

US COMPANIES DOING BUSINESS IN ALGERIA

Air Express International Corporation
120 Tokeneke Rd.
Darien, CT 06820
Gunter Rohrmann, CEO
203/655-7900
Operating in Algiers
Frieght Forwarders

Anadarko Petroleum Corporation
17001 Northchase Drive
Houston Texas, 77060
http://www.anadarko.com/anadarko/default.htm

Bechtel

50 Beale
San Francisco, CA 94119
Riley P. Bechtel, CEO
415/768-1234
Operating in EIBIAR
General Contractors

Citicorp
399 Park Ave.
New York, NY 10043
John S. Reed, Chairman
212/559-1000

Colgate Palmolive
300 Park Ave.
New York, NY 10022
William Shanhan, CEO
212/310-2000

Deloitte Touche, Tohmatsu International
P.O. Box 820
Wilton, CT 06897
J. Micheal Cook, President

GTE Corporation
One Stamford Forum
Stamford, CT 06904
Charles R. Lee, CEO
203/965-2000

Norton Company
1 New Bond Street
Worcester, MS 01606
Pierre Andre Di Chalendare, CEO
508/795-5000
Operating in Algiers
Braces, drill bits

Weatherford International, Inc.
1360 Post Oak Blvd.
Houston, TX 77227-7608
Phillip J. Burguieres, CEO
713/439-9400
Operating in Algiers
Oil field service equipment

Western Atlas International, Inc.
10205 Westheimer
Houston, TX 77251-1407
John R. Russel, CEO
713/266-5700
Oil Industry service

Xerox Corporation

800 Long Ridge Rd.
Stamford, CT 06904
Paul A. Allaire
203/968-3000

INDUSTRIAL AND TRADE ASSOCIATIONS

CLUB OF INDUSTRIAL CONTRACTORS AND THE MIT ... Equine Club Avenue Mokhtar Kritli, 09000 Blida-Algeria www.ceimi.org

WORLD TRADE CENTER ASSOCIATION ALGIERS (WTCAA) 70, Chemin Larbi Allik BP 539 Hydra Algiers-Algeria www.wtcalgeria.com

BUSINESS LEADERS FORUM (FCE) Villa No. 69, Plot Benhaddadi, Cheraga Algiers Algeria www.fce.dz

NATIONAL FREIGHT FORWARDERS IN UNION ALGEX building, RN No. 05 Five Houses Mohamadia Algiers www.untca.org

Full name	Function	Phone	E-mail
KHEFFACHE Meziane	President	021 52 00 55	mkheffache@untca.org
HAYOUN Ali	Secretary General	021 52 00 55	hayoun@untca.org
BENABDELLAH Fares	Deputy Secretary General	021 52 00 55	benabdellah@untca.org
FERNANE Salah	General Treasurer	021 52 00 55	fernane@untca.org
Ould Hocine MOHAND	Assistant Treasurer	021 52 00 55	ouldmohand@untca.org
REBAI Messaoud	Vice President Centre	021 52 00 55	rebai@untca.org
MELIANI Bouabdellah	Vice President Western	021 52 00 55	meliani@untca.org
HAMADACHE Arezki	Vice President South	021 52 00 55	hamadache@untca.org
TEITACHE Bashir	Assessor Member	021 52 00 55	teitache@untca.org
Ahmed Triki	Assessor Member	021 52 00 55	triki@untca.org
AOUIDETTE Djelloul	Assessor member AND / Secretary General P I	021 52 00 55	aouidette@untca.org
Kaci CHAOUECHE Amokrane	Assessor Member	021 52 00 55	kacichaoueche@untca.org
Rachid Méridji	Assessor Member	021 52 00 55	meridji@untca.org
BELARBI Tayeb	Assessor Member	021 52 00 55	belarbi@untca.org

Idres Boualem	Assessor Member	021 52 00 55	idres@untca.org

GENERAL CONTRACTORS ASSOCIATION Algerians (AG ... Copérative Echarifa Bt A, No. 03 BP 186 Alger Bab Ezzouar www.agea-dz.org

NATIONAL ASSOCIATION OF CONDITIONERS AND EXPORTING ... # 53 Zone D'equipment Biskra

PROFESSIONAL ASSOCIATION OF BANKS AND educational ... 03 Roman Way Val d'Hydra Algiers

NATIONAL ASSOCIATION EDUCATION INSTITUTIONS A. .. 08 Road Brn Aknoun El Biar Algiers New Castle www.anefa-dz.org

17 Results found.CONFEDERATION OF INDUSTRIAL AND PRODUCERS Algerians ... 118 Chemin de la Wilaya Industrial Zone of Oued Smar Algiers

CONFEDERATION OF EMPLOYERS OF ALGERIA (CAP) Hotel AURASSI Level C Office No. 07 Algiers

EAN ALGERIA ASSOCIATION / GS 1 ALGERIA BU: 10-16, 10th floor Commercial and Business Centre "El Quds" Cheraga - Algiers www.gs1.dz

PRODUCERS ASSOCIATION OF ALGERIA BEVERAGES (APA. .. Residence of the 21st century. Ain Allah Bt 3, Apt 01 Dely Brahim www.apab-algerie.org

Residence of the 21st century.
Ain Allah
Bt 3, Apt 01
Dely Brahim
Tel.: 00 213 (0) 21 37 51 43
Fax:. 00 213 (0) 21 37 51 43
Mobile: 00 213 (0) 6 61 56 67 05
E-mail: contac@apab-algerie.org

ASSOCIATION OF WOMEN BUSINESS LEADERS

NATIONAL UNION OF CARRIERS (UNAT)

CIRCLE OF ACTION AND REFLECTION ABOUT THE COMPANY ...

NATIONAL OPERATORS OF PHARMACY UNION (UNOP)

OIL AND GAS SECTOR: CONTACTS AND BUSINESS OPPORTUNITIES

STRATEGIC CONTACTS

AGENCIES AND ORGANISATIONS

National Agency for the Promotion and Rationalization of the use of energy (APRUE) Adresse : 02, rue Chenoua BP 265 Hydra. Alger.Algérie http://www.aprue.org	National Agency for Development and Investment (ANDI) 28 rue Ahmed OUAKED Dely -Ibrahim http://www.andi.dz
National office of the Statistics (ONS) 8 & 10 Rue des moussebilines Alger Algérie E.mail: ons@onsieg.ons.dz Web: http://www.ons.dz	Algerian institute of Standardization (IANOR) 5, Rue Abou Hamou Moussa BP104 RP Alger Algérie http://www.ianor.org.dz/

HYDROCARBONS

Company	Activity	Address	Phone	Fax
SONATRACH See also Sonatrach Petroleum Corporation. (UK) & Fondation Sonatrach Tassili	Research, exploitation, transport and marketing of liquid and gas hydrocarbons.	Djenane Al-Malik. Hydra. Alger	+213-21 54 70 00 +213-21 54 80 11 +213-21 54 90 22 sonatrach@sonatrach.dz +213-21 54 77 00	
NAFTEC	Treatment of the crude oil.	130, Sidi Arcine, Baraki, Alger.	+213-21 67 21 12 +213-21 67 21 96 +213-21 67 22 01	
NAFTAL	Marketing and distribution of petroleum products and derived, in particular fuels and lubricants.	Route des dunes Chéraga. Tipaza BP 73	+213-21 38 13 13 +213-21 38 19 19	
SNTM HYPROC	Naval transport of Hydrocarbons and chemicals.	130, Sidi Arsine, Baraki, Alger. Siège Social : B.P 60 ARZEW - Algérie	+213-41 47 48 55 à 59 +213-41 47 34 45	
ENIP	Production and marketing of petrochemical products.	B.P 215 Zone Industrielle. Skikda	+213-38 75 68 62 +213-38 75 70 82 +213-38 75 61 46	

ELECTRICITY AND GAS DISTRIBUTION

Company	Activity	Address	Phone	Fax

SONELGAZ	Production and marketing of electricity and public distribution of natural gas	02 Boulevard Krim Belkacem. Alger	+213-21 72 31 00 +213-21 72 26 90
AEC Algerian Energy Company	Production of electricity, Marketing, transport and distribution of energy. Desalination of sea water and telecommunication.	12 Boulevard Krim Belkacem. Alger	+213-21 72 27 75 +213-21 72 31 58 +213-21 72 25 65
TRANSMEX	Company of transport and handling of industrial and electric plants	RN 28 Gué de Constantine Kouba 16260 Alger	+213-21 83 90 56 +213-21 83 90 51
KAHRAKIB	Study and realization of electric work of infrastructures (high voltage).	127 Bd Krim Belkacem. Alger	+213-21 74 21 28 +213-21 74 14 67
KAHRIF	Electrification work	Villa Malvalle, quatier Ain D'hab. Médéa	+213-25 58 31 14 +213-25 58 31 14
KANAGHAZ	Studies and achievements of gas transport pipes	Route nationale n° 24 B.P 115. Boumerdès	+213-24 81 18 83 +213-24 81 62 92

MINING

Company	Activity	Address	Phone	Fax
ORGM	Research and promotion of mining resources	B.P 102. Boumerdès.	+213-24 81 91 42 +213-24 81 85 25 +213-24 81 83 79	
AQUAMINES	Hydrogeologic, mining and geotechnical Drilling. Hydrogeologic, geophysical, geotechnical, Topographic Studies.	8 Rue des Aurès - El Harrach - Alger.	+213-21 52 31 76 aquamines@wissal.dz +213-21 52 32 55	
GOLDIM	Exploitation of noble metal deposits, industrial minerals, Marketing of exploitation products.	8 Rue des Aurès - El-Harrach - Alger.	+213-21 52 31 76 +213-21 52 32 55	
ENOR	Extraction and processing of gold ore.		enor@wissal.dz +213-21 92 21 77	
ENAMARBRE	Extraction, transformation, production and marketing of marble and its derived.	B.P 228. Zone industrielle Pont Saf-Saf. Skikda	+213-38 75 64 08 à 10 +213-38 75 61 61 +213-38 75 62 19 +213-38 75 64 10	
ENASEL	Exploitation of industrial and domestic salt careers and marketing of salts	Zone Industrielle le Rhumel. BP 18. boussouf Constantine	info@enasel.com +213-31 66 48 84 à 85	
ASMIDAL	Production of fertilizers and nitrogenized phosphate	Route des Salines	+213-38 52 29 83 et 90 +213-38 52 30 29	

		Annaba	+213-38 52 24 00
ENG	Production and marketing of aggregates, carbonate of calcium	Z.I Gué de constantine BP 04 Kouba Alger	+213-21 83 93 86 +213-21 86 93 50
			+213-21 53 70 71 +213-21 83 93 84
ENOF	Production and marketing of the non-ferrous mining products	31 Rue Mohamed Hattab, Belfort.. Alger	info@enof-mines.com
			+213-21 52 15 27
FERPHOS	Exploitation, marketing and export of iron and phosphate	ZHUN II. BP 122 12000 Tébessa, Algérie	+213-37 49 47 82 +213-37 49.19.27 ferphos@ferphos.com
			+213-37 49 25 50 +213-37 49 10 50

REFINING AND PETROCHEMICAL UNITS

Units	TEL	FAX	Address
Refinery of Algiers (RAI G)	021.82.31.60/63	021.67.12.86	BP N-185, Sidi Arcine, Baraki Alger.
Refinery of Skikda (RAI K)	038.74.52.29	038.74.52.28	BP N-108, Zone Industrielle, SKIKDA.,
Refinery of Hassi-Messaoud (RHM).	029.73.26.90	029.73.26.90	SH DP, Base Irara, BP 50. Hassi-Messaoud.
Refinery of Arzew (RAIZ)	041.47.39.55	041.47.47.34	Route Tlélat, BP N-37, ARZEW.
Industrial Complex CP 1Z, Methanol and derived	041.47.17.16	041.47.36.36 Zone Industrielle Arzew BP 33 Arzew -31200 ALGERIE.	
Industrial Complex CP 1K, Ethylene and derived	038. 75.68.62	038.75.20.40 Zone Industrielle Skikda BP 115 Skikda-21 000 ALGERIE.	
FERTALGE Industries	041.47.17.08 041.48.05.03	041.47.17.09 041.37.62.63	Unité de production Zone Industrielle BP 68 Arzew.

SERVICE COMPANIES

ompany	Activity	Address	Phone	Fax
NEAL New Energy Algeria	Promotion and development of new and renewable energies.	10 rue du Sahara Hydra. Alger	+213-21 60 18 44	
			+213-21 60 18 44	
ETTERKIB	Assembly and maintenance of industrial works.	B.P 6 Route Nationale N° 1 Boufarik. 09400.	+213-25 47 32 56	
			+213-25 47 32 52	
ENAFOR	Drilling	BP 211 Hassi Messaoud. Ouargla	+213-29 73 75 40 +213-29 73 71 35 +213-29 73 74 21 +213-29 73 81 85	

			+213-29 73 80 26
ENAGEO	Processing of seismic data, Studies of prospection and research of hydrocarbons and other mineral substances.	B.P 140 Hassi Messaoud. 30500 Ouargla	+213-29 73 84 12 +213-29 73 45 74 +213-29 73 81 03
			+213-29 73 78 01
ENGTP	Study and realization of industrial projects for hydrocarbons sector	BP 9 zone industrielle de Reghaia. Boumerdes	+213-21 84 89 85 à 87 +213-21 84 86 26
			+213-21 84 80 34 +213-21 84 89 61
ENTP	Oil and hydraulic drilling	B.P 206 Hassi Messaoud. Ouargla	+213-29 73 88 50
			+213-29 73 84 06
ENSP	Realization of wells services	B.P 83 Hassi - Messaoud. Ouargla	+213-29 73 73 33 +213-29 73 87 88
			+213-29 73 82 01
NAFTOGAZ	Formation, study and scientific research	BP 54 Hassi Messaoud. Ouargla	+213-29 73 71 36 +213-29 74 21 55
			+213-29 73 77 02
ENGCB	Design and realization of work of civil engineering, building and roads for the energy sector.	B.P 23 Route de Corso. Boudouaou. Boumerdès	+213-24 84 35 26 à 29 +213-24 81 89 99
			+213-24 84 30 09
INERGA	Energy infrastructures and buildings work.	B.P 104 Route Nationale N° 1 Boufarik. Blida	+213-25 47 33 37 +213-25 47 33 82 +213-25 47 33 15 +213-25 47 14 52
ENAC	Engineering realization, installation, maintenance and reparation of liquid hydrocarbons transport pipes	BP 54, Rue Ben Youcef Khettab. Mohammadia. Alger	+213-21 53 85 49
			+213-21 53 89 59 +213-21 53 85 53
ENGI	Production and distribution of Industrial Gas	2 Av. ALN, Hussein dey BP 270 Alger	+213-25 49 75 81 +213-25 49 85 99
			+213-25 49 71 94
EGZIK	Maintenance and industrial safety.	B.P 129 Zone Industrielle. Skikda	+213-38 75 75 60 +213-38 75 77 50 +213-38 75 91 08
			+213-38 75 79 08
KAHRAMA	arzew region water desalination.	EGZIA (Zone industrielle d'Arzew)	+213-21 72 27 75
			+213-21 72 27 75

EGZIA	Maintenance and industrial safety.	B.P 1 Zone Industrielle d'Arzew. Oran	+213-41 47 19 24 +213-41 47 28 27 +213-41 47 11 68 +213-41 47 14 06 +213-41 47 19 24
			+213-41 47 11 94

FOREIGN OIL EXPLORATION AND PRODUCTION COMPANIES

AGIP	28. Rue Med Amallal - El-Biar - Alger
Burlington	
SINOPEC	
Gulf Keystone	10 Rue des Pins Hydra, Alger
Repsol	26. Rue Hadj Ahmed Mohamed -Hydra - Alger
Cepsa	13,Lotissement Altitude ,chemin de la madelaine -Hydra-Alger
BHP/Billiton	5, Chemin Macklay - El-Biar -Alger
Petronas	Hotel Sheraton Club Des Pin -Alger
Rosneft Stroytransgaz	67, rue des idrissides (ex.Rue Badin) El-Biar -Alger
Total Fina Elf	17, Chemin de la Madeleine 16030 -El-Biar -Alger
First Calgary Petroleum	
Gaz de France	48, Rue des Frères Benali (ex Parmentier), Hydra, Alger
Petrocanada	172, Rue Hassiba Ben-Bouali
Anadarko	4, Chemin des Glicines, El-Biar -Alger
BP	12, Rue Slimane Amirat, Colonel Voirol, Aler
Amerada hess	Hôtel Sheraton, Club des Pins, Alger
Medex	
PIDC	
Maersk	

N.B. Many others companies of services are present, such as Schlumberger and others, in joint Societies or Algeria subsidiary.

OIL PRODUCTS STORAGE AND DISTRIBUTION

AGIP	28. Rue Med Amallal - El-Biar - Alger
Burlington	
SINOPEC	
Gulf Keystone	10 Rue des Pins Hydra, Alger
Repsol	26. Rue Hadj Ahmed Mohamed -Hydra - Alger
Cepsa	13,Lotissement Altitude ,chemin de la madelaine -Hydra-Alger
BHP/Billiton	5, Chemin Macklay - El-Biar -Alger
Petronas	Hotel Sheraton Club Des Pin -Alger

Rosneft Stroytransgaz	67, rue des idrissides (ex.Rue Badin) El-Biar -Alger
Total Fina Elf	17, Chemin de la Madeleine 16030 -El-Biar -Alger
First Calgary Petroleum	
Gaz de France	48, Rue des Frères Benali (ex Parmentier), Hydra, Alger
Petrocanada	172, Rue Hassiba Ben-Bouali
Anadarko	4, Chemin des Glicines, El-Biar -Alger
BP	12, Rue Slimane Amirat, Colonel Voirol, Aler
Amerada hess	Hôtel Sheraton, Club des Pins, Alger
Mecex	
PIDC	
Maersk	

INVESTMENT AND BUSINESS OPPORTUNITIES AND CONTACTS

Ministry of Energy and Mining
http://www.mem-algeria.org
B.P 677 AlgerGare 80 Av. Ghermoul. Algiers, Algeria
Tel+213 (0)21 65 22 22 / **Fax** +213(0)21 65 19 04
info@mem-algeria.org

HYDROCARBONS (GAS AND LIQUIDS)

The upstream sector of the hydrocarbons national industry is mainly characterized by the following factors:

- An extreme richness and diversity of the oil and gas potential
- An oil potential still to be developed
- The existence of sedimentary basins unexplored or under-explored
- A clear and flexible legislation offering various advantages to operators.

These quite competitive characteristics, comparatively to other regions in the world containing hydrocarbons resources, are likely to attract and foster investments from national and foreign operators.
Ancillary oil activities and services are, for their part, governed by the common legislation and more particularly the Investments Code.
Moreover, the national and foreign investors in the upstream sector of the hydrocarbons national industry may benefit from a number of incentives and advantages:

- the prime quality of hydrocarbons produced (light crudes, without sulfur content),
- the sector has accumulated a significant amount of quality data covering the whole national mining field and easily available to investors,
- most major international service companies (Schlumberger, Halliburton, Weatherford, Baker,..) are established in Algeria,

- the country has a very wide pipe transportation system of hydrocarbons, many refineries, liquefaction plants, LPG separation units as well as oil ports from which liquid productions can be shipped,
- the petroleum legislation provides for a number of royalty and tax allowances applicable in regions with particular difficulties,
- the diversity of investment projects proposed is likely to attract both large multinationals and medium sized companies,
- investors benefit from guarantees in accordance with the various international agreements and treaties to which Algeria is a party,
- the country has a dense industrial base (small and medium industries, various services, consulting, manufacturing, works, construction,..) likely to give a support to oil activities at a competitive cost. The same facilities are currently opened to direct investments or partnerships with national operators,
- existence of a skilled and experimented workforce,
- the core infrastructure is solid, well distributed throughout the country (airports, roads, rail network,..).

☐ **Hydrocarbons exploration**

The hydrocarbons mining domain is very wide and covers an area of 1.5 million km^2 representing in fact 60% of the national territory.
It is a very rich and diversified field, both of the Mesozoic / Paleozoic and Cenozoic eras, containing oil potential confirmed by Sonatrach together with foreign partners.
Except some basins where significant hydrocarbon deposits have been discovered, this domain remains unexplored as wide regions only experienced preliminary works to this day.
Even the basins considered as known are currently subject to studies and analyses for the purpose of new programs. It is the case for example, of the Hassi-R'Mel region producing in the Trias, where an exploratory drilling has been located, targeting the Cambrian reservoir.
Sonatrach are currently booting promotion campaigns at the international level and organizing data rooms for foreign oil companies wishing to invest in Algeria in the exploration sector.
A number of blocks are thus periodically offered to the interested companies.
Two call for bids have already been made and resulted in the signature of two R&P partnership agreements through the first call and in five contracts through the second one.
The perimeters where Sonatrach is currently operating alone are also opened to partnership.
Thus, the interested companies may contact:

SONATRACH
Division Exploration
Avenue du 1er novembre 1954
Immeuble IAP
Boumerdes
Tel : +213-24 81 91 70 / 81 91 79
Fax : 213-24 81 91 75 / 74 84 37

Ministry of Energy and Mines,
Hydrocarbons General Direction, Hydrocarbons Mining Field Direction

☐ **Hydrocarbons exploitation**
Various investment opportunities are offered in this sector:

- Development and exploitation of already discovered fields.
- Improvement of the operating fields recovery rate.
- Development and exploitation of wet gas fields.
- Exploitation of marginal fields.
- Partnerships for the development and production of the new gas reserves.

SONATRACH has already concluded many agreements with foreign companies that may only intervene in association with the former. On these grounds, a call for bids for the operation of five fields was introduced during 2001.
The interested companies may contact:

SONATRACH
Chemin du Réservoir
Hydra
Tel : 213-21-60 92 00 / 60 72 44
Fax : 213-21-60 18 95

Ministry of Energy and Mines
Hydrocarbons General Direction

☐ **Ancillary oil activities and services**
Investment opportunities in this field are quite numerous and varied. They are governed by the Investment Code and benefit from a number of incentives and advantages granted to the sector. Available niches market are diversified:

- Geophysical works,
- Drilling and well services
- Construction,
- Labours
- Engineering,
- Equipment manufacturing
- Consulting,
- ...etc.

A lot of companies are already operating in these fields and a number of projects about to start. Such are then the opportunities of investment in Algeria offered to operators who can take profit of. Actually, these are only the major lines of the subject considered, but experience showed that domestic and foreign operators once in Algeria progress rapidly in the targeted niche(s) market and are proposed other investment opportunities with much more interesting development prospects.

MINING

MINING LAW N°01-10

The new Mining law enacted on the 3rd of July 2001, establishes :

- Separation of the ground and underground ownership.
- Non differentiation of the mineral substances.

- Open access to mining activities for any operator.
- The same treatment for all investors.
- The legal value of mining title :
    - Prospecting and exploration Mining Titles : a personal estate, which can be transferred and assigned.
    - Exploitation Mining Title : a real estate, which can be transferred, assigned, leased or mortgaged.

- Automatic right to exploitation shall be granted to the holder of an Exploration Mining Title who has discovered a mineral deposit.
- Stability of fiscal, legal and social conditions during the validity of the Mining Concession.
- Enhancement on environmental management.
- International arbitration.
- Mining Title granted by bid in the case of mineral deposits discovered under public financing.
- Setting up of the Geological data bank and its free access.
- Setting up of a single authority for granting mining Titles.

WHO CAN INVEST ?

Mining activities are commercial acts exercised exclusively by natural or legal entities of private law.
Prospection:
Any legal entity of private law can apply for a Prospecting Title.
Exploration:
Any legal entity possessing the relevant financial and technical capacities can apply for an Exploration Title:

- Any Holder of a valid Prospecting authorisation, or for the awarded bidder,
- The first comer is the first served, if the area has never been prospected.

Mining Exploration :
Concession : granted to a legal entity

- holding an Exploration Permit,
- the awarded bidder.

Small or medium scale exploration : granted to a legal entity.

- holding an Exploration Permit.
- the awarded bidder.

Artisanal Exploitation :
Legal or natural entities according to the following priorities:

1. the holder of an Exploration Permit,
2. the holder of a Prospecting authorisation,
3. the awarded bidder.

Documents to Provide

In 4 (four) copies
Decree n°02-65 of the 06/02/2002

Mining exploration:
Prospection :

- Company by-laws.
- Map at 1: 50 000 or 1: 200 000 scale showing the requested area and its location.
- General programme of projected works.

Exploration:

- Company by-laws.
- Documents proving the financial and technical capacities.
- Map at 1 : 25 000 or 1 : 50 000 scale showing the perimeter boundaries.
- According to the case, a copy of the Prospecting Authorisation.
- Environmental impact assessment.

Mining exploitation:
Concession / small or medium scale mining:

- Previous exploration Permit or the awarding act.
- Documents proving the financial and technical capacities.
- Report on the general development programme, planning of the intended works, and the financial amount to be invested.
- Map at the 1: 25 000 or 1: 50 000 scale showing the perimeter boundaries, the corners coordinates and the reference points.
- Report on the Prospecting and Exploration results.
- The feasibility study.
- Development plan of exploitation (1: 1 000 or 1: 5 000 scale).
- Environmental impact assessment.

TWO POSSIBLE WAYS

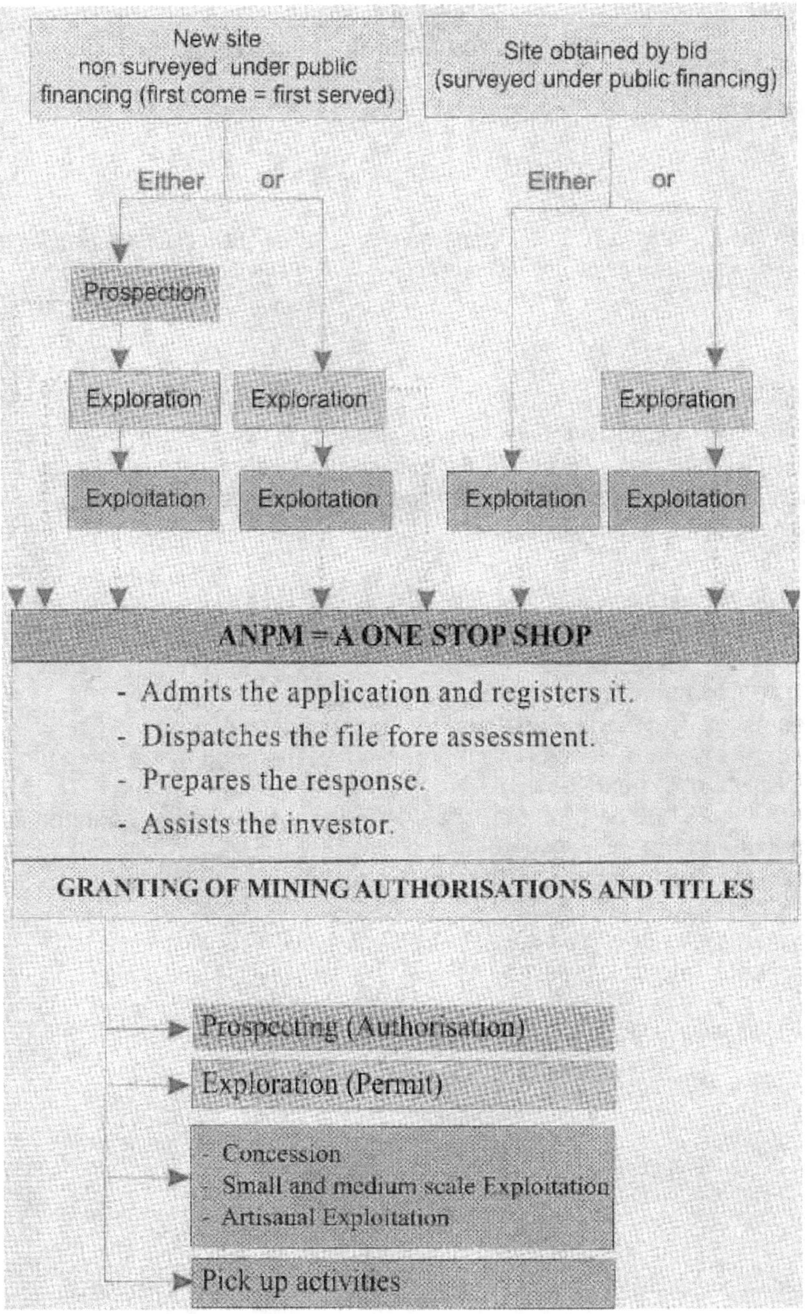

Artisanal exploitation

- Previous Prospecting Authorisation or Exploration Title,
- Prospecting or exploration results,
- Information on financial capacities,
- Delimitation of the site at the map 1: 25 000 or 1: 50 000 scale,
- Exploitation method on the map at 1: 5 000 or 1: 10 000 scale,

- Intended production and estimated cost.
- Environmental impact study and mitigating actions

The applications are deposited at:

- **Mining Patrimoine National Agency (ANPM).**
- **Mining General Directorate (during transitional period).**

PROCEDURES

I)- Case of a new site which has not been surveyed under public financing, principle of first come = first served according to the chronological order of the registered applications.
- Either :

- **Apply for a Prospecting authorisation for defining the area to explore and,**
- **Apply for an Exploration Permit, for delimiting the mineral deposit and obtaining the automatic right to an exploitation title or,**
- **Apply for an Exploitation Title.**

- Or :

- **Apply for an Exploration Permit for delimiting the deposit and obtaining the automatic right to an exploitation title or,**
- **Apply for an Exploitation Mining Title.**

II)- Case of a site which has been surveyed under public financing or a released perimeter. Titles awarded following a bidding process (decree N°02-66) :

- **An Exploration mining Title for confirming the existence of the mineral deposit and obtaining the automatic right to an Exploitation mining Title.**
- **An Exploitation mining Title when the deposit is already known and surveyed or when the Exploitation is an open area.**

MINING TITLES - TYPES AND GRANTING

Mining Research:
1 - Prospectiing Authorisation:
Initial Period 1 Year + 2 Renewal Periods Of Six (6) Months Each One.
2 - Exploration Permit:
Initial Period 3 Years + 2 Renewal Periods Of Two (2) Years Each One With Possibility Of A Grace Period Of 2 Years In The Case Of An Unfavourable Situation.
Mining :
3 - Mining Concession:
Duration 30 Years + Renewal According To The Deposit Reserves.
4 - Exploitation Permit For Small Or Medium Scale Mining:
Duration 10 Years + Renewal According To The Deposit Reserves.
5 - Artisanal Mining Authorisation:
Duration 5 years + renewal according to the deposit reserves.
Mining titles are granted after a prior administrative review :

- **Either for the first applicant (as certified by registration date and hour), if the deposit has not been surveyed under public funds.**
- **or to the awarded bidder when the deposit has been surveyed under public financing or the exploitation area has been released.**

Applications handling

- **1 (one) month for Prospecting**
- **3 (three) months for Exploration**
- **5 (five) months for Exploitation**

FISCAL INCENTIVES

The mining law n°01 - 10 of the 03/07/2001 offers:

1. **Exemption from professional activity tax.**
2. **Exemption from the VAT on goods specifically for acquired or imported for mining activity,**
3. **Exemption from custom duties for equipment, material and products used in mining surveying.**
4. **Exemption from the built property tax.**
5. **Exemption from all the taxes related to exploitation results, except the mining profit tax (IBM).**
6. **Depreciation of the Prospecting and Exploration costs in the case of Exploitation.**
7. **Abatements of the mining royalties according to the exploitation type, surveying efforts and exploitation location.**
8. **Transfer warranty of the invested capital and resulting incomes.**
9. **Loss carry-over on 10 years.**
10. **Possibility for setting up a provision of 1% from the turnover (excluding taxes), deductible from the gross renewing for rebuilding the reserves.**

ELECTRICITY AND GAS DISTRIBUTION

OPPORTUNITIES

Energy infrastructures investment requirements (electricity and gas) in the country are still very important ($US 12 bn for the next ten years). These are dictated by :

- high expectations for economic growth in all sectors considered,
- a sharp population growth
- strong needs for new housings

The importance of these investments is still increased when allowing for the energy options developed, encouraging natural gas consumption and the follow-up of rural electrification, more particularly for the development of the high plains regions.

On these grounds, the new law on electricity and public distribution of gas through pipelines has been adopted recently, changing the statute of Sonelgaz to joint-stock company, carrying out the activities of gas public distribution and electricity, will allow :

- the opening of production to private investments for domestic needs and exports,

- the access to networks (exports, supplying of eligible customers),
- the opening up of capital of the future Sonelgaz subsidiaries.

INVESTMENT NICHES MARKET BY 2010

A. Electricity

Transportation system
The additional capacity of transmission and interconnection lines to bring on stream is estimated at 5350 km for the VHT (Very High Tension) and 2750 km for the HT. The achievement of around 140 power stations and substations will be required.

Distribution network
Power distribution provided through the medium (10 and 30 KV) and low tension systems (220-380 V) should record an important development.
More than 100,000 km of networks and around 50,000 transforming stations (100 to 400 KVA) should thus be commissioned.
The number of meters to install is of 3,500,000 (new consumers and replacement of old meters).

Production
In order to meet the future needs of the various customers and more particularly the industrial ones, electricity production should double and rise from 24,400 GWH currently to around 46,000 GWH in 2010.
In this regard, the additional requirements in production capacity are estimated at 6000 MW for the period mentioned. It should be noted that the new law on electricity and public distribution of gas adopted in 2002, removed the state monopoly concerning the electricity production.

B. Gas
The evolution of natural gas consumption by 2010 will require a development plan for the transportation and distribution infrastructures. The expected investments for the period are as follows:

Transportation system
Networks of 4,500 km, 3,000 km of which for the implementation of the public distribution programs.

Distribution networks
The connection of 40 new locality/year on average for the public distribution of natural gas; approximately 500 additional towns will be connected to the natural gas NG network by 2010.
These new stations correspond to the achievement of around 9,000 km of distribution networks, to which 7,500 km will be added for the extensions and the intensification of the already supplied towns systems.
On these grounds, it is worth mentioning the adoption by the Government in April 2002 of a 2002-2004 three-year gas program aiming at the natural gas connection of 188 new towns, gathering over 358,000 homes, and requiring the achievement of about 1,800 km of transportation systems and 6,200 km of distribution networks. The project cost is estimated at 35,700 million dinars.

OIL PRODUCTS DISTRIBUTION

The opening to competition of petroleum products distribution activities is not only meant to make up for lack of infrastructure, but also and chiefly to make consumers profit from competitiveness.

1. Offered advantages

- Existence of a market of 8.5 million tons/year of petroleum products.
- The distributor may import his products, get his supplies from local sources or produce his own needs from high grade oil and LPG available in large quantities.
- Foreign investments are given a guarantee of transfer of invested capital and derived income (contact the ANDI Agency for more details).
- Tax aids are allowed by the State to local and foreign investors (see ANDI).
- Cheap managerial staff and labour.
- Public companies transportation and storage capacities may be used by the distributors.

2. Investment niches market in the marketing of petroleum products

The opening to competition of the national market offers large parts to the local and foreign investment in the field of marketing of petroleum products.

These investments concern the following activities :

1. distribution of fuels including the LPG fuel,
2. distribution of LPG for domestic use,
3. distribution of lubricants,
4. distribution of bitumen,
5. pipe transportation of LPG and fuels,
6. storage of LPG and fuels,
7. LPG bottling,
8. Bitumen formulation,
9. CNG distribution.

3. Undeveloped infrastructures
a) Deficiencies in the field of fuel distribution

- massive pipe transportation connecting the big consuming centres to the production sources.
- The fuel storage to increase autonomy and supply the wilayates (regions) in need.
- Development of rail transportation,
- Increase in the transportation rolling stack for the delivery of fuels.
- Densification of the distribution network.

b) Distribution deficiencies of LPG as a fuel

- shortage of storage capacities in consuming areas to secure demand.
- reinforcement of the transportation network to satisfy the growing demand.
- further upgrading of the distribution network.

c) Distribution deficiencies of LPG as a domestic fuel
- butane

- development of massive pipe transportation linking the production sources to the regional distribution areas.
- increase in storage capacities mainly in the regional station of the Centre and the filler centres.

- conditioning : butane gas filling capacities to be achieved in deficient or deprived Wilayates (regions). The setting up of mobile monopost fillers with one post is to be developed in Algeria.
- bulk transportation of butane : the supply of the barreling stations with bulk butane requires the use of additional tankers and in the future of railways.
- transportation development of conditioned butane deliveries involving increasingly private carriers.

- propane

- development of small zones endowed with propane to supply towns and urban areas deprived of natural gas.
- the minor bulk business is not very developed in Algeria.

4. Interchangeability of the gas LPG bottles
The investors in LPGs filling activity may use LPG bottles available on the market of a third promoter and in particular the ones from the public enterprise Naftal, against the conclusion of a convention between the concerned operators initialed by the Ministry in charge of hydrocarbons, according to the Decree fixing the terms and conditions for interchangeability of butane bottles between operators carrying on the activity of filling liquefied petroleum gases.

☐ **5. The required conditions**
The exercise of one or more activities, regulated hereabove, is subject to the authorisation of the Minister in charge of Hydrocarbons in accordance with the provisions of the decree 97-435.
This authorisation is issued to any operator having the necessary funds to achieve the infrastructures, facilities and other means required to carry out his activity.

☐ **6. Administrative procedures**
The application for an authorisation to exercise one or more activities is addressed by registered letter with acknowledgement of receipt to the Minister in charge of Hydrocarbons who deals with it within a maximum of three months from the date of reception of the application (decree 97-435).
This application should be accompanied by the following documents:

- the agreements and permits granted by the local authorities for the achievement of the infrastructures required for the operations,
- an outline map to scale 1/1000 of infrastructures to be achieved, representing on a minimal ray of 100 m, neighboring infrastructures, works and dwellings,
- of a plan of mass of the project with 1/250th representing the various equipment and facilities, particularly the refilling and storage surfaces, traffic areas, access roads and safety systems,
- the total amount of investment and its destination according to each item,
- estimated lead time,
- a statement of estimated achievements for the first five years (optional).
- Chart of the principal equipment by specifying their storage and outputs per product,
- Description of the safety device of the project (preventive, average means of fight against the fire, lighting, lightning protector, put at the ground of equipment etc).

STRATEGIC INFORMATION FOR CONDUCTING BUSINESS

Prior to independence in 1962 Algeria's economy had been dominated by agriculture for a millennium and was known as 'the breadbasket of the Roman empire'. However, with rising oil revenues throughout the 1960s and 1970s, the government embarked on a major program of industrialization which has transformed the economy, making Algeria one of the wealthiest nations in Africa. Fuelled by oil revenues, Algeria's economy grew dramatically throughout this period.

Declining oil prices during the 1980s drastically reduced economic growth of the now oil-dependent country. Annual per capita income fell from $2,360 in 1988 to $1,541 in 1992. As a socialist country, Algeria's entire oil industry is controlled by the state.

Although agriculture no longer dominates the economy it remains an important sector. During the first half of the 1990s the national budget registered expenditures of $14.6 billion as against revenues of $14.4 billion annually.

AGRICULTURE

Prior to independence Algeria provided 93% of its agricultural requirements. Today, the country must import over 60% of its cereal requirements. By the late 1980s agriculture only contributed 15% of Algeria's Gross Domestic Product.

Cereals including wheat, barley, oats, maize, and sorghum, comprise the country's main agricultural crops. Vegetables are also important: crops include beans, lentils, potatoes, peas, cucumbers, tomatoes, onions, carrots, melons, artichokes, sunflowers, sugar beets and tobacco. Grapes and a variety of citrus fruits including oranges, mandarins, lemons, grapefruit and clemencies are also grown. Exports include olives, figs, dates, wine and tobacco.

The agricultural sector has suffered from lack of effective government support. The government favored industry until agricultural output became a critical issue, but by the time there was administrative will to address the problem, financial resources had fallen as a result of declining oil revenues.

TRADE AND INDUSTRY

Algeria's main exports are natural gas, petroleum, iron ore, vegetables, tobacco, phosphates, fruit, cork and leather hides. Principal imports are machinery, textiles, sugar, cereals, iron and steel, coal and gasoline.

Almost two-thirds of all Algeria's export trade is with European Union countries, with the United States and Japan taking much of the remainder. Annual exports during the early 1990s amounted to about $11.6 billion, mostly in the form of petroleum, natural gas and lubricants, while imports totaled about $8.2 billion.

The sale of natural gas and petroleum provided Algeria with 87% of its foreign exchange earnings during 1992. Petroleum and natural gas industries generated 38.1% of the government's income and contributed about 17.7% of the country's Gross Domestic Product. However, with only 9,200 million barrels of proven reserves, Algeria's petroleum will be depleted within 21 years and the government has emphasized the exploitation of its natural gas reserves which, as of 1993, were 3,600 million cubic meters and estimated to last for 71 years.

Algeria has developed a petrochemical and refining industry based in Arzew, Bijaya and Skikda but thus far these projects have been costly and inefficient and have yet to contribute to the economy in a significant way.

The mining industry contributes 17% to Algeria's Gross Domestic Product. Mineral production includes mercury, iron ore, phosphates, zinc, silver, gypsum, and barite. The manufacturing industry contributes 14% to the GDP and includes construction materials (cement, bricks, structural steel), steel production, automobile manufacturing and consumer goods manufacturing.

The centrally controlled Algerian government has a large service sector encompassing industries like water supply, sewage, telecommunications and transport. Much of Algeria's financial resources have been channeled toward non-commercial projects and to finance a bloated socialist military and civilian bureaucracy. The services industry sector comprises 36% of the GDP.

ALGERIAN ECONOMY: IMF EVALUATION

Over the past four years, Algeria has implemented a comprehensive program of economic adjustment and structural reform, supported by a stand-by arrangement and subsequently, since May 1995, by an extended arrangement that expired on May 21, 2004. In addition to Fund resources, Algeria's program was supported by other multilateral and bilateral donors including the Arab Monetary Fund and the World Bank, and by debt relief from Paris and London club creditors. The objectives of the program included achieving macroeconomic stabilization and assisting Algeria in a process of reforms aimed at reinvigorating growth by creating a market-based and private sector-led economy integrated with the rest of the world.

Under the Fund-supported programs, Algeria was successful in restoring macroeconomic balances: inflation was lowered to 5 percent and international reserves exceeded nine months of imports at the beginning of 2004. At the same time, backed by a broad consensus between government, labor, and the private sector, a large number of reforms were implemented to dismantle the existing centrally planned system, open up the economy, and establish market mechanisms, including the liberalization of all prices and the elimination of generalized food subsidies. Moreover, the state started to withdraw from production activities, and a large number of local public enterprises have been closed or privatized. However, progress in privatizing the large public enterprises (EPEs) has been slow. This significant change in Algeria's economic direction was achieved against a backdrop of civil unrest that muted the supply response to economic reforms.

In 1997, despite the robust performance of the hydrocarbon sector, real GDP growth slowed to 1.2 percent after two consecutive years of growth at 4 percent. Agricultural output fell in the wake of a severe drought, and industrial production continued to decline due to the ongoing restructuring process in the public sector and low foreign and domestic investment. These developments put further strain on the labor market as unemployment remained high at around 28 percent. Meanwhile, tight fiscal and monetary policies, coupled with a relatively high level of oil prices, led to a strengthening of public finances and the external position. Indeed, the authorities, as in 1996, saved most of the oil windfall. As a result, the budget surplus reached 2.4 percent of GDP while the external current account showed a surplus equivalent to 7.3 percent of GDP, contributing to a further accumulation of international reserves. Economic reforms focused on restructuring public enterprises. More than half of the small local public enterprises were liquidated or privatized, while the public sector withdrew almost completely from distribution and importing activities. In addition, in the second half of 1997 Algeria accepted the obligations of the Fund's Article VIII and established the full convertibility of the dinar for current account transactions.

For 2004, while economic growth is likely to rebound, financial balances are expected to deteriorate due to the sharp decline in oil prices. Agricultural output should rebound in response to more favorable weather conditions and industrial production is projected to recover. Moreover, despite cuts in output to support international oil prices, hydrocarbon production is estimated to grow by about 6 percent. Nonetheless, with lower oil prices, the budget balance was projected to deteriorate. To preserve the gains obtained on the stabilization front, the authorities have taken measures to compensate for lower than expected budgetary receipts and to deal with needed additional capital expenditure on infrastructure that had been previously postponed. As a result, the outcome for 2004, on the basis of present policies, would be a budget deficit limited to 1.9 percent of GDP. As far as the external accounts are concerned, and despite lower export receipts and a projected import recovery, only a small current account deficit is expected for the year. Despite the end of external debt rescheduling as of June 2004, international reserves would decline only slightly in 2004. Structural reforms are expected to focus on the privatization of the 250 EPEs that comprise the government's program for 2004–99, and legislation is expected to clarify private ownership rights over agricultural land. Privatization of large public enterprises should help consolidate financial sector reforms, in particular the development of the stock exchange that was opened at the beginning of 2004. Meanwhile steps to increase private participation in and modernize the operations of banks, notably the payments system, should enhance their efficiency. Efforts will continue to establish an adequate institutional and legal framework to protect property rights and to reform the public housing sector.

Although recent discoveries have boosted prospects for hydrocarbon production, Algeria's medium-term economic prospects are clouded by the risk of low oil export prices. Therefore, creating an environment conducive to increased private sector investment and growth in thenonhydrocarbon sector is essential for employment creation and a sustained improvement in living standards.

EXECUTIVE BOARD ASSESSMENT

Executive Directors commended the authorities for their steadfast implementation, under very difficult circumstances, of an ambitious program of macroeconomic adjustment and structural reform supported by the Extended Arrangement. They noted that over the past four years, tight macroeconomic management, favorable oil prices, and the timely implementation of a comprehensive program of structural reforms had resulted in the substantial deceleration in inflation, a strengthening of the fiscal and external position of Algeria, and further progress toward a market-oriented economy.

However, Directors expressed concern about the sluggish economic growth in 1997 in the nonhydrocarbon sector and the resulting further tensions in the labor market, and about the potential impact on the budget and the external position of the recent fall in oil prices. In that connection, they emphasized the need to maintain a tight stance of fiscal and monetary policies to preserve the stabilization gains of recent years and to accelerate structural reforms to achieve the ambitious growth and employment objectives outlined in the government's medium-term program.

Executive Directors praised the authorities' determination to save the windfall from higher oil prices in 1996 and 1997 which, coupled with firm expenditure restraint, had led to fiscal and external current account surpluses. They underscored that those prudent policies would make Algeria better prepared to weather the current external oil price shock.

Directors recognized the unavoidable deterioration in the budgetary and external position, owing to the recent fall in oil prices. They therefore supported the authorities' revised fiscal plan for 2004. However, they emphasized the need for the authorities to be ready to take supplementary spending and revenue measures in the event of a further deterioration in oil prices, so as to contain the internal and external imbalances that might emerge. Over the medium term and in order to reduce the budget's heavy dependence on hydrocarbon revenues, Directors also emphasized the importance of further broadening the tax base through reform of the value-added tax and reducing tax and customs exemptions. They also recommended that the authorities contain public sector wages and pursue the reform of the civil service so as to allow adequate budgetary allocation for priority expenditure in key social sectors.

Directors endorsed the authorities' intention to pursue a prudent monetary policy geared toward keeping inflation low and strengthening external reserves, while providing adequate financing to the private sector. They welcomed the authorities' intention to conduct monetary policy mainly through open market operations.

Directors recognized the difficult political and social context that had slowed to a certain extent the current structural reform process. Nevertheless, they underscored the need to deepen and accelerate structural reforms, in particular the privatization of public enterprises, land, financialintermediaries, and housing. Those reforms would help to promote private sector participation in the economy. In that regard, Directors welcomed the progress made in dismantling and privatizing local public enterprises and the courageous measures aimed at restructuring all public enterprises, while noting that those actions had resulted in numerous liquidations and widespread labor retrenchment. They were concerned about delays in privatizing the 250 public enterprises announced in September 1997, and especially the large ones, and urged the authorities to move swiftly in that area. They stressed that a rapid implementation of the program would help boost confidence and signal the government's commitment to reform. Directors also underscored the beneficial role that the law on privatization of agricultural land could have in promoting investment in the agriculture sector, and urged the authorities to act promptly to adopt that legislation.

Directors welcomed the measures taken in recent years to strengthen the financial position of banks. They encouraged the authorities to speed up the auditing process of state-owned banks in order to proceed rapidly with their privatization and to preserve a sound financial system, as a key element for improved resource allocation and economic development. In that regard, Directors stressed the need to strengthen banking supervision. Directors welcomed the steps taken to deepen financial markets, including the establishment of a stock market and the associated regulatory institutions for its operations. Those developments should help promote investment, especially foreign direct investment, and encourage savings.

Directors emphasized the need to preserve an adequate social safety net, which would also help to maintain the social consensus in support of economic reforms. In particular, they emphasized the need to maintain the financial viability of the unemployment insurance scheme, which had come under pressure in the wake of higher unemployment following the restructuring of the industrial public sector. In addition, Directors urged the authorities to take rapidly the required steps to restore the financial soundness of the pension system. Also, Directors underscored the critical role of the housing sector for employment creation, promoting private-sector-based growth and alleviating urgent social needs. While Directors welcomed the creation of new financial institutions, they urged the authorities to pursue the needed reforms in that sector.

Directors welcomed the strengthening of the external accounts, with the official foreign exchange reserves reaching almost a year of imports at end-March 2004. They underscored, however, that the medium-term balance of payments prospects are now less favorable than at the time of the last review under the Extended Arrangement, because of the much lower prevailing oil prices, while alternative sources of external financing remain scarce as Algeria has yet to regain full access to foreign financing on appropriate terms. These developments illustrate the vulnerability of Algeria's external position and underscore the need to develop nonhydrocarbon exports. Directors stressed the need for an exchange rate policy in line with the economic fundamentals so as to avoid a real effective appreciation of the dinar on a sustained basis, in order to support the diversification of the economy and increased openness without undermining the inflation objective. They welcomed the steps taken to open the economy and commended the authorities for the removal of all restrictions on the convertibility of the dinar for current transactions. Directors encouraged the authorities to undertake furthernonpreferential tariff reductions to increase competition, improve resource allocation, lay the basis for export development, and pursue the opening of the economy.

Directors observed that major challenges remain to be addressed in order to ensure the transformation of Algeria into a full market economy. They hoped that the continued close cooperation with the Fund, including further technical assistance, would contribute to the transition process. In that context, some Directors indicated that the Fund should remain open to a request from the authorities for a more intensive policy dialogue.

Public Information Notices (PINs) are issued, at the request of a member country, following the conclusion of the Article IV consultation for countries seeking to make known the views of the IMF to the public. This action is intended to strengthen IMF surveillance over the economic policies of member countries by increasing the transparency of the IMF's assessment of these policies.

[1]Under Article IV of the IMF's Articles of Agreement, the IMF holds bilateral discussions with members, usually every year. A staff team visits the country, collects economic and financial information, and discusses with officials the country's economic developments and policies. On return to headquarters, the staff prepares a report, which forms the basis for discussion by the Executive Board. At the conclusion of the discussion, the Managing Director, as Chairman of the Board, summarizes the views of directors, and this summary is transmitted to the country's authorities. In this PIN, the main features of the Board's discussion are described.

ALGERIA MINING INDUSTRY

Algeria has major deposits of phosphates and iron ore, as well as smaller deposits of coal, lead and zinc. All of these are mined as well as some mercury and copper. Mining and beneficiation operations in Algeria are owned and operated by the government.

A bonanza of high-grade gold has been found in the Hoggar desert hills of southern Algeria. Five vast geological provinces, each about 600 km long, have been identified. Exploration drilling at two deposits have produced yields graded at 25,1 g/t and 16,49 g/t. In South Africa's declining gold industry, 6,4 g/t is considered good. The Algerians are looking for foreign companies with expertise to come in and do some exploration, increase the reserves and actually start mining.

The industry is regulated by the
Ministry of Mines and Industry,
4 rue Ahmad Bey,

Immeuble le Colisee, Algiers.
The telephone number is +213 (0)2 60-1326.

LARGEST COMPANIES

ENTREPRISE NATIONALE DU FER ET DU PHOSPHATE

General Information

Organization Type:	Company
Registered in:	Algeria
Nick name/Abbrev.:	FERPHOS
Business Sector(s):	Mining & Quarrying Chemical & Fertilizer Mineral Mining

SOCIETÉ NATIONALE DE RECHERCHES ET D'EXPLOITATION MINIERES

General Information

Organization Type:	Parastatal
Registered in:	Algeria
Nick name/Abbrev.:	SONAREM
Business Sector(s):	Mining & Quarrying Mining Industry

OIL AND GAS SECTOR

Following years of civil war and continuing political unrest, Algeria now is experiencing a significant economic upturn, in large part aided by strong oil and natural gas export revenues since 1999. Real gross domestic product (GDP) growth is expected to reach 6.4% in 2004, following estimated growth of 7.4% in 2003. The sharp increase in oil export revenues which Algeria has enjoyed during the past few years has led the country's foreign reserves to rebound sharply (to over $30 billion by late 2003, compared to $12 billion at the end of 2000), external debt to fall (to the lowest level in a decade), the current account balance to improve dramatically, and pressures on government finances to decrease.

Despite the recent good news, Algeria continues to face serious economic, social, and political problems, including: high unemployment (officially around 30%, but possibly much higher); continued political violence by Islamic fundamentalists and others; labor unrest; a large black market (possibly 20% of the country's GDP); continued weakness in the non-oil economy; natural disasters (a severe drought hurt the agricultural sector in 2000; heavy flooding struck northern Algeria in November 2001; a major earthquake hit Algeria in May 2003); and slow progress on economic reform efforts (largely due to opposition by labor unions and the armed forces). Periodically, there have been protests by the country's restive Berber minority demanding greater autonomy, increased employment opportunities, and better living conditions. The unrest has centered on the Kabyle region of northeastern Algeria.

In early November 2003, Algeria unveiled its draft budget for 2004. The budget calls for increased social spending and assumes economic growth of 5.1%, inflation of 2.0%, and a $19 per barrel price for Algerian oil. The oil price assumption appears to be extremely conservative, considering that prices in 2003 averaged around $10 per barrel higher than this. Algeria remains highly dependent on oil and natural gas exports, which account for more than 90% of Algerian export earnings, and about 30% of GDP.

With rapid population growth, Algeria's top priority is to reduce the country's extremely high unemployment rate (estimated at around 50% for the "under-30s" age group). Regardless of fluctuating oil revenues, structural reforms and fiscal discipline appear to remain important parts of the government's economic program, as urged by the IMF. To date, however, little progress in this regard appears to have been made. For instance, an important hydrocarbons reform bill, which among other things would "corporatize" state oil company Sonatrach, had gone nowhere as of early 2003. In February 2003, a two-day strike among oil and gas workers was launched in protest of the proposed legislation. Algeria is scheduled to hold Presidential elections in April 2004, meaning that any new reform initiatives will probably have to wait until mid-2004. Meanwhile, it is likely that Algeria will pursue expansionary economic policies ahead of the elections.

In January 2004, the International Monetary Fund (IMF) issued its annual "Article IV" assessment of the Algerian economy, urging that the government proceed with privatization and banking reform, while lowering tariffs aimed at protecting domestic industry and reducing dependence on hydrocarbons. The IMF praised the Algerian government for its strong macroeconomic discipline, while pointing out that high oil prices provide Algeria with an opportunity to make progress on implementing reforms and addressing the country's many problems.

In late 2001, an important new hydrocarbons reform bill was introduced, but progress stalled in 2002 and 2003. The bill would open Algeria's all-important energy sector to private (including foreign) investment, although state oil and gas company Sonatrach (see below) most likely would remain in public hands. The law faces opposition from trade unions and others, and already has been watered down somewhat from its original form, while Energy and Mines Minister Chekib Khelil has stated that "it is not necessary to privatize" Sonatrach. One study, by Bayphase, estimates that Algeria's oil and gas sectors will require total capital investment of $50-$73 billion over the next 10 years.

In December 2002, Algeria signed a cooperation pact with the European Free Trade Association (EFTA), providing for expanded and liberalized trade with EFTA members (Iceland, Liechtenstein, Norway, and Switzerland). Algeria also is pursuing membership in the World Trade Organization, with the latest negotiations concluded in Geneva during November 2002. In late 2001, Algeria and the EU reached an Association Agreement after years of negotiations, and the deal was ratified by the European Parliament in October 2002. Under the accord, Algeria is to cut tariffs on EU agricultural and industrial products over the next 10 years. In exchange, the EU will eliminate duties and quotas on many Algerian agricultural products.

President Abdelaziz Bouteflika, elected President on April 15, 1999 for a 5-year term, has attempted to implement plans for national reconciliation and economic reforms (i.e., deregulation, privatization). More than 100,000 rebels, soldiers and civilians have died in Algeria's civil war, which began in 1992 following the military's nullification of a national election won by the Islamic Salvation Party. On July 13, 1999, President Bouteflika offered amnesty to rebel groups, and on September 16 a national referendum was held in which voters approved the offer. Although the government claimed that nearly 80% of rebels (including members of the Islamic Salvation Army) accepted amnesty, the level of violence appeared to rise once again, with the most violent groups apparently stepping up attacks. In August 2000, President Bouteflika replaced Prime Minister

Ahmed Benbitour with Ali Benflis. Parliamentary elections were held in May 2002, resulting in a strong showing for the president's party, the FLN. On February 19, 2004, President Bouteflika announced that he would stand for re-election in April 2004.

OIL

Although oil was first discovered in Algeria at the Hassi Messaoud oil field in 1956, Algeria is considered to be underexplored. Algeria's National Council of Energy believes that the country still contains vast hydrocarbon potential. Over the last few years, significant oil and gas discoveries have been made, largely by foreign companies (in partnership with state-owned Sonatrach, as required by current Algerian law). Sonatrach and its foreign partners hope to increase Algeria's crude oil production capacity significantly over the next few years.

In order to accomplish this, Algeria will require significant amounts of foreign capital and expertise. Energy Minister Chekib Khelil has stated that his goal is "to double the number of companies operating in Algeria over the next five years" to 40 companies. Khelil also has expressed his view that the industry needs to be restructured in order to survive, and that new regulatory bodies independent of the Energy and Mining Ministry might be needed as well. Algeria's oil sector, unlike that of most OPEC producers, has been open to foreign investors for more than a decade.

Algeria's proven oil reserves are estimated at 11.3 billion barrels, although "recoverable oil resources" may range as high as 43 billion barrels. With recent oil discoveries, plans for more exploration drilling, improved data on existing fields, and use of enhanced oil recovery (EOR) systems, proven oil reserve estimates are expected to be revised upward in coming years. Algeria should also see a sharp increase in crude oil exports over the next few years due to a rapid shift towards domestic natural gas consumption and planned increases in oil production by Sonatrach and its foreign partners. In December 2003, Energy Minister Khelil stated that he hoped to see a total of 54 wells drilled during 2004, up from 43 in 2003 and 29 in 2002.

Approximately 90% of Algeria's crude oil exports go to Western Europe, with Italy as the main market followed by Germany and France. The Netherlands, Spain and Britain are other important European markets. Algeria's Saharan Blend oil, 45° API with negligible (0.05%) sulfur content, is considered among the highest quality in the world.

As mentioned above, the Algerian parliament has been considering a law which would restructure the state oil company, Sonatrach (and Sonelgaz, the state utility) in order to attract private international investment. One possibility would be for Sonatrach to remain the national oil company but eventually be forced to compete for new projects. Non-core subsidiaries of Sonatrach also could be privatized if the law passes. In January 2001, Algeria's oil and gas industry labor unions announced their opposition to any government plans to open up the country's hydrocarbon sector to foreign investors.

Oil Production

Algeria's average crude oil production during 2003 was around 1.2 million bbl/d. Together with 445,000 bbl/d of lease condensate and 250,000 bbl/d of natural gas plant liquids, Algeria averaged about 1.86 million bbl/d of total oil production during 2003, up sharply from 1.57 million bbl/d in 2002. Algeria's crude oil production is running well above its OPEC quota of 782,000 bbl/d (as of November 1, 2003; only crude oil production is subject to the OPEC quota). Algeria had estimated net oil exports (including crude oil, lease condensate, and natural gas liquids) of around 1.65 million bbl/d in 2002, most of which went

Algeria's Oil Production and Consumption, 1980-2003E

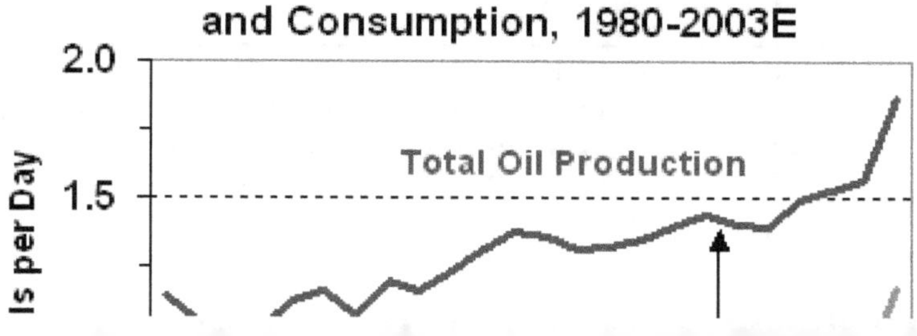

For additional an
please c
at (202) 546

to Europe and the United States. Domestic oil consumption is around 212,000 bbl/d.

In coming years, it is likely that Algeria's oil production capacity will be increasing rapidly as the country invests billions of dollars into exploration and development efforts. Currently, the country is targeting crude oil production capacity of 1.5 million bbl/d by 2005 and 2.0 million bbl/d by 2010.

Much of Algeria's increased production capacity will come from foreign independent oil companies, such as Amerada Hess (the El-Gassi field), Anadarko (Berkine, Ourhoud), Burlington Resources (Block 405), BHP Billiton (ROD), and Cepsa (Ourhoud, Rhourde El Krouf). Sonatrach accounts for more than half of Algeria's crude oil output. Anadarko is the largest foreign oil producer in Algeria, with current output of around 530,000 bbl/d of oil (300,000 bbl/d at Berkine, 230,000 bbl/d at Ourhoud). Anadarko is developing seven oil and gas fields in Block 208 of the Berkine Basin. First production from the fields (EKT, El Merk, El Merk N, El Merk E, El Merk C, El Kheit, and El Tessekha) is possible in 2004, with output eventually reaching 150,000-200,000 bbl/d of crude oil and condensate.

By far, the largest oil field in Algeria is Hassi Messaoud, located in the center of the country, which produces about 350,000-400,000 bbl/d of 46° API crude, down from 550,000 bbl/d in the 1970s, but up from 300,000 bbl/d in 1989. The Hassi Messaoud area contains an estimated 6.4 billion barrels, just under 60% of the country's proven oil reserves. Sonatrach hopes to double production at the field to 700,000-750,000 bbl/d within 5-7 years.

Besides Hassi Messaoud, Sonatrach operates Algeria's other major oil fields, including Rhourde el-Baguel (Algeria's second largest oil field, located to the northeast of Hassi Messaoud), Tin Fouye Tabankort Ordo, Zarzaitine (30,000 bbl/d), Haoud Berkaoui/Ben Kahla, el-Gassi el-Agreb and Ait Kheir. The Hassi R'Mel gas field (north of Hassi Messaoud, south of Algiers) also produces around 18,000 bbl/d of 46.1° API crude. In February 2004, Sonatrach announced that it had discovered a new oilfield near Rhourde El Baguel, with possible oil reserves of 360 million barrels.

In April 2000, Amerada Hess announced that it had acquired (for $55 million) the Gassi el-Agreb Redevelopment Project from Sonatrach. Amerada Hess will form a joint operating company with Sonatrach, to be called Sonahess, and will invest $500 million over 5 years to enhance recovery from the el-Gassi, el-Agreb, and Zotti fields. Currently, the three fields produce around 30,000 bbl/d, and the redevelopment project aims to increase production to 45,000 bbl/d.

BHP has stated that it will spend $190 million on oil field development at the ROD integrated oil development project in the Berkine Basin in eastern Algeria. Production is expected to commence in mid- to late-2004 at 35,000 bbl/d, and peak at 80,000 bbl/d. In July 2000, several companies (Burlington Resources, Talisman, and Sonatrach) announced that they would develop the MLN (Menzel Ledjmat North) field in Block 405a. MLN is expected to produce around 35,000-40,000 bbl/d when completed (initial output of 14,000 bbl/d began in early July 2003). Exploration success rates in the Berkine Basin have been high, and several billion barrels of oil may lie within 15 miles or so of the area.

In early January 2003, Sonatrach announced that it had brought the 1-billion-barrel, $1.3 billion Ourhoud oil field online, ahead of schedule, with initial production of 75,000 bbl/d. Output at the field reportedly reached 230,000 bbl/d by April 2003, when all three oil treatment trains came online. Ourhoud is divided into three blocks operated by Anadarko (Block 404), Cepsa of Spain (Block 406a), and Burlington Resources (Block 405). Ourhoud is operated by Cepsa, Anadarko, ENI, Maersk, Burlington, and Sonatrach.

Although Algeria has experienced a significant influx of foreign investment in recent years, it still has many oil fields in need of additional foreign capital and EOR investment. Halliburton has an eight-year contract to provide EOR services and boost production at Hassi Messaoud, for instance, which saw production fall sharply beginning in the mid-1980s. Algeria's second largest oil field, Rhourde El Baguel, already has received foreign investment to boost its production capacity. Rhourde El Baguel contains about three billion barrels of 42.6° API oil, of which less than 450 million barrels has been produced since 1963. In February 1996, Arco (now owned by BP) signed a $1.3-billion production sharing agreement (PSA) with Sonatrach to increase production at the field. BP expects to raise the field's output from 27,000 bbl/d to 125,000 bbl/d by 2010.

During 2004, Algeria is planning to open its fifth licensing round for oil and gas. The country received bids from nearly 40 companies in its fourth licensing round, although it awarded only 12 blocks for exploration. In September 2003, Brazil's Petrobras signed a deal with Sonatrach to explore for oil in Algeria, and in December 2003, Algeria and China's CNPC reached a similar agreement. Also in December 2003, Cepsa and Total won drilling and exploration rights on the Bechar block in the Sahara desert.

Sinopec reportedly was awarded a $525 million contract in October 2002 to help increase the crude oil recovery rate at Zarzataine, near Hassi Messaoud. In November 2002, the Kuwait Foreign Petroleum Exploration Company (KUFPEC) and Anadarko announced a partnership to explore the Berkine Basin. KUFPEC has not been active in Algeria for over 10 years.

Downstream
Algeria has four oil refineries, with combined capacity of 450,000 bbl/d, which supply most of the country's refined oil product needs (Algeria also imports around 20,000-35,000 bbl/d of sour crudes and specific products). The 30,000-bbl/d Hassi Messaoud plant supplies products to southern Algeria. The 60,000-bbl/d Algiers refinery processes crude from Hassi Messaoud. Finally, the coastal 60,000-bbl/d Arzew refinery, which uses Algerian Saharan blend as feedstock, produces products for domestic consumption and export. In January 2001, Algeria issued a tender for a new refinery in the central Adrar region near the Sbaa basin, and in May 2003 contracted with China's CNODC to build it (for $350 million, including upstream development as well). Algeria also is looking at upgrading the In Amenas refinery, currently idle.

Although Algeria has a substantial petrochemical and fertilizer industry, low capacity utilization rates mean continued reliance on imports. The majority of Algeria's petrochemical plants are located at Annaba (a 550,000-ton- per-year (t/y) - ammonium phosphate fertilizer plant and ammonium nitrate and nitric acid complex), Arzew (365,000 t/y ammonia, 146,000 t/y urea, and 182,500 t/y ammonium nitrate), and Skikda (a 130,000 t/y high-density polyethylene unit, 120,000-t/y ethylene cracker, and a substantial aromatics complex). Sonatrach has undertaken a number of petrochemical and fertilizer expansion projects, including a new methyl tertiary butyl ether (MTBE) complex and a polyester resin complex.

Algeria uses seven coastal terminals for crude oil, refined product, NGL, and liquefied natural gas (LNG) exports. These are located at Arzew (Algeria's largest crude oil export port), Skikda (Algeria's second largest crude oil export port), Algiers, Annaba, Oran, plus the Tunisian facilities of Bejaia and La Skhirra. Arzew handles about 40% of Algeria's total hydrocarbon exports (including all of its NGL exports), and Algeria has ambitious plans for the port area. Among other things, the government would like to build a petrochemicals complex at Arzew, as well as a condensate refinery and desalination plant. Work also needs to be done to maintain and upgrade Arzew's crude oil loading capacity. A refurbishment project on the port began in 2004. Skikda port is limited to 80,000-ton tankers and will require dredging and other maintenance work in order to accommodate larger tankers.

NATURAL GAS

Commercial production of natural gas began in 1961, with output in 2000 of 2.8 trillion cubic feet (Tcf). Algeria has 160 Tcf of proven natural gas reserves, primarily associated (with oil), ranking it in the top 10 worldwide. Algeria's recoverable natural gas potential may, however, be as high as 282 Tcf. In 2000, natural gas (including natural gas liquids) accounted for about 60% of Algeria's total hydrocarbons production. Algeria also is a major natural gas exporter, accounting for one-fifth of EU natural gas imports in 2000 (Russia accounted for 39% in that year). As of 2002, Algeria's total natural gas export capacity, via pipeline and LNG tanker, was over 2 Tcf per year. This is expected to increase rapidly in coming years as major new gas fields, export pipelines, and LNG facilities come online. Algeria's goal is to export 3 Tcf per year or more by 2010. Algeria is a founding member of the Gas Exporting Countries' Forum, a loose group of 15 gas producing countries formed in Tehran in May 2000.

Algeria's largest gas field (by far) is the super-giant Hassi R'Mel, discovered in 1956 and holding proven reserves of about 85 Tcf. Hassi R'Mel accounts for around 1.35 billion cubic feet (Bcf) per day, or about a quarter of Algeria's total dry gas production. The remainder of Algeria's gas reserves are located in associated and non-associated fields in the southeast, and in non-associated reservoirs in the In Salah region of southern Algeria. (Note: flaring of natural gas at Algeria's associated gas fields is slated to end in 2010). The Rhourde Nouss region holds 13 Tcf of known reserves in the Rhourde Nouss, Rhourde Nouss Sud-Est, Rhourde Adra, Rhourde Chouff, and Rhourde Hamra fields. Smaller gas reserves are located in the In Salah region (5-10 Tcf) as well as at the Tin Fouye Tabankort (TFT; 5.1 Tcf), Alrar (4.7 Tcf), Ouan Dimeta (1.8 Tcf), and Oued Noumer fields. In October 2003, Sonatrach announced a major natural gas discovery in the Reggane Basin in southwestern Algeria.

Algeria's natural gas pipeline export capacity includes around 900 Bcf/y via the 667-mile Trans-Mediterranean (Transmed, renamed Enrico Mattei) line from Hassi R'Mel via Tunisia and Sicily to mainland Italy, and 280 Bcf/y via the 1,013-mile Maghreb-Europe Gas (MEG, renamed Pedro Duran Farell, onstream since November 1996) line via Morocco to Cordoba, Spain, where it ties into the Spanish and Portugese gas transmission networks. Given that over the past decade, natural gas has been the fastest growing fuel source in the EU, with natural gas - mainly imported -- expected to account for 26% of EU energy consumption by 2010, Algeria has plans to increase its natural gas export capacity significantly in coming years. In August 2001, Sonatrach awarded ABB a $93 million contract to build a natural gas compressor station on the Pedro Duran Farrell (MEG) line in order to raise capacity to nearly 400 Bcf/y by late 2004 (and 650 Bcf/y by 2006). There also are plans to expand Transmed capacity to more than 1 Tcf per year by 2005.

One complication in Algeria's natural gas export strategy to Europe has been EU liberalization, which has complicated the legality of traditional "destination clauses" for gas deliveries. Such clauses prevent the offtaker of the gas from reselling it to another EU state, and this has complicated Algeria's attempts at signing agreements with EU purchasers, such as ENEL.

In late July 2001, Spain's Cepsa and Algeria's Sonatrach (with 20% shares each) agreed to move ahead with a new natural gas pipeline (Medgaz) linking Algeria directly to Spain, and onwards to France. Since then, several other companies -- BP, Endesa, Eni, Gaz de France, and TotalFinaElf -- have acquired 12% shares in Medgaz. In September 2002, the consortium completed a study of the line's feasibility, but work did not begin in 2003 as had been expected. The $1.3 billion, 280-Bcf/y (initial capacity) Medgaz line most likely would go from Hassi R'Mel through the port of Arzew to Almeira, Spain, and include a power cable as well. Medgaz could be operational by 2006. In November 2002, Cepsa said that it had signed a letter of intent to purchase 35 Bcf/y of natural gas via Medgaz. In October 2003, Iberdrola announced that it had taken over Eni's 12% share in the Medgaz project. In January 2004, Algeria asked Spain's Enagas to join the project.

In December 2001, Sonatrach signed a deal with Italy's Enel and Germany's Wintershall on a feasibility study of another new natural gas pipeline, this one from Algeria under the Mediterranean Sea to Sicily and onwards to the Italian mainland and also southern France. Initial capacity on this line could be in the 280-350 Bcf per year range. Possible routes include one to Sardinia and Corsica, entering mainland Italy at La Spezia. An alternative route would run through Sardinia to the Italian mainland at Castiglione della Pescaia. The project could cost $2 billion and possibly be operational by 2008. A power line is to be built along the route as well.

Another possibility that has been mentioned recently is a Trans-Sahara natural gas pipeline from Nigeria, across the Sahara, and north through Algeria to the Mediterranean coast. The pipeline could cost $5-$7 billion and utilize the Medgaz line to Spain.

Aside from exports to Italy, Spain, Portugal, etc., Algeria has a policy of using its natural gas reserves as a source of domestic energy and as a raw material for the petrochemical industry. Algeria consumes around 400 Bcf of natural gas per year. Approximately 95% of the country's electricity is generated by natural gas.

Development of the In Salah region is one of the lynchpins in Algeria's plan to increase its natural gas exports. In February 2000, BP Amoco (now BP) and Sonatrach signed a $2.5 billion deal to develop seven of the twelve existing fields in the In Salah region, including the Garat al-Bafinat, Teguentour, Krechta, Reg, In Salah, Hassi Moumeme, and Gour Mahmoud fields. These fields contain estimated dry natural gas reserves of 6 Tcf, with a potential for 10 Tcf total. In addition, the joint venture, called In Salah Gas, will appraise existing wells and explore for new gas reserves in the In Salah region. In Salah Gas is the first major natural gas joint venture between Sonatrach and a foreign partner. Production from the region originally was expected to come online in late 2003, after the drilling of up to 200 production wells and construction of a $1 billion, 48-inch pipeline link to Hassi R'Mel. However, progress has been slowed due to several factors, including EU rules on natural gas re-exports (see above) and slower-than-expected natural gas demand growth in potential importing countries such as Spain, and production now is expected to begin in mid-2004. In July 2003, Statoil agreed to buy 49% of BP's interest in the In Salah project, plus 50% of BP's stake in the In Amenas development (see below), for a total of $740 million.

In May 1997, In Salah Gas sealed its first natural gas sales deal with Italian electricity generator Enel. The deal enables In Salah Gas to take over an existing contract to supply Enel with 141 Bcf/y of gas. Sonatrach will continue supplying the Italian power giant with natural gas supplies until In Salah is ready. The deal represents In Salah's first step towards achieving its sales goal of 315 Bcf/y. Besides Enel, the venture is also marketing gas to other potential clients in Europe, Turkey and North Africa.

Besides In Salah, three other important Algerian natural gas and condensates projects are Ohanet, In Amenas, and Gassi Touil. Ohanet is located in the Illizi province on the northern edge of the Sahara desert about 60 miles west of the Libyan border. Ohanet is being developed -- at a cost of around $1 billion -- by Australia's BHP (with a 45% share), Woodside Petroleum (15%), Japan Ohanet Oil and Gas, Swiss-Swedish ABB, and U.S.-based Petrofac. Natural gas production from Ohanet began in October 2003, with natural gas liquids and liquefied petroleum gas (LPG) production expected as well. The Ohanet project includes construction of a natural gas processing plant, with capacity of 30,000 bbl/d of condensate, 26,000 bbl/d of LPG, and around 700 million cubic feet (Mmcf)/day of natural gas -- as well as a pipeline. BHP is to operate the fields in partnership with Sonatrach.

In November 2002, Sonatrach and BP signed a deal to develop natural gas production in the In Amenas region. The $1.8 billion project is due to come onstream in 2005 and to produce around 900 million cubic feet per day of "wet" (i.e., associated with oil) natural gas, plus 50,000 bbl/d of condensate and LPG. The project also includes construction of three pipelines to carry the hydrocarbons to the Sonatrach distribution system at Ohanet.

In May 2002, Algeria issued and international tender for development of Gassi Touil, which is believed to contain natural gas reserves of 9 Tcf. In January 2004, Energy Minister Khalil said that Algeria intended to award a contract for Gassi Touil development by March 2004. Bidders include Amerada Hess, BHP Billiton, ExxonMobil, Marathon, Occidental, Petronas, Repsol, Shell, Total, and others. Gassi Touil is expected to have eventual production capacity of 580 Mmcf/d, much of which will be exported as LNG, with development to cost $2 billion.

LIQUEFIED NATURAL GAS (LNG) EXPORTS

With the start-up of the Arzew GL4Z plant in 1964, Algeria became the world's first LNG producer. Algeria is the second largest exporter of LNG (behind Indonesia), with around 17% of the world's total, exported mainly to Western Europe (France, Belgium, Spain, Turkey, Italy, and Greece) and the United States (about 5% of Algeria's LNG exports go there). Sonatrach has LNG export contracts with Gaz de France, Belgium's Distrigaz, Spain's Enagas, Turkey's Botas, Italy's Snam, and Greece's DEPA.

On January 19, 2004, a boiler exploded at the Skikda LNG export terminal, Algeria's second largest next to Arzew, killing at least 27 people and shutting down operations at several adjacent facilities, including a refinery and crude oil and petroleum product loading terminals. Three liquefaction trains (out of six) at Skikda were heavily damaged, accounting for 11% of Algeria's total LNG capacity. Overall, Skikda handles about one-quarter of Algeria's total LNG exports, with a nameplate capacity of 230 billion cubic feet (Bcf) per year prior to the accident. Most of the LNG exported from Skikda currently is earmarked for markets in Western Europe (mostly France, with smaller quantities going to Greece, Italy and Spain). Algeria has 44 Bcf per year of spare capacity available at its Arzew liquefaction complex, which accounts for the other three-quarters of the country's LNG exports. Energy Minister Khelil has promised to build two new LNG trains in Skikda, with double the capacity of the three destroyed units and utilizing the most advanced technology. The cost of rebuilding could approach $800 million.

In 1999, Sonatrach completed a total renovation of its LNG facilities, raising the country's LNG production capacity to around 1 Tcf per year. This refurbishment program focused on the 400-Bcf/year Arzew GL1Z, 440-Bcf/year Arzew GL2Z, and 275-Bcf/year Skikda GL1K plants. Also, Algeria's original 60-Bcf/y Arzew GL4Z, or "Camel," plant, which was slated for decommissioning by 1997, has been refurbished to keep the plant operational for reserve purposes until at least 2003. Sonatrach plans to expand its exports, especially to Europe. In September 2001, Spain's second largest power company, Iberdrola, purchased a spot LNG cargo from Algeria, the first such purchase by a Spanish utility.

ELECTRICITY

Algeria's electricity demand is growing at a rapid, 5%-7% annual rate, and will, according to Sonelgaz, require significant additional capacity -- possibly 8,000 MW by 2010 -- in coming years. Currently, Algeria has around 6,000 MW of installed power generating capacity, but this has not been sufficient to reach demand during peak cooling periods in the summer. In July 2003, power and water shortages led to rioting and demonstrations in the country. Currently, the Algerian government is pushing power conservation measures. In the longer-term, however, Algeria's power sector will need to grow. This will require billions of dollars worth of investments in new generating capacity, plus transmission and distribution infrastructure (i.e., lines and sub-stations).

In February 2002, legislation passed by Algeria's parliament ended Sonelgaz's monopoly over electric power generation, transmission, and distribution, converted the company into a joint-stock company, and cleared the way for Algeria's first independent power projects (IPPs). However, further legislation which would allow Sonatrach to operate along commercial lines is stalled at the moment.

In May 2001, Sonatrach and Sonelgaz established a joint venture -- the Algerian Energy Company (AEC) -- to export electricity. Among other projects, AEC is examining the feasibility of establishing a trans-Mediterranean power link to Italy. In December 2001, Sonelgaz signed a joint venture agreement with Italian power grid manager GRTN on the possibility of constructing an undersea power cable to export electricity to Europe via Sardinia or Sicily. In November 2001, Sonelgaz signed a similar deal with Spain's power group Red Electrica de Espana to build an underwater power line between Algeria and Spain. Currently, Algeria has two links to the Moroccan electricity grid and supplies over 550 gigawatthours (GWh) of electricity to Morocco. In December 2003, a draft agreement on integrating the Maghreb and European power grids was signed in Rome.

Sonatrach has a $107 million contract with Anadarko and Italy's GE Nuovo Pignone to build the country's first privately financed natural-gas-fired power plant at Hassi Berkine. GE Nuovo Pignone, a subsidiary of General Electric, will also provide a gas treatment system, liquid fuel gas turbine storage and services. In July 2003, Canada's SNC Lavalin was awarded contracts to design and build an 825-MW combined cycle power plant in Skikda. The U.S. Export-Import Bank has agred to provide export guarantees, since a U.S. subsidiary of Lavalin is exporting GE gas-fired turbines and providing engineering services for the project, which is expected to come online in the third quarter of 2005. In August 2003, France's Alstom won a contract to construct a 300-MW power plant at F'Kirina, around 300 miles east of Algiers.

In July 2002, Sonatrach and Sonelgaz formed a new, renewable energy joint venture company, called New Energy Algeria (NEAL). NEAL will look at development of solar, wind, biomass, and photovoltaic (PV) energy production. One project reportedly under consideration is a 120-MW hybrid natural gas/solar power plant and a wind/diesel/PV facility at Timimoun. In January 2003, Algeria and the International Energy Agency agreed on technological cooperation in developing solar power. Overall, Algeria is aiming at a 5% share for solar in the country's electricity mix by 2010.

ALGERIA LARGEST OIL & GAS COMPANIES

SONATRACH (ENTREPRISE NATIONALE SONATRACH)

Nature of Business

Enterprise Nationale Sonatrech, founded in 1963, is the national oil company of Algeria. It is responsible for the management of the country's oil industry which encompasses organization of Algerian exploration, production, transport, refining, processing, marketing and distribution of oil, gas and related products. Included in this portfolio is management of exploration bidding rounds for oil and gas. Sonotrach also has an important role in the chemicals industry of Algeria, owning fertilizer plants and petrochemical facilities.

Sonatrach is structured as a holding company with five major operating subsidiaries which encompass: Exploration, production and marketing of oil, gas and chemicals Management of the Algerian oil refineries Transport, including pipeline operation and maintenance Gas liquefaction and operation of the Arzew and skilda LNG and LPG plants International operations, including management of foreign investments and overseas sales offices Sonatrach has begun an 18 billion US dollar, 5 year investment plan which includes a 25 year oil recovery enhancement project with Arco.

General Information

Organization Type:	Company
Registered in:	Algeria
Nick name/Abbrev.:	Sonatrach
Business Sector(s):	Oil And Gas Industry Exploration & Production

Directors/Managers

Director General: Mr NCE Zouioueche (Nazim)

Chairperson: Mr A Attar (Abdeknadhud)

CONTACT INFORMATION

Sonatrach (Entreprise Nationale Sonatrach)

Tel: +213 (0)2 663300

Office Address: 80 Ave Ahmed Ghermoul
Algiers
Algeria

AFRICA OPERATIONS

TOTAL has extensive assets in Africa encompassing both upstream and downstream investments. TOTAL has business activities in at least 38 African countries and its trademark is present in 32 of these. The company distributes six million tones of petroleum products in Africa annually and it employs 3,800 employees. It's upstream activities are centered in Algeria, Angola, Cameroon, Gabon and Tunisia.

TOTAL is one of the largest oil marketers in Africa, operating 2,300 service stations in 32 African countries and boasting an overall market share of roughly 15%. TOTAL's largest affiliate in Africa is that in South Africa which has an extensive marketing network as well as refining, lubricant base oil and blending assets. Through the South African operation, the company is also active in neighboring countries by means of subsidiary companies which include TOTAL Namibia, TOTAL Botswana, TOTAL Lesotho, and TOTAL Swaziland.

TOTAL Cote d'Ivoire operates no less than 95 stations in the country, including 35 former Esso stations acquired two years ago (along with the stations in Senegal), giving it a 20.8% share of the road network market. In addition, TOTAL Cote d'Ivoire holds a 10.1% stake in SIR, where it acts as technical assistant, and 15% in Sifal (lubes). TOTAL has over the past two years been the upgrading the standards of some 700 of its stations across Africa at a reported cost of Ffr800 million.

Refining is carried out in Africa through its 34% share in Natref Refinery in South Africa and through various equity shares in smaller units located in the Ivory Coast (Abidjan). Cameroon (Limbe), Gabon (Port Gentil), and Senegal (Dakar).

ARZEW REFINERY

The oil refinery at Arzew, Algeria, is a topping and reforming refinery with a nameplate distillation capacity of 3,000 ktonnes per annum (60,000 bpd). It was built by a consortium of Japanese contractors and completed in 1973. It processes Saharan crude piped to it along the Haoud El Hamra/Arzew pipeline. Half of its output is consumed locally with the remainder being exported. The refinery is owned by the Algerian national oil company, Sonatrach.

Following the country's expansion of its gas exports, the Arzew refinery is undergoing a major rehabilitation of its GL1-Z and GL2-Z gas liquefaction plant. Contractors are Bechtel and the Japanese companies, IHI and Itochu, who have been awarded contracts to install new equipment and expand existing facilities.

REFINERY UNITS

The refinery has the following main production units (capacities in barrels per day):

Refinery Units	Capacity (bpd)
Crude unit	60,000
Vacuum unit	5,500
Catalytic reformer	11,600
Catalytic hydrotreater	11,000
Lubes production	2,400
Asphalt production	2,400

CONTACT DETAILS

Postal Address: P O Box 37, Arzew, Algeria
Street Address: Emir Abdel Kader St, Arzew, Algeria

SONATRACH AN INTERNATIONAL PETROLEUM GROUP

A far-reaching scope

Sonatrach is the Algerian oil and gas company. According to the Petroleum Intelligence Weekly, it is ranked as the twelveth company in the world.

It is the first oil company in the Mediterranean, the fourth world largest exporter of natural gas and the second one for LPG.

A leading role
Upon its creation in december 1963, Sonatrach role was, essentially, to contribute in the national development of Algeria. It was mostly targeted to generate external payment means, but also to meet the existing and future hydrocarbons requirements of Algeria.

An impressive growth
For purposes of maximizing the long term value of the Algerian hydrocarbons resources, Sonatrach undertook a tremendous development of activities.
Production has been multiplied by four since 1970 and is expected to be twice as much by 2007.

Significant assets
- A highly qualified human potential.
- A very competitive and attractive law on hydrocarbons.
- An important reserve base.
- Sedimentary basins with a high potential and still largely under-explored.
- An expertise of thirty years operations in field exploitation and development.
- A great experience in gas industry.
- A privileged geo-economic situation, neighbouring the important European Union market and open to the remainder of the world.
- A most positive partnership track record.

Exports

Given the privileged geo-economic situation of Algeria, Sonatrach has developed a strong commercial relationship with Western Europe and the United States and is particularly interested in the Mediterranean countries and the Maghreb.

(In millions of toe)

Product	1995	1996	1997	2004	1999	2000
Crude oil	15.42	18.17	17.35	19,3	19,3	21,4
NGL (condensate)	17.44	18.16	17.85	17,3	17,1	17,7
Refined products	14.64	13.91	15.81	14,1	14,9	14,9
Natural gas	18.58	20.08	22.88	26,4	32,1	32,9
Liquefied natural gas	17.59	19.63	24.07	24,5	26,0	26,6
Liquefied petroleum gas	4.03	4.52	5.82	6,8	7,8	8,5
Total	87.70	94.47	103.78	108,3	117,2	122,1

SCHEMA ORGANISATIONNEL ET FONCTIONNEL DE LA MACROSTRUCTURE SONATRACH 11 Juin 2002

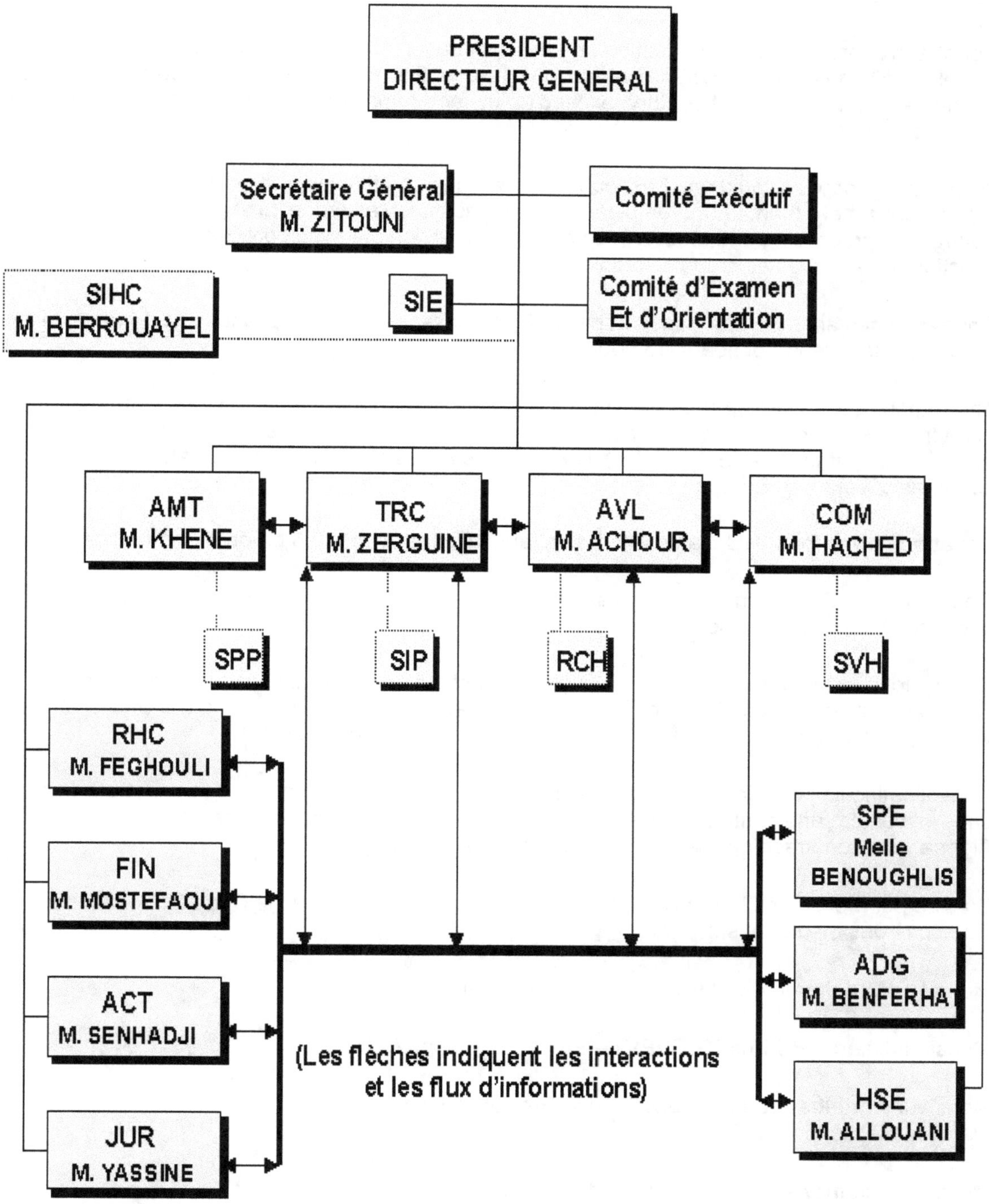

The important exploration efforts of Sonatrach have resulted in 30 important discoveries in the last few years in 1994 and 1995, 15 discoveries were made, followed by 10 others in 1996.

Algeria was ranked as one of the most important oil discovering country. 5,680 billion barrels of oil, 200 million barrels of condensate and 71 billion m3 of natural gas represent the total of what has been discovered in the last few years.

Sonatrach is present in the production and the exploration of deposits with more than 3.9 million barrels of oil equivalent / day. The production of crude oil is forecast to exceed 60 million tonnes by the beginning of the next century, exceeding by far the maximum achieved in 1978 which was 54 million tonnes

.Sonatrach produces liquid and gaseous hydrocarbons on 75 fields and nearly. It 200 wells, it also exploits more than a hundred plants and facilities such as crude oil separation centers, natural gas processing and recovry plants, LP.G extraction units, compression gas and water injection units as well as crude oil refining plants.

Sonatrach has an important transport network composed of 11 ags pipelines and 14 oil pipelines reaching a total lengh of nearly 13 000 Km.

The transport capacity of Sonatrach has increased thanks to the entry into service of new infrastructures among which are those particulary designed for exports such as the G.M.E and the doubling of the TRANSMED which links the gas deposits of the Algerian Sahara to the countries of southern Europe.

Sonatrach owns four LNG plants with a total annual capacity of 30.5 billion m^3 natural gas.

Concerning LPG, Sonatrach has two separation plants (butane and propane) totaling an annual capacity of 4.6 million tonnes.

Thanks to its priveliged geographic position with respect to the great consuming markets, Sonatrach has developed its marketing actions towards Western Europe and the United States with a particular attention to the Mediterranean and Maghrebine countries.

Consolidating its position on the international markets, Sonatrach managed to penetrate new ones in western and central Europe and Asia. In order to meet a growing demand in energy, Algeria with Sonatrach envisage export growth and diversification.

Présidé par Monsieur **Chakib KHELIL**, Président Directeur Général, le Comité Exécutif est Composé des membres suivants :

Monsieur **Abdelmalek ZITOUNI**Secrétaire Général

Monsieur **Djamel Eddine KHENE**Vice-Président Amont (AMT)

Monsieur **Abdelhamid ZERGUINE** Vice-Président Transport: par Canalisations (TRC)

Monsieur **Bachir ACHOUR**Vice-Président Aval (AVL)

Monsieur **Ali HACHED**Vice-Président
Commercialisation (COM)

Monsieur **Abdelhafid FEGHOULI** Directeur Général Adjoint
Ressources Humaines
et Communication (RHC)

Melle **Fatma-Zohra BENOUGHLIS** Directrice Exécutive Stratégie,
Planification et Economie (SPE)

Monsieur **Ahmed MOSTEFAOUI** Directeur Exécutif
Finances (FIN)

Monsieur **Mohamed SENHADJI** Directeur Exécutif
Activités Centrales (ACT)

Monsieur **Rabah Nadir ALLOUANI** Directeur Central Santé,
Sécurité et environnement (HSE)

ALGERIA SKIKDA REFINERY

The oil refinery at Skikda, Algeria, built by Snamprogetti and which became fully operational in 1981, is the country's largest being capable of processing 15 million tons of Saharan crude and 300,000 tons of imported reduced crude annually. The refinery is supplied with Saharan crude by the Haoud El Hamra/Skikda pipeline and with imported crude from the oil terminal at Skikda.

The refinery is owned by the Algerian state oil company, Sonatrach

REFINERY UNITS

The refinery has the following main production units (capacities in barrels per day):

Refinery Units	Capacity (bpd)
Crude unit	320,000
Vacuum unit	9,000
Catalytic reformer	30,000
Isomerisation unit	1,900
Asphalt unit	2,900

ALGERIA EL DJAZAIR REFINERY (ALGIERS)

The El Djazair Refinery at Maison Carree, Algiers, Algeria, came on stram in 1964 with an initial capacity of 1,400 ktonnes per year (28,000 bpd) but has been progressively increased to its present nameplate distillation capacity of 3,000 ktonnes per annum (60,000 bpd). The refinery processes crude from the Hassi Massaoud oilfields piped to it along the Haoud El Hamra/Algiers pipeline. The refinery's output is distributed to the central part of Algeria for local consumption except for naphtha which is exported. The refinery is owned by the Algerian national oil company, Sonatrach.

REFINERY UNITS

The refinery has the following main production units (capacities in barrels per day):

Refinery Units	Capacity (bpd)
Crude unit	60,000
Catalytic reformer	15,000
Catalytic hydrotreater	15,000

ALGERIA HASSI MESSAOUD REFINERY COMPLEX

The refinery complex at Hassi Messaoud in the middle of the oilfields of Algeria, comprises 2 refineries. The first refinery, originally opened in 1962, is a topping and reforming refinery with a nameplate distillation capacity of 1,700 ktonnes per annum (30,000 bpd). A second refinery with a capacity of 1,200 ktonnes per annum came on stream in 1979 and supplies a large part of southern Algeria.. The refinery complex is owned by the Algerian national oil company, Sonatrach.

PRODUCT RANGE

The product spread of the Hassi Messaoud Refinery complex includes :

- Gas oil
- Gasoline (premium and regular grades)
- Paraffin
- Krosene
- Butane

ALGERIA CHEMICAL INDUSTRY

Algeria's's chemical and plastics industries have been developed using the hydrocarbon feedstock from its well-developed oil industry. The country's aim is to produce an integrated, broad-based petrochemical industry to reduce Algeria's dependence on imports and increase the volume of petrochemicals and fertilizers available for export. The Algerian chemicals industry is one of the largest in Africa and contributes substantially to the country's economy.

The Algerian chemical industry is dominated by Sonatrach, the Algerian national oil company which is responsible for the management of the country's oil and associated industries. This includes an important role in the chemicals where its chemicals subsidiary, Entreprise Nationale d'Industrie Petrochimique (ENIP) is active. Through its subsidiary activities Sonatrach owns petrochemical facilities and fertilizer plants.

- **Petrochemicals**
- **Fertilizers**

- **Other chemicals**

PETROCHEMICALS

The Algerian chemicals industry is based in three centres which include Skikda, Arzew and Annaba. These sites are industrial and refining centres which include the Arzew refinery and the Skikda refinery. The refinery at Skikda has an aromatics complex which supplies the following products:

Product	Capacity (1,000 year/year)
Benezene	90
Toluene	5
Xylenes	245
Paraxylenes	40
Linear alkyl benzene	50

ENIP has a large petrochemical complex at Skikda which is geared towards the production of polymers and plastics. The range of products produced at Skikda includes:

- ethylene (120 ktpa)
- chlorine (35 ktpa) & caustic soda
- hydrochloric acid (10 ktpa)
- Vinyl chloride monomer (VCM) (40 ktpa)
- Polyvinyl chloride (PVC) (35 ktpa)
- LDPE (48 ktpa)
- HDPE (130 ktpa)

ENIP has been progressing the expansion of its ethane cracking capacity at Skikda from 120 thousand year/year to 220 thousand year/year. Other developments at Skikda include a petrochemicals plant with a capacity of 30 thousand year/year orthoxylene, 71 thousand year/year paraxylene and 25 thousand year/year phthalic anhydride. Another development includes a 130 thousand tonne/year polyethylene plant joint venture between Repsol Quimica (Madrid) and ENIP.

The petrochemical centre at Arzew produces petrochemicals including fertilizers. Apart from fertilizer components and finished products, Arzew is the source of methanol and associated products. The range of products and capacities are as follows:

- Methanol (100-115 thousand year/year)
- Phenol resin (6 thousand year/year)
- melamine resins (0.5 thousand year/year)
- Urea resins (0.8 thousand year/year)

An expansion of the methanol capacity at Arzew through the establishment of a new 660 thousand tonne/year plant has been subject of agreements between Sonatrach and Itochu Corporation. Reservations have been the price of the gas feedstock. An objective has been to use one-third of the output in a downstream methyl tert-butyl ether plant planned by Sonatrach, Ecofuel, and Total and the remainder would be exported

Expansion and devlopment projects at Arzew include a $1.45-billion petrochemical complex with a 500 thousand tonne/year ethane cracker, and downstream units for; 110 thousand year/year of linear low-density polyethylene (LDPE); 90 thousand year/year of high-density (HDPE); 20 thousand year/year of polypropylene; and 40 thousand year/year of vinyl acetate monomer. Also in development is a 10 thousand tonne/year polyester resins complex which would use imported feedstocks.

FERTILIZERS

Algeria produces both nitrogenous and phosphate fertilizers mainly for the domestic market. Local fertilizer production can meet most of the domestic demand which is over 600 thousand tones per year. Algeria tends to be stronger in nitrogenous fertilizers than in the phosphate products. Nitrogenous fertilizers are produced at a plant in Arzew using natural gas as feedstock. The plant has a capacity of 800 thousand tones per year.

There is a second fertilizer complex at Annaba. This site produces 550 ktpa ammonium phosphate, sulphuric acid (495 ktpa), phosphoric acid (165 ktpa) and diammonium phosphate (330 ktpa). Sodium tripolyphosphate (STPP) (40 ktpa) produced at Annaba is supplied to the Société Nationale des Industries Chimiques (SNIC) for detergent manufacture.

OTHER CHEMICALS

Other recent chemical projects include a helium and nitrogen plant which is a joint venture between Sonatrach, Air Products & Chemicals Inc (USA) and L'Air Liquide (France). It is situated in the natural gas liquefaction complex at Béthious, near Arzew and has a liquid helium capacity of 16 million m^3/a and liquid and gaseous nitrogen capacity of 33 ktpa respectively. Liquid helium from this plant and from Oran are to be exported to Europe. Air Products and Chemicals has built a distribution center in Rognac, near Marseilles in France for supply of bulk helium to Europe.

Algeria has plans to develop the manufacture of pharmaceuticals by means of joint ventures with various international partners. Plans include the construction of a plant near Algiers to manufacture a range of drugs, a joint venture between Novo-Nordisk Pharmaceuticals (Denmark) and Enterprise Nationale d'Approvisionnement en Produits Pharmaceutiques. Other joint ventures, with Pfizer (USA) and Rhône-Poulenc Rohrer (France) are also in the pipeline.

The principal trade union in the chemical industry is Secteur Energie et Pétrochimie, which is affiliated to Union Générale des Travailleurs Algériens (UGTA).

ECONOMIC REFORMS AND DEVELOPMENT: GOVERNMENT STRATEGY

THE GOVERNMENT'S LATEST ECONOMIC strategy was unveiled in the spring of 2001 in the form of the Plan de soutien à la relance. In an attempt to make use of Algeria's oil-driven financial health, the plan commits around $7 billion (approximately 14% of GDP) in expenditure over a four-year period from 2001 to 2004.

The plan's broad objective – increasing economic activity – comes in four parts: stimulating demand, focusing on developing labor-intensive activities via increased support for agricultural production such as fisheries and animal production as well as small and medium-sized enterprises, engaging in public infrastructure works and, finally, developing human resources.

Proponents of the plan expect it to generate an annual GDP growth of 5% to 6% in the following years, with the majority of the stimulus package scheduled for disbursement by the end of this year (see table above).

The IMF, Algeria's principle donor, has in the main endorsed the plan, arguing that a more expansionary fiscal policy is consistent with Algeria's strong financial position and its growing social demands. Nevertheless, it expects Algerian authorities to maintain a cautious monetary stance and fulfill a commitment to adjust fiscal policy to future developments in the oil market. The inability of OPEC to convince other major oil producers, such as Russia, to cut output will be a continuing worry for the government. The falling oil price – $19 in early 2002 – will most likely force a more limited implementation of the 2001-2004 economic plan.

Overall, the plan is designed as a supplement to the government ongoing structural reforms, which must remain the focus. Some notable positives have been the liberalization of the hydrocarbons sector, telecommunications deregulation and customs tariff reform, a crucial part of the government's Association Agreement with the European Union and for its attempt to gain membership to the World Trade Organization.

The ongoing pursuit of these reforms will depend on the government's ability to override vested interests, while at the same time alleviating the poor living standards of its people. In truth, of course, there are many more questions than just the price of oil.

The last four years illustrate the pattern. In 2004, the average annual price of crude oil was just under $13 per barrel. By 2000, the price was $28.5, dropping slightly in 2001 to approximately $26.

Over the same period, the government's total budget revenue and grants increased from $10.1 billion to approximately $21 billion, the current account from a deficit of –1.9% of GDP to a massive surplus of 16.8% in 2000 and 12% in 2001, gross official reserves from $6.8 billion to $17.9 billion, while total debt as a percentage of GDP dropped from 64.3% to around 40%. Financially, Algeria has never been so good.

However, the capacity of the hydrocarbons sector to transform the state's public finances highlights Algeria's vulnerability; its spending policies and domestic economic growth are hostage to fluctuations in international energy prices. This dependence also illustrates how crucially important Algeria's reform agenda is in order to rehabilitate and diversify the economy.

Economic reform, in place since a balance of payments crisis in 1994, has had mixed results. Stringent fiscal measures undertaken in coordination with an IMF-sponsored stabilization program resulted in the sharp drop in inflation, the balance of payments regime was workably restored, while the negative trend in economic growth was reversed. Testimony to this change was the ability of the Algerian government to maintain – albeit sluggish – economic growth in 2004-1999, a time of severely depressed oil prices.

But, while the tightening of domestic demand has helped to decrease Algeria's vulnerability to external shocks, economic growth as a whole has not been strong.

Despite surging oil prices since 1999 and a strong increase in hydrocarbon exports, overall economic growth dropped from 3.2% in 1999 to 2.4% in 2000, with growth in 2001 hovering around the 3% mark. This is insufficient to meet Algeria's social and material demands. Most estimates argue that the Algerian economy needs to grow at approximately 7% per annum in order to at least make some inroads into the country's acute unemployment problem – which stands at around 30% to 35%, 60% of which are young and unskilled – and improve the generally poor level of living standards. It is estimated that poverty affects approximately two-thirds of the total population, 20% of whom live on less than a dollar a day.

GDP:	**$57 billion**
GDP PER CAPITA:	**$1,620**
2001 GDP GROWTH:	**3%**
EXPECTED 2002 GDP GROWTH:	**4.9%**
INFLATION:	**4.5%**
POPULATION:	**30 million**
Thanks to high oil prices in 2000-2001, Algeria's financial situation is strong. Increased levels of social unrest in 2001, high unemployment, housing shortages, and severe urban floods mean the government will spend much of that money on stimulating the economy in 2002	

Algeria has a relatively broad industrial base. Iron and steel, cement, food processing, textiles, pharmaceuticals and electromechanical engineering are all key industries.

It is paying the costs, however, of centrally funded development. Under the command economy of the 1960s and 1970s, the private sector was marginalized, while public industry was protected from competition through high customs duties and structural monopolies, sustained by guaranteed credit from state-owned banks.

The crunch came in the mid-1980s, the time in which Algeria's sustained economic recession began. The recession – and the corresponding fiscal crises – saw successive devaluations of the Algerian dinar. State industries, particularly dependent on raw material imports, began racking up increasing levels of debt. Excessively high wage bills, inefficient management, and outdated equipment and machinery prevented state firms from successfully fighting their way out of debt and modernizing their operations.

As part of the transition to a market economy, the state has been focusing on restructuring its public industry and opening up the sector to foreign investors. According to the Minister of Industry and Restructuring, Mr. Abdelmajid Menasra, so far the government has injected more than $15 billion in restructuring efforts, involving liquidating non-viable state firms, shedding staff and implementing financial recovery schemes such as debt-equity swaps, capital injections, debt forgiveness, refinancing and so on.

Despite these efforts, the industrial sector as a whole still remains in recession. Although private sector industry continues to show positive growth (6.8% in the first quarter of 2001), it still remains small in relation to public industry. Because privatization has by and large not taken place, the sector remains dominated by state-owned firms (around 75%). Industrial production, which has been in decline since the early 1990s, continued to fall in 2000 and 2001 despite record earnings in hydrocarbon exports. Excluding the oil and gas sector, total public sector growth fell by over 1% in 2000, an increase over the 0.5% in negative growth in 1999. For 2001, first quarter public industry output fell by 2.5% over the same period in 2000.

THE ONLY POSITIVE GAINS were made by the heavy industrial sector. First quarter production in 2001 in the steel and metal industry was up 11.9% over the same period last year. Manufacturing of metal mechanized products was up 18.2%, while the electromechanical industry was up 11.7%, despite heavy import competition.
Otherwise, most other areas reported negative results. Construction materials were down 1.9%,

agro-industry down 11.6%, textiles and leather down 24.9%, chemical, pharmaceutical and pesticides down 2.1%, while wood and paper industries were down 4%.

INDUSTRY: **10% of GDP**
EMPLOYEES: **14% of total workforce**

2002 will see yet more money put towards restructuring the inefficient state sector. The 2001-2004 economic plan commits a portion of the designated $7 billion to finance public industry reforms, including the cost of liquidation and employee reduction schemes. The situation for Algeria's industrial sector will become increasingly critical as the government's efforts to gain admission to the WTO will force unpopular tariff reductions and expose state firms to greater competition.

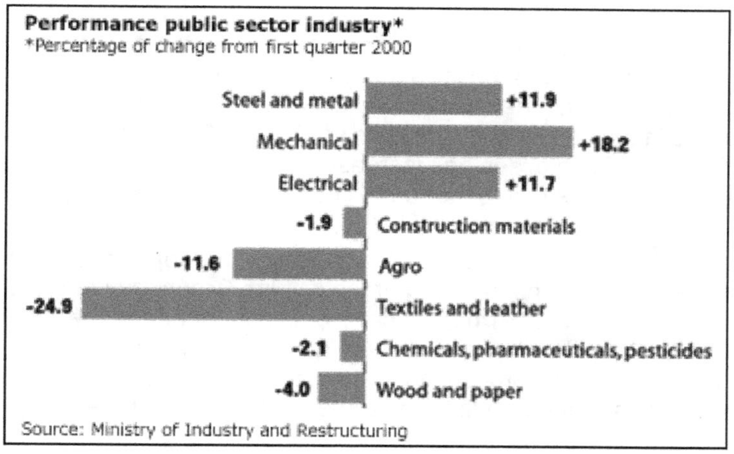

Private industry. Grew 6.8% in the first quarter last year.

Public industry. Production dropped 2.5% in the first quarter of 2001; so too did total investment (2%) and added value (6%). The number of employees dropped by a meager 0.4%.

Saidal, state-owned pharmaceutical producer. Contrary to the rest of the sector, it has actually recorded strong growth. Bankrupt in maceutical firm, and profitable too. In the face of heavy imports and growing local competition, Saidal has increased its market share from 10% four years ago to 40% today and saw a 2001 turnover of $85 million. CEO, Mr. Ali Aoun, has also confirmed a production partnership with American pharmaceutical giant, Pfizer.

Public industry finances have also become more critical. According to the Ministry of Industry and Restructuring, the net treasury balance at the end of March 2001 registered a bank overdraft of $582 million, a deterioration of $139 million from the end of December 2000.
In the face of continued disappointments in the sector, the government is hoping that persistence in structural reform will eventually see results. The 2001-2004 economic program commits another $7 billion in spending, some of which will be used to finance restructuring of public industry and prepare its firms for privatization. Mr. Menasra also points to some notable successes as an example of what they can achieve. SIDER, one the country's largest iron and steel producers and heavily in debt at the end of the 1990s, was financially restructured and cut its staff from 22,000 to 12,000.

The fruit of this achievement was the deal negotiated with ISPAT – an Indian iron and steel producer – to take control of 70% of SIDER's capital. If concluded, this will be the first real privatization to take place in the industrial sector and, hopes the government, point the way in the right direction.

ONE SUCH PUBLIC FIRM PUSHING in that direction is the Paper and Cellulose Industrial Group (GIPEC). Formed in 2004, GIPEC represents the incorporation of two key paper manufacturers, CELPAP, which produces stationary for schools and offices, and ENEPAC, which specializes in packaging paper. With an average annual turnover of $70 million and around 4,000 employees (which the company is in the process of rationalizing), GIPEC has attempted to restructure its operations via a process of subsidiarization, forming its profitable platforms into sister businesses that will be more responsive to market conditions and more competitive.

Although private sector industry continues to show positive growth, it still remains small in relation to public industry

Aside from the pursuit of partners for public companies, Mr. Menasra also points to the continuing emergence of the private sector as a positive source of growth. "Between 1992 and 1997," he says, "the number of private industrial enterprises was actually decreasing because the government had not relinquished its socialist policies. Since 2004, the number of private enterprises with 10 or more employees has increased at a rate of 50 to 70 annually, a trend that is particularly seen in agro-industries, construction materials and electronics."

Business leaders from the private sector are also making a greater impact on the international scene. Mr. Rafik Abdelmounem Khalifa, CEO of the Khalifa Group, a diversified business with interests in banking, aviation and pharmaceutical production, attended the World Economic Forum this year in New York. Mr. Khalifa is emblematic of private Algerian industrialists, who are forcing change. For example, the competition for business generated by the group's airline, Khalifa Airways, is largely attributed to the government's decision last year to privatize the state airline, Air Algérie.

Oil and gas is the unconditional wealth of Algeria. Hydrocarbon exports have financed Algeria's post-independence development and they're the key reason why the country's GDP per capita is three times that of its neighbors to the south.

But Algeria is also highly dependent on the industry. Despite years of effort to diversify its export and revenue bases, oil and gas traditionally represent 95% of total exports, 60% of state revenue and 25% to 35% of GDP.

In view of this dominance, it is somewhat ironic that Algeria is considered under-explored in terms of hydrocarbon resources. According to the Ministry of Energy and Mines, Algeria has only eight exploration wells per 10,000 km2, compared to the world average of 100 wells. With a total territory of over 1.5 million km2, the potential of this sector is indeed enormous.

The result has been intense efforts at restructuring the sector to encourage competition and increase the level of foreign investment. Most fundamental in this is reforming the country's national oil and gas company, Sonatrach. In terms of turnover – $22 billion in 2000 – Sonatrach is far-and-away Africa's largest corporation.

It ranks as the 12th largest petroleum corporation in the world and its gas exports, both of LPG (liquid petroleum gas) and natural gas, are among, if not the, world's largest. With over 48,000 employees and approximately 120,000 when including its subsidiaries, reorganizing the firm is no easy task.
The prospect of outright, or partial, privatization of Sonatrach has not been greeted warmly in

Algeria. The powerful labor confederation, UGTA, last year threatened industrial action if Dr. Chekib Khelil, Algeria's Minister for Energy and Mines (and formerly OPEC President in 2001), pushes forward divestment legislation. Nevertheless, the essential objective of the minister's reforms has not wavered. The intention, proposed in a new draft law for liberalization of the hydrocarbons sector, is to fully commercialize the company by separating its operational procedures and responsibilities from those of its owner, the state, and expose it to full competition. "The only responsibility Sonatrach should have," says Dr. Khelil, "is to make money, create employment and be competitive."

THE MOST IMPORTANT STEP will be to establish two independent agencies. The first, called ALNAFT, will exist to award future exploration and production contracts to investors through an open bidding process and provide information on investment opportunities; a 0.5% share of oil royalties will finance it. Sonatrach, which currently performs this role, will no longer be in the position to award the contract and therefore will operate on an equal footing with other investors in the sector. The second agency, the Regulatory Authority, will be responsible for administrative and regulatory activities in the sector, such as ensuring each player has access to oil and gas transportation infrastructure and so on; it will be financed by charging a service fee. Removing these activities from Sonatrach and handing them to independent, self-financed agencies will erase potential conflicts of interest Sonatrach may have in its partnerships with foreign investors.

The changes will also put Sonatrach on a much more sound commercial footing. With its future income contractually based, it will not need to haggle with the government's budget committee each year, allowing it to plan for the long term.
The requirement upon Sonatrach to build and maintain transportation pipelines will also be removed, with new construction being offered to any investor on an open bidding basis. Pipelines are not high-return operations and giving Sonatrach the right to pick and chose will reinforce the firm's ability to improve financial management.

MORE CONTROVERSIAL, however, is the draft law's proposal to limit Sonatrach's share in all future commercial discoveries and pipelines to 25% (with the maximum duration of 32 years for exploration and production concessions, 50 years for transport concessions). This will most likely lower the government's take over the long term when compared to the current production-sharing system. The point, says the government, is that this is the price to be paid for increased private investment in the sector, especially in the currently unexplored basins or small and marginal fields.
Anti-privatization proponents are afraid, of course, that the broad aim of the draft law – to expose Sonatrach to full competition – is merely the thin end of wedge. Like other national oil and gas companies whose monopoly fell in the face of economic reform, reduced opportunity in Sonatrach's home market will more than likely lead to a strategy of international expansion. Sonatrach already has an international presence: a contract for pipeline construction and another for gas field development, both in Latin America. It has a joint venture with Agip in Yemen, it is developing a polypropylene plant in Spain with BASF and it owns a trading company in Singapore. Nonetheless compared to other of the world's large oil and gas firms, this is still a very small portfolio.

The question, then, will be how to finance greater expansion. The most obvious way will be to raise funds on the international capital markets by selling shares and issuing bonds. Separating the operations of the state from Sonatrach will be the first step in demonstrating that it is acting in a more commercially oriented way; opening its capital to investors may well be the next logical step.

THE REFORM PROCESS will also affect Sonatrach's subsidiary companies that operate both upstream and downstream in the oil and gas industry. One example is the National Enterprise for Well Works (ENTP). Although ostensibly created in 1983, it actually took shape 33 years ago as a branch of Sonatrach that was subsequently made into a subsidiary company. Today it is commercially independent, free to make its own joint-venture agreements and operates in competition with foreign powers such as Schlumberger and Halliburton.

Drilling both for Sonatrach and for foreign companies in Algeria with exploration contracts, such as BHP, Cepsa and Anadarko Petroleum, ENTP commands around 40% to 45% of the market. It has also entered into a joint venture with the Dutch firm, Deutag. Mr. Abdelaziz Krissat, the firm's CEO, says that opportunities for increased business and partnership will come fast thanks to the upcoming deregulation of the sector. "Fifteen years ago, we would never have believed where we are today. In the 1980s, there was speculation that our wells would go dry by 2005 and hence business would dry up too. But today, with new discoveries, we still have the same level of reserves we had in the 1970s; we still have at least 30 years ahead of us. So for us, we think of it as starting from square one, only we now have 30 years of experience behind us."

PROVEN OIL RESERVES:	**9.2 billion barrels***
TOTAL OIL EXPORTS:	**Around 1.15 billion barrels per day in 2001**
	Western Europe and the United States
MAIN MARKETS:	**773,000 barrels per day (crude oil), a cut of 4.1%**
OPEC QUOTA:	**as of September 2001**
PROVEN NATURAL	
GAS RESERVES:	**3.7 trillion cubic meters**
GAS EXPORTS:	**32 billion cubic meters per year**
MAIN MARKETS:	**Western Europe, mostly via two submarine pipelines to Italy and Spain**

*Official estimate

The hydrocarbons sector, which saw huge returns in 2000 and 2001, will be preparing for deregulation in 2002. The Minister of Energy and Mines, Dr. Chekib Khelil, prepared a draft law in 2001 that calls for the introduction of competition in the oil and gas industry, mining and energy production.

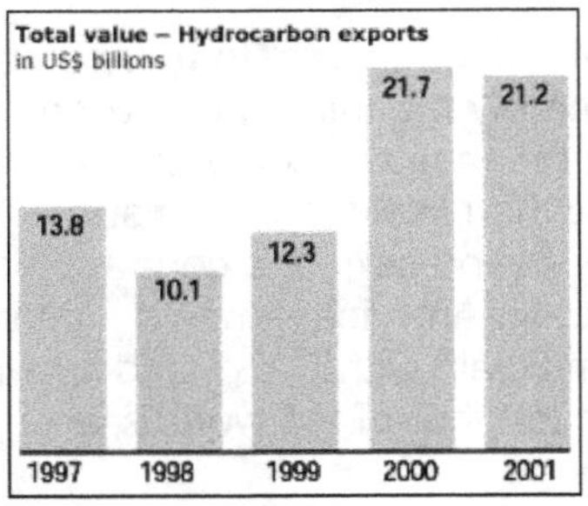

Source: IMF

ALSO SOON TO EXPORT
Sonelgaz, the state electricity provider. Installed capacity is currently 6,000 megawatts, while a further 1,200 megawatts is under construction just for export to the European Union.

Gas exports to Europe. Algeria accounts for around one quarter of the European Union's gas consumption and is the region's largest single supplier along with Russia and Norway. However, the country believes it can improve on that figure, projecting to increase its gas exports by around 20 billion cubic meters per year within the short term. A massive $2.5 billion deal with BP to develop the In Salah region is expected to generate exports of 9 billion cubic meters per year alone.

ECONOMIC AND FINANCIAL GOVERNMENT PROGRAM

During the week from august 9 to 15, 1997 the program of the government of Mr.Ouyahia was examined by the National Popular Assembly. The economic and financial section of this text which has liberal overtones advocates the implementation and strengthening of the process of structural reforms of the Algerian economy. There are two main thrusts which shape the overnment's proposals ; reduction of the role of the state (which would entail the gradual rivatization of major public services) and a readjustment of public policy dealing with housing construction, agricultural development and employment subsidies.

A. REDUCTION OF THE ROLE OF THE STATE IN ECONOMIC MATTERS

On the one hand, reduction of the role of the state will first begin by controlling the evolution of the public spending, and on the other, by the stabilization and privatization of the competitive public sector and the financial system. Replacing the "operator" state by a "regulatory" state will be the second phase with gradual externalization of the public services which are onopolies and at the same time, strengthening the ability to observe and control the economic activities of the administration.

CONTROLLING THE EVOLUTION OF PUBLIC SENDING

It looks as if public sending has brought under control and is on the right track in 1993, the budget was almost 9% of GNP, in 1996 a surplus of 3% of GNP was recorded and the budged should record a surplus of about 1.5% in 1997. There are, however, three mid-term risk which affect public finance. In 2004, servicing the external debt (which stands at 33 billion dollars) will be further burdened by the withdrawal of the window for rescheduling. The state will also have to face several deadlines of internal debts which have increased substantially as a result of the restructuring of production and banking systems, currently almost 25% of GNP (9 billion ollars). Ultimately, the social impact of the economic reforms will result in substantial costs for all of the organizations involved in social welfare (especially the national insurance company for unemployment) and the local organizations. In order to be able to rein in the mounting expenses, the government program recognizes the need to implement a more stringent and austere budget as well as decentralization or "partitioning" public expenses which are difficult to manage (local public finances, social welfare, servicing the foreign debt)

- The program therefore advocates a "rationalization of public manpower" and a move to reduce the total salary of the administration which was already reduced from 10% of GNP in 1993 to 8.5% in 1996. - A substantial shift towards decentralization will affect local public revenues (around 8% of GNP) ; the regional organizations will especially have the possibility to develop and manage local taxes. - The government program also recognizes the need for contracts to define the relations between health organizations and social security coffers, as well as "heightened economic truth for certain national insurance benefits." Transfers for health care abroad are being gradually reduced. - The exterior financial balance which ultimately brought to the surface the economic crisis of 1992-1993 will continue to be the object of great scrutiny by the Algerian authorities. The policy of prudent management for bilateral credit which was applied in 1996 will be continued. Exports not including hydrocarbons will be systematically encouraged. New foreign debt management techniques will be proposed such as converting part of the debt to buy shares in private companies. New methods for foreign financing will be encouraged such as B.O.T. techniques.

MODERNIZATION OF ECONOMIC FINANCING

Measures aimed at restructuring the financial sector should be implemented in the coming months within the general framework of stabilization and restructuring of the production system. In particular, the five public banks which are currently unable to secure a stable reserve will be obliged to confirm in the mid term to stabilization plans for their investments and management modernization which were recommended following audits conducted under the auspices of the World Bank, in order to ensure production financing. In the short term, the configuration of the banking system will undergo different arrangements. The BDL (Bank for Local Development) will be privatized. The BADR (Bank for Agricultural and Rural Development) will be merged with the Agricultural Mutual Credit so as to develop financing for agro-alimentary activities.

The BAD (Algerian Bank for Development) will be split up into an investment bank and a leasing bank. The CNEP (national Saving and Reserve Bank) will specialize in financing housing construction. In order to accelerate the reforms of banks and insurance companies of Algeria, private institutions and the establishment of branches for foreign banks will be encouraged. The government also intends to hasten the transformation from an economy of intermediary financing to an economy of direct financing (non-inflationary and conducive to productive investment) by pursing the modernization of republic shares and establishing a financial market.

Consequently, after having well managed the reforms of treasury bonds and after having "worn down" the investors (banks, insurers, social security banks) to the subscriptions by allocation, the Treasury will have to develop a secondary market for public shares and emergence of specialists in treasury stocks. After having established the regulatory and legislative framework needed to operate the Bourse of Algiers in the future, the COSOB (Commission for the Organization and Supervision of Stock Exchange Operations) will have to attend to the first stock transactions from now till the end of 1997. In view of this rapid establishment of primary and secondary markets for stocks and shares, markets which will eventually become attractive to foreign investment, the government has appealed for international corporation, not only for training personnel but also for the acquisition of needed technological support (regulatory delivery systems and share quotations).

RATIONALIZATION AND PRIVATIZATION OF THE COMPETITIVE PUBLIC SECTOR

The establishment of a financial system which would no longer be a simple intermediary between the treasury and private companies will, in the mid-term, benefit from a productive system. In the short term, however, the adoption by the banks of cautious credit management will emphasize the need to rapidly stabilize the public industrial sector, linked until now, almost exclusively with financial auditing. The "bank-companies" mechanism which was reactivated at the end of 1996, will thus allow public companies to obtain bank credit to counterbalance the effective application of structural recovery (reduction of total value,
transfer of shares, establishing branch offices, readjustment of basic jobs). To face the critical lack of productive investment in Algeria and awaiting the restructuring of the financial system, the choice was made to systematically open the capital of public companies to national and foreign private capital. The principle of complete privatization of companies in competitive sectors is clearly outlined in this program.

This privatization can, if necessary, be conducted through public privatization, by distributing complimentary coupons to certain categories of mthe population (mujahidins, workers who have been laid off because of the restructing, victims of terrorism, young, first-time jobseekers).

Gradual Externalization of Public Services Operated as Monopolies

Demonstrating the determination of the Algerian executive branch to pursue true liberalization of the economy regardless of eventual public reaction, the government program announced that state would gradually abandon public service funtions. The state will therefore progressively delegate the production in network industries (characterized by increasing returns) on a contractual basis. The retaind operators will recieve subsides to compensate for the eventual losses resulting from the tarification of certain collective goods that they will have to produce. The railway company SNTF will thus be branched out before some of its activities are privatized. In the same way, SONELGAZ (gas-electricity), during the first phase, will become EPIC basing its work on contractual work. The reorganization of the PTT (postal services and telecommunications) will consist of the separation of postal services and telecommunications; amorg its activities, the profit-making ones will be delegated to private operators on a contactual basis while the regulatory, standization and control functions will remain the domain of public authcrities.

Strengthening the Observation Capacity and Adminstration Control

The gradual withdrawal of the state as operator will eventually be compensated by the strengthening of its regulatory activities. The government program outlines throughout the text, the development of the adminstrative control bodies: general inspection of finances, inspection of labor, inspection of urbanism, water and forestry police etc. It also recognizes a marked inprovement in the public statistical office as well as the development of the analytical capabilities and economic forecasts of the adminstration, especially within the framework of developing plans for a five-year law for economic trends 2000-2005 which will constitute the first phase.

B. THREE NEW PRIORITIES IN PUBLIC POLICES

While awaiting for optimal regulation to result from market mechanisms which is what the program aims for, public policy will continue to support housing construction, agricultural development and job creation. According to this program, this support is temporary and should not become permanent nor compromise the prospects for midterm growth by delaying the application of indispensable reforms.

Housing Construction

In order to solve the very serious housing crisis from within, the government is particularly concerned about quickly setting up regulatory mechanisms for housing offers as dictated by the market (which presents an unmet demand of 1.5 million units). According to the government program, by providing the conditions which stimulate cintruction, 800,000 units will be delivered in three years, which will cover additional demand for the same period (at 250,000 houses per year). Without budgetary constrains, the government is committed to finalize the program for social housing in progress which plans delivery of 238,000 units in 2004.

The first axis of reforms will be implemented by restructuring the financial system. As mentined above, the CNEP will become a housing bank; also to be established is a fund for mortgage gurantees, a refinancing company, a bank to gurantee public markets which would allow the confining rules of Algeria's public accounting to become more flexible. The state will also encourage real estate developers through tax exemptions and will support the self-construction by individuals through a system of subsides. The second axis of reforms will constitute the reestablishment of truth in rental pricing, which is indispensable for real estate construction to be profitable. "Social" rent will be gradually suppressed and replaced by housing allowances assigned to households.

GOVERNMENT SUPPORT FOR EMPLOYMENT

Unemployment which affects almost 80% of those under thirty and represents 28% of the active population, constitutes, along with the housing crisis, the great social problem of Algeria. While awaiting the slow long-term absorption of the demographic shock of the years 1970-1980 and the establishment in the mid-term of a sustained growth rate (the government program predicts 7% growth of GNP in the year 2000, or 4% more than the natural growth rate of the population) through structural reforms, the government plans to develop an active policy to support employment. Public works (renovation of railway tracks, reforestation of mountainous regions, completion of the trans-saharan etc.) will constitute the first axis of this policy. Collective utility works will be developed with the financial support of the World Bank. Ultimately the first step in the fight against youth unemployment will be to support the creation of companies which are the first employ workers.

AGRICULTURAL DEVELOPMENT

Agriculture, today considered one of the sectors which contributes the most to the development of Algeria, will also be the object of special government attention. The growth of agricultural production (at about 5% per year since 1986, while the GNP not including hydrocarbons stagnated in volume during the same period) will result in a decrease in "the cost of food" and keep a considerable portion of the population employed. The government will first focus on stabilizing production conditions, especially by clarifying the legislative framework. The bill on the privatization of public agricultual land, adopted by the Council of Ministers in December 1996, should therefore be quickly presented before Parliament. The holding company entrusted with agro-alimentary industries will have to establish a finance company to support agricultural investment. Finally (to emphasize the main measures) numerous public works will be completed from now to the year 2000, which will result in the construction of 29 new dams which will increase by almost 30% the capacity of existing reservoirs.

THE INVESTMENT PROMOTION, SUPPORT AND MONITORING AGENCY

NATIONAL AND INTERNATIONAL PREQUALIFICATION NOTICE FOR THE CONCESSION, THE OPERATION AND MANAGEMENT OF THE INDUSTRIAL EXPORT FREE ZONE OF BELLARA

(WILAYA OF JIJEL, ALGERIA)

In accordance with the Executive Decree n° 97-06 dated 5th April 1997 enacted on 6th April in the Algerian Official Journal n° 20 relating to the creation of the Bellara industrial export free zone (Wilaya of Jijel), the Investment Promotion, Support and Monitoring Agency (APSI) informs interested bidders that a prequalification notice is issued for the concession, operation and management of the Bellara I E F Z. The prequalification technical documents can be collected against payment of 500 US dollars for foreign bidders or the equivalent in Algerian dinars for local bidders on the exchange rate basis of the day of transmission at the following address :

Agence de promotion, de soutien et de suivi des investissements (APSI) Boulevard du 11 Decembre 1960, El-Biar 16030 - Algiers - Algeria

The documents may be delivered on request by express mail to the bidder's adress after confirmation of receipt of payment and confirmation of payment to APSI of the amount mentionned above. In the case of payment by cheque, the cheque should be drawn on favour of :

Monsieur l'Agent comptable de l'APSI compte trésor n°197-822, or through Bank transfer to CCP n°32.1976/63 Algiers, Algeria.

Application for prequalification together with the required mandatory documents referred to in the presentation note of the free zone found in the technical file of the prequalification are to be submitted in a double sealed envelope without any specific external markings on the outside envelope to :

Agence de promotion, de soutien et de suivi des investissements (APSI) BP 336 EL-BIAR Boulevard du 11 Decembre 1960, El-Biar 16030 - Algiers - Algeria

With the following written on the top of the envelope :

Avis de présélection nationale et internationale, relative à la concession de la zone franche industrielle d'exportation de Bellara.

The date limit for the receipt of prequalification application is 120 days starting from the 21 st June 2004 date of the pre-qualification notice.

ALGERIA MEMBERSHIP IN INTERNATIONAL ORGANIZATIONS

- African Development Bank
- Arab Bank for Economic Development in Africa
- Arab Fund for Economic and Social Development
- Arab Maghreb Union
- Arab Monetary Fund
- Association of Iron Ore Exporting Countries
- Customs Cooperation Council
- Economic Commission for Africa
- Food and Agriculture Organization
- Group of 77
- International Atomic Energy Agency
- International Bank for Reconstruction and Development (World Bank)
- International Civil Aviation Organization
- International Criminal Police Organization
- International Development Association
- International Finance Corporation
- International Fund for Agricultural Development
- International Labor Organization
- International Lead and Zinc Study Group
- International Maritime Organization
- International Mobile Satellite Organization
- International Mercury Producers Association
- International Monetary Fund
- International Organization for Standardization
- International Telecommunications Satellite Organization
- International Telecommunications Union
- Islamic Development Bank League of Arab States
- League of Red Cross and Red Crescent Societies
- Non-Aligned Movement Organization of African Unity

- Organization of American States (observer)
- Organization of Arab Petroleum Exporting Countries
- Organization of the Petroleum Exporting Countries
- Organization of the Islamic Conference
- United Nations United Nations Conference on Trade and Development
- United Nations Educational, Scientific and Cultural Organization
- United Nations Industrial Development Organization
- Universal Postal Union
- World Health Organization
- World Intellectual Property Organization
- World Meteorological Organization
- World Tourism Organization

PRACTICAL INFORMATION AND CONTACTS FOR BUSINESS AND INVESTMENTS[1]

The biggest exports in Algeria are either mined or manufactured in the country. Agriculture plays a comparatively minor role in the country's overall economy. The vast majority of highly profitable mining or manufacturing concerns are owned and operated by the government and Algeria's government also oversees the instituting of economy-related laws and other necessary planning. In recent years there has seen a trend towards foreign investment and an increase in Algerian exports.

Petroleum and natural gases are the country's most important mineral resources. Algeria currently exports about 90% of its crude oil to parts of Western Europe. Its largest gas and petroleum deposits are found mainly in the Eastern Sahara and these are transported to various sea ports by means of pipelines. Algeria also extracts iron ore, phosphates, zinc, coal, salt, uranium and lead.

When it comes to farming, the most fertile areas of the country can be found in the north and in the oases of the Sahara. Algeria's principle farm crops are wheat, oats, citrus fruit, wine grapes, olives, figs, tobacco, dates and barley. Of these, the most notable products are olive oil, wine and other beverages and tobacco. The country is also involved in the export of some construction materials, chemicals, textiles, clothing and metals, but its involvement in this is limited. A number of Algerians farm sheep, chickens, cattle, and goats while a small fishing industry supplies the country with seafood.

The option of exporting large portions of the country's national products is becoming more and more attractive since the annual earnings from exports are considerably higher than that of importing. Algeria trades mainly with France, Italy, the US, Spain and Germany. However, exporting also has a downside in that many Algerians face a decrease in supply, higher food costs and even possible unemployment that is either directly or indirectly related to Algerian exports.

EXPORT INCENTIVES

ADVANTAGES AND FACILITATIONS GRANTED TO EXPORT OIL OUT
TAX BENEFITS : Algerian tax law provides many advantages for export operations:

Exemption in relation to direct taxes

Permanent exemption from income tax (CIT) and removal of the requirement to reinvest their profits or income, for sales operations and services for export (Article 138 of the Code direct taxes and amended by Section 06 of Finance Act 2006) similar taxes;
Exclusion from the tax base of the tax on professional activity of TAP turnover export: is not included in the revenue base for the TAP amount of sales transactions, transportation or brokering on objects or goods for direct export, including all processing operations and processing operations for the manufacture of petroleum products for direct export (Article 220-3 of the code direct taxes and similar taxes);
Removal of lump sum VF (Article 209-3 CID repealed by Article 13 of the LF 2006). This exemption applies in proportion to the turnover in foreign currencies.
Exemption of taxes on sales

VAT exemption for business sales and so on goods exported under certain conditions (Article 13 of the Code of taxes on sales;

[1] This section based in part on the material of the US Department of Commerce

VAT exemption for purchases or imports of goods made by an exporter for either export or re-export in the state, or to be incorporated in the manufacture, composition, packaging or packaging products for export and services directly related to the export transaction (Article 42-2 of the Code of taxes on sales;
VAT refunds for merchandise export operations, works, services or delivery of products for which duty-free purchases are authorized by Article 42 of the VAT Code (Article 50 of the Code of taxes turnover);

Clearance formalities

(Source Site Customs: www.douane.gov.dz)

The record clearance

The customs declaration must necessarily be accompanied by the following documents:
Invoice domiciled with an approved bank in Algeria.
Copy of the trade register of Algerian law
Copy of the tax card issued by the tax authorities territorial jurisdiction.
Any other document required as a special administrative formalities, or for, the benefit of preferential treatment related tax benefit.
The clearance procedure

The clearance process is the set of formalities to enable and ensure the implementation of various regulatory measures, customs or other, which are subject imported or exported goods.
I. The declaration of goods

Before lodging the customs declaration, all merchandise is subject to mandatory driving operations, presentation and implementation customs are the obligations of the carrier vis-à-vis the customs services.

a) The conduct and the customs

Driving is the transaction routing imported or exported to the office closest to the border of the customs territory customs goods, the carrier must borrow, for this road legal.
The following operation is the application that allows Customs to Customs to identify, support and keep under his supervision the goods to customs clearance or removal.

b) The establishment and verification of the accounting

The Customs Code expressly states that: "All goods imported or reimported, to be exported or re-exported must be an accounting. "
the establishment of the accounting
a) Definition of Accounting

The accounting is the act by which the declarant is the customs procedure applied to the goods and communicate the information required for the application of duties and taxes and for the purposes of customs control. Customs procedures which can be placed under the goods are: - the consumer; - filing Customs; - transit; - transhipment; - warehouses, - plants exercised; - temporary; - replenishment franchise - the returned goods; - final export - temporary export - re-export; - shipbuilding.

Suspensive CUSTOMS PROCEDURES FOR EXPORT
Economic customs procedures allow companies that transform products to benefit from suspension of rights and duties, able to promote exports.

Algerian legislation laid, and set these plans in Law No. 79-07 of 21 July 1979 as amended and supplemented by Law No. 98-10 of 22 August 1998 on the Customs Code Chapter 07. These plans include:
The customs warehouse : under sections 129 to 164 of the Customs Code "the customs warehouse is a customs procedure which allows the storage of goods under customs control in approved by the customs authorities suspended premises duties and taxes and prohibition measures of an economic nature. " The terms and conditions for the exercise of public and private warehouse shall be determined by the decisions of the Director General of Customs No. 05 and No. 06 of 3 February 1999. Click here (source: www.douane.gov.dz)

Temporary : Articles 174-185 of the Customs Code and the decisions of the Director General of Customs No. 04 and No. 16 of 3 February 1999 stipulate the terms and conditions under which temporary admission for inward processing and export in the state. Click here (source: www.douane.gov.dz)

Free replacement of goods : is a customs procedure which allows import free of duties and taxes on imports, goods equivalent in description, quality and technical characteristics to those taken on the domestic market were used to obtain products previously exported outright (Articles 186, 187 and 188 of the Customs Code and the Implementing Decision of the Director General of Customs No. 17 of 3 February 1999).. Click here (source: www. douane.gov.dz)

Temporary export : is a customs procedure which allows the temporary export without the application of prohibitions and economic nature for a purpose, of goods to be re-imported within a specified time in the same state or after undergoing a transformation a working, additional labor or repair (Articles 193 to 196 of the Customs Code and the decision of the Director General of Customs No. 13 of 3 February 1999 on the temporary export). Texts relating to the temporary export are listed in Annex Plans (Excise)
Transit : Click here (source: www.douane.gov.dz)

Exchange control PDF Print Send

Banking legislation has granted benefits to exporters for transfer delays of export earnings and the return of export currency amounts.

1. repatriation time (Official Journal No. 08 of 15 February 2012 / shown here) :

Regulation No. 2011-06 of 19 October 2011 amending and supplementing Regulation n ° 07-01 of 15 Muharram 1428 corresponding to 3 February 2007 on common rules applicable to foreign transactions and foreign currency accounts.

Article 1 st : modify and supplement the Regulation n ° 07-01 of 3 February 2007 on common rules for transactions with foreign currency and accounts This Regulation aims.

Article 2 : Article 61 of Regulation No 07 -01 of 3 February 2007 referred above is amended to read as follows:

" Article 61 :

The non-hydrocarbon export contract can be established for cash or credit.

Exporters must repatriate revenue from exports in a period not exceeding one hundred eighty (180) days from the date of shipment for goods or completion date for services. When payment of export is due within more than one hundred eighty (180) days, the export can take place only after authorization of the competent services the Bank of Algeria. " Article 3 : This Regulation shall be published in Official Journal of the Democratic and Popular Republic of Algeria.

Governor

Mohammed Laksaci

2. Surrender of export earnings:

Instruction No. 05-2011 of 19 October 2011 amending the provisions of Instruction No. 22-94 of 12 April 1994 as amended and supplemented fixing the percentage of non-hydrocarbon and mineral products export receipts which give entitlement to enrollment (x) account (s) foreign legal persons

Article 1 : Article 2a of the instruction n ° 22-94 of 12 April 1994 as amended and supplemented, fixing the percentage of export earnings excluding hydrocarbons and mining products eligible for inclusion in the (x) has (s) foreign legal persons, is amended as follows:

"Article 2a: An amount limited to currency 40% , levied on the share of export earnings excluding hydrocarbons and mining products actually repatriated and eligible for inclusion in the (x) account (s) foreign legal persons, can be freely used at the discretion of the exporter under its responsibility in the framework of the promotion of exports. "

Article 2: This instruction comes into force on the date of its signature.

Governor

Mohammed Laksaci

3. Export of products under Logging: It is exporting products to be sold by a custodian or commission established abroad at a price fixed by the exporter. It is called "price maintenance" or in the interests of the exporter, it is called "the best." It applies only to fruit and vegetables. In terms of exchange control, Article 12 of the Rules of the Bank of Algeria n ° 91-13 of 14 August 1991 on the clearance of non-oil exports defines the methods for carrying out this type of operation.

Under the provisions of this Regulation, the exporter must provide the paying bank operation a record of sales accounts accompanied final invoices from foreign buyers.

FINANCIAL PROVISIONS CONCERNING FOREIGN TRADE

Are considered as foreign trade transactions transactions in goods and services covered by a trade contract, and related services to processing, processing way, manufacture or repair (Art.25 of Regulation N ° 07-01 of 03/02/2007 the Bank of Algeria concerning common rules for transactions with foreign currency and accounts).

The changes introduced by the Regulation No. 07-01 of 03/02/2007 the Bank of Algeria concerning the rules applicable to foreign trade transactions on goods and services have eased the financial provisions applicable to exports as follows:

1 - Exports exempted from direct debit:

- Export without payment, samples, gifts, goods received under warranty and exports worth less than the FOB value against 100,000 DA.

- Exports against repayment of a value less than or equal to the value of 100,000 against DA made through Algeria post.

Customs declarations for exports above, must bear the endorsement ' Export non-domiciled "(Art.33 and 58 of Regulation n ° 07-01 of BA).

2 - Domicile of exports of fresh, perishable and / or dangerous:

It can take place during the five (05) working days of shipping and customs declaration dates.

These exports are authorized customs under the guise of incomplete declaration, of non domiciled bill (Art. 60 and 63 of the Regulations).

3 - export consignment:

- The obligation to sell or import the product within a maximum period of one year from the date of shipment is deleted.

- Payment of the export consignment shall be payable as and when the sales made by the custodian or agent.

- Repatriation to be made within the prescribed time counted (180 days) from the date of sales.

- A monthly statement of accounts together with duplicate sales invoices from foreign buyers (Art. 68 of the Regulations).

4 - The responsibility for repatriation of export earnings:

The obligation to repatriate export revenue falls to the exporter for the repatriation within more than 180 days, exemptions may be granted, subject to a substantiated request to submit to the Bank of Algeria

REGULATORY AND INSTITUTIONAL FRAMEWORK

Sending samples: In the general scheme, the conditions of export samples whose value does not exceed 30000 DA are defined by the Ministerial Decision No. 216 of 15 November 1997. In the case of samples whose value is greater than 30,000 Da and no commercial coating can be exported under a license called "Export Without Payment Authorization" issued by the Ministry of Commerce, by way of derogation. This export is exempt from the process debit and repatriation of export earnings.

Creation of the National Advisory Council for the Promotion of Exports: The composition and functioning of the Board are defined by Executive Decree No. 04-173 June 12, 2004 (OJ No. 39 of June 16, 2004) made under the said Act ;

Creating ALGEX: The organization and functioning of the National Agency for the Promotion of Foreign Trade have been defined by Executive Decree No. 04-174 DU12 June 2004 (OJ No 39 of 16 June 2004).

Creativity is of the Algerian Company Insurance and Guarantee Exports (CAGEX) , which dates back to 1996. Its mission is to support the insurance business and political risk.

The Pest Control

Legislative and regulatory framework put in place by the government focuses on the phytosanitary border control for the export of agricultural products.

Following the conventions and agreements that govern trade, phytosanitary control that is sanctioned by the establishment of phytosanitary certificate's purpose, to give the plants for export phytosanitary safeguards required by the importing country.

Agricultural products can be exported from 27 official border crossings (8 airports, 11 seaports, land border crossings 8), the list is:

- Post Air : Airport Tlemcen (Zenata), Oran (Senia), Algiers (Houari Boumediene): Constantine (Boudiaf) Annaba (El Malaha) Tébessa; Ghardaia (Noumerat) and Biskra (Khider Mohamed).

- Maritime Jobs : Port Ghazaouet; Arzew, Oran, Mostaganem, Tenes; Algiers Dellys, Bejaia, Skikda, Annaba and Djen Djen.

- Land Border Crossings : Akid Lotfi - Tlemcen, El Kala - Taref; Souk Ahras, and Ain Tine Zaouatine Guezzam - Tamanrrasset; Bordj Badji Mokhtar - Adrar; Bouchabka - Tébessa; Taleb Larbi - El Oued and Deb Deb - Illizi.

Registration of exporters in the commercial register:

411101 exports of food products

411,102 export of manufactured industrial products Nonhydrocarbon

411103 exports of all products, excluding hydrocarbons not defined elsewhere.

AGREEMENTS AND CONVENTIONS PDF Print Send

1 - ASSOCIATION AGREEMENT WITH THE European Union (EU) :

When exporting to the EU agricultural products (Chapter 1-24)

Protocol 1: agricultural products

117 tariff lines benefit from duty-free access tariffs unlimited quantities

26 tariff lines are duty free tariff quotas under customs,

15 tariff lines are admitted free of customs duties under reference quantities.

Protocol 3: fishery products.

20 tariff lines covered by the exemption of customs duty.

Protocol No. 5: agricultural products (Annex 1)

Free of customs unlimited quantities

Free of customs duty, taxation of agricultural components,

Free of customs under quotas:

pasta (2000T/An)

couscous (2000T/An)

preparing fermented milk (1500T/An)

2 - For export to the EU for industrial products (Chapter 25-97)

decommissioning is immediate from the implementation of the Association Agreement (1 September 2005).

2 - BILATERAL AGREEMENTS WITH THE ARAB :

Tunisia:

The agreement between Algeria and Tunisia in 1981 which provides for the exemption from taxes and customs duties between the two countries has been frozen by the Algerian side in 1996. This agreement is being updated.

Libya:

The 1973 agreement between the two parties that provides for the exemption of taxes and customs duties is not applied by Algeria. However, the Libyan party grants, under domestic law, the exemption of customs duties on all originating goods of Arab countries, including Algeria.

Jordan:

The agreement for commercial cooperation between Algeria and Jordan signed in Algiers in 1997 and applied by both parties, provides for exemption from customs duties and taxes having equivalent effect to customs duties, except the goods listed on a negative list appended to the Convention.

Mauritania:

A trade and tariff agreement was signed between Algeria and Mauritania in 1996, stipulating that both parties agree to remove all customs duties and charges having equivalent effect for all products origins Algeria and Mauritania. Ratified by Algeria in September 2005, the agreement has been implemented, the instruments of ratification has not yet exchanged between the diplomatic authorities of both countries.

Morocco:

The agreement provides for the exemption from duties and taxes between the two countries was signed in March 1989, was frozen in 1996.

3 - GREAT ARAB FREE TRADE ZONE "GAFTA"

4 - GENERALIZED SYSTEM OF TRADE PREFERENCES (GSP) WITH U.S. : expired December 31, 2010

Since 2004, the Algerian products are eligible for U.S. GSP is a system by which the United States shall exempt from customs duties for a number of products (more than 3000) from eligible countries to the system.

The list of these products can be found on the website:

http://www.ustr.gov/gsp/general.shtm

In the Harmonized Tariff Schedule of the USA, the letter A in the column Special indicates that the product is eligible, and therefore admitted free of customs duties on the territory of the United States of America.

The entitlement to these benefits is determined by:

direct export: the product must be exported from Algeria to the United States without passing through the territory of any other country, except in transit.

All documents: invoices, bills of lading and other documents ... shall indicate the U.S. as the final destination. -

Rules of origin: an essential condition for the product to be eligible for GSP rule of origin. Thus, the sum of the cost of raw materials from Algeria and direct processing costs (labor ...) must represent at least 35% of the price paid by the importer U.S..

Generalized System of Trade Preferences with the U.S.

THE SGP: BACKGROUND AND OBJECTIVES

In 1964, Algeria, on behalf of the Group of 77 developing countries (DCs), proposed the convening of an international conference to prepare a "new world economic order." A few years later, in order to promote growth in developing countries, industrialized countries agreed to let their markets, free of customs duties, certain products from developing countries. This mechanism is called "Generalized System of Trade Preferences" GSP (1) . The modalities of work of SGP different depending industrialized countries, as developing countries that can benefit from the GSP.

(1) English: GSP (Generalized system of preferences)

ALGERIA NOW ELIGIBLE TO GSP UNITED STATES

The United States decided to grant Algeria to their GSP, both because of the quality of relations between the two countries to take account of economic reforms by Algeria in recent years, including human rights intellectual property. Concretely, this means that the Algerian producers of certain products may be exported to the U.S. without having to pay customs duties in the USA.

YOUR BUSINESS CAN BENEFIT FROM SGP / USA?

Your products can enter the United States duty-free customs in the GSP mechanism, if three main conditions are met:

1 / The letter "A" appears in the last column ("Special" column) of the Harmonized System tariff in the U.S., for the eight-digit code corresponding to your products. The harmonized system of USA can be found on the Internet (website: www.ustic.goy / tata / hts).

2 / For your products meet the condition above, the total "value added Algeria + cost of raw materials of Algerian origin" represents more than 35% of the price paid by U.S. importers, excluding delivery costs in the USA.

3 / The products satisfying the two conditions above must be exported directly to the U.S. without transformation, modification or packaging in a third country (single transit through third countries is, however, allowed).

THE SGP / USA: A SIMPLE MECHANISM

GSP mechanism / USA is managed by the U.S. Customs. Its implementation is simple. If your products meet the conditions above, just in the document for U.S. Customs, to include the letter "A" before the eight-digit harmonized system for your products (The only exception handmade textiles woven by hand to which a seal of authenticity is required).

MECHANISM SGP / USA: A MECHANISM OF EMERGENCY

The lowering of customs duties granted by the USA as part of free trade agreements cover all of the Harmonized System. Instead, as mentioned above, the SGP / USA only applies to a limited number of products. Moreover, the SGP / USA can be questioned, especially if, for a type of product allowed the U.S. duty-free GSP imports into the U.S. from a given country accounted for more than half of total imports (all countries) of this product in the U.S., or more than a certain amount of imports ($ 120 million in 2005).

LEADING SECTORS FOR U.S. EXPORT AND INVESTMENT

OIL AND GAS – HYDROCARBONS

- Since the early 1970s this key industrial sector has heavily dominated the economy and placed the country among the top world producers in both products.

- Algeria is still vastly under-explored among producing countries generally. The potential for further exploration and development is sizable.

- State-owned Sonatrach plans to invest over $32.4 billion between 2006 and 2010. Around two-thirds of this investment ($21 billion) will go to upstream activities split between gas and oil; midstream and pipelines are slated for $6.4 billion; and $5 billion for downstream investment.

- Recent amendments to the hydrocarbon law mandate Sonatrach's required 51 percent shareholder position in upstream and oil/gas transportation projects. While we are waiting for detailed regulations from the government of Algeria, it appears that foreign investors will now be obligated to split taxes, royalties and transport fees for these types of projects with Sonatrach. Most downstream projects remain open to foreign-majority participation.

Background: Algeria's hydrocarbons sector is relatively young, with oil first commercially extracted in 1956 and natural gas in 1961. Exploration density is very low so far, with only eight to nine exploration wells per 10,000 sq km, while the international average is 100. The potential for further exploration and development is great, creating opportunities not only for foreign players but also for Algeria's own increasingly world-class oil and gas industry. Foreign involvement in the sector has grown rapidly. In 1995, just 2 percent of Algeria's crude oil was produced under production-sharing contracts. This rose to 25 percent in 2001 and 51 percent in 2004.

Oil: Algeria has an estimated 11.8 billion barrels of proven oil reserves. With recent oil discoveries and plans for more exploration, proven oil reserve estimates could climb upwards in coming years. Algeria's oil production capacity is likely to rise in the coming years, as the country plans to increase investments in exploration and development efforts. Algeria's current production is 1.5 million b/d of crude oil in 2006. The goal is to increase production to 2.0 million b/d by 2010. Over the last few years, there have been significant new oil and gas discoveries, largely by foreign companies and more recently by Sonatach, the Algerian parastatal. Under the new hydrocarbon legislation, foreign companies can have 100 percent ownership of downstream projects, with the exception of refining. Refining and pipeline projects require at least 51 percent Sonatrach participation.

A system of international tenders was adopted in 2002, with six licensing rounds through April 2005, allocating over 30 blocks. We expect a seventh round of block licensing by mid-2007.

Enhanced Oil Recovery investments, EOR, is a rapidely developing subsector with strong potential for U.S. technology. Very successful projects were awarded to U.S. firms to provide advanced EOR services and boost production in Hassi Messaoud and Rhourde El Baguel, Algeria's second largest site of proven oil reserves.

NATURAL GAS: Algeria's proven natural gas reserves are around 4.5 trillion cubic meters, though total recoverable reserves could be up to 75 percent higher. The largest field is Hassi R'Mel. Other significant reserves exist at Rhourde Nouss basin, In Amenas, In Salah and the Reggane Basin. Gas extraction has grown considerably in the last decade, from 115 billion cubic meters in 1995 to a record 144 billion cubic meters in 2004. Around three-quarters of Algeria's gas is exported (partly by pipeline, partly as LNG). The primary market is the European Union, especially France and Italy, but the U.S. is rapidly gaining importance.

Liquid Natural Gas: Algeria is the second-largest exporter of LNG behind Indonesia, with around 17 percent of the world's total LNG exports. Sonatrach exports almost 12 percent of U.S. LNG imports and is the U.S. second-largest source of LNG behind Trinidad and Tobago. Algeria's largest LNG export terminal is the Arzew facility (western coastal area of Algeria).

Pipeline: There are two existing natural gas export pipeline connections between Algeria and Europe. One is the 670-mile TransMediterranean (Transmed, also called Enrico Mattei) running from Hassi R'Mel to Italy via Tunisia and Sicily. The second is the Maghreb-Europe Gas line (the MEG) from Hassi R'Mel to Cordoba, Spain. The 1,000 mile, 820-Mmcf/d line operated by an international consortium, led by Spain's Enagas, Morocco's SNPP, and Sonatrach, ties into the Spanish and Portuguese gas transmission networks. In addition to the two existing Natural Gas pipelines, three main projects are underway to increase natural gas exports form Algeria mainly to Western Europe:

MEDGAZ : In July 2001, a multinational consortium led by Spain's Cepsa and Algeria's Sonatrach agreed to build a new natural gas pipeline linking Algeria and Europe. The 120-mile Medgaz will link Beni Saf, Algeria to Almeria, Spain with a possible extension to France. In September 2002, the consortium completed a study for the line's feasibility. The $ 1.3 billion Medgaz project, which should be completed by 2008 or 2009, will have an initial capacity of 390 Mmcf/d, increasing to a maximum of 1.55 Bcf/d.

GALSI : In 2002, Sonatrach signed a deal with Italy's Enel and Germany's Wintershall to form Galsi, a consortium to build a natural gas pipeline from Algeria to Italy. Current plans call for an offshore pipeline from Hassi R'mel to El Kala (close to Tunisia) and an underwater section to Cagliari, Sardinia. This is to be followed by an on-shore section to Olbia, Sardinia and a final offshore pipeline to C.D. Pescaia, Italy. Galsi estimates initial capacity of the 910-mile line at 770-990 Mmc/d. The $2-billion project could come on-stream by 2009.

NIGEL : Sonatrach and NNPC, the Nigerian state oil company, formed the Trans-Saharan Natural Gas Consortium (NIGEL), in 2002. The NIGEL consortium plans to construct a 4,550-mile natural gas pipeline from Warri, Nigeria to Hassi R'Mel, via Niger. The NIGEL pipeline would utilize the proposed Medgaz and existing Transmed pipeline to carry Nigerian gas to European markets. The Nigerian and Algerian governments have sought financial assistance for this $7 billion project from the World Bank and the New Economic Program for Africa's Development (NEPAD). Both governments expressed their continued commitment to the project, promising concrete action by the end of 2006 or mid-2007.

Downstream: Naftec, a subsidiary of Sonatrach, operates Algeria's crude oil refineries. The country has four refineries, with combined capacity of 450,000 bbl/d, supplying most of the country's refined oil products needs. Although Algeria has a substantial petrochemical and fertilizer industry, low capacity utilization rates mean continued reliance on imports. There are plans to expand refining considerably, since it is underdeveloped relative to extraction.

Coastal terminals: For the export of crude oil, refined products such as liquefied petroleum gas, (LPG) and liquid natural gas, (LNG) there are facilities located at Arzew (Algeria's largest crude oil export port), Skikda (Algeria's second largest crude oil export port), Algiers, Annaba, Oran and Bejaia. Arzew handles about 40 percent of Algeria's total hydrocarbon exports, including all of its LNG, LPG and oil condensate exports. The Algerian government has ambitious plans for the expansion of the Arzew port area, including the construction of a petrochemicals complex, a condensate refinery, and a desalination plant.

Recent policy changes: Energy Minister Chakib Khelil has stated that his goal is to double the number of companies operating in Algeria in the next 3 to 4 years, restructure the domestic oil industry, and establish new regulatory bodies independent of the Ministry of Energy & Mines. In late 2001 President Bouteflika introduced a hydrocarbons reform bill which was rejected by industry partners. The Algerian government re-introduced the hydrocarbons bill in 2004 producing consensus with the dominant labor union, UGTA. In February 2005, the Council of Ministers approved the bill, followed by parliamentary approval in March. The law was to be an important and concrete step towards Algeria's goal of increasing crude oil production. However, implementing legislation has never emerged. In July 2006, the president amended the 2005 law to return Sonatrach to its dominant role in the hydrocarbons landscape by mandating it hold 51 percent of any upstream or pipeline contract with foreign investors.

Sonatrach investment programs: $1.3 billion in 2005 (upstream: $780 million, 32 wells drilled, eight new discoveries and 18 percent growth over 2004; midstream: $260 million, and downstream: $260 million). Sonatrach's investment program drastically increased to $8.6 billion in 2006 (upstream: $5.1 billion, midstream: $1.9 billion, and downstream: $1.3 billion). For 2006-2010, Sonatrach is planning to invest over $32.4 billion (around two-thirds of this, $21 billion, will go to upstream activities split roughly half for gas and half for oil; $6.4 billion for midstream and pipelines; and $5 billion for downstream.) Sonatrach, with its foreign partners, will invest around $600 million per year in exploration alone.

BEST PRODUCTS/SERVICES

Sub-sector products & services include:

- Drilling equipment
- Catering services
- Temporary structures

OPPORTUNITIES

Opportunities for U.S. investment include:

- Enhanced Oil Recovery investments: EOR is a rapidly developing sub-sector with strong potential for U.S. technology.
- A seventh round of exploration and development block licensing expected to occur by early 2007.
- The Algerian government's ambitious plans for the expansion of the Arzew port area, including the construction of a petrochemicals complex, a condensate refinery, and a desalination plant.

RESOURCES

- For upcoming industry-specific trade shows and expositions, please visit www.worldoil.com
- Ministry of Energy website: www.mem-**algeria**.org
- Sonatrach website: www.**sonatrach**-dz.com
- Upcoming events in Algeria include:
    - The second Conference and Exhibition on Renewable Energy (CEER 2007) to be held in Algiers on June 18-20 2007 (http://www.ceer-algeria.com), and
    - The 1st International Conference and Exhibition on Mining in Algeria (CIRMA 1) also to be held in Algiers on 2-4 December 2007.

BANKING AND FINANCIAL SERVICES

- Banking modernization and reform programs include:
- Recapitalizing state-owned banks and cleaning out their portfolios
- Holding inter-bank workshops to establish new services (new product lines, international payment cards, data transmission networks, electronic banking)
- Increased focus on client needs, particularly households and individuals, developing mortgage and consumer loans and capital lease loans.
- There are more than 33 different banks and financial institutions, with the private sector currently representing 5 to 6 percent of the market and growing steadily.
- The acceleration of banking reforms will provide opportunities for private banks with the required expertise and know-how to promote new products and services and contribute to the development and deepening of the financial markets.
- Foreign banks are expected to play a major role in the modernization of the banking system, but the lack of branch networking capabilities poses a challenge.
- We expect an increase of more diversified foreign direct investment inflows as a result of political and economic stability in Algeria as well as Algeria's eventual accession to the WTO.

- The government has begun the privatization of three major state-owned banks. CPA is the first bank to be privatized; we expect the RFP to be launched in the upcoming weeks.

Background:

Before the early 1990's, the Algerian banking system operated as a privileged instrument of state-owned companies and central planning authorities. Banking activity centered exclusively on aiding the smooth functioning of state-owned enterprises, which at the time were the main source of economic growth. Following the enactment of Law 86/12, governing banking and credit, and especially after the 1990 Currency and Credit Law, however, Algerian banking began to undergo significant reforms. With this law, the Bank of Algeria became the country's official monetary authority, and a new banking and financial system was established to go along with the deregulated economy. Banks and financial institutions can now offer a complete range of services to domestic and foreign clients.

The banking sector consists of six state-owned banks which account for 95 percent of the banking sector's deposits and 10 foreign banks account for less than 6 percent of all deposits. Of the public banks, three have been selected for privatization. The first of which, Credit Populaire d'Algerie (CPA bank) is expected to be sold by mid-2007. The Local Development Bank (BDL) and the National Bank of Algeria (BNA) are scheduled to undergo the privatization process in 2007 and 2008 respectively.

The branches of major foreign banks such as Citibank, Société Generale, the Arab Banking Corporation, BNP-Paribas etc., that came to Algeria originally to accompany foreign investment gradually opened up the Algerian market. They are still very far, however, from meeting all the country's banking needs. There are a few private Algerian banks but their minimum capital requirements, set by Bank of Algeria regulations more than ten years ago, remain inadequate to provide significant financing to the economy.

Market influence: The continued high price of petroleum in the international marketplace means Algeria will continue to be flush with dollars for the foreseeable future. Algeria's foreign exchange reserves are near $80 billion and a government-controlled stabilization fund holds an additional $40 billion. The inflow of dollars has created a situation of excess liquidity on the market which the government has dealt with so far by paying down its external debt and controlling dollars on the market via exchange controls such as import and export license restrictions and revenue exchange requirements (exporters outside of hydrocarbons may only retain 50 percent of earnings in dollars and must receive the other 50 percent in Algerian dinars; 100 percent of hydrocarbon revenue is remitted to the central bank and Sonatrach's share is credited to its accounts 100 percent in dinars at the Central Bank set exchange rate).

Future spending on large government infrastructure projects could lead to inflation locally. The government could introduce a free float of the currency causing an appreciation of the exchange rate, increase the reserve requirements in the banks, and/or introduce new financial instruments carrying higher interest rates, to absorb dinars in the market. So far, the government has not started any of these initiatives, but a U.S. Treasury Department technical team is working with the Algerian Finance Ministry and the Central Bank on policy options.

Algeria's generally small and ill-financed private sector needs better access to credit. The lack of credit history in Algeria (since it has been a cash-based society for so long) presents a unique challenge to mid-level banking officials and lending officers who have no history to base risk assessments on and very little, if any, training in portfolio diversification and risk management.

The long-time practice of the government using public banks to finance failing state-owned enterprises was abolished only recently in the 2005 budget when a line item was established to provide subsidies to these SOEs instead of continuing to tap on public banks for mandatory financing and continuing the trend of non-performing loans.

Algeria's opening of its markets to international banks for corporate banking was a good start and the 2006 opening for new commercial banking possibilities is a positive continuing trend of banking liberalization. However, the 2002 executive decree requiring state-owned enterprises to borrow only from public banks must be rescinded, not only for the health of public banks but to accord with WTO national treatment requirements.

Opportunities

- Private banking institutions will play an increasing role in extending credit and advisory services for local businesses, especially in retail banking, insurance and leasing.
- The acceleration of banking reforms will provide opportunities for private banks with the required expertise and know-how to promote new products and services and contribute to the development and deepening of the financial markets.

Resources

For additional information on the banking sector, please visit the following websites:
Banque d'Algerie: www.bank-of-algeria.dz
Ministry of Finance: www.finances-algeria.org
International Monetary Fund: www.imf.org

HOUSING AND CONSTRUCTION

- The government is struggling to meet the enormous demand for real estate and housing units. The Algerian government dominates the country's housing market with its national housing programs.
- The government wants no less than one million housing units built by 2009, complete with electricity, water supply, roads and hospitals. This is unlikely to end the shortage as the construction industry also lacks the capacity to implement the program in the first place.
- The actual need for housing is estimated to range between 250,000 and 300,000 units per year, as 250,000 new households are entering the market each year. Analysts widely agree that the Algerian construction sector does not have the capacity to deliver this number of units, as there are not enough raw materials locally available.
- The state has a 60-percent market share in the sector's financing, although mostly executed by private architects, engineers and contractors. With the one million housing unit programs, this share is expected to increase up to 75 percent by 2008/2009.
- The narrow coastal strip is congested, particularly around large cities. It is estimated that 80 percent of the country's population live on five percent of its surface. To remedy this situation, the government is planning on launching the construction and/or expansion of 10 new cities countrywide.
- Local construction is still below international standards. The industry learned this the hard way during the May 2003 earthquake. U.S. expertise and construction techniques can address this very serious problem. Analysts point out the urgent need for specialists in certain fields, with environmental issues being increasingly of concern for local construction entrepreneurs.

Background:

Construction is one of the most important sectors in the economy, representing about 8.5 percent of total added value. Housing remains the most essential segment for the Algerian construction sector. The political crisis of the 1990's saw the industry declining as government spending shifted to security-related programs. As migration to major cities continued through the decade, ramshackle private dwellings were constructed on the out skirts of urban areas.

The share of state-owned companies in the sector has recently declined mainly due to weak commercial performance and archaic management practices. Yet according to state statistics, they still represent almost a third of the sector's activity.

Roughly 130,000 housing units are built yearly. Of these, 30,000 to 40,000 are privately constructed. In addition to the need for new houses, there is also strong demand for the rehabilitation of older housing units (an estimated two million housing units date from the colonial era). Independent experts estimate the deficit to total about two million housing units at least. According to analysts, the gap is expected to rise to three million housing units over the next 15 years.

Government efforts to improve the housing situation are largely jeopardized by the archaic and inefficient bureaucracy. Despite the absence of modern urban planning, real estate in Algeria is registered. According to the Ministry of Housing 90 to 95 percent of real estate property in the capital is registered with the authorities.

Construction Specialization: There are over 22,000 registered contractors, of which an overwhelming majority are small-scale enterprises. The sector offers little specialization, which has decreased its capacity to respond to the market needs, such as after the 2003 Boumerdes earthquake.

Quality control: Local construction is still below international standards. The industry learned this the hard way when, as a result of the May 2003 earthquake, hundreds of buildings collapsed and countless more were damaged. Although questionable quality control and regulation are problems, the industry suffers especially from the lack of qualified construction workers.

Financing: The deficiencies of the national banking sector constitute a hurdle for the industry. The government has increased its efforts to find investors abroad to participate in huge construction projects, especially from the capital-rich Gulf. Help is needed; senior government officials have expressed hope that multinational construction firms will bridge the capacity gap.

Too low price per square meter: During 2005, tenders for construction projects to be built in 2007 and 2008 were issued, suited to international suppliers, but at low offering prices. Cost average stands at $218 per square meter, and neared $254 in spring 2005. The price is expected to soon top $300, but industry insiders say that the State will probably need to offer at least $325 to attract more Chinese and Turkish contracting firms. It seems unlikely that companies from other countries will take a significant part in the program. The only attractive selling point for foreign firms is quick payment from the Algerian government.

Mega Projects: Until recently, the mega-projects of the sector relied on the large-scale investments made by the country's oil and gas industries. But with large multinational suppliers present – including U.S., French, Italian, Japanese and Canadian companies – this segment will also prove to be highly competitive. The Algerian construction sector will continue to benefit from infrastructure projects and mega-projects, both for local industry and international suppliers.

Algeria might be the only country where orders far exceed capacity, requiring a massive inflow of foreign construction companies.

Building materials and construction techniques: The growth of construction in Algeria has been followed by a similar increase in demand for building materials. There was a significant increase in the price of cement, amounting to five percent of construction cost. In 2004, domestic consumption reached 12 million tons, up from 10.5 million tons in 2003. This is expected to reach 13 million tons in 2005, and to stabilize at around 15 million tons per year over the next four years.

OPPORTUNITIES

Opportunities for U.S. Investment include:

- Cement and construction materials plants
- Modern building techniques
- Construction and expansion of 10 new cities countrywide
- Urban planning projects and investments

RESOURCES

Ministry of Public Works: www.mtp-dz.com
National Agency for the Development of Investment (ANDI): www.andi.dz

TELECOMMUNICATIONS & INFORMATION TECHNOLOGY

- The Algerian telecom market remains one of the most active sectors in the country, with estimated revenues of $2.5 billion in 2005.
- With penetration rates of only 7.6 percent, 40.3 percent and 1.8 percent in the fixed, mobile and internet markets respectively, there is ample space for growth in all telecom sub-sectors.
- The upcoming privatization of the country's previous monopoly service provider Algerie Telecom, and the recently licensed, second fixed-line telephone operator should further stimulate the telecom market.
- The number of fixed lines is forecast to increase by an average of 18 percent in the next five years, to reach 5.9 million subscribers by the end of 2010. The number of mobile customers is expected to grow by an average of 19.4 percent yearly through the end of 2010, to reach 31.6 million subscribers and a penetration rate of 86 percent.
- Opportunities for U.S. investment and exports include: ***Privatization of Algerie Telecom (AT), privatization of internet provider Djaweb, PC Penetration and Government Program "OUSRATIC" (A PC in every home), Wi-FI/ Wimax Technologies, Voice over IP technologies, and regional call centers.*** For additional information, please see "Opportunities" section below.

Background:

After years of lagging behind other North African countries, the market has seen a remarkable rally since 2001, notably in the mobile sector. All telecom subsectors are now open to some level of competition, with the fixed market under a duopoly status.

Fixed Telephony: Law 200/3 passed in August 2000 split the overwhelmed Ministry of Post and Telecommunications into Algerie Poste and Algerie Telecom and created a Telecom Regulatory Authority (ARPT) that began operations in May 2001. The number of fixed lines owned by the parastatal monopoly Algerie Telecom has been growing at an average of 8.0 percent in the last five years, reaching 3.5 million at the end of 2005.

While Algerie Telecom currently enjoys a monopoly on fixed-line services, in March 2005 a consortium of two Egyptian companies, Egypt Telecom and Orascom Telecom, obtained a second fixed-line license for $65 million that will enable the consortium to build and operate its own fixed-line network. The consortium plans to invest $1 billion in the network over the 15-year duration of the license. It started operations in the three major Algerian cities in the second quarter of 2006, and is expected to acquire a significant market share.

Orascom Telecom, which also has an ISP and a very small aperture terminal (V-SAT) license, has announced that it will deploy an undersea cable connecting Algiers and Marseilles. The project's estimated cost is over $30 million and has been awarded to French telecom supplier Alcatel.

While the fixed-line penetration rate is currently below the regional average, it is catching up, and analysts anticipate added momentum resulting Egyptian players investment in the sector, which should also spur growth in others sectors of the economy, including banking, IT, and the service industry. The number of fixed lines is forecast to increase by an average of 18 percent in the next five years, to reach 5.9 million subscribers by the end of 2010.

Mobile Telephony: The mobile sector has been booming for the last four years since the arrival of foreign competition in 2002 in the form of the Egyptian operator Djezzy and the third operator, Nedjma, a Kuwaiti operator. From 2001 to 2005 the sector grew by an average rate of 247 percent. By the end of 2005 there were 13.7 million mobile subscribers. This dynamic expansion trend should continue in the next five years, albeit at a slower pace, as mobile penetration is still relatively low. The number of mobile customers is expected to grow by an average of 19.4 percent yearly through the end of 2010, to reach 31.6 million subscribers and a penetration rate of 86 percent.

Internet Market: Algeria's internet market is far behind most countries in the region, with an estimated 613,000 internet subscribers and 1.9 million users at the end of 2005, representing a penetration rate of 1.8 percent. The arrival of a competing fixed-line operator should improve the situation with further expansion of the fixed network and reductions in connection fees. The number of internet subscribers is therefore forecast to grow by an average of 20 percent in the next five years to reach 1.5 million and a penetration rate of 4.2 percent.

ADSL services: Launched as late as 2003 in Algeria, ADSL services are relatively limited but now starting to grow in popularity. At the end of 2005, there were 195,000 broadband subscribers in the country, representing 31.8 percent of all Internet connections. Broadband services are forecast to grow significantly in the coming years to reach 1.5 million at the end of 2010, representing 99.4 percent of all internet customers.

OPPORTUNITIES

Opportunities for U.S. investment and exports include:

- ***Privatization of Algerie Telecom (AT):*** AT has 4.9 million active mobile subscribers representing 35.9 percent of the total market. It has 91 offices, almost 30,000 multifunction kiosks, and a backbone network of 10 GBs. Its satellite service, Algerie Telecom Satellite (ATS), has 45 domestic ground stations, three international stations, an INMARSAT station and VSAT Network.

- ***Djaweb,*** an internet provider **owned by AT,** has 7,000 subscribers, 3,000 accesses through private lines and 25,000 customers using ADSL. Algerie Telecom also runs 4,046 internet cafes.

- ***PC Penetration and Government Program "OUSRATIC" (a PC in every home):*** At the end of 2004 there were only 290,000 PCs in Algeria, representing a penetration rate as low as 0.87 percent. To solve this problem, in 2005 the Algerian government launched a campaign with the objective of installing a computer in every home by 2010. The program is called "OUSRATIC".

- ***Wi-FI/ Wimax Technologies:*** This is a virgin sector of Algeria's IT market. There are currently only two known wireless providers in Algeria. Smart Link Communication (SLC) was the first company to deploy WiMAX to provide broadband wireless services in Algeria. SLC's goal is to build a wireless broadband backbone covering the national territory, to develop the metropolitan broadband networks, and to set up an independent new generation telecom infrastructure. On July 25, 2005, SLC launched the first national multi-services network. The deployment of this network makes it possible to develop services based on Broadband Wireless Access (BWA), VoIP, and Virtual Private Network (VPN-IP MPLS). Algeria's tough and mountainous terrain makes it an ideal candidate for wireless connectivity solutions.

- ***VoIP:*** A key element in the government's telecom market liberalization strategy was the liberalization of the VoIP market in 2005 and the allocation of ten 5-year licenses. Six VoIP licenses have been already authorized.

- ***Call Centers:*** Development of call centers in Algeria is still in its infancy; Algeria lags behind Morocco, Tunisia and Egypt, all of which have well developed call center industries. Low labor costs and good French language skills are the main reasons why international clients might outsource operations in Algeria. To date, in Algeria only Algerie Telecom is running a small commercial operation and several private GSM operators are serving their own customers.

RESOURCES

ARPT: www.arpt.dz
Algerie Telecom: www.algerietelecom.dz

INFRASTRUCTURE DEVELOPMENT PROJECT OVERVIEW:

- In a major new initiative, the government of Algeria is investing over $110 billion in infrastructure projects to boost economic growth and address infrastructure problems.

- The focus is on four areas: (a) Improve living conditions for people in general; (b) modernize infrastructure; (c) promote growth in basic economic sectors and (d) modernize of the Algerian administration.

- Major opportunities for U.S. investment and exports include: ***Transport Infrastructure:*** from 2005-2009 Algeria is expected to spend $9.6 billion in large transport infrastructure projects such as railways, ports and airport modernization; ***Public Works*:** $8.2 billion in large public works projects such as the East-West Highway and an upgrade of secondary roadways; ***Water Resources*:** $5.4 billion in large water projects, mainly dams and water treatment facilities; ***Housing and Health:*** $11 billion for housing units and heath projects such as hospitals; ***For the southern region*:** an additional $ 8.5 billion will be dedicated to projects in southern Algeria, including housing, water resources management, irrigation and agricultural development, and the creation of a new city.

- These amounts do not include the regular government-sector investment program budgeted in the ordinary budgets for 2006, 2007, 2008 and 2009, estimated at roughly $6 billion yearly. All together, the government investment programs are expected to amount to over $110 billion.

Background:

From 1991 to 2001 government investment programs almost stopped. The massive rural exodus caused by lack of employment opportunities and terrorist threats worsened the housing, environment and unemployment crisis in and around major cities. The infrastructure, construction and transport sectors are currently undergoing much-needed, substantial changes. It is too early to judge the government's ability to design a sustainable transport network that will able to carry the country's future economic development. The implementation of inter-modal concepts between different means of transport from the very beginning will be crucial. Whether the government and the implementing authorities can meet this challenge remains doubtful. The modernization of infrastructure needs to be followed by consolidation of commercial market structures.

Transport Infrastructure From 2005 to 2009, Algeria is expected to build three new airports; conduct studies and construct an airspace management system for the entire territory; modernize the 1,220-km East-West railway; build subway systems for Algiers and Oran, and tramway systems for major cities; and undertake the electrification of the existing 2,000-km railway, all for a total of roughly $9.6 billion. New roads are already under construction and the modernization of the railway network is in full swing. Maritime transport is booming as well. Overall, transportation has been opened to the private sector.

The geography of Algeria creates enormous challenges for the country's transport sector. Most transport of goods and people take place along the narrow northern coast. The high plateaus are relatively easy to connect with the East-West highway and rail connections. Establishing connections to the vast desert areas in the south and its integration into the national transport system will be challenging. The Algerian government has made transport a top priority within the $110 billion investment budget. The axis Bordj Bou Arreridj-Chlef will be the starting phase of the huge East-West Highway project. This axis accounts for about two thirds of the domestic road traffic. Completion of this project is expected in 2009. Connections to coastal roads and to the high plateaus will be added over the next few years.

For ***maritime transport***, Algeria has a 1,200-km maritime coastline. Over the past years, maritime traffic has increased by an annual growth rate of 20 to 30 percent, surprising local authorities and overwhelming existing capacities. The Port of Algiers accounts for 60 percentof Algeria's port traffic, followed by Bejaia, Oran and Annaba. One-quarter of this traffic is domestic, and another quarter is trade just with France. Located in the city center of Algiers, the port essentially has not been upgraded since the 19th century. Because of this, depending on their size, vessels often wait three to four days before they can enter the port.

Rail: Railways remain a state monopoly. The 4,200-km network rail system is in bad shape and its basic configuration dates from colonial times. The majority of the railways is not electric and only single track. The trains themselves run slowly, between 60 and 80 km/h.

The Algerian railway company (SNTF) has been in decline. The overall efficiency of its operations is very low, generating 80 percent of its passenger revenues from traffic around the greater Algiers. The bulk of its cargo revenues are from the country's mining, oil and gas sectors.

Beyond revenues, its market share is minimal, as road transport often proves more efficient. The government has reacted to this and allocated $7.4 billion to the railways under the five-year public spending program.

Public Works: Algeria is expected to build a 1,216-km East-West highway to connect the Tunisian border to Morocco, modernize and upgrade existing 6,000-km road grid, and develop three secondary but important highways. The overall cost for these projects is estimated at $8.2 billion, though this figure is recently reported to have increased to $11 billion.

Water Resources: Algeria plans to build eight dams, interconnect eight existing dams with considerable and sophisticated water transfer systems, build nine waste water treatment plants, and rehabilitate 11 existing large wastewater treatment plants all over the country. The overall amount for these projects is estimated at $5.4 billion.

Housing and Health: The government announced plans to build one million housing units, 17 major hospitals, connect an additional one million houses with natural gas and install electricity to 400,000 existing homes. The government estimates this project will cost around $11 billion.

For the southern region: The government plans an addition $1 billion for a housing program/construction projects, $600 million to improve water resources management and distribution, $800 million to connect houses to electrical power and natural gas grids, $700 million to modernize and expand irrigation systems for agricultural development, $400 million for the development of the new city of Boughezoul, and about $ 3.5 billion for the high-plateau highway project. All told, $8.5 billion is planned for southern Algeria projects.

Estimated magnitude of business opportunities: The most promising prospects for U.S. investments and exports are in transport equipment and design, infrastructure, water resources and housing/hospital construction for which planned spending is expected to reach $42.7 billion. According to analysts, domestic capacities will only be able to absorb at most 20 percent of these outlays. This leaves the potential for close to $35 billion for international companies. Main international suppliers and anticipated competition to U.S. firms in transport, infrastructures, wastewater treatment, housing and hospital construction projects comes from France, Italy, Germany, China, Japan, Canada, Turkey and Egypt.

Opportunities

Major opportunities for U.S. investment and exports include:

- ***Transport Infrastructure:*** From 2005-2009 Algeria is expected to spend $9.6 billion in large transport infrastructure projects such as railways, ports and airport modernization;
- ***Public Works:*** $8.2 billion in large public works projects such as the East-West Highway and an upgrade of secondary roadways;
- ***Water Resources:*** $5.4 billion in large water projects, mainly dams and water treatment facilities;
- ***Housing and Health:*** $11 billion for housing units and heath projects such as hospitals;
- ***For the southern region:*** An additional $ 8.5 billion will be dedicated to projects in southern Algeria, including housing, water resources management, irrigation and agricultural development, and the creation of a new city.

Resources

For further information on these projects please check out the following websites:
Ministry of Public Works: www.mtp-dz.com
Ministry of Finance: www.finances-algeria.org

HEALTHCARE

- The healthcare sector is a buoyant market for foreign investors. The demand for pharmaceuticals and medical equipment is considerable and depends largely on imported goods.
- The living standard of the population is improving slowly but there has been an increased incidence in reporting of hypertension, respiratory and cardiovascular diseases, and allergies.
- The pharmaceutical sector is developing, and the market is very competitive. Government favoritism for generics and other measures have caused problems for international pharmaceutical companies operating in Algeria.
- Total pharmaceutical imports to Algeria reached $1 billion by the end of 2005 compared to $967 million in 2004. Officially, Algeria produces just 30 percent of its needs in pharmaceutical products, one of Algeria's largest import categories.
- The medical equipment market is estimated at about $750 million for 2005 with very little local production. The market relies entirely on imports and is open to U.S companies because of the advanced technology and the associated training.
- U.S. products have an advantage over European products in the medical sector due to their high quality and globally recognized reputations in the Algerian market. Moreover, demand for these products is increasing due to the strength of the value of the Euro over the dollar.
- Opportunities for U.S. exports to Algeria's medical equipment and services markets are substantial and cut across the entire spectrum of medical activities.
- Strongest opportunities for U.S. companies include: ***biotechnology, high-tech, anti-cancer and cardiovascular drugs, medical equipment, disposable products, advanced medical and surgical equipment, radiology, pathology, optical devices, vaccines, and software for hospital management and internal networks.*** For additional information, please see "Opportunities" section below.

Background:

Algeria has an active healthcare sector that employed 196,000 people in 2002, including 30,000 doctors. There are 185 hospitals, 32 specialized centers and 13 university hospital centers with a estimated total of 54,000 beds. The health care system's infrastructure is not very well developed. Algeria represents a potential important market for medical equipment. Most equipment in public hospitals was broadly upgraded in the 1980s but not since. The breakdown rate of diagnostic equipment is estimated at 32 percent, and 24 percent for the imagery, sterilization and disinfection equipment. Private hospitals are better equipped than public hospitals.

Estimates indicate that up to 95 percent of the medical equipment is imported. Most equipment comes from Germany, Italy, the UK, the U.S. and Japan.

The sector is developing rapidly due to the recent decree issued by the government that allows private and public investment, either national or foreign, in the establishment of private hospitals. Currently there are 91 private clinics in operation and 125 clinics are in the works. Plans for 45 additional projects are being studied. Imports of medical equipment are expected to increase.

OPPORTUNITIES

Opportunities for U.S. companies include:

- ***Biotechnology, high-tech, anti-cancer and cardiovascular drugs:*** U.S. products have an advantage over European products in pharmaceuticals. Moreover, any new leading American drug that is not yet manufactured in Europe is well received in Algeria. Competition from generics has been a major problem.

- ***Medical equipment:*** Private sector demand for sophisticated medical equipment is growing. With a population of over 32 million inhabitants, reduced local production, hospital establishments under renovation, and the development of the private hospital sector, Algeria represents an important market for medical equipment, a market 95 percent dominated by imports.

- ***Most desired products***: Disposable products, advanced medical and surgical equipment, radiology, pathology, optical devices, vaccines, and software for hospital management and internal networks.

- Hospital Reform and transformation of the heath care sector in Algeria with the new Hospital Reform policy and the on going hospital projects of the Ministry of Health will also bring export opportunities.

RESOURCES

Healthcare sector links: www.ands.dz

POWER GENERATION

- In 2005, installed capacity for power generation was 6732 megawatts, around 800 megawatts more than in late 2002. Ninety-three percent of the power generation plants are gas-fired. The rest are hydroelectric and diesel fired plants.

- Recent years have seen the start of sector reform. A special law on electricity and gas distribution was passed in 2002. This provided for abolition of Sonelgaz's legal monopoly over power production and the establishment of an independent regulatory authority.

- Total installed capacity for power generation is expected to total 10,250 megawatts by the end of 2010. This is a 52 percent increase from 2004. This capacity is expected to further increase to 12,000 megawatts by 2012 .

- Sonelgaz expects investments in the power sector in 2005-2009 to total $7.1 billion, of which $2.7 billion is for power generation, $2 billion to modernize, expand and maintain the grid and around $2.4 billion for the distribution system.

- Opportunities for U.S. investment include p***ower distribution, power generation – security reserves, and power generation – European export*** (please see opportunities below for additional information).

Background:

Established is 1969, Sonelgaz operates a virtual monopoly on Algeria's gas energy sector. Sonelgaz has been responsible for power generation, all aspects of national grid (including investment, maintenance and operation) and low-voltage distribution of electricity. It also runs gas distribution, though high-pressure gas transport is Sonatrach's domain.

Like the hydrocarbons industry, Algeria's power industry faces the challenge of ensuring the necessary growth of production to meet the developing economy's fast-increasing needs. To do so, it must invest heavily, partly by attracting foreign investment.

In recent years there has been some initial sector reform. A special law on electricity and gas distribution was passed in 2002 that abolished Sonelgaz's legal monopoly over power production, established an independent regulatory authority, and provided for an eventual transition to a European-style of regulated third-party access in the power sector. Unsurprisingly, progress has been somewhat slower than originally envisaged. The law talked of a 30 percent market opening within three years of implementation, but more recent timetables schedule the first stage of market opening – a system of bilateral contracts between Independent Power Production (IPP) – for 2007. There are no concrete plans for the privatization of Sonelgaz itself, though the 2002 law provides for the possibility of opening its capital. Most likely, Sonelgaz Group will remain the majority shareholder in generation JVs.

Total installed capacity for power generation is expected to reach 10,250 megawatts by the end of 2010. This is a 52 percent rise from 2004. This capacity is expected to increase further more by 2010, as the installed capacity will total 12,000 megawatts. This means excellent opportunities for foreign contractors and investors. The capacity coming online in 2005, for example, included a 300 megawatt gas-fired plant in F'krina, and a larger, combined-cycle 800 megawatt facility in Skikda, a 500 megawatt plant in Berrouaghia as well as the 1,200 megawatt gas-fired Hadjret Ennous power plant in Cherchell.

The main additional power generation plants to be brought online by 2010/2012: Koudiet Edraouch (1200 MGW) east of the country, Tiaret (100 MGW) west of the country, Terga (600 MGW) west of the country, and M'Sila (200 MGW) center-east of the country.

OPPORTUNITIES

Opportunities for U.S. investment include:

- ***Power distribution:*** Power distribution is divided between four regional units which will move from autonomy to full subsidiary where the system operator will be given increased autonomy. Sonelgaz plans to open equity for private investment when a variety of players, possibly including private firms, will be invited to purchase shares of 10 percent each with Sonelgaz' own share reduced to just 10 percent by late 2008.

- ***Power generation – security reserves:*** Despite interconnection of all power generation plants north of the country, the current security reserve level is considered to be low -- less than 10 percent. The Algerian government wants to increase the security reserve level to 20 percent, knowing that the annual domestic electricity demand increases 8 percent per year.

- ***Power generation – European export:*** Because Algerian domestic gas prices are far lower than international prices, Algeria already sells some surplus power to its neighbors and has wider electrical power-export ambitions. A project of underwater lines for 3000 megawatts will run alongside the planned gas pipelines to Spain and Italy, connecting Algeria to European power systems. This is an excellent opportunity for the U.S. power generation industry to generate electrical power from gas-fired plants in Algeria, export, and market electricity in the rapidly expanding European market.

RESOURCES

Ministry of Mines and Energy: www.mem-algeria.org
Sonatrach: www.sonatrach-dz.com

TOURISM

- Algeria has a potential to develop its tourism sector. The country offers a broad variety of landscapes: sea, mountains, high plateau, desert, dunes, rock mountains, oases, rich historical and cultural heritage with Phoenician, Roman, Arab and Ottoman vestiges.

- Algeria lacks sufficient hotels and resorts meeting international standards, and requires further development in internal transportation, tourist attractions and activities.

- Algeria earned just $115 million in tourism receipts in 2005, compared to $4 billion in tourism income enjoyed by its neighbors Tunisia and Morocco.

- According to the Ministry of Tourism, Algeria hosted 1,443,000 tourists in 2005, an increase of 15 percent compared to 2004.

- Opportunities for U.S. companies include: ***Tourism projects, Tourism Expansion Zones (ZETs) for infrastructure development and investment incentives, hotels and resort areas, restaurants, tour organization and leisure activity guides.*** For additional information, please see "Opportunities" section below.

Background:

The following statistics provide a snapshot of the Algerian tourism sector:

- 67 percent of foreign tourists are from Europe, mainly France.
- 70 percent of Algeria's hotels are privately owned.
- Foreign investment:
  - Accor Group with one Sofitel and one Mercure
  - Sheraton: one in Algiers and one in Oran.
  - Hilton Hotel in Algiers
- Algeria has 81 000 tourist beds, whereas in Morocco there are 220,000 and in Tunisia 222,000.
- Accor, the French chain, has signed a joint-venture agreement between Accor and the private Algerian Group Mehri, owned by billionaire Djilali Mehri. Accor and Mehri each hold half of the joint venture which was launched with an initial capital of $13 million since 1992.

After a market study carried out by the Accor group revealed that Algerian cities critically lacked accommodation, it concluded that Algeria needed around 36 mid-market (three-star) hotels to satisfy accommodation demand. The group plans to begin construction of the first series of Ibis and Novotel hotels in Algeria's larger cities (Algiers, Oran, Annaba, Constantine) starting in 2007.

The total investment should reach $21 million per hotel. With this, Accor moved into a solid position in the hotel sector as the country opens to tourism and foreign investment. Algerians hope that such ambitious projects will send a positive signal to tourism developers worldwide.

PERSPECTIVE BY 2013:

- Algeria intends to attract 3 million tourists by 2013.
- Create 230,000 jobs.
- Reach 187,000 bed capacity.
- Develop deep Sahara tourism.
- Develop sports tourism

OPPORTUNITIES

OPPORTUNITIES FOR U.S. COMPANIES INCLUDE:

- ***Tourism projects:*** The Algerian government has set up a Tourism Development Program identifying 174 **Tourism Expansion Zones (ZETs) for infrastructure development and investment incentives**. Foreign companies can develop projects in these zones from the sunny coastline of Kabylia to Algiers and Oran to Jijel and Annaba, to the ski resorts in the interior. The ZET are the bases from which the government hopes the sector will grow.

- ***Hotels:*** The government has also launched a privatization program to privatize hotels via a tendering process that should generate attractive investment opportunities.

- With the $110-billion public spending plan for the 2005-2009, **$42 million has been allocated to improve the tourism sector, mainly the ZET.**

- U.S companies have opportunities in all aspects of the tourism business, from hotels and restaurants to tour organization and guide and leisure activities.

RESOURCES

Ministry of Tourism: www.mta.gov.dz
Ministry of Participation and the Promotion of Investments: www.mppi.dz

AGRICULTURAL SECTOR

Agriculture Environment

Agriculture represents an average of 9.6 percent of Algeria's GDP (1997-2004) and provides a means of livelihood for at least 20 percent of the Algerian population. The country's arable land or useful agricultural land is about 8 million hectares, which is about 3 percent of its total area (238 million hectares). Only 7 percent of this arable land is irrigated. Agriculture is a rainfall-dependent sector and suffered from drought for several consecutive years. However, agricultural production has been increasing steadily since 2000, with an 8 percent growth in 2005. This is mainly due to the launch of an ambitious plan of farmland conversion as part of the new agriculture development program (PNDA). In order to better manage occasions of drought, reduce the food imports bill, and improve food safety, the Ministry of Agriculture began an ambitious plan of agriculture development (PNDA) in 2000 to launch the sector again. The main objectives of this program consist of:

- Grains intensification and farmland conversion; grain production focused in the most productive regions (eastern and central plains with rainfall between 450 mm-800 mm. More traditional dry land crops (vineyards, fruit trees) are being encouraged for the regions that receive less rainfall such as the western regions, the steppe and the Sahara.
- Development, valorization, commercialization and storage as well as packaging and export of the agricultural productions.
- Improvement of irrigation in agriculture and reforestation
- Improvement of Breeding (Dairy cattle, Apiculture, Poultry)
- Development and protection of animal and plant genetics.
- Grant land for exploitation

The main agricultural products Algeria exports are: dates, grapes and wine, olives and olive oil as well as vegetables.

Algeria relies on imports to meet some food needs. Algeria imported about $3.8 billion of foodstuffs in 2005, of which 39 percent were cereals and 20 percent were dairy products, 7 percent sugar and confectionaries, and 6 percent meat. Imported foodstuffs represent about 18 percent of 2005 total imports and ranked third behind equipment goods and semi-finished goods for industry.

The European Union continues to be Algeria's major trading partner. About 55 percent of its total imports come from European countries, France in particular (40 percent), Germany (16 percent), Italy (14 percent), and other EU countries (30 percent). About 54 percent of Algerian exports go to the EU: Italy (29 percent), France (19 percent), Spain (21 percent) and (31 percent) to the rest of the EU.
Competition from the EU is intense due to its geographical advantage. Proximity to Europe makes transit from Europe necessary, especially with no direct shipping lines with the U.S. Prices offered to Algeria by European exporters are often lower than U.S. goods because of the subsidies. However, Algeria remains a potential market for U.S. products. The total U.S. two-way trade exchange with Algeria reached $11 billion in 2005, making the U.S. Algeria's largest overall trading partner and third largest supplier for 2005 behind France and Italy. Total Algerian 2005 CY imports from the U.S. reached $1.3 billion, of which $271 million were agricultural products. (Source: Algerian Customs).

U.S. market share for foodstuffs constitutes roughly 7.5 percent. Major agricultural products imported from the United States are bulk commodities, including corn (57 percent), oils (5 percent), soybean meals (8 percent), and wheat (16 percent). U.S. CY imports of Algerian agricultural products are minimal but increasing; $830,000 in 2004 and $929,000 in 2005. The average for five-year period (2001-2005) reached $475,000.

MARKET STRUCTURE AND TRENDS

In the field of agribusiness, since privatization in 1997 local private investment has risen sharply and taken a substantial share of the market. Most of the agricultural imports are received by the private sector.

Private processors continue to grow and many processing plants appeared to offer products with lower prices by importing raw material and processing it locally. This is especially evident in milling, dairy processing, biscuit, fats and soybean products industry, as well as vegetable oil refinery, snacks and beverage processing.

Since the economy was liberalized, consumers have become more accustomed to seeing imported products and semi-processed products sold in stores and small private supermarkets. These opened later after the closing of the former state-owned distribution chain in 1996. Consumers can now find bulk, packaged, and high value products, both local and imported, in these rapidly growing supermarkets. The super market industry is still in its infancy, however, and needs further development.

BEST PROSPECTS FOR AGRICULTURAL PRODUCTS

Grain and Feed (Wheat, Barley, Oats and Corn)

Algeria is one of the world's largest importers of wheat (4 million MT imported per year minimum) and the largest importer of durum wheat. In the first six months of CY 2006 alone, Algeria imported 2.2 million MT of wheat, of which 948,000 MT was durum and 1.3 million MT was soft wheat. The average production level for 2000-2004 was 2.7 million MT and the maximum level reached for the best years was 4 million MT. Harvests as well as production are always affected by either drought or poor weather.

U.S. market share for durum declined significantly over the past years due to competition from French and Canadian wheat. Excellent durum yields and good quality crops, as well as proximity and good prices, have enabled France to become the largest supplier of wheat to Algeria. In CY 2005, Algeria imported 1.5 million MT of durum from France (50 percent of total durum imports). That same year, the U.S. was ranked the fourth largest supplier of durum with 172,000 MT behind France (1.5 million MT), Canada (360,000 MT) and Mexico (295,000 MT).

France still remains the main supplier of soft wheat as well, with 977,000 MT for CY 2005 followed by Russia (670,000 Mt), and Ukraine (336,000 MT).

For the first two months of CY 2006, Algeria imported 157,000 MT of durum and 294,000 MT of soft wheat from France. For the same period, the United States ranked third for durum (62,000 MT) behind France and Canada. Soft wheat is mostly imported from France, Ukraine, the Czech Republic, and Russia.

Barley is usually imported exclusively in small shipments by private importers from Europe and Eastern Europe because of the proximity and low freight costs. Exceptional climatic conditions affected crops in CY 2005, generating a shortage of pasture lands and increasing barley imports. That same year, Algeria imported 142,000 MT of barley, of which an exceptional 23,000 MT originated from the U.S. This made the U.S. the second largest supplier behind Russia (62,000 MT). Ukraine ranked third with 22,000 MT.

Algeria imported 2.3 million MT of corn in CY 2005. The United States remains the largest supplier of Algeria's corn imports with 1.08 million MT, followed by Argentina (961,000 MT) and Ukraine (206,000 MT). The animal feed manufactures and storage facilities operations expect a continued high demand for corn even though avian influenza disease is disturbing the poultry sector and despite current high world prices.

	2001	2002	2003	2004	2005
	(1000 Metric tons)				
A. Total market	9,734	10,419	11,085	10,864	11,787
B. Total local production	2,584	1,951	4,268	4,001	3,525

C. Total Imports	7,150	8,468	6,817	6,863	8,262
E. Total imports from U.S.	1,462	287	1,204	1,521	1,290

Exchange rates (U.S. $1.00= AD 72.366)
The statistics above are unofficial estimates.

Vegetable Oil and Other Oilseeds Products (Soybean, Sunflower seed, Rapeseed and Palm Oil).

Algerian oilseed cultivation is not well developed. Aside from olive oil production, which remains traditional, Algeria does not crush any oilseeds. Most of the commercialized oil is produced domestically from imported crude oil, which is refined locally by the state-owned operator ENCG Group, and the main private operator CEVITAL.

The most used oils are sunflower oil and olive oil. Soybean oil represents the second most commonly used oil in other industries, such as baked goods, pastry, chocolate, cheese, biscuits, chips, candies, cosmetics, and canned fish. Several new Algerian entrepreneurs are looking to increase production in the snack and soybean consumer goods industry. In addition to bakeries and biscuit industries, these newly established enterprises should generate an increase in both the importation of raw materials and general consumption.

	2001	2002	2003	2004	2005
		(1000 Metric tons)			
A. Total market	870	482	560	807	60
B. Total local production	0	0	0	0	0
C. Total Imports	870	482	560	807	60
E. Total imports from U.S.	270	62	21	212	26

The statistics above are unofficial estimates.

Dairy Products (Non-fat Dry Milk, Whole Milk Powder, Butter oil, Butter, Cheddar Cheese)

The estimated need for milk in Algeria is about 3 million MT annually. Domestic production of fresh milk reached 2 million MT in 2005 and only 17 percent of fresh milk is collected. Algeria remains one of the largest importers of dairy products ($500 million per year).

The dairy processing sector has grown these four past years. Private importers and processors import whole milk powder, non-fat dry milk, and cheddar in order to produce reconstituted milk and dairy products such as yogurt, cheese, butter, fermented milk, and dairy desserts.

Major suppliers for whole milk powder are France, Argentina, Belgium, and New Zealand. France, Poland, the U.S. and the Czech Republic are the major suppliers of non-fat dry milk. Butter and cheese are mostly imported from Spain, the Netherlands, New Zealand, Ireland, Australia and France. Imports from U.S. have decreased tremendously, although there is considerable interest in purchasing from the United States. High U.S. prices and a lack of responsiveness on the part of U.S. suppliers hamper imports of U.S. dairy products.

	2001	2002	2003	2004	2005
		(1000 Metric tons)			
A. Total market	1842	1959	2419	2119	2186
B. Total local production	1690	1690	1690	1900	2000

C. Total Imports	152	269	729	119	286
E. Total imports from U.S.	2	0	0.60	0.63	11

The statistics above are unofficial estimates.

Export of Seafood Products to Algeria:

Algeria is looking for partners in order to improve the seafood and fishing sector. Algerian consumes 3.2 kg of fish products per year per capita and produces 70,000 - 100,000 tons of fish per year. Most canned seafood sold in supermarkets is imported, as is frozen fish. Fresh fish is primarily sold in open markets.

Algeria has 15 ports for fishing and 50 percent of the flotilla is 20 years old. In the markets, seafood is very expensive and out of reach for many households. For example, prawns cost at least 500 AD ($6.50) per kilogram, and the most popular and cheapest seafood, sardines, cost 100 AD ($1.30) per kilo.

TRADE REGULATIONS AND STANDARDS

Algeria has liberalized its trade regime. Its desire for membership in the World Trade Organization and for an association agreement with the European Union may lead to yet freer trade. The import categories that remain subject to restrictions are firearms, explosives, narcotics, and pork products, which are prohibited on security or religious grounds.

TRADE BARRIERS

Algeria's procurement practices have little adverse effect on U.S. exports to the country. It makes little use of countertrade, laws to encourage local production, and non-competitive bidding practices. Algeria is a member of the Arab League. We know of no instance of U.S. firms having been disadvantaged in Algeria because of the League's anti-Israel boycott.

Algeria's Customs Service uses the Harmonized System of product classification. Customs operations are being modernized, but administrative procedures remain burdensome in some instances. Algerian imports are subject to payment of customs duties ranging from 5 percent to 45 percent ad valorem. The rates will be lowered to between 3 to 40 percent in 2004. A value-added tax (VAT) is levied on imports 7, 14, or 21 percent. Imports are subject to another import tax, the Taxe Spécifique Additionnelle (TSA), which ranges from 20 percent to 110 percent. The VAT is based on the purchase price of the imports plus customs duties whereas the TSA excludes the latter in its calculation and applies mainly to luxury goods.

SERVICES BARRIERS

Algeria's Post, Telephone, and Telecommunications Ministry has a monopoly on all telecommunications services. It operates telephone, telex, telegraph, and facsimile networks, a mobile telephone system, a public data communications network, and a maritime radio service. The production, importation, and distribution of equipment are activities open to the private sector. DHL operates a courier service in several cities.

Algeria's stock exchange is not yet open for business. No barriers affect other service sectors.

IMPORT LICENSES

No import licenses are required, but the importation of some items, essentially luxury goods, remains restricted to certain importers owing to the state-owned banks' unwillingness to provide to all importers the documents that are necessary to clear such items through customs.

EXPORT CONTROLS

Almost all export restrictions have been removed. The main exceptions relate to palm seedlings, sheep, and historical and archaeological artifacts. The Government is encouraging non-hydrocarbons exports. The GOA has established the Algerian Export Insurance and Guarantee Company. It offers the kind of insurance normally underwritten by such companies. The agency hopes that its resources will help quadruple such exports by the year 2000.

TEMPORARY ENTRY

Equipment and machinery brought into Algeria temporarily for the purpose of a specific project or exhibition are exempt from payment of customs duties and taxes. To obtain waivers, importers fill out a customs form which they must present to the authorities when the goods are re-exported.

LABELING, MARKING REQUIREMENTS

All imported products, particularly consumer goods, must be labeled in Arabic. Imported drugs can be distributed in Algeria only with the prior authorization of the Ministry of Health and Population. Such drugs must have been marketed in their country of origin before they can be sold in Algeria. Algeria's Customs Service has established strict controls over food imports and enforces a regulation specifying the minimum validity period of imported food products.

FREE TRADE ZONES/WAREHOUSES

In April 1997 the Government designated the site of Bellara (wilaya of Jijel, new port of Djendjen) as a free trade zone. It is possible that another zone will be established at the Algiers International Fairgrounds next year. Foreign investors in these zones will be exempt from taxes and customs duties. Foreign suppliers can establish customs depots to stock goods for sale in Alger a.

MEMBERSHIP IN FREE TRADE ARRANGEMENTS

Algeria, Tunisia, Morocco, Mauritania, and Libya formed the Arab Maghreb Union (known by its French acronym UMA) in 1989. They agreed on a free trade zone but did not establish a timetable. Algeria is negotiating the establishment of a free trade zone with the European Union. Agreement may be reached in 2004. Algeria plans to become a member of the World Trade

TRADE STRUCTURE

MAIN EXPORTED AND IMPORTED PRODUCTS

Main exported products	Main imported products
Fuels and lubricants	Industrial supplies NA
Industrial supplies NA	Foodstuffs
Foodstuffs and beverages	Machinery and other capital goods
Machinery and other capital goods	Transport equipment

Consumption goods NA	Consumption industrial goods
Transport equipment and accessories	Fuels and lubricants.

TRADING PARTNERS:

Main suppliers	Main customers
France	Italy
Italy	United States of America
Spain	France
United States of America	Spain
Germany	Germany
Canada	Netherlands

FOREIGN TRADE REGULATIONS:

IMPORTS REGULATIONS:

Algeria classifies its imports according to the Harmonized Commodity Description and Coding System.
Products prohibited for imports are the following : firearms, explosives, narcotics, pork products, pornographic materials, and other items prohibited for reasons of health, safety, national security or religion. The sale of alcohol is prohibited.
Restricted products are as follows: some agricultural products (cheese, honey), luxury products (such as yachts, perfumes and automobiles). The list of products subject to restrictions is revised every six months. Imported consumer goods must have a warranty of six months to eighteen months depending upon the type of products.

REQUIRED DOCUMENTS

***Commercial invoice*:**
A commercial invoice in duplicate is required including a detailed description of products, the total value of the invoice and terms (FOB, CIF, etc.) and names and addresses of the exporter, importer, the consignee and the manufacturer. The invoice must be signed by the shipper and legalized by the consular services of the Algerian Embassy. In case the products contain foreign components the country of origin must be indicated along with the percentage of the foreign component.

***Certificate of origin*:**
A separate certificate of origin is not required unless the importer requests it. In this case two copies are required. The certificate must be signed by an official of the exporting company and certified by a recognized chamber of commerce.

***Packing list*:**
The packing list should be in French and included with ocean freight shipments to facilitate

customs processing. The packing list should describe the contents of each case or container while mentioning the gross weights together with the CIF value of each commodity.

Bill of lading:
The bills of lading should the gross weight and measurements, the name of the shipper, port of destination, number of bills of lading in the full set, and date and signature of the carrier's official. Shipping marks and numbers should correspond to those shown on the invoices and the packages. The airway bill replaces the bill of lading on air cargo shipments.

EXPORTS REGULATIONS

Sanitary certificate:
Plants, plant product seeds and animals and animal products require a sanitary certificate. There are also special requirements for potatoes and special documentary and sterilization for chestnut trees and wood.

Imports must be insured with an Algerian firm

OTHER FORMALITIES AND DOCUMENTS:

Importers must be registered in the commercial register and have the necessary Dinar to import goods. All import licenses and the "specifications" system have been abolished.
Items intended as samples and having no commercial value are admitted free of duty but should be accompanied by a pro forma invoice. Advertising material is subject to customs duties except for single catalogues sent as printed matters.

Labeling:
The containers of fruit and vegetables should be labeled as to country of origin, variety of fruit, or vegetable and quality class.

Marking:
Marks of origins requirements mainly apply to wines, nuts , canned foods, prunes, honey, margarine and various milk products.

Packing:
Goods should be packed to withstand weather conditions, rough handling and pilferage.

FINANCIAL REGULATIONS OF FOREIGN TRADE OPERATIONS

Banking system:
The banking system includes an issuing bank, five commercial banks, an investment bank and a savings bank. The central bank of Algeria (Bca) has the preference of issue. It executes operations relating to the management of reserves and exchange regulations. It finances deposit banks through rediscount and by taking bills in pawn.

Deposit banks are the following:
Banque Nationale d'Algérie (Bna) which deals with industrial sectors, transport other than maritime, trade and distribution.
Banque Algerienne de Développement Rural which deals with the agricultural sector and agro-food industry.
Banque de Développement Local (Bdl) which deals with local economic units.

Banque Algérienne de Développement (Bad) which finances long term investments of public enterprises.
Crédit Populaire d'Algérie (Cpa) which deals with tourism, handicraft, fishery, trade and distribution sectors.

Caisse Nationale d'Epargne et de prévoyance which finances the programmes of accession to individual property or co-operative and construction.

FOREIGN EXCHANGE SYSTEM

Foreign currencies are always available for importers. All imports must be domiciled through an authorized intermediary bank, to which the importer must present a commercial contract or pro forma invoice and through which all payments related to the transaction must be made.
Very limited acceptance of Visa, American Express, Diners Club and access/MasterCard but top class hotels accept traveler's checks.

METHODS AND MEANS FOR INTERNATIONAL SETTLEMENT

Thanks to domiciliation, it is possible to have a pro forma invoice to facilitate payments. The bank may effect payments for imports by public enterprises, public agencies, or government ministries before the completion of trade and exchange formalities if the imports are considered urgent.

Banks may require a deposit in dinars up to the full value of the imports before the import payments are effected. Imports of gold, other precious metals and precious stone must be paid for from foreign currency accounts.
The imports of private automobiles must be paid from the importer's own foreign exchange resources.

Advance payments may not exceed 15% of the import value without the approval of the central bank. Import Payments for countries with which no payment agreements have been concluded are made in convertible currency.

CUSTOMS TAXATION

APPLICABLE DUTIES AND TAXES:

Ad valorem duties: Ad valorem duties are assessed on a CIF basis that includes wholesale value of goods in the country of origin, transport charges, Export duties, insurance, commissions, freight, and all other costs incurred before the goods reach Algerian customs control. Customs duties and warehouse charges are not included in the dutiable value.

PREFERENTIAL DUTIES:

There are preferential duties between Algeria and the European Union countries that are similar to those included within the framework of the EU's convention with African, Caribbean and Pacific developing countries. There are also preferential duties with the Arab Maghreb Union countries 5Libya, Morocco, Mauritania and Tunisia). the imports of products originating in the AMU countries are exempted from customs duties.

CUSTOMS SURCHARGES AND INDIRECT TAXES:

Since April 1992 an added value tax has replaced the production and services taxes.

The rates are as follows:

7% on necessities, 13% on almost all goods, and 21% on finishes goods and luxury items and finally an extra superior rate of 41% that was discontinued in 1993. There is an additional tax on the customs value of the goods plus duties and VAT. It ranges from 10% to 80% depending upon the item in question.

SPECIAL PROVISIONS:

A basic standard tariff is levied on (tariff de droit commun) is levied on goods originating in all countries that accord Algeria most-favored nation treatment (MFN). Customs duties are highest on luxury goods. Strategic and vital products are exempted from customs duties.

FOREIGN TRADE LOGISTIC

INTERNATIONAL TRANSPORTS:

Maritime transports:

The main ports are located in Algiers, Annaba, Arzew, Béjaia Oran, Ghazahouet, Béni Saf, Ténès, Djedjen, Mostaghanem, Cherchell, Zemmouri, Djijel and in Skida. Other maritime companies of Mediterranean ports serve Algiers. The two major shipping lines are Entreprise Nationale de Transport Maritime de Voyageurs ferries (ENTMV) and Compagnie de Navigation Mixte.

Air transports:

Algeria's national airline is Air Algérie (AH). Other airlines serving Algeria are Air France, Alitalia, Balkan, Egyptair, Jamahirya Libyan Arab Airlines, Royal Air Maroc, Saudia, Syrian Arab Airlines and Tunis Air. International airports: Algiers (ALG) (Houari Boumedienne) in Dar-el-Beida is 20 km East of Algiers, Oran airport (ORN) in ESSénia is 10 km from Oran, Annaba airport in El Mellah is 12 km from the city and Constantine airport in Ain El Bey is 9 km away from the city. There are other airports in Ouargla and Tlemcen.

Land transports:

*** Railways:** There is one daily train connecting Algier to Tunis via Constantinae and Annbaba. A railway network links large cities. In 1995 the Algerian railway network was 4,290 km long.*

*** Road:** There are roads which lead to Morocco (Mahdia), Tunisia (Souk Ahras, Tébessa and El Kala), Libya (Fort Thiriet), Niger (Guezzam), and Mali (Bordj Mokhtar). Coastal regions and Northern Sahara are provided with paved roads. In 1994, the road network reached 60,000 km. In 1995, the number of cars reached 2700997 vehicles of 57% are individual cars.*

TELECOMMUNICATIONS:

Automatic telephone, telex and mail services are available in Algeria. In 1995, Algeria was provided with 3,145 post offices and with 1164000 telephone lines.

Distribution system:
The distribution system in Algeria is traditional like in most of its Maghreban neighbors.

ALGERIA CUSTOMS OFFICE: BASIC ACTIVITIES AND FUNCTIONS

CUSTOMS MODERNIZATION PROGRAMME 2011-2015

Building on the achievements of the modernization program 2007-2010, the new strategy to support the modernization will benefit from the greatest care in its definition, design, definition of these areas and its implementation and this, in the wider consultation structures. For this purpose, a new approach to support the modernization spread over five (5) years will be launched in 2011. The main objective of the program 2011-2015 is:

- Increase organizational effectiveness and operational customs while encouraging the development of human resources;
- Develop staff capacity to improve its own functioning with a capacity to anticipate and be proactive while moving in a positive and constructive;
- To have specific tools for planning, analysis and problem solving, realistic and high performance to ensure progress permanance.

The reflection on this process is a shared responsibility between all the structures of Customs: " **Together for a new strategy geared towards better performance. "**

CUSTOMS PROCEDURES

Upon arrival of products in the Algerian territory, the carrier is responsible for making a preliminary declaration with the customs office concerned after which the goods are placed under the control of the Direction Gènèrale des Douanes (Customs). Besides the owner of the shipment and the transport agent, only so called "transitaires", who are accredited by the Ministry of Finance, are allowed to carry out import formalities.

All imported merchandise must be declared through the customs automated system via the detailed import declaration. The Import Declaration is a single administrative document, which the importer or transitaire must fill out by hand if the electronic interface is not available.

Since 1995, Algerian Customs has used the Automated Customs Management System (SIGAD) to codify merchandise and for the management of tax and fee collection systems. The declaration is entered electronically into SIGAD and automatically transmitted to the CNIS (National Center for Statistics Information) for statistics purposes and in order to check whether the allocated quota for the imported products has not been reached.

The Import Declaration, whether submitted electronically or manually, and accompanying documents are checked by the Customs officer responsible for verification and control. The system then prints the paper declaration and assigns the channel which it must go through (red, orange, green) according to the risk management program. The amount of taxes and duties to be recovered is entered and the form is processed for payment.

Foodstuffs will be subject to a quality control prior to their release for free circulation. For this control, it is necessary to submit the appropriate certificates issued in the country of origin, e.g. Certificate of Analysis or sanitary certificates. For animal products or foodstuffs containing substances of animal origin, the submission of the Halal Certificate is required, proving that they correspond to the food standards required by Islamic rules concerning the contents and the manufacturing process of these goods.

Goods entering under the regime of import for local consumption are cleared from customs once the customs duties and taxes on the imports are paid. The declarant is then provided with a Clearance Attestation and clearance authorization is given by the customs officer in charge.

At the request of the importer or his broker, a copy of the declaration stamped with the stamp of the Direction Gènèrale des Douanes can be provided as proof of import for domestic consumption. This stamp is also used to authenticate circulation certificates EUR.1.

Imported goods can remain in bond in the customs depot while waiting for payment of required fees and taxes and/or presenting the administrative authorization for up to two months. This condition can be extended up to four months for goods subject to a special administrative authorization.

The removal authorization can not be given until all duties and taxes are paid, deposited or secured. After the authorization is issued, the declarant must proceed to remove the goods within 15 days.

CUSTOMS REGIMES

1. Clearance for local consumption Under this regime goods are imported into the customs territory of Algeria for local consumption and remain in this territory with no obligation to export. The Import Declaration, is accompanied by the following general documents:

Commercial invoice

Bill of lading for goods transported by sea, or airway bill for air cargo shipments or CMR

Certificate of origin: for goods originating in the European Community, original of the certificate EUR1 issued by the Customs authorities of the exporting country

Insurance policy,

Packing list

For products subject to specific regulations, any other documents required (in particular phytosanitary and sanitary certificates)

Importers must show evidence of their registration with the Companies Registry: copy of the certificate of registration and copy of the tax identification card.

Customs bonded warehousing Under this regime goods imported into the customs territory of Algeria are stored under in warehouses customs control without payment of customs duties or VAT and taxes until released for local consumption or placed under another customs regime.

Inward processing Using this regime eligible companies carry out, under the customs control, the production, transportation, refining and processing of a number of products, mainly hydrocarbons and chemicals. Imported goods are admitted to the customs territory of Algeria with a full conditional exemption from customs duties and taxes on the condition that the products are exported from the territory of Algeria. If the processed goods are exported, no customs duty or VAT is payable on the import of the goods.

Imported goods that have been processed under this regime are released for local consumption after the customs authorities have assessed the amount of import duties payable and import duties and taxes have been fully paid.

Free admission This regime allows the import of goods without payment of customs duties or VAT and taxes: such imported goods must be identical to goods obtained on the local market and used for manufacturing products which have been exported.

Temporary admission Temporary admission applies to goods imported to be used in Algeria for the purpose of a specific project or exhibition which will be re-exported in the same state: such goods enjoy a full relief from customs duty and VAT.

Transit Under this Customs regime foreign goods are moved within the customs territory of Algeria under customs control between one customs office and another customs office either by air or by land;

LIST OF CUSTOMS PROCEDURES CODES

The Customs Procedure Code appears in Box 1 of the Import Declaration:

code	Regime available for imports
1000 1033 1078	Local consumption Import for local consumption Import for local consumption from customs warehousing Import for local consumption from Temporary admission
3300	Customs storage
1500	Transit
1167	Transhipment
3301 3302 3303 3304 3378 3320	Private warehouses Public warehouses Industrial warehouses Extension of warehousing Entrance in warehouse further to temporary admission Transfer of warehousing
3604	Inward Processing
7801 7802 7803 7804 7805 7806 7878	Temporary Admission: Temporary Admission for works and services Temporary Admission for improvement Temporary Admission for Fairs and Exhibitions Temporary Admission Extension of temporary admission Foreigner authorised to reside in Algeria Transfer of Temporary Admission
1007	Free admission

The Customs Procedure Name appears in Box 2 of the Import Declaration. "la mise à la consummation" corresponds to an entry for home consumption.

LIST OF ENTRY PORTS AND CODES

The customs port of entry name appears in Box 5 of the Import Declaration Form. The import of animal products is only allowed at the customs offices of entry marked in Bold:

Alger oust – Direction Régionale Inspection divsionnaire Chlef:

02201. Tenes

09201. Inspection divsionnaire Blida 42201. Inspection divsionnaire Tipaza

Alger-Est Direction Régionale Inspection divsionnaire Aeroport H. B.

16200. Aeroport H. B.

16205. Alger voyageurs 16203. Alger contentieux 16202. Alger entrepôt 16204. Dar .El .beida contentieux

Inspection divsionnaire Alger-Exterieur-Est: 16206. Zone .industr alger Inspection divsionnaire Boumerdes: 35203. Boumerdes

35201. Dellys

15201. Inspection divsionnaire Tizi ouzou

Annaba Direction Régionale Inspection divsionnaire Annaba:

23201. Annaba

23202. Annaba contentieux 23203. Annaba les salines 23204. El hadjar

Inspection divsionnaire El-tarf: 36201. El aioun 36202. El kala contentieux 36203. Oum teboul

Inspection divsionnaire Souk Ahras: 41201. Souk ahras 41202. El hadada

Oran Direction Régionale Inspection divsionnaire Oran-port:

31201. Oran port

31202. Oran entrepot 31203. Oran contentieux

Inspection divsionnaire Oran exterieur: 31206. Es senia 31209. Oran voyageurs 31204. Inspection divsionnaire Arzew 31208. Bethioua Inspection divsionnaire Mostaganem:

27201. Mostaganem

29201. Mascara

Tébessa Direction Régionale

Inspection divsionnaire Tebessa: 12201. Tebessa contentieux 12202. Tebessa

Inspection divsionnaire Bouchebka: 12203. Bouchebka 12206. Ras el aioun 12205. El meridj 12204. Inspection divsionnaire Bir el ater

Tlemcen Direction Régionale 13201. Inspection divsionnaire Tlemcen Inspection divsionnaire Ghazaouet:

13202. Ghazaouet

13205. Boukanoun

Inspection divsionnaire Maghnia: 13203. Maghnia contentieux 13204. Akid lotfi

46202. Inspection divsionnaire Ain temouchent

Inspection divsionnaire Sidi Bel Abbes: 22201. Sidi bel abbes 20201. Saida

Bechar Direction Régionale

Inspection divsionnaire Bechar: 08201. Bechar Inspection divsionnaire 08202. Beni ounif

01201. Inspection divsionnaire Adrar 45202. Inspection divsionnaire Naama 37201. Inspection divsionnaire Tindouf 01202. Inspection divsionnaire Bordj badji mokhtar

Ouargla Direction Régionale

Inspection divsionnaire Ouargla: 30201. Ouargla 30203. Touggourt

30202. Inspection divsionnaire Hassi messaoud 47201. Inspection divsionnaire Ghardaia Inspection divsionnaire Laghouat:

03201. Laghouat 17201. Djelfa

Inspection divsionnaire El oued: 39201. El oued 39202. Taleb larbi

Tamanaghasset Direction Régionale 11201. Tamanrasset Inspection divsionnaire 11202. In guezzam Inspection divsionnaire

Sétif Direction Régionale 19201. Inspection divsionnaire Setif

06201. Inspection divsionnaire Bejaia

18201. Inspection divsionnaire Jijel

Inspection divsionnaire Constatine: 25201. Constantine 25202. Aeroport m.boudiaf

Inspection divsionnaire Skikda:

21201. Skikda

21203. Skikda el djadid 05201. Inspection divsionnaire Batna 04201. Inspection divsionnaire Oum el bouaghi 07201. Inspection divsionnaire Biskra

SPECIMEN DOCUMENTS

Import Declaration

Purpose – Import declaration for customs clearance Issuing Authority – Algerian Customs Where entry number is marked – Box 5 Where procedure code is marked – Boxes 1 and 2 Where duty amount is marked – Box P9 (reverse page) Where stamps are posted – Box 6

English Translation

Declaration Code
Description
Sheet
Total/articles
Registration No. Date/Time Office Code
Official stamp
Actual importer:
SJ
Fiscal code
Postal code
Type of operation
Method of financing
IJV conditions
Method of transport
Actual supplier/recipient
Total print net invoice/ Currency/ Amount
Other costs/Currency/Amount
Freight/Currency/Amount
Insurance/Currency/Amount
Country of sale/Code
Country of Destination/Code
Relation of sale
Adjustment co-efficient
Balance other items (total invoice prince, net)
Exchange rate
Declarant License No.
Value in Dinars
Banking details
Manifest/Code/Document No.
Record line/Date
Total number packages
Transport to/from/ Type
Total gross weight
Description of Merchandise
Domestic transport
Localization of merchandise
Country of origin
Fiscal regime
Origin
Statistical code

Net weight
Value in Dinars
Preferential tariff
Extra quantity
Codes with documents
Accompanying documents
Warehouse
Previous customs regime
Time period
Suspension rate
Value added
Characteristics of private vehicles
Bond amount
Discount amount
Payment – tax code
Quota
Tax base
Amount
SIGAD – Payment summary
Transit/Seals applied
Authorized by:
Border office:
Office at destination
Commitments
Commitments subscribed
Deposit receipt
Fine receipt
Signature of cashier

I, the undersigned, wish to place the goods described in this declaration under the authority of the present customs regime. Signed at_____dated_______. Signature of the Customs Clearance Agent

Reverse

Controlling officer

Apparent volume/Date/Temperature/Density/Actual volume L Box – Service check M Box – Certificate Verification N Box – Settlement of Deposits O Box

Returned following customs clearance Documents, samples Signed at/Dated/Clearnace Agent

P Box - Liquidation

Description taxes and duties

Liquidation prior to contesting taxes and duties

Liquidation post contesting taxes and duties

Additional taxes and duties to be recovered Total

Supplementary payment No. Dated/Amount

Payment of reimbursement No.

CLEARANCE ATTESTATION

Purpose – Proof of customs clearance and release Issuing Authority – Direction Gènèrale des Douanes (Customs). Where entry number is marked – No. Declaration (marked Box 1) Where procedure code is marked – Regime (marked Box 2)

English Translation

ALGERIAN CUSTOMS THE GOODS DESCRIBED BELOW AUTHORISED BY :

OFFICE CODE NAME | REGISTRATION OF DECLARATION REGIME 2 N° DECLARATION 1 DATE | DATE OF ISSUE

REAL IMPORTER / EXPORTER

DECLARANT

MANIFEST YEAR TYPE REGISTRATION NUMBER

LINE NUMBER OF PARCELS NATURE AND LABELING OF PARCELS - IDENTIFICATION OF GOODS

COMMENTS

THE GOODS SHOULD BE REMOVED WITHIN THE TIME SET BY APPLICABLE REGULATIONS

CUSTOMS STAMP

Purpose – Proof of Customs clearance for home consumption Issuing Authority – Direction Gènèrale des Douanes (Customs). Where stamps are posted – Import Declaration, Box 6, upper right corner "cachet du bureau. Clearance Attestation.

TRADE AND PROJECT FINANCING

BANKING SYSTEM

The Algerian banking system comprises the Central Bank (Banque d'Algérie), six state-owned banks, one public development bank, and one private bank. An

Islamic bank is owned jointly by one of the state banks and the Saudi Al-Baraka Group. Algeria's first private bank, Union Bank, has been operating nearly two years. It concentrates on merchant banking. Algeria's banking system remains inefficient because its banks were no more than mere depository institutions for many years. They lent mainly to the public sector, which left the banks a legacy of non-performing debt and managerial problems. Algeria's implementation of IMF and World Bank reform programs led to their recapitalization and to the liberalization of the banking system. The Government wants to see reputable foreign private banks establish themselves in Algeria.

FOREIGN EXCHANGE CONTROLS AFFECTING TRADING

Aside from a few exceptions the Government prohibits Algerians from holding real and financial assets abroad. It does make foreign exchange available to Algerians provided they have the dinar equivalent of the hard currency cost of the imports.

GENERAL FINANCING AVAILABILITY

Local importers have access to foreign exchange through the five state-owned commercial banks. Foreign exchange reserves of the Central Bank stood at $6.2 billion at the end May 1997.

EXPORT SUBSIDIES

About 95 percent of Algeria's export earnings derive from oil and gas exports. The government provides small indirect subsidies to Algerian firms for market research facilitating non-hydrocarbon exports.

EXPORT IMPORT BANK FINANCING

ExIm cover is open for short-term transactions (i.e., repayment terms not exceeding 180 days) involving the five Algerian state banks and Sonatrach. ExIm guaranteed a $150 million Citibank loan for services being provided to Sonatrach by Halliburton Company. ExIm remains one of Algeria's leading creditors since its exposure approximates $2.2 billion. Further information regarding ExIm programs in Algeria can be obtained by calling 202-566-8945.

In autumn 1996 the U.S. Department of Agriculture guaranteed $265 million of commodity import financing. More than half of the guarantees was for loans maturing in less than a year.

OTHER EXTERNAL FINANCING

France's Export Credit Guarantee Agency, the Coface, covers about $1 billion of imports. Spain and Germany guarantee almost as much. The other major guarantors of credit to Algeria are Belgium, Italy, the Netherlands, and the United Kingdom.

PROJECT FINANCING AVAILABLE

The World Bank and the African Development Bank are active in Algeria. Both finance infrastructure and social projects. The World Bank is funding Algeria's economic restructuring programs. The European Union is funding major investments through the European Investment Bank.

BANKS WITH U.S. CORRESPONDENT ARRANGEMENTS

Each of the state-owned Algerian banks maintains correspondent banking relationships with several U.S. banks.

Banque Extérieure d'Algérie Banque Nationale d'Algérie

Bank of New York American Express Bank
BankAmerica International Bank of America
Bankers Trust Bank of New York
Chase Manhattan Bank Bankers Trust
Chemical Bank Chase Manhattan Bank
Citibank Citibank
First Chicago CoBank Denver
First Interstate Bank
Crédit Populaire d'Algérie of California
Citibank Mellon Bank
Arab American Bank Pittsburgh national Bank
Chemical Bank United Bank for Africa
Mellon Bank
Banque de l'Agriculture Banque de Développement Local
et du Développement Rural Citibank
Bank of America NY Crédit Lyonnais NY
CoBank Denver Rabo Bank
Citibank United Bank for Africa
Bankers Trust
First Chicago
Rabo bank

AFRICAN DEVELOPMENT BANK PROJECT APPROVED CONCERNING THE TELECOMMUNICATIONS SECTOR IN ALGERIA.

The African Development Bank (ADB) has approved a loan of 120.313 million US $ to finance the telecommunications sector upgrading and support project in Algeria. The project is in keeping with the Government's reform and investment policy for the 2000-2005 period, which aims to liberalize the entire telecommunications sector through the establishment of new structures and the arrival of new private operators.

The project's objective is to increase the contribution of telecommunications and information technologies to the country's gross fixed capital formation (GFCF) from 1.16% in 1999 to at least 5% by 2005. It specifically seeks to qualitatively and quantitatively increase telephone density from 5.95 lines per one hundred inhabitants in 2001 to 10 lines per one hundred inhabitants by 2005. The project will also involve the operating capacities building of the Posts and Telecommunications Regulatory Authority (ARPT) to ensure it rapidly becomes autonomous and efficient and the technical upgrading of the national telecommunications network in order to meet demand in terms of interconnection capacity and subscriber connections.

The project will contribute to the dissemination of new information technologies that have an increasing number of relevant applications to education (distance training/distance education), and health (telemedicine) in Algeria. Support to the ARPT will contribute significantly to the establishment of a competitive environment, which will attract private investments required for the upgrading of the telecommunications network with all the ensuing economic and social benefits.

In order to minimize the social cost of the project, the Government prepared a mechanism for the restructuration of the Ministry of Posts and Telecommunications involving a voluntary redundancy scheme for applicants for early retirement as well as training programmes to upgrade the remaining staff.

The ADB loan will be used to finance 86% of the foreign exchange costs of the project whose total cost is estimated at UA 120.87 million Units of Account (UA)* – about US $ 152 million.

Bank Group operations in Algeria started in 1971. To-date, the Group has committed a total of about US$ 2.24 billion on 32 operations. Of this amount, approximately US$ 1.38 billion has been disbursed.

* 1UA = US$ 1.25673 as at January 1st, 2002

Description: Support to the Posts and Telecommunications Regulatory Authority; Upgrading of National Telecommunications Network

Beneficiary: Government of the People's Democratic Republic of Algeria

Executing Agency:Posts and Telecommunications Regulatory Authority (ARPT) Ministry of Posts and Telecommunications/AlgérieTélécom

Starting date: August 2002

Duration: 48 months

Procurement: International competitive bidding: equipment; shortlist: consultancy services.

TRAVEL TO ALGERIA

US STATE DEPARTMENT SUGGESTIONS

WARNING: The United States Department of State warns U.S. citizens to evaluate carefully the implications for their security and safety before deciding to travel to Algeria. Although the level of terrorist incidents in Algeria is lower than in recent years, unpredictable attacks continue to occur in crowded urban areas, in rural villages and roadsides, and on public transport.

For those Americans who decide to travel to Algeria despite this warning, the Department urges maximum caution, including the following measures: minimize use of regularly scheduled commercial flights, be met and accompanied by pre-arranged local contacts upon arrival and departure at airports, and have armed protection while traveling overland. Nighttime travel outside the central urban areas should be strictly avoided. Visitors to the capital of Algiers should reside only in one of the several large, internationally recognized hotels where security is provided. U.S. citizens should not travel or walk anywhere in Algeria unless accompanied by a known Algerian companion. This measure applies to walking the streets of Algiers and other cities. U.S. Embassy personnel take all of these precautions.

Most recent terrorist activity has occurred in northern Algeria. U.S. oil companies operating in the desert region south of the Saharan Atlas Mountains have experienced no attacks in the past year. The Algerian Government and the companies themselves take maximum security precautions, including the measures described above, to ensure safety in the oil-producing region.

COUNTRY DESCRIPTION: Algeria is a republic and a developing economy. Facilities for travelers are widely available, but sometimes limited in quality. The workweek in Algeria is Saturday through Wednesday.

ENTRY REQUIREMENTS: Passports and visas are required for U.S. citizens traveling to Algeria. Algerian Embassies may not give visas to persons whose passports indicate travel to Israel. For more information concerning entry requirements, travelers may contact the Embassy of the Democratic and Popular Republic of Algeria at 2137 Wyoming Avenue N.W., Washington, D.C. 20008, telephone (202) 265-2800.

AVIATION SAFETY OVERSIGHT: As there is no direct commercial air service at present, or economic authority to operate such service, between the U.S. and Algeria, the U.S. Federal Aviation Administration (FAA) has not assessed Algeria's Civil Aviation Authority for compliance with international aviation safety standards for oversight of Algeria's air carrier operations. For further information, travelers may contact the Department of Transportation within the U.S. at 1-800-322-7873, or visit the FAA Internet home page at http://www.faa.gov/avr/iasa/index.htm. The U.S. Department of Defense (DOD) separately assesses some foreign air carriers for suitability as official providers of air services. For information regarding the DOD policy on specific carriers, travelers may contact DOD at 618-256-4801.

AREAS OF INSTABILITY: Political, social, and economic problems have created an environment in which acts of terrorism are regularly perpetrated. A state of emergency has been in effect since early 1992. Since September 1993, terrorist actions against foreigners have resulted in the deaths of more than 120 foreigners. Thousands of Algerians from all walks of life and classes of Algerian society, including women and children and retirees, have been and continue to be viciously assassinated. Car bombings, shoot-outs between government forces and armed groups, and other violence often occur. In the localities in which large number of American expatriates reside, Algerian military and other security personnel offer generally adequate protection, but in many other localities, especially in remote hamlets and the poorer sections of urban areas, protection is not assured.

Although the Government of Algeria has discontinued a late-night curfew in the central area around Algiers, it continues to maintain roadblocks at many major intersections. Security personnel at roadblocks and intersections expect full cooperation. In response, terrorist groups occasionally put up false roadblocks as ambushes.

Banditry and assault involving foreigners often occur in the far southern region of Algeria near the border with Niger. Bandits have robbed, assaulted, kidnapped, and killed travelers in Algeria south of Tamanrasset.

Travel overland is treacherous in many parts of Algeria. The Department of State recommends that American citizens in Algeria have substantial armed protection while traveling overland, on their work sites, and at their accommodations.

TERRORIST ACTIVITIES: Slightly more than 120 foreigners have been kidnapped and murdered in Algeria since September 1993, sometimes in assaults involving dozens of attackers. For example, in 1996, a group of seven Catholic monks (none U.S. citizens) residing some 300 miles southwest of Algiers were taken hostage and decapitated by a group of terrorists with whom the monks had had previous peaceful contact. Terrorists have threatened to kill all foreigners who do not leave Algeria. In response to these threats, the U.S. Government has substantially reduced the number of U.S. government personnel in Algeria. Dependents of U.S. Government personnel may not accompany employees to Algeria. An Air France flight was hijacked at Algiers Airport on December 24, 1994, by heavily armed terrorists who threatened to blow up the aircraft. The U.S. Embassy in Algiers has specifically identified ports, trains, and airline terminals as terrorist targets and warns against traveling on regularly scheduled commercial transport. U.S. Embassy personnel have suspended their use of regularly scheduled commercial flights.

MEDICAL FACILITIES: Hospitals and clinics in Algeria are available, but of doubtful quality. Doctors and hospitals often expect immediate cash payment for services. U.S. medical insurance is not always valid outside the United States. Supplemental medical insurance with specific overseas coverage, including provisions for medical evacuation, has proven useful. For further information, travelers can contact the Centers for Disease Control and Prevention's international travelers hotline at 1-888-232-3228, or their autofax service at 1-888-232-3299, or their Internet site at http://www.cdc.gov.

INFORMATION ON CRIME: The crime rate in Algeria is moderately high, and is increasing. Serious crimes have been reported in which armed men posing as police officers have entered homes of occupants, held them at gunpoint, and robbed them. Armed carjacking is also a serious problem. Petty theft and home burglary occur frequently. Theft of contents and parts from parked cars, pickpocketing, theft on trains and buses, theft of anything left in a hotel room, and purse snatching are common. Most residences of foreigners are protected by alarms, grills, watchdogs, and/or guards.

The loss or theft of a U.S. passport abroad should be reported to local police and the nearest U.S. Embassy or consulate. Useful information on safeguarding valuables, protecting personal security, and other matters while traveling abroad is provided in the Department of State pamphlets, *A Safe Trip Abroad* and *Tips for Travelers to the Middle East and North Africa*. They are available from the Superintendent of documents, U.S. Government Printing Office, Washington, D.C. 20402.

CURRENCY REGULATIONS: Travelers checks and credit cards are acceptable in only a few establishments in urban areas. The Government of Algeria requires all foreigners entering the country to exchange $200 into local currency. Documentary proof of legal exchange of currency is needed when departing Algeria.

DRUG PENALTIES: U.S. citizens are subject to the laws of the country in which they are traveling. Penalties for possession, use, or dealing in illegal drugs in Algeria are severe, and convicted offenders can expect jail sentences and fines.

EMBASSY LOCATION/REGISTRATION: The U.S. Embassy in Algeria is located at 4 Chemin Che kh Bachir El-Ibrahimi, B.P. 549 (Alger-gare) 16000, in the capital city of Algiers. The telephone number is (213)(2) 691-425/255/186. The fax number for the U.S. Embassy is (213)(2) 69-39-79. The former U.S. Consulate in Oran is closed.

U.S. citizens are encouraged to register and obtain current information on travel and security within Algeria at the Consular Section of the U.S. Embassy. They also may register with the Embassy's emergency alert network.

AMERICAN EMBASSY, ALGIERS

Telephone: 011-213-2) 69-31-17, 69-18-54, or 69-12-55
Telex: (011-213-2) 69-37-72
Telemail: AGR@ist.cerist.dz
FAX: (011-213-2) 69-37-72
Office Hours: Saturday - Wednesday 8:00 A.M. - 5:00 P.M.
Internet Email: agr@ist.cerist.dz

Mailing Address to Staff with Diplomatic Status	Embassy Address and Mailing Address to Other FAS Employees
US EMBASSY ALGIERS US DEPARTMENT OF AGRICULTURE FAS WASHINGTON DC 20250-6000	4, Chemin Cheikh Bachir Ibrahim 16001 Alger Gare Algiers, Algeria
Quintin Gray (Attache) Resident in Rabat	Anice MOUSSA (Agrl Spec) Tayeb FOUFA (Clerk)

SUPPLEMENTS

IMPORTANT WEBSITES

I. FINANCE, CUSTOMS, BANKS

Ministry of Finance: www.mf.gov.dz

Directorate General of Forecasting and Policies: www.dgpp.mf.gov.dz

Directorate General of Taxes: www.mfdgi.gov.dz

Directorate General of Customs: www.douane.gov.dz

Bank of Algeria: www.bank-of-algeria.dz

Foreign Bank of Algeria: www.bea.dz

National Bank of Algeria: www.bna.dz

National Fund for Savings (CNEP): www.cnepbanque.dz

Stock Exchange of Algiers : www.sgbv.dz

Commission for Organisation and Monitoring of Stock Exchange Operations: www.cosob.dz

II. TRADE AND ASSOCIATIONS OF FAIRS AND EXHIBITIONS

Ministry of Commerce: www.mincommerce.gov.dz

Algerian Chamber of Commerce and Industry: www.caci.dz

Algerian Society of Fairs and Exportation: www.safex.com.dz

National Trade Registry: www.cnrc.org.dz

National Agency for the Promotion of Foreign Trade: www.algex.dz

Algerian Company for Export Insurance and Guarantees: www.cagex.com.dz

III. INDUSTRY AND INVESTMENT PROMOTION

Ministry of Industry, Small and Medium-Sized Enterprises and Investment Promotion:www.mipmepi.gov.dz

National Agency for Investment Development (ANDI): www.andi.dz

National Agency for Intermediation and Land Regulation (ANIREF): www.aniref.dz

IV. Energy and mining

Ministry of Energy and Mining: www.mem-algerie.org

Hydrocarbons Regulatory Authority: www.arh.gov.dz

Electricity and Gas Regulatory Commission: www.creg.gov.dz

Bulletin of tenders in the energy and mining sector: www.baosem.com

Sonatrach (Algeria's national oil and gas company): www.sonatrach-dz.com

Sonelgaz (Algeria's national electricity and gas company): www.sonelgaz.dz

Algerian Energy Company: www.aec.dz

Algerian gold-mining company (ENOR): www.enor.dz

National Agency for the Promotion and Rationalisation of Energy Use: www.aprue.org.dz

National Agency for Mining Patrimony:

V. OTHER MINISTERIAL DEPARTMENTS

Ministry for Agriculture and Rural Development: www.minagri.dz

Ministry of Water Resources: www.mre.gov.dz

Ministry for Tourism and Handcraft: www.mta.gov.dz

Ministry of Postal Services and Telecommunications: www.mptic.dz

Ministry of Higher Education and Scientific Research: www.mesrs.dz

VI. OTHER NATIONAL ORGANISATIONS

National Office of Statistics: www.ons.dz

Algerian Accreditation Centre: www.algerac.org

Algerian Institute of Standardisation: www.ianor.org

VII. LINKS TO RESOURCES FOR FINDING ALGERIAN BUSINESSES

Site for the Algerian Chamber of Commerce and Industry: www.elmouchir.caci.dz

Site for Algerian businesses: www.entreprisesalgeriennes.com

Directories of Algerian businesses: www.algerieclic.com

and www.rea-dz.com

ALGERIA PORTS

EL KALA PORT

Country:	Algeria	Latitude:	36° 54' N
Geographic Region:	ALGERIA	Longitude:	8° 27' E

Publication	131	Tugs Salvage	Lifts
Chart	52200	Tugs Assist	200 Tons Plus
Harbor Size	V	Quarantine	50-200 Tons
Harbor Type	OR	Pratique	25-49 Tons
Shelter Afforded	P	Deratt Cert	0-24 Tons
Entrance Restrictions		Other	Services
Tide		Communications	Longshore
Swell		Telephone	Electrical
Ice		Telegraph	Steam
Other	Y	Radio	Navig Equip
Overhead Limits		Radio Tel	Elect Repair
Channel Depth	O	Air	Supplies
Anchorage Depth	C	Rail	Provisions
Cargo Pier Depth	O	Load/Offload	Water
Oil Terminal Depth		Wharves	Fuel Oil
Tide		Anchor	Diesel Oil
Maximum Size Vessel		Med Moor	Deck
Good Holding Ground	N	Beach Moor	Engine
Turning Area		Ice Moor	Repair
First Port of Entry		Medical Facilities	Drydock
U.S. Representative		Garbage Disposal	Railway
ETA Message		Degauss	
Pilotage		Dirty Ballast	
Compulsory		Cranes	
Available		Fixed	
Local Assist		Mobile	

Advisable		Floating	

ANNABA PORT

Country:	Algeria	Latitude:	36° 54' N
Geographic Region:	ALGERIA	Longitude:	7° 46' E

Publication	131	Tugs Salvage	Y	Lifts
Chart	52202	Tugs Assist	Y	200 Tons Plus
Harbor Size	M	Quarantine		50-200 Tons
Harbor Type	CB	Pratique		25-49 Tons
Shelter Afforded	F	Deratt Cert	Y	0-24 Tons
Entrance Restrictions		Other		Services
Tide		Communications		Longshore
Swell	N	Telephone		Electrical
Ice	N	Telegraph		Steam
Other	N	Radio	Y	Navig Equip
Overhead Limits	N	Radio Tel	Y	Elect Repair
Channel Depth	J	Air	Y	Supplies
Anchorage Depth	C	Rail	Y	Provisions
Cargo Pier Depth	K	Load/Offload		Water
Oil Terminal Depth	K	Wharves	Y	Fuel Oil
Tide	2	Anchor	Y	Diesel Oil
Maximum Size Vessel	L	Med Moor	Y	Deck
Good Holding Ground	Y	Beach Moor		Engine
Turning Area		Ice Moor		Repair
First Port of Entry		Medical Facilities	Y	Drydock
U.S. Representative		Garbage Disposal		Railway
ETA Message	Y	Degauss		
Pilotage		Dirty Ballast	Y	
Compulsory		Cranes		
Available	Y	Fixed		
Local Assist		Mobile		

Advisable	Y	Floating	Y	

CHETAIBI PORT

Country:	Algeria	**Latitude:**	37° 4' N
Geographic Region:	ALGERIA	**Longitude:**	7° 23' E

Publication	131		Tugs Salvage				Lifts	
Chart	52200		Tugs Assist				200 Tons Plus	
Harbor Size	V		Quarantine				50-200 Tons	
Harbor Type	CB		Pratique				25-49 Tons	
Shelter Afforded	F		Deratt Cert				0-24 Tons	
Entrance Restrictions			Other				Services	
Tide			Communications				Longshore	
Swell	Y		Telephone				Electrical	
Ice			Telegraph				Steam	
Other	Y		Radio				Navig Equip	
Overhead Limits			Radio Tel				Elect Repair	
Channel Depth	K		Air				Supplies	
Anchorage Depth	K		Rail				Provisions	
Cargo Pier Depth	N		Load/Offload				Water	
Oil Terminal Depth			Wharves	Y			Fuel Oil	
Tide			Anchor	Y			Diesel Oil	
Maximum Size Vessel			Med Moor	Y			Deck	
Good Holding Ground			Beach Moor				Engine	
Turning Area			Ice Moor				Repair	C
First Port of Entry			Medical Facilities				Drydock	

U.S. Representative			Garbage Disposal				Railway	
ETA Message			Degauss					
Pilotage			Dirty Ballast					
Compulsory			Cranes					
Available			Fixed					
Local Assist			Mobile					
Advisable			Floating					

SKIKDA PORT

Country: Algeria **Latitude:** 36° 53' N

Geographic Region: ALGERIA **Longitude:** 6° 55' E

Publication	131	Tugs Salvage	Y	Lifts
Chart	52223	Tugs Assist	Y	200 Tons Plus
Harbor Size	S	Quarantine		50-200 Tons
Harbor Type	CB	Pratique	Y	25-49 Tons
Shelter Afforded	F	Deratt Cert	Y	0-24 Tons
Entrance Restrictions		Other		Services
Tide	N	Communications		Longshore
Swell	N	Telephone		Electrical
Ice	N	Telegraph	Y	Steam
Other	Y	Radio	Y	Navig Equip
Overhead Limits	N	Radio Tel	Y	Elect Repair
Channel Depth	A	Air	Y	Supplies
Anchorage Depth	A	Rail	Y	Provisions
Cargo Pier Depth	G	Load/Offload		Water
Oil Terminal Depth	H	Wharves	Y	Fuel Oil
Tide	1	Anchor		Diesel Oil
Maximum Size Vessel	L	Med Moor	Y	Deck
Good Holding Ground	Y	Beach Moor		Engine
Turning Area	Y	Ice Moor		Repair
First Port of Entry	Y	Medical Facilities	Y	Drydock

U.S. Representative	N	Garbage Disposal	N	Railway
ETA Message	Y	Degauss		
Pilotage		Dirty Ballast	Y	
Compulsory		Cranes		
Available	Y	Fixed		
Local Assist		Mobile		
Advisable	Y	Floating	Y	

ALGERIA EXPORT

ALGERIA EXPORT BY PRODUCTS

HS4	Name	Value	Percent
2709	Petroleum oils, crude	$24,566,899,141	40.74%
2711	Petroleum gases	$24,223,058,560	40.17%
2710	Petroleum oils, refined	$8,541,381,891	14.17%
2707	Oils and other products of the distillation of high temperature coal tar	$625,348,106	1.04%
8703	Cars	$477,702,274	0.79%
2814	Ammonia	$354,393,076	0.59%
1701	Raw sugar, cane	$256,950,970	0.43%
2510	Natural calcium phosphates	$122,931,195	0.20%
7204	Ferrous waste and scrap	$101,371,864	0.17%
2804	Hydrogen, rare gases and other nonmetals	$75,033,380	0.12%
7901	Unwrought zinc	$73,362,367	0.12%
2922	Oxygen-function amino-compounds	$40,072,553	0.07%
7801	Lead refined unwrought	$29,465,951	0.05%
2905	Acyclic alcohols	$29,171,122	0.05%
2202	Waters flavored or sweetened	$28,342,439	0.05%
2902	Cyclic hydrocarbons	$25,005,694	0.04%
7005	Float glass	$24,429,371	0.04%
0804	Dates, figs, pineapples, avocados, guavas and mangoes	$24,256,961	0.04%
4801	Newsprint	$23,292,014	0.04%
7208	Hot rolled iron or non-alloy steel, coil,w >600mm, t >10mm, myp 355 mpa	$22,644,028	0.04%
4804	Uncoated kraft paper and paperboard	$21,465,139	0.04%
7108	Gold	$17,635,841	0.03%

1001	Wheat and meslin	$16,552,125	0.03%
7305	Other tubes and pipes of iron or steel having circular cross section	$16,542,922	0.03%
7210	Flat rolled iron or non-alloy steel, coated with tin, w >600mm, t >0.5m	$16,052,418	0.03%
4105	Tanned skins of sheep or lambs	$14,579,880	0.02%
2901	Acyclic hydrocarbons	$13,729,425	0.02%
7209	Cold rolled iron or non-alloy steel, coil, width >600mm, t >3mm, 355 mp	$12,794,424	0.02%
2523	Cement	$12,478,186	0.02%
2904	Sulfonated, nitrated or nitrosated derivatives of hydrocarbons	$12,019,002	0.02%
4011	New pneumatic tires, of rubber	$12,016,847	0.02%
8471	Automatic data processing machines	$11,785,107	0.02%
0305	Fish flours, meals & pellets for human consumption	$11,551,745	0.02%
8704	Motor vehicles for transporting goods	$11,339,210	0.02%
8515	Electric laser or other light or photon beam	$11,083,653	0.02%
8803	Parts of goods of other aircraft	$10,971,076	0.02%
8414	Air or vacuum pumps; ventilating or recycling hoods	$9,918,868	0.02%
7112	Scrap of precious metal	$9,897,723	0.02%
7201	Pig iron	$9,815,438	0.02%
7601	Unwrought aluminum	$9,111,142	0.02%
8483	Transmission shafts	$8,991,286	0.01%
9025	Hydrometers and similar floating instruments, thermometers, pyrometers, barometers, hygrometers and psychrometers	$8,789,396	0.01%
8426	Ships' derricks; cranes	$8,698,463	0.01%
4805	Other uncoated paper and paperboard	$7,628,615	0.01%
7007	Safety glass	$7,582,770	0.01%
1512	Sunflower-seed or safflower oil, crude	$6,717,229	0.01%
8429	Self-propelled bulldozers, excavators and road rollers	$6,311,443	0.01%
8517	Telephones	$5,836,991	0.01%
9607	Slide fasteners and parts thereof	$5,658,035	0.01%
0306	Crustaceans	$5,651,742	0.01%
2620	Slag, ash and residues	$5,578,815	0.01%
8702	Motor vehicles for the transport of > 10 persons	$5,575,453	0.01%
7404	Copper waste and scrap	$5,505,194	0.01%
0709	Other vegetables	$5,414,394	0.01%
3402	Cleaning products	$5,146,483	0.01%
4707	Recovered paper and paperboard	$5,025,643	0.01%

7304	Tubes, pipes and hollow profiles, seamless, of iron or steel	$4,913,165	0.01%
4104	Tanned hides and skins of bovine or equine animals	$4,750,392	0.01%
3915	Plastic waste, parings and scrap	$4,562,658	0.01%
2716	Electrical energy	$4,492,559	0.01%
7326	Other articles of iron or steel	$4,374,529	0.01%
3923	Packing of goods	$4,351,044	0.01%
6908	Glazed ceramic flags and pavers including glazed ceramic mosaic cubes	$4,292,402	0.01%
8411	Turbojets, turbo propellers and other gas turbines	$4,205,977	0.01%
8708	Parts and accessories of the motor vehicles	$4,171,018	0.01%
1212	Locust beans, locust seeds	$4,077,458	0.01%
7207	Semifinished products of iron or nonalloy steel	$3,992,001	0.01%
3920	Other not reinforced plastic plates, sheets, film, foil and strip	$3,928,070	0.01%
3206	Other coloring matter	$3,907,726	0.01%
2818	Artificial corundum	$3,874,792	0.01%
8479	Machines and mechanical appliances having individual functions nes	$3,822,810	0.01%
1703	Molasses	$3,734,813	0.01%
8504	Electrical transformers	$3,720,255	0.01%
0307	Molluscs	$3,600,292	0.01%
8529	Parts of radios, telephones and TVs	$3,493,410	0.01%
8408	Compression-ignition internal combustion piston engines	$3,478,567	0.01%
8413	Pumps for liquids	$3,451,859	0.01%
4411	Fiberboard of wood	$3,399,055	0.01%
8431	Parts for use with hoists and excavation machinery	$3,338,843	0.01%
7403	Refined copper and copper alloys	$3,274,808	0.01%
8543	Electrical machines and apparatus with individual functions not elsewhere specified	$3,270,165	0.01%
4503	Articles of natural cork	$3,246,402	0.01%
8705	Special purpose motor vehicles	$2,983,369	0.00%
9014	Direction finding compasses	$2,967,579	0.00%
6809	Plaster articles	$2,922,437	0.00%
3102	Mineral or chemical fertilizers, nitrogenous	$2,902,079	0.00%
2715	Bituminous mix, mastic from asphalt, bitumen/tar/pitc	$2,804,310	0.00%
4101	Raw hides and skins of bovine or equine animals	$2,801,533	0.00%
8207	Interchangeable tools for hand tools	$2,798,099	0.00%
4110	Waste of leather	$2,710,693	0.00%

1804	Cocoa butter, fat, oil	$2,601,486	0.00%
4102	Raw skins of sheep or lambs	$2,581,092	0.00%
2607	Lead ores	$2,562,058	0.00%
3004	Medicaments, packaged	$2,556,541	0.00%
8905	Floating or submersible drilling platforms	$2,431,155	0.00%
3921	Other plastic plates, sheets, film, foil and strip	$2,332,363	0.00%
4016	Other articles of vulcanized rubber	$2,315,272	0.00%
4818	Toilet paper of a kind used for household or sanitary purposes	$2,283,554	0.00%
8512	Electrical lighting or signaling equipment used for motor vehicles	$2,256,661	0.00%
3214	Glaziers' putty	$2,240,293	0.00%
9015	Surveying, hydrographic, oceanographic, hydrological, meteorological or geophysical instruments and appliances	$2,208,680	0.00%
8716	Trailers and semi-trailers	$2,135,712	0.00%
8430	Other moving, excavating, extracting or boring machinery for earth, minerals or ores; pile-drivers; snowplows and snowblowers	$2,111,671	0.00%
7308	Structures and parts thereof (bridges, lock gates, towers, etc)	$2,022,246	0.00%
1522	Residues from treatment animal & veg waxes	$1,994,668	0.00%
0703	Onions and shallots	$1,982,997	0.00%
8907	Other floating structures (for example, rafts, tanks, buoys and beacons)	$1,974,145	0.00%
2401	Tobacco, raw	$1,942,861	0.00%
2204	Wine of fresh grapes	$1,902,746	0.00%
8502	Electric generating sets and rotary converters	$1,845,278	0.00%
2207	Ethyl alcohol > 80% by volume	$1,781,942	0.00%
3926	Other articles of plastic	$1,735,382	0.00%
3204	Synthetic organic coloring matter	$1,723,172	0.00%
8481	Appliances for thermostatically controlled valves	$1,666,687	0.00%
1003	Barley	$1,642,561	0.00%
7802	Lead waste or scrap	$1,637,264	0.00%
7320	Springs of iron or steel	$1,616,236	0.00%
2501	Salt	$1,592,642	0.00%
9104	Instrument panel clocks and clocks of a similar type for vehicles, aircraft, spacecraft or vessels	$1,582,681	0.00%
8474	Machinery for working earth, stone, and other mineral substances	$1,515,029	0.00%
8505	Electromagnets	$1,499,644	0.00%
4009	Tubes, pipes and hoses, of vulcanized rubber	$1,495,281	0.00%

4819	Cartons, boxes, cases, bags and other packing containers of paper	$1,481,666	0.00%
8432	Agricultural, forestry machinery for soil preparation	$1,298,623	0.00%
8437	Machines for cleaning, sorting or grading seed; machinery used in the milling industry or for the working of cereals or dried leguminous vegetables	$1,297,530	0.00%
9013	Liquid crystal devices	$1,264,697	0.00%
8526	Radar and radio navigational aid apparatus	$1,258,227	0.00%
3208	Paints and varnishes, nonaqueous	$1,239,549	0.00%
8424	Mechanical appliances for dispersing liquids or powders; fire extinguishers; spray guns; steam or sand blasting machines	$1,236,109	0.00%
2713	Petroleum coke	$1,149,215	0.00%
3916	Monofilament	$1,138,340	0.00%
7307	Tube or pipe fittings of iron or steel	$1,112,414	0.00%
9031	Measuring or checking instruments, appliances and machines	$1,092,396	0.00%
4504	Agglomerated cork	$1,068,280	0.00%
4106	Tanned skins of other animals	$1,067,039	0.00%
5211	Woven fabrics of cotton of < 85% weighing > 200 g/m2	$1,046,266	0.00%
5603	Nonwoven textiles	$1,032,706	0.00%
2603	Gold content	$990,468	0.00%
8406	Steam turbines and other vapor turbines	$971,299	0.00%
4902	Newspapers, journals and periodicals	$964,030	0.00%
8511	Electrical ignition or starting equipment	$950,767	0.00%
9007	Cinematographic cameras and projectors	$936,646	0.00%
0403	Fermented milk and cream products	$920,439	0.00%
1905	Bread, pastry, cakes, biscuits and other baked goods	$906,551	0.00%
0304	Fish fillet or meat	$882,203	0.00%
1604	Prepared or preserved fish	$874,676	0.00%
4802	Paper, uncoat, for writing etc, rolls, handmade paper	$866,472	0.00%
3704	Photographic plates, film, paper, exposed but not developed	$857,267	0.00%
2807	Sulfuric acid; oleum	$823,345	0.00%
2002	Tomatoes, prepared or preserved	$802,662	0.00%
2836	Carbonates; peroxocarbonates (percarbonates); commercial ammonium carbonate containing ammonium carbamate	$801,102	0.00%
8544	Insulated wire; optical fiber cables	$790,390	0.00%
8438	Machinery, not specified for the industrial preparation or manufacture of food or drink	$770,702	0.00%

8425	Pulley tackle and hoists; winches and capstans; jacks	$765,289	0.00%
8422	Dishwashing machines; machinery for cleaning or drying containers; machinery for filling, closing, sealing or labeling containers	$764,556	0.00%
8409	Parts suitable for use with spark-ignition engines	$763,953	0.00%
4901	Printed books, brochures, leaflets and similar printed matter	$760,659	0.00%
2618	Granulated slag	$750,255	0.00%
8536	Apparatus protecting electrical circuits for < 1k volts	$641,370	0.00%
9018	Medical, surgical, dental or vet instruments	$639,786	0.00%
3823	Industrial monocarboxylic fatty acids; acid oils from refining; industrial fatty alcohols	$639,751	0.00%
9026	Instruments and apparatus for measuring or checking the flow, level, pressure or other variables of liquids or gases	$631,762	0.00%
1519	Stearic acid	$630,228	0.00%
3303	Perfumes and toilet waters	$629,449	0.00%
8524	Recorded gramophone records	$620,893	0.00%
8506	Primary cells and primary batteries	$572,452	0.00%
1902	Pasta	$570,303	0.00%
8707	Vehicle Bodies	$557,569	0.00%
7606	Aluminum plates, sheets and strip > 0.2 mm	$555,250	0.00%
0302	Fish, excluding fillets	$553,918	0.00%
1006	Rice	$552,324	0.00%
0303	Frozen fish, excluding fillets	$533,388	0.00%
4501	Natural cork, raw	$527,397	0.00%
8525	Transmission apparatus for radio, telephone and TV	$525,927	0.00%
8421	Centrifuges	$483,027	0.00%
8604	Railway or tramway maintenance or service vehicles	$473,615	0.00%
8407	Spark-ignition reciprocating or rotary internal combustion piston engines	$471,659	0.00%
9030	Oscilloscopes, spectrum analyzers and other instruments and apparatus for measuring or checking electrical quantities	$458,746	0.00%
8538	Parts for use with apparatus for protecting electrical circuits	$455,142	0.00%
9406	Prefabricated buildings	$454,620	0.00%
8519	Sound recording apparatus	$454,465	0.00%
1507	Soya-bean oil, crude	$451,483	0.00%
1702	Other sugars	$446,386	0.00%
8307	Flexible tubing of base metal with or without fittings	$444,251	0.00%
6910	Ceramic sinks	$442,742	0.00%

3902	Polymers of propylene or of other olefins, in primary forms	$427,730	0.00%
2106	Food preparations not elsewhere specified	$426,998	0.00%
8412	Other engines and motors	$412,319	0.00%
1101	Wheat or meslin flour	$406,101	0.00%
4823	Other paper, paperboard cut to size or shape	$405,843	0.00%
5903	Textile fabrics impregnated with plastics	$399,054	0.00%
3307	Shaving products	$395,657	0.00%
3901	Polymers of ethylene, in primary forms	$380,096	0.00%
9027	Instruments and apparatus for physical or chemical analysis	$375,556	0.00%
7321	Stoves, ranges, barbecues and similar appliances of iron or steel	$370,969	0.00%
5911	Textile fabric for card clothing, technical use	$362,208	0.00%
6307	Other made up articles, including dress patterns	$361,698	0.00%
4012	Retreaded or used pneumatic tires of rubber	$353,812	0.00%
9028	Gas, liquid or electricity supply or production meters	$346,763	0.00%
2009	Fruit juices	$342,651	0.00%
8477	Machinery for working rubber or plastics	$337,294	0.00%
4412	Plywood, veneered panels and similar laminated wood	$329,319	0.00%
8205	Hand tools (including glass cutters) not elsewhere specified	$315,293	0.00%
7306	Other tubes and pipes of iron or steel	$314,031	0.00%
2844	Radioactive chemical elements and radioactive isotopes	$313,419	0.00%
5901	Textile fabrics coated with gum or amylaceous	$311,733	0.00%
2610	Chromium ore	$311,651	0.00%
7213	Hot rolled bar/rod grooved iron or non-alloy steel in irregular coils	$298,974	0.00%
8418	Refrigerators, freezers	$295,183	0.00%
9703	Original sculptures and statuary	$292,595	0.00%
7605	Aluminum wire	$289,814	0.00%
7604	Aluminum bars, rods and profiles	$289,731	0.00%
9006	Photographic cameras	$282,902	0.00%
7615	Table, kitchen or other household articles of aluminum	$281,644	0.00%
8427	Fork-lift trucks	$278,844	0.00%
2508	Clays	$257,219	0.00%
2606	Aluminium ores	$256,728	0.00%
7318	Screws, bolts, nuts and similar articles of iron or steel	$251,527	0.00%
8609	Containers for carriage by one or more modes of transport	$247,521	0.00%

3003	Medicaments, not packaged	$245,855	0.00%
0402	Milk and cream, concentrated	$242,778	0.00%
2817	Zinc oxide and peroxide	$238,851	0.00%
8507	Electric storage batteries	$238,168	0.00%
1515	Linseed oil, crude	$236,920	0.00%
8701	Tractors	$223,499	0.00%
8415	Air conditioners	$219,357	0.00%
8542	Electronic integrated circuits	$217,563	0.00%
0202	Bovine meat (frozen)	$217,544	0.00%
7322	Radiators for central heating of iron or steel	$212,631	0.00%
9404	Mattress supports; articles of bedding	$208,655	0.00%
4103	Other raw hides and skins	$202,097	0.00%
7309	Tanks etc, over 300 liter capacity, iron or steel	$194,470	0.00%
6907	Unglazed ceramic flags and pavers including unglazed ceramic mosaic cubes	$193,200	0.00%
9403	Other furniture and parts thereof	$192,138	0.00%
9405	Lamps and lighting fittings	$185,817	0.00%
1516	hydrogenated animal and vegetable fats, oils	$185,473	0.00%
2516	Granite	$185,030	0.00%
8443	Printers and copying machines	$184,316	0.00%
8903	Yachts	$183,647	0.00%
3815	Reaction initiators, reaction accelerators and catalytic products	$179,340	0.00%
7503	Nickel waste and scrap	$178,979	0.00%
8485	Ships or boats propellers and blades	$173,187	0.00%
6301	Blankets and traveling rugs	$171,489	0.00%
8501	Electric motors and generators	$170,915	0.00%
8523	Storage devices, smart cards, discs, tapes etc	$170,134	0.00%
9032	Automatic regulating or controlling instruments and apparatus	$169,991	0.00%
3103	Mineral or chemical fertilizers, phosphatic	$167,573	0.00%
4803	Toilet etc household, sanitary stock	$167,501	0.00%
8534	Electronic printed circuits	$167,312	0.00%
4013	Inner tubes of rubber	$164,097	0.00%
2918	Carboxylic acids with additional oxygen function	$162,582	0.00%
7312	Stranded wire, ropes, cables of iron or steel, not electrically insulated	$159,192	0.00%
8537	Electrical Boards and panels for protecting electrical circuits	$158,338	0.00%

3301	Essential oils	$158,035	0.00%
8204	Hand-operated spanners and wrenches	$155,630	0.00%
8482	Ball or roller bearings	$153,148	0.00%
8428	Other lifting, handling, loading or unloading machinery (for example, elevators, escalators, conveyors, teleferics)	$151,025	0.00%
8503	Parts for use with electric generators or converters	$149,985	0.00%
9017	Drafting tables and machines	$147,058	0.00%
4005	Compounded rubber	$144,200	0.00%
8545	Carbon electrodes or other articles of graphite or carbon used for electrical purposes	$142,510	0.00%
2505	Natural sands	$138,794	0.00%
7405	Master alloys of copper	$136,935	0.00%
8473	Parts and accessories for office machines	$133,952	0.00%
0803	Bananas and plantains	$132,442	0.00%
6802	Worked monumental or building stone (except slate)	$132,307	0.00%
8528	Monitors and projectors; reception apparatus for television	$130,864	0.00%
3806	Rosin and resin acids	$130,400	0.00%
7315	Chain and parts thereof, of iron or steel	$129,444	0.00%
3207	Prepared pigments	$126,985	0.00%
2201	Waters natural	$126,507	0.00%
3814	Organic composite solvents and thinners	$123,827	0.00%
9401	Seats	$123,809	0.00%
7407	Copper bars, rods and profiles	$123,471	0.00%
1209	Seeds, fruits and spores for sowing	$122,675	0.00%
7216	Angles, shapes and sections of iron or nonalloy steel	$122,306	0.00%
0104	Sheep	$121,226	0.00%
3917	Tubes, pipes and hoses and fittings	$121,208	0.00%
0802	Other nuts	$120,096	0.00%
7616	Other articles of aluminum	$119,470	0.00%
4911	Other printed matter	$119,152	0.00%
8607	Parts of railway locomotives	$119,059	0.00%
7602	Waste or scrap, aluminium	$118,334	0.00%
7010	Glass carboys, bottles, flasks, jars, pots or other containers	$117,303	0.00%
7323	Table, kitchen or other household articles of iron or steel	$116,469	0.00%
8531	Electric sound or visual signaling apparatus	$113,810	0.00%

5803	Gauze	$113,508	0.00%
1806	Cocoa powder, sweetened	$112,874	0.00%
3603	Safety or detonating fuses	$111,707	0.00%
2005	Homogenized vegetable preparations	$108,541	0.00%
5705	Other carpets and other textile floor coverings	$104,149	0.00%
8602	Other rail locomotives; locomotive tenders	$102,062	0.00%
1509	Olive oil, virgin	$101,018	0.00%
6204	Women's suits, not knit	$99,315	0.00%
6109	T-shirts	$98,854	0.00%
9610	Slates and boards, with writing or drawing surfaces	$96,409	0.00%
8419	Machinery, plant or laboratory equipment involving a change of temperature such as heating, cooking, roasting	$96,117	0.00%
8509	Electromechanical domestic appliances	$94,761	0.00%
6305	Sacks and bags, used for packing goods	$92,570	0.00%
2803	Carbon, nesoi	$92,272	0.00%
8480	Molding boxes for metal foundry	$92,078	0.00%
9701	Paintings, drawings and pastels done by hand	$91,571	0.00%
2403	Cigarettes	$85,780	0.00%
4001	Natural rubber	$82,514	0.00%
8440	Bookbinding machinery	$76,895	0.00%
7314	Cloth of iron or steel wire	$76,776	0.00%
8453	Machinery for preparing, tanning or working hides, skins or leather	$76,574	0.00%
7608	Aluminum tubes and pipes	$74,457	0.00%
8516	Electric instantaneous or storage water heaters	$73,521	0.00%
4706	Pulps of fibers derived from recovered paper or paperboard	$73,210	0.00%
3304	Beauty or make-up preparations	$72,782	0.00%
0701	Potatoes	$72,156	0.00%
7219	Flat-rolled products of stainless steel of a width > 600 mm	$70,838	0.00%
1105	Potato flour or meal	$69,621	0.00%
7110	Platinum	$68,340	0.00%
8302	Base metal mountings, fittings and similar articles suitable for furniture; base metal hat racks; castors with mountings	$67,874	0.00%
8539	Electrical filament	$67,250	0.00%
3002	Human or animal blood prepared for therapeutic uses	$67,035	0.00%
3302	Mixtures of odoriferous substances and mixtures	$64,783	0.00%

6203	Men's suits, not knit	$64,471	0.00%
8450	laundry-type washing machines	$62,398	0.00%
4202	Trunks or cases of any kind	$61,530	0.00%
1103	Cereal groats, meal and pellets	$60,678	0.00%
2302	Bran, sharps (middlings) and other residues	$60,164	0.00%
9023	Instruments, apparatus and models, designed for demonstrational purposes	$59,114	0.00%
1211	Plants used in perfumery, in pharmacy or for insecticide	$56,812	0.00%
6310	Used or new rags textile scraps	$56,129	0.00%
2524	Asbestos	$56,007	0.00%
2942	Other organic compounds	$53,020	0.00%
3201	Tanning extracts of vegetable origin	$52,223	0.00%
8484	Gaskets and similar joints of metal sheeting	$51,717	0.00%
3913	Natural polymers	$51,485	0.00%
6807	Asphalt	$51,007	0.00%
0713	Dried legumes	$49,340	0.00%
9019	Mechano-therapy appliances	$48,934	0.00%
0808	Apples	$48,755	0.00%
1302	Vegetable saps and extracts	$47,524	0.00%
8433	Harvesting or agricultural machinery	$46,370	0.00%
4808	Paper and paperboard, corrugated	$45,869	0.00%
8466	Parts and accessories for metal working machines	$44,860	0.00%
7117	Imitation jewelry	$44,243	0.00%
2517	Pebbles, gravel, broken & crushed stone for aggregate	$44,232	0.00%
3605	Matches	$43,510	0.00%
2714	Bitumen and asphalt, natural	$42,539	0.00%
6810	Cement articles	$41,330	0.00%
8464	Machine tools for working stone	$41,329	0.00%
2917	Polycarboxylic acids	$41,244	0.00%
2923	Quaternary ammonium salts and hydroxides	$40,964	0.00%
9021	Orthopedic appliances, including crutches; splints and other fracture appliances; artificial parts of the body; hearing aids	$40,672	0.00%
3105	Mineral or chemical fertilizers, mixed	$40,582	0.00%
8309	Stoppers, caps and lids	$38,723	0.00%
2915	Saturated acyclic monocarboxylic acids	$38,478	0.00%

8540	Thermionic, cold cathode or photocathode tubes	$38,058	0.00%
6402	Other footwear of rubber or plastics	$37,530	0.00%
7013	Glassware for interior decorative use	$36,889	0.00%
8904	Tugs and pusher craft	$36,708	0.00%
6208	Women's undergarments, not knit	$36,388	0.00%
3405	Polishes and creams	$36,324	0.00%
0207	Poultry	$36,026	0.00%
5601	Wadding of textile materials	$35,409	0.00%
9029	Revolution counters; speedometers and tachometers	$34,700	0.00%
3209	Paints and varnishes, aqueous	$34,291	0.00%
2941	Antibiotics	$34,228	0.00%
6217	Clothing accessories not elsewhere specified, not knit	$33,970	0.00%
8467	Tools for hand working, pneumatic, hydraulic motors	$33,951	0.00%
6309	Used clothes and textiles	$33,553	0.00%
7419	Other articles of copper	$33,519	0.00%
0711	Vegetables provisionally preserved	$33,312	0.00%
9020	Other breathing appliances and gas masks	$33,049	0.00%
0511	Animal products not elsewhere specified	$32,462	0.00%
7018	Glass beads	$32,332	0.00%
6913	Statuettes and other ornamental ceramic articles	$32,278	0.00%
8206	Tools of two or more types of hand tools, for retail sale	$31,482	0.00%
0401	Milk and cream	$31,090	0.00%
3808	Insecticides, rodenticides, fungicides, herbicides	$31,024	0.00%
7418	Table, kitchen or other household articles of copper	$29,645	0.00%
8203	Files, rasps, pliers, pincers, tweezers, metal cutting shears, pipe cutter, and base metal parts thereof	$29,448	0.00%
7607	Aluminum foil < 0.2 mm	$29,326	0.00%
2008	Fruit, nuts and edible plants preserved with sugar	$29,136	0.00%
2103	Sauces and seasonings	$29,098	0.00%
2936	Vitamins	$28,942	0.00%
8901	Cruise ships and similar vessels for the transport of persons	$28,843	0.00%
0206	Edible offal of animals	$28,579	0.00%
0106	Live animals, except farm animals	$28,463	0.00%
4203	Articles of apparel of leather	$28,240	0.00%
2903	Halogenated derivatives of hydrocarbons	$28,121	0.00%

8208	Knives and cutting blades for machines	$27,918	0.00%
2309	Preparations of a kind used in animal feeding	$27,905	0.00%
9101	Wrist watches and pocket watches in cases of precious metal	$27,839	0.00%
7413	Stranded wire, cables and similar articles of copper	$27,835	0.00%
2912	Aldehydes	$27,767	0.00%
8447	Knitting machines	$27,581	0.00%
3924	Plastic tableware, kitchenware or other household products	$27,275	0.00%
0708	Legumes	$27,042	0.00%
8439	Machinery for making pulp of cellulosic material or for making paper	$26,616	0.00%
5701	Carpets, knotted	$26,379	0.00%
9304	Arms nes, (spring/air/gas guns, truncheons, etc)	$26,128	0.00%
3401	Soap	$25,790	0.00%
8527	Reception apparatus for radio broadcasting	$24,828	0.00%
8301	Padlocks of base metal	$24,605	0.00%
4811	Paper, paperboard, cellulose wadding and webs of cellulose fibers	$24,288	0.00%
9102	Wrist watches and pocket watches	$23,174	0.00%
8541	Diodes, transistors, semiconductor devices; photosensitive semiconductor devices, including photovoltaic cells	$22,676	0.00%
9506	Articles and equipment for general physical exercise	$22,595	0.00%
8714	Parts and accessories of motorcycles, bicycles or carriages	$22,305	0.00%
9601	Worked ivory, bone, tortoise-shell, horn, antlers, coral, mother-of-pearl and other animal carving material	$22,117	0.00%
2519	Natural magnesium carbonate	$21,366	0.00%
3006	Pharmaceutical goods	$21,274	0.00%
1802	Cocoa shells	$21,077	0.00%
0910	Ginger	$21,062	0.00%
5704	Carpets of felt	$20,541	0.00%
4002	Synthetic rubber	$20,257	0.00%
6306	Tarpaulins, awnings and sunblinds	$20,125	0.00%
3212	Pigments, nonaqueous	$19,991	0.00%
4502	Natural cork, debacked	$19,818	0.00%
8532	Electrical capacitors	$19,741	0.00%
8441	Other machinery for making paper pulp, paper or paperboard	$19,571	0.00%
6110	Sweaters, pullovers, sweatshirts, etc	$19,532	0.00%
8462	Machine tools for working metal by forging; machine tools for working	$19,356	0.00%

	metal by bending, folding, straightening or flattening		
3811	Anti-knock	$18,723	0.00%
4006	Other forms of unvulcanized rubber	$18,251	0.00%
7311	Containers for compressed or liquified gas	$18,119	0.00%
2512	Siliceous fossil meals and earths	$18,043	0.00%
3925	Plastic builders' ware	$17,834	0.00%
5703	Carpets, tufted	$17,797	0.00%
8445	Machines for preparing textile fibers	$17,024	0.00%
2520	Gypsum	$16,906	0.00%
9001	Optical fibers	$16,738	0.00%
2824	Lead oxides	$16,165	0.00%
3403	Lubricating products	$16,088	0.00%
8533	Electrical resistors	$16,023	0.00%
2007	Jams, jellies	$16,022	0.00%
7014	Signaling glassware	$15,927	0.00%
6304	Bedspreads, textile material, not elsewhere specified, knit or crochet	$15,924	0.00%
1602	Homogenized preparations of meat	$15,887	0.00%
0710	Frozen vegetables	$15,710	0.00%
7113	Jewelry of precious metal	$15,635	0.00%
6403	Footwear, with leather body	$15,470	0.00%
6103	Men's suits	$15,285	0.00%
0809	Apricots	$15,248	0.00%
6506	Other headgear	$15,136	0.00%
8448	Auxiliary machinery for use with knitting and textile machines	$15,005	0.00%
3203	Coloring matter of vegetable or animal origin	$14,842	0.00%
2835	Phosphinates and phosphonates	$14,595	0.00%
6201	Men's overcoats, not knit	$14,564	0.00%
6202	Womens overcoats, not knit	$14,490	0.00%
0405	Butter	$14,401	0.00%
4302	Other tanned or dressed furskins	$14,380	0.00%
7316	Anchors, grapnels and parts thereof, of iron or steel	$13,883	0.00%
3305	Hair products	$13,712	0.00%
8436	Other agricultural, horticultural, forestry equipment; poultry incubators and brooders	$13,517	0.00%
8420	Calendering or other rolling machines	$13,374	0.00%

0409	Honey	$13,281	0.00%
6116	Gloves, mittens and mitts	$13,257	0.00%
8442	Machinery for making printing components	$13,251	0.00%
1704	Confectionery sugar	$12,795	0.00%
8461	Machine tools for planing, shaping, slotting, gear cutting, or sawing	$12,706	0.00%
6206	Women's shirts, not knit	$12,165	0.00%
8522	Parts and accessories for video or sound equipment	$12,096	0.00%
7016	Glass paving blocks, slabs, bricks, squares, tiles or other molded products	$11,915	0.00%
6404	Footwear, with textile body	$11,845	0.00%
8458	Lathes for removing metal	$11,610	0.00%
0901	Coffee, not roasted	$11,430	0.00%
9010	Equipment for photographic laboratories	$11,406	0.00%
4820	Registers, account books, notebooks	$11,098	0.00%
6401	Waterproof footwear	$10,965	0.00%
3005	Wadding, gauze and bandages	$10,494	0.00%
1518	Processed animal, vegetable oils	$10,429	0.00%
4909	Printed or illustrated postcards	$10,243	0.00%
4418	Builders' joinery and carpentry of wood	$10,085	0.00%
8311	Wire, rods, tubes, plates, electrodes and similar products of base metal	$9,981	0.00%
9603	Brooms, brushes, floor sweepers, mops	$9,818	0.00%
3909	Amino-resins, phenolic resins and polyurethanes, in primary forms	$9,551	0.00%
9106	Time of day recording apparatus and apparatus for measuring	$9,527	0.00%
5515	Other woven fabrics of synthetic staple fibers	$9,504	0.00%
6902	Refractory bricks, blocks, tiles and similar refractory ceramic constructional goods	$9,429	0.00%
6914	Other ceramic articles	$9,342	0.00%
8478	Machinery for preparing or making up tobacco	$9,262	0.00%
8547	Insulating fittings for electrical machines, appliances or equipment	$9,228	0.00%
0601	Bulbs, tubers, corms, crowns and rhizomes, dormant	$9,163	0.00%
0406	Fresh cheese	$9,137	0.00%
0407	Birds eggs, in shell	$8,904	0.00%
3215	Ink	$8,721	0.00%
1904	Cereal foods	$8,708	0.00%
2515	Marble and travertine	$8,627	0.00%
2530	Other mineral substances	$8,474	0.00%

0702	Tomatoes		$8,201	0.00%
6104	Women's suits		$7,952	0.00%
1517	Margarine, not liquid		$7,703	0.00%
0204	Lamb meat		$7,682	0.00%
8451	Machinery for washing, cleaning or drying fabrics		$7,553	0.00%
4602	Basketwork, wickerwork and other articles, made directly to shape from plaiting materials		$7,318	0.00%
8709	Works trucks, self-propelled		$7,122	0.00%
9706	Antiques older than one hundred years		$7,060	0.00%
4414	Wooden frames for paintings, photographs, mirrors		$6,767	0.00%
2506	Quartz		$6,707	0.00%
8706	Vehicle chassis fitted with engines		$6,654	0.00%
8306	Bells and gongs		$6,617	0.00%
7324	Sanitary ware and parts of iron or steel		$6,528	0.00%
2209	Vinegars		$6,464	0.00%
9503	Toys, scale models, puzzles		$6,388	0.00%
8468	Machinery and apparatus for soldering, brazing or welding, whether or not capable of cutting		$6,282	0.00%
0812	Preserved fruit and nuts		$6,099	0.00%
7310	Tanks and similar containers, of iron or steel, not exceeding 300 liters		$6,015	0.00%
0805	Citrus fruit		$5,927	0.00%
6911	Porcelain or china tableware or other household articles		$5,906	0.00%
2004	Other vegetables, prepared or preserved		$5,833	0.00%
0813	Apricots, dried		$5,649	0.00%
6211	Active wear, not knit		$5,607	0.00%
6912	Ceramic tableware or other household articles		$5,604	0.00%
4010	Conveyor or transmission belts of vulcanized rubber		$5,424	0.00%
0101	Horses		$5,302	0.00%
9005	Binoculars, monoculars, other optical telescopes, and mountings		$5,299	0.00%
9704	Postage or revenue stamps		$5,299	0.00%
1511	Palm oil, crude		$5,216	0.00%
9022	Apparatus based on the use of X-rays or of alpha, beta or gamma radiations		$5,154	0.00%
4407	Wood sawn or chipped of a thickness exceeding 6 mm		$4,997	0.00%
2402	Cigars		$4,994	0.00%

8712	Bicycles	$4,990	0.00%
6806	Slag wool, rock wool and similar mineral wools	$4,917	0.00%
3802	Activated carbon	$4,888	0.00%
8417	Industrial or laboratory furnaces and ovens, including incinerators	$4,709	0.00%
6214	Shawls, scarves, etc, not knit	$4,586	0.00%
2833	Sulfates; alums; peroxosulfates (persulfates)	$4,234	0.00%
8460	Machine tools for finishing metal or cermets	$4,110	0.00%
2701	Coal; briquettes	$4,019	0.00%
8209	Tool plates/tips/etc, sintered metal carbide & cermet	$3,976	0.00%
4822	Bobbins, spools, cops of paper pulp	$3,961	0.00%
7226	Flat-rolled products of other alloy steel of a width < 600 mm	$3,843	0.00%
0712	Dried vegetables	$3,554	0.00%
3810	Metal pickling preparations	$3,519	0.00%
7009	Glass mirrors	$3,416	0.00%
8711	Motorcycles	$3,328	0.00%
4813	Cigarette paper	$3,232	0.00%
9033	Parts and accessories for machines, appliances, instruments or apparatus	$3,107	0.00%
5203	Cotton, carded or combed	$3,104	0.00%
6205	Men's shirts, not knit	$3,076	0.00%
2846	Compounds, inorganic or organic, of rare-earth metals	$3,075	0.00%
1008	Buckwheat	$3,052	0.00%
2712	Petroleum jelly	$3,047	0.00%
8416	Furnace burners for liquid fuel	$3,047	0.00%
2839	Silicates; commercial alkali metal silicates	$3,036	0.00%
8211	Sets of different knives, cutlery sets	$3,016	0.00%
0806	Grapes	$2,899	0.00%
9004	Spectacles, goggles, corrective, protective	$2,811	0.00%
5604	Rubber textiles	$2,809	0.00%
5208	Woven fabrics of cotton of > 85% weighing < 200 g/m2	$2,662	0.00%
9606	Buttons, press-fasteners, snap-fasteners and press-studs, button molds	$2,662	0.00%
3816	Refractory cements, mortars	$2,654	0.00%
4910	Calendars	$2,651	0.00%
8608	Railway or tramway track fixtures and fittings; safety equipment	$2,651	0.00%
5101	Wool	$2,594	0.00%

8508	Vacuum cleaners	$2,561	0.00%
4008	Plates, sheets, strip, rods and profile shapes, of vulcanized rubber	$2,555	0.00%
0706	Carrots, turnips and beets	$2,544	0.00%
4415	Packing cases, boxes, crates, drums of wood	$2,481	0.00%
6212	Brassieres and parts thereof, not knit	$2,448	0.00%
4821	Paper and paperboard labels	$2,392	0.00%
2203	Beer	$2,334	0.00%
8518	Microphones; loudspeakers; headphones	$2,301	0.00%
6909	Ceramic wares for laboratory uses; ceramic troughs used in agriculture; ceramic pots, jars and similar articles for packing of goods	$2,300	0.00%
4015	Articles of apparel and clothing accessories of vulcanized rubber	$2,254	0.00%
4401	Fuel wood	$2,179	0.00%
6112	Active wear	$2,123	0.00%
7806	Other articles of lead	$2,122	0.00%
8535	Apparatus protecting electrical circuits for > 1k volts	$1,975	0.00%
7114	Articles of goldsmiths' or silversmiths' wares	$1,868	0.00%
5808	Braids in piece	$1,853	0.00%
6216	Gloves, mittens and mitts	$1,843	0.00%
8403	Central heating boilers	$1,767	0.00%
6107	Men's undergarments	$1,763	0.00%
9016	Balances of a sensitivity of 50 milligram or better	$1,754	0.00%
6901	Bricks, blocks, tiles and other ceramic goods	$1,634	0.00%
7211	Hot box roll iron or non-alloy steel, flat, w 150-600mm, t >4mm, myp>35	$1,598	0.00%
1207	Other oil seeds	$1,553	0.00%
1601	Sausages	$1,500	0.00%
8434	Milking and dairy machines	$1,441	0.00%
4107	Leather further prepared after tanning of bovine or equine animals	$1,429	0.00%
7408	Copper wire	$1,363	0.00%
5702	Carpets, woven, not tufted or flocked, hand-woven rugs	$1,347	0.00%
2601	Iron ores and concentrates	$1,334	0.00%
8202	Handsaws, and metal parts thereof	$1,327	0.00%
6210	Garments made of textile felts and nonwoven fabric	$1,326	0.00%
3706	Motion-picture film, exposed and developed	$1,325	0.00%
3822	Diagnostic or laboratory reagents	$1,325	0.00%
4420	Wood marquetry, statuettes and other ornaments of wood	$1,325	0.00%

7610	Aluminum structures (bridges, towers etc)	$1,325	0.00%
7613	Aluminum containers for compressed or liquefied gas	$1,325	0.00%
9024	Machines and appliances for testing the hardness, strength, compressibility, elasticity or other mechanical properties of materials	$1,325	0.00%
9402	Medical, surgical, dental or veterinary furniture	$1,325	0.00%
0801	Coconuts, Brazil nuts and cashew nuts	$1,288	0.00%
7612	Aluminum cans and similar containers	$1,273	0.00%
0902	Tea	$1,193	0.00%
5810	Embroidery in piece	$1,188	0.00%
4421	Other articles of wood	$1,165	0.00%
2521	Limestone	$1,152	0.00%
6117	Other clothing accessories, knitted or crocheted	$1,144	0.00%
0707	Cucumbers	$1,117	0.00%
8215	Cutlery sets plated with precious metal	$1,045	0.00%
0704	Cabbages, cauliflower, kohlrabi, kale, broccoli	$1,045	0.00%
8423	Weighing machinery	$1,012	0.00%
8452	Sewing machines	$1,012	0.00%
4903	Children's picture, drawing or coloring books	$1,002	0.00%

ALGERIA EXPORT BY COUNTRY

Abbrv	Name	Value	Percent
USA	United States	$13,558,313,225	22.49%
ITA	Italy	$9,618,863,041	15.95%
ESP	Spain	$5,980,894,887	9.92%
NLD	Netherlands	$3,957,977,604	6.56%
FRA	France	$3,440,787,460	5.71%
TUR	Turkey	$3,326,855,511	5.52%
CAN	Canada	$3,015,357,546	5.00%
BRA	Brazil	$2,375,483,694	3.94%
BLX	Belgium-Luxembourg	$2,164,614,672	3.59%
IND	India	$1,570,655,173	2.60%
CHN	China	$1,195,510,237	1.98%
GBR	United Kingdom	$1,086,022,716	1.80%
PRT	Portugal	$967,728,913	1.60%

MAR	Morocco		$925,335,060	1.53%
TUN	Tunisia		$918,138,934	1.52%
NGA	Nigeria		$781,471,645	1.30%
KOR	Korea, Rep.		$754,963,700	1.25%
DEU	Germany		$646,636,324	1.07%
ISL	Iceland		$482,440,524	0.80%
EGY	Egypt		$432,530,332	0.72%
JPN	Japan		$411,083,670	0.68%
THA	Thailand		$319,397,804	0.53%
CHE	Switzerland		$293,698,574	0.49%
GRC	Greece		$274,930,719	0.46%
CUB	Cuba		$195,052,641	0.32%
MLT	Malta		$152,042,094	0.25%
AUS	Australia		$140,314,271	0.23%
SVN	Slovenia		$120,781,307	0.20%
IDN	Indonesia		$115,322,496	0.19%
SWE	Sweden		$92,222,560	0.15%
DNK	Denmark		$83,169,889	0.14%
SYR	Syrian Arab Republic		$74,333,402	0.12%
ARE	United Arab Emirates		$71,887,603	0.12%
SGP	Singapore		$65,226,473	0.11%
CRI	Costa Rica		$57,741,091	0.10%
ROU	Romania		$55,454,945	0.09%
CHL	Chile		$54,259,066	0.09%
SDN	Sudan		$52,436,355	0.09%
CYP	Cyprus		$41,495,571	0.07%
AUT	Austria		$41,106,347	0.07%
LBY	Libya		$30,736,601	0.05%
CZE	Czech Republic		$27,885,122	0.05%
LBN	Lebanon		$27,259,899	0.05%
JOR	Jordan		$26,647,928	0.04%
RUS	Russia		$26,151,918	0.04%
MEX	Mexico		$23,025,720	0.04%
XXG	Asia NES		$21,673,145	0.04%

NER	Niger	$21,126,631	0.04%
PHL	Philippines	$20,694,853	0.03%
ZWE	Zimbabwe	$18,784,358	0.03%
POL	Poland	$17,528,404	0.03%
GIN	Guinea	$12,588,251	0.02%
HRV	Croatia	$9,289,594	0.02%
SAU	Saudi Arabia	$9,126,964	0.02%
PAK	Pakistan	$7,605,071	0.01%
DOM	Dominican Republic	$6,651,491	0.01%
LKA	Sri Lanka	$6,158,973	0.01%
BGR	Bulgaria	$5,998,394	0.01%
GHA	Ghana	$5,616,054	0.01%
ALB	Albania	$5,600,810	0.01%
UKR	Ukraine	$4,721,070	0.01%
IRN	Iran	$4,390,254	0.01%
IRQ	Iraq	$4,285,110	0.01%
IRL	Ireland	$4,226,050	0.01%
TZA	Tanzania	$3,156,024	0.01%
SLE	Sierra Leone	$2,519,305	0.00%
URY	Uruguay	$2,171,537	0.00%
LBR	Liberia	$2,118,047	0.00%
	So. African Customs Union	$1,900,217	0.00%
GMB	Gambia	$1,726,713	0.00%
CMR	Cameroon	$1,635,867	0.00%
GEO	Georgia	$1,604,303	0.00%
MLI	Mali	$1,546,464	0.00%
DJI	Djibouti	$1,422,915	0.00%
MRT	Mauritania	$1,268,644	0.00%
KEN	Kenya	$1,236,942	0.00%
MOZ	Mozambique	$1,214,431	0.00%
CPV	Cape Verde	$1,127,572	0.00%
SEN	Senegal	$1,112,082	0.00%
QAT	Qatar	$1,084,636	0.00%
BHR	Bahrain	$981,937	0.00%

NPL	Nepal		$909,731	0.00%
MDG	Madagascar		$901,552	0.00%
AGO	Angola		$832,629	0.00%
NOR	Norway		$791,114	0.00%
BLR	Belarus		$786,879	0.00%
MYS	Malaysia		$740,465	0.00%
OMN	Oman		$692,019	0.00%
BIH	Bosnia and Herzegovina		$552,150	0.00%
CIV	Cote d'Ivoire		$389,206	0.00%
NZL	New Zealand		$372,598	0.00%
HUN	Hungary		$361,000	0.00%
PAN	Panama		$318,671	0.00%
GNQ	Equatorial Guinea		$303,797	0.00%
ETH	Ethiopia		$303,500	0.00%
YEM	Yemen		$205,297	0.00%
KWT	Kuwait		$205,021	0.00%
SVK	Slovak Republic		$193,057	0.00%
MUS	Mauritius		$181,223	0.00%
TJK	Tajikistan		$178,809	0.00%
HKG	Hong Kong		$168,121	0.00%
MNE	Montenegro		$138,836	0.00%
PSE	Palestinian Territory, Occupied		$134,409	0.00%
ARG	Argentina		$130,497	0.00%
VEN	Venezuela		$129,718	0.00%
VNM	Viet Nam		$117,974	0.00%
STP	Sao Tome and Principe		$105,352	0.00%
AZE	Azerbaijan		$84,359	0.00%
COL	Colombia		$74,780	0.00%
LTU	Lithuania		$69,870	0.00%
FIN	Finland		$53,229	0.00%
GAB	Gabon		$48,132	0.00%
BEN	Benin		$43,109	0.00%
UGA	Uganda		$37,784	0.00%
NCL	New Caledonia		$31,676	0.00%

TCD	Chad		$27,732	0.00%
KAZ	Kazakhstan		$26,714	0.00%
PYF	French Polynesia		$23,462	0.00%
BFA	Burkina Faso		$17,558	0.00%
SRB	Serbia		$17,514	0.00%
MHL	Marshall Islands		$16,785	0.00%
MWI	Malawi		$15,481	0.00%
ECU	Ecuador		$12,181	0.00%
BOL	Bolivia		$8,980	0.00%
SLV	El Salvador		$8,270	0.00%
SYC	Seychelles		$6,745	0.00%
XXM	Europe NES		$3,812	0.00%
MDA	Moldova		$3,756	0.00%
HTI	Haiti		$1,680	0.00%
PRY	Paraguay		$1,435	0.00%

Explore More Years »

ALGERIA IMPORTS

ALGERIA IMPORT BY PRODUCTS

HS4	Name	Value	Percent
3004	Medicaments, packaged	$1,130,017,140	5.90%
8411	Turbojets, turbo propellers and other gas turbines	$880,438,658	4.60%
8703	Cars	$822,686,411	4.29%
7304	Tubes, pipes and hollow profiles, seamless, of iron or steel	$795,831,426	4.15%
8704	Motor vehicles for transporting goods	$756,153,400	3.95%
8414	Air or vacuum pumps; ventilating or recycling hoods	$579,365,558	3.02%
2710	Petroleum oils, refined	$559,444,148	2.92%
1701	Raw sugar, cane	$538,228,791	2.81%
8481	Appliances for thermostatically controlled valves	$440,622,083	2.30%
1005	Maize (corn) seed	$411,389,120	2.15%
8413	Pumps for liquids	$346,225,942	1.81%
2304	Soybean oilcake	$318,804,964	1.66%
8708	Parts and accessories of the motor vehicles	$291,672,425	1.52%
7308	Structures and parts thereof (bridges, lock gates, towers, etc)	$253,790,445	1.32%
8705	Special purpose motor vehicles	$248,134,753	1.30%
8471	Automatic data processing machines	$237,028,106	1.24%
1507	Soya-bean oil, crude	$225,126,116	1.17%

8431	Parts for use with hoists and excavation machinery	$218,353,322	1.14%
8479	Machines and mechanical appliances having individual functions nes	$217,435,682	1.13%
8415	Air conditioners	$206,485,899	1.08%
8544	Insulated wire; optical fiber cables	$198,723,321	1.04%
8429	Self-propelled bulldozers, excavators and road rollers	$197,451,644	1.03%
8421	Centrifuges	$191,723,899	1.00%
8517	Telephones	$187,890,249	0.98%
8701	Tractors	$183,568,267	0.96%
8504	Electrical transformers	$165,984,590	0.87%
4011	New pneumatic tires, of rubber	$158,283,423	0.83%
8474	Machinery for working earth, stone, and other mineral substances	$157,593,708	0.82%
2713	Petroleum coke	$157,015,417	0.82%
8537	Electrical Boards and panels for protecting electrical circuits	$146,681,420	0.77%
1001	Wheat and meslin	$141,197,525	0.74%
8526	Radar and radio navigational aid apparatus	$140,429,908	0.73%
0402	Milk and cream, concentrated	$135,546,301	0.71%
8443	Printers and copying machines	$129,817,033	0.68%
8528	Monitors and projectors; reception apparatus for television	$129,229,018	0.67%
0713	Dried legumes	$123,585,577	0.64%
8422	Dishwashing machines; machinery for cleaning or drying containers; machinery for filling, closing, sealing or labeling containers	$120,604,482	0.63%
7208	Hot rolled iron or non-alloy steel, coil,w >600mm, t >10mm, myp 355 mpa	$108,431,533	0.57%
8536	Apparatus protecting electrical circuits for < 1k volts	$105,900,700	0.55%
0901	Coffee, not roasted	$100,682,357	0.53%
8702	Motor vehicles for the transport of > 10 persons	$97,079,752	0.51%
0202	Bovine meat (frozen)	$97,016,463	0.51%
8525	Transmission apparatus for radio, telephone and TV	$95,770,594	0.50%
8901	Cruise ships and similar vessels for the transport of persons	$94,554,719	0.49%
7306	Other tubes and pipes of iron or steel	$93,927,089	0.49%
9403	Other furniture and parts thereof	$88,700,322	0.46%
7305	Other tubes and pipes of iron or steel having circular cross section	$87,083,713	0.45%
2523	Cement	$84,334,529	0.44%
3822	Diagnostic or laboratory reagents	$82,870,812	0.43%
9018	Medical, surgical, dental or vet instruments	$79,873,768	0.42%
8418	Refrigerators, freezers	$79,578,865	0.42%
7326	Other articles of iron or steel	$78,983,483	0.41%
8716	Trailers and semi-trailers	$74,164,631	0.39%
8426	Ships' derricks; cranes	$73,532,962	0.38%
8502	Electric generating sets and rotary converters	$73,080,580	0.38%
8419	Machinery, plant or laboratory equipment involving a change of temperature such as heating, cooking, roasting	$69,557,564	0.36%
7213	Hot rolled bar/rod grooved iron or non-alloy steel in irregular coils	$68,324,847	0.36%

8501	Electric motors and generators	$65,707,562	0.34%
7303	Tubes, pipes and hollow profiles, of cast iron	$64,021,821	0.33%
7604	Aluminum bars, rods and profiles	$63,947,344	0.33%
3907	Polyacetals	$63,363,669	0.33%
8408	Compression-ignition internal combustion piston engines	$60,495,905	0.32%
2401	Tobacco, raw	$60,458,947	0.32%
8409	Parts suitable for use with spark-ignition engines	$59,783,165	0.31%
0808	Apples	$59,631,608	0.31%
0102	Bovines	$59,015,039	0.31%
8483	Transmission shafts	$58,497,561	0.31%
8430	Other moving, excavating, extracting or boring machinery for earth, minerals or ores; pile-drivers; snowplows and snowblowers	$55,128,146	0.29%
7307	Tube or pipe fittings of iron or steel	$54,726,825	0.29%
8207	Interchangeable tools for hand tools	$54,498,307	0.28%
4407	Wood sawn or chipped of a thickness exceeding 6 mm	$53,893,499	0.28%
3002	Human or animal blood prepared for therapeutic uses	$53,450,716	0.28%
9026	Instruments and apparatus for measuring or checking the flow, level, pressure or other variables of liquids or gases	$51,036,669	0.27%
8473	Parts and accessories for office machines	$49,703,218	0.26%
9031	Measuring or checking instruments, appliances and machines	$49,211,217	0.26%
8477	Machinery for working rubber or plastics	$48,504,371	0.25%
5407	Woven fabrics of synthetic filament yarn	$48,081,499	0.25%
8542	Electronic integrated circuits	$45,853,115	0.24%
9015	Surveying, hydrographic, oceanographic, hydrological, meteorological or geophysical instruments and appliances	$45,759,451	0.24%
3920	Other not reinforced plastic plates, sheets, film, foil and strip	$45,656,759	0.24%
8529	Parts of radios, telephones and TVs	$45,390,578	0.24%
3823	Industrial monocarboxylic fatty acids; acid oils from refining; industrial fatty alcohols	$43,671,480	0.23%
7210	Flat rolled iron or non-alloy steel, coated with tin, w >600mm, t >0.5m	$41,993,317	0.22%
3901	Polymers of ethylene, in primary forms	$41,801,126	0.22%
9027	Instruments and apparatus for physical or chemical analysis	$41,071,765	0.21%
7214	Other bars and rods of iron or nonalloy steel, not further worked than forged	$39,721,180	0.21%
3923	Packing of goods	$39,690,950	0.21%
3917	Tubes, pipes and hoses and fittings	$38,622,656	0.20%
9405	Lamps and lighting fittings	$37,113,664	0.19%
8511	Electrical ignition or starting equipment	$36,943,264	0.19%
7013	Glassware for interior decorative use	$36,487,500	0.19%
8205	Hand tools (including glass cutters) not elsewhere specified	$36,223,846	0.19%
8450	laundry-type washing machines	$35,895,589	0.19%
8535	Apparatus protecting electrical circuits for > 1k volts	$35,680,717	0.19%
4412	Plywood, veneered panels and similar laminated wood	$35,308,733	0.18%

2002	Tomatoes, prepared or preserved	$35,038,410	0.18%
7318	Screws, bolts, nuts and similar articles of iron or steel	$33,952,675	0.18%
8538	Parts for use with apparatus for protecting electrical circuits	$33,484,405	0.17%
4819	Cartons, boxes, cases, bags and other packing containers of paper	$33,438,388	0.17%
6908	Glazed ceramic flags and pavers including glazed ceramic mosaic cubes	$32,980,014	0.17%
2106	Food preparations not elsewhere specified	$32,380,923	0.17%
8424	Mechanical appliances for dispersing liquids or powders; fire extinguishers; spray guns; steam or sand blasting machines	$32,027,859	0.17%
3926	Other articles of plastic	$31,276,263	0.16%
8543	Electrical machines and apparatus with individual functions not elsewhere specified	$30,554,801	0.16%
5603	Nonwoven textiles	$29,901,066	0.16%
9032	Automatic regulating or controlling instruments and apparatus	$29,414,548	0.15%
8402	Steam or other vapor generating boilers	$29,195,074	0.15%
4901	Printed books, brochures, leaflets and similar printed matter	$29,019,762	0.15%
8406	Steam turbines and other vapor turbines	$28,472,756	0.15%
8515	Electric laser or other light or photon beam	$28,472,134	0.15%
3906	Acrylic polymers in primary forms	$26,833,264	0.14%
3808	Insecticides, rodenticides, fungicides, herbicides	$26,345,928	0.14%
4202	Trunks or cases of any kind	$25,559,816	0.13%
1202	Ground-nuts in shell	$25,436,672	0.13%
8427	Fork-lift trucks	$24,857,984	0.13%
7225	Flat-rolled products of other alloy steel of a width > 600 mm	$24,619,366	0.13%
8803	Parts of goods of other aircraft	$24,608,293	0.13%
4818	Toilet paper of a kind used for household or sanitary purposes	$24,280,517	0.13%
8516	Electric instantaneous or storage water heaters	$24,101,033	0.13%
7607	Aluminum foil < 0.2 mm	$24,100,553	0.13%
8438	Machinery, not specified for the industrial preparation or manufacture of food or drink	$23,816,946	0.12%
2008	Fruit, nuts and edible plants preserved with sugar	$22,943,238	0.12%
4016	Other articles of vulcanized rubber	$22,376,407	0.12%
4801	Newsprint	$22,050,268	0.12%
7321	Stoves, ranges, barbecues and similar appliances of iron or steel	$21,936,760	0.11%
6104	Women's suits	$21,750,534	0.11%
8507	Electric storage batteries	$21,212,009	0.11%
6301	Blankets and traveling rugs	$21,128,466	0.11%
6405	Other footwear	$20,955,875	0.11%
2929	Compounds with other nitrogen function	$20,693,258	0.11%
8531	Electric sound or visual signaling apparatus	$20,023,902	0.10%
8417	Industrial or laboratory furnaces and ovens, including incinerators	$19,991,217	0.10%
0201	Bovine meat	$19,906,063	0.10%
8480	Molding boxes for metal foundry	$19,689,905	0.10%

2836	Carbonates; peroxocarbonates (percarbonates); commercial ammonium carbonate containing ammonium carbamate	$19,657,311	0.10%
8462	Machine tools for working metal by forging; machine tools for working metal by bending, folding, straightening or flattening	$19,540,350	0.10%
0902	Tea	$19,505,559	0.10%
8475	Machines for assembling electric lamps	$19,357,393	0.10%
7411	Copper tubes and pipes	$18,992,959	0.10%
4802	Paper, uncoat, for writing etc, rolls, handmade paper	$18,965,147	0.10%
6802	Worked monumental or building stone (except slate)	$18,833,848	0.10%
6211	Active wear, not knit	$18,632,052	0.10%
8302	Base metal mountings, fittings and similar articles suitable for furniture; base metal hat racks; castors with mountings	$18,563,801	0.10%
1209	Seeds, fruits and spores for sowing	$18,550,571	0.10%
8452	Sewing machines	$18,486,393	0.10%
6402	Other footwear of rubber or plastics	$18,335,434	0.10%
8482	Ball or roller bearings	$18,153,881	0.09%
9401	Seats	$17,884,502	0.09%
8508	Vacuum cleaners	$17,770,950	0.09%
3811	Anti-knock	$17,640,172	0.09%
3105	Mineral or chemical fertilizers, mixed	$17,568,884	0.09%
4009	Tubes, pipes and hoses, of vulcanized rubber	$17,511,402	0.09%
4804	Uncoated kraft paper and paperboard	$17,324,270	0.09%
7323	Table, kitchen or other household articles of iron or steel	$17,254,243	0.09%
2103	Sauces and seasonings	$17,060,289	0.09%
6902	Refractory bricks, blocks, tiles and similar refractory ceramic constructional goods	$17,002,292	0.09%
3402	Cleaning products	$16,994,665	0.09%
7312	Stranded wire, ropes, cables of iron or steel, not electrically insulated	$16,893,535	0.09%
8428	Other lifting, handling, loading or unloading machinery (for example, elevators, escalators, conveyors, teleferics)	$16,854,441	0.09%
7605	Aluminum wire	$16,412,581	0.09%
8425	Pulley tackle and hoists; winches and capstans; jacks	$16,190,301	0.08%
6203	Men's suits, not knit	$16,069,705	0.08%
4005	Compounded rubber	$15,975,768	0.08%
7216	Angles, shapes and sections of iron or nonalloy steel	$15,528,285	0.08%
6103	Men's suits	$15,471,699	0.08%
3401	Soap	$15,397,093	0.08%
7408	Copper wire	$15,208,535	0.08%
6302	House linen	$15,088,521	0.08%
7322	Radiators for central heating of iron or steel	$15,038,519	0.08%
5516	Woven fabrics of artificial staple fibers	$14,562,837	0.08%
1806	Cocoa powder, sweetened	$14,421,588	0.08%
8441	Other machinery for making paper pulp, paper or paperboard	$14,376,506	0.08%

2102	Yeasts, active	$14,313,648	0.07%
9022	Apparatus based on the use of X-rays or of alpha, beta or gamma radiations	$14,074,868	0.07%
4810	Paper and paperboard, coated on one or both sides with kaolin	$13,870,396	0.07%
8711	Motorcycles	$13,638,772	0.07%
6204	Women's suits, not knit	$13,560,058	0.07%
8301	Padlocks of base metal	$13,224,777	0.07%
3304	Beauty or make-up preparations	$13,121,564	0.07%
3817	Mixed alkylbenzenes and mixed alkylnaphthalenes	$12,921,011	0.07%
3206	Other coloring matter	$12,707,860	0.07%
7601	Unwrought aluminum	$12,623,382	0.07%
9402	Medical, surgical, dental or veterinary furniture	$12,578,925	0.07%
9406	Prefabricated buildings	$12,538,263	0.07%
0701	Potatoes	$12,314,582	0.06%
8485	Ships or boats propellers and blades	$11,998,307	0.06%
4418	Builders' joinery and carpentry of wood	$11,801,510	0.06%
8530	Electric signal, safety & traffic controls, railways, waterways, parking or airfields	$11,732,998	0.06%
8539	Electrical filament	$11,467,202	0.06%
6912	Ceramic tableware or other household articles	$11,136,975	0.06%
8412	Other engines and motors	$11,021,926	0.06%
8512	Electrical lighting or signaling equipment used for motor vehicles	$10,948,477	0.06%
4008	Plates, sheets, strip, rods and profile shapes, of vulcanized rubber	$10,746,651	0.06%
9603	Brooms, brushes, floor sweepers, mops	$10,471,388	0.05%
9030	Oscilloscopes, spectrum analyzers and other instruments and apparatus for measuring or checking electrical quantities	$10,365,695	0.05%
3006	Pharmaceutical goods	$10,223,790	0.05%
6110	Sweaters, pullovers, sweatshirts, etc	$10,100,356	0.05%
7325	Other cast articles of iron or steel	$9,851,059	0.05%
8466	Parts and accessories for metal working machines	$9,722,276	0.05%
0703	Onions and shallots	$9,631,213	0.05%
3815	Reaction initiators, reaction accelerators and catalytic products	$9,596,538	0.05%
9304	Arms nes, (spring/air/gas guns, truncheons, etc)	$9,556,700	0.05%
3903	Polymers of styrene, in primary forms	$9,498,938	0.05%
9014	Direction finding compasses	$9,470,046	0.05%
9021	Orthopedic appliances, including crutches; splints and other fracture appliances; artificial parts of the body; hearing aids	$9,445,064	0.05%
7616	Other articles of aluminum	$8,998,411	0.05%
6403	Footwear, with leather body	$8,963,216	0.05%
7007	Safety glass	$8,947,084	0.05%
7615	Table, kitchen or other household articles of aluminum	$8,764,592	0.05%
8523	Storage devices, smart cards, discs, tapes etc	$8,734,262	0.05%

8607	Parts of railway locomotives	$8,444,272	0.04%
8518	Microphones; loudspeakers; headphones	$8,426,386	0.04%
9506	Articles and equipment for general physical exercise	$8,423,173	0.04%
9023	Instruments, apparatus and models, designed for demonstrational purposes	$8,400,858	0.04%
6910	Ceramic sinks	$8,340,092	0.04%
3302	Mixtures of odoriferous substances and mixtures	$8,332,683	0.04%
2941	Antibiotics	$8,302,825	0.04%
5903	Textile fabrics impregnated with plastics	$8,271,499	0.04%
1801	Cocoa beans, whole	$8,186,269	0.04%
7005	Float glass	$8,038,857	0.04%
7309	Tanks etc, over 300 liter capacity, iron or steel	$8,006,839	0.04%
9608	Pens	$7,988,471	0.04%
7010	Glass carboys, bottles, flasks, jars, pots or other containers	$7,952,286	0.04%
0303	Frozen fish, excluding fillets	$7,920,869	0.04%
3303	Perfumes and toilet waters	$7,902,180	0.04%
6109	T-shirts	$7,852,537	0.04%
7606	Aluminum plates, sheets and strip > 0.2 mm	$7,848,473	0.04%
9503	Toys, scale models, puzzles	$7,827,455	0.04%
7610	Aluminum structures (bridges, towers etc)	$7,816,931	0.04%
0304	Fish fillet or meat	$7,740,017	0.04%
3925	Plastic builders' ware	$7,613,484	0.04%
8546	Electrical insulators of any material	$7,574,907	0.04%
9617	Vacuum flasks and other vacuum vessels	$7,539,561	0.04%
8407	Spark-ignition reciprocating or rotary internal combustion piston engines	$7,536,365	0.04%
6112	Active wear	$7,465,944	0.04%
6208	Women's undergarments, not knit	$7,464,632	0.04%
8608	Railway or tramway track fixtures and fittings; safety equipment	$7,401,942	0.04%
5402	Synthetic filament yarn	$7,365,462	0.04%
2918	Carboxylic acids with additional oxygen function	$7,328,917	0.04%
1511	Palm oil, crude	$7,272,593	0.04%
7311	Containers for compressed or liquified gas	$7,263,659	0.04%
6115	Panty hose, tights, stockings, socks and other hosiery	$7,228,612	0.04%
4001	Natural rubber	$7,218,981	0.04%
6907	Unglazed ceramic flags and pavers including unglazed ceramic mosaic cubes	$7,198,309	0.04%
7209	Cold rolled iron or non-alloy steel, coil, width >600mm, t >3mm, 355 mp	$7,121,493	0.04%
6404	Footwear, with textile body	$7,058,263	0.04%
8503	Parts for use with electric generators or converters	$7,014,568	0.04%
3921	Other plastic plates, sheets, film, foil and strip	$6,984,172	0.04%
3904	Polymers of vinyl chloride or of other halogenated olefins, in primary forms	$6,886,320	0.04%
7019	Glass fibers	$6,784,965	0.04%

3912	Cellulose not elsewhere specified	$6,778,345	0.04%
8447	Knitting machines	$6,771,635	0.04%
8524	Recorded gramophone records	$6,763,980	0.04%
6201	Men's overcoats, not knit	$6,763,019	0.04%
3919	Self-adhesive plates, sheets, film, foil, tape	$6,631,887	0.03%
8458	Lathes for removing metal	$6,610,753	0.03%
7614	Stranded wire, cables of aluminum slings and similar articles	$6,512,211	0.03%
6001	Pile fabrics, including long pile fabrics and terry fabrics, knitted or crocheted	$6,484,347	0.03%
3204	Synthetic organic coloring matter	$6,453,521	0.03%
8307	Flexible tubing of base metal with or without fittings	$6,335,828	0.03%
9404	Mattress supports; articles of bedding	$6,300,768	0.03%
4010	Conveyor or transmission belts of vulcanized rubber	$6,188,992	0.03%
4410	Particle board	$6,177,569	0.03%
1302	Vegetable saps and extracts	$6,157,162	0.03%
8455	Metal-rolling mills	$6,105,989	0.03%
6307	Other made up articles, including dress patterns	$6,031,112	0.03%
3924	Plastic tableware, kitchenware or other household products	$6,027,010	0.03%
6002	Knit or crochet fabric, width <30 cm >5% elastomer	$6,025,864	0.03%
5803	Gauze	$5,993,142	0.03%
8311	Wire, rods, tubes, plates, electrodes and similar products of base metal	$5,910,368	0.03%
3307	Shaving products	$5,860,442	0.03%
8521	Video recording apparatus	$5,823,546	0.03%
6506	Other headgear	$5,812,881	0.03%
3003	Medicaments, not packaged	$5,804,993	0.03%
2905	Acyclic alcohols	$5,671,092	0.03%
6809	Plaster articles	$5,653,798	0.03%
8532	Electrical capacitors	$5,610,736	0.03%
8467	Tools for hand working, pneumatic, hydraulic motors	$5,606,810	0.03%
8509	Electromechanical domestic appliances	$5,569,243	0.03%
8440	Bookbinding machinery	$5,553,804	0.03%
0406	Fresh cheese	$5,451,071	0.03%
7117	Imitation jewelry	$5,417,045	0.03%
1601	Sausages	$5,390,264	0.03%
2716	Electrical energy	$5,386,604	0.03%
8714	Parts and accessories of motorcycles, bicycles or carriages	$5,353,484	0.03%
3909	Amino-resins, phenolic resins and polyurethanes, in primary forms	$5,252,249	0.03%
2601	Iron ores and concentrates	$5,245,759	0.03%
3505	Dextrins and other modified starches	$5,230,545	0.03%
6911	Porcelain or china tableware or other household articles	$5,224,154	0.03%
2903	Halogenated derivatives of hydrocarbons	$5,208,019	0.03%

8484	Gaskets and similar joints of metal sheeting	$5,174,981	0.03%
1516	hydrogenated animal and vegetable fats, oils	$5,160,737	0.03%
1108	Starches	$5,101,811	0.03%
0813	Apricots, dried	$5,031,864	0.03%
3506	Glues and adhesives	$5,018,877	0.03%
1704	Confectionery sugar	$5,012,414	0.03%
3214	Glaziers' putty	$4,980,253	0.03%
8465	Machine tools for working wood	$4,961,292	0.03%
4811	Paper, paperboard, cellulose wadding and webs of cellulose fibers	$4,934,903	0.03%
2009	Fruit juices	$4,922,429	0.03%
4411	Fiberboard of wood	$4,877,932	0.03%
6108	Women's undergarmnets	$4,834,858	0.03%
1702	Other sugars	$4,832,664	0.03%
7612	Aluminum cans and similar containers	$4,770,739	0.02%
2924	Carboxyamide-function compounds	$4,766,587	0.02%
5515	Other woven fabrics of synthetic staple fibers	$4,765,831	0.02%
7217	Wire of iron or nonalloy steel	$4,764,027	0.02%
9102	Wrist watches and pocket watches	$4,747,371	0.02%
8404	Auxiliary plant for use with boilers; condensers for steam or other vapor power units	$4,670,920	0.02%
5810	Embroidery in piece	$4,670,366	0.02%
7302	Railway or tramway track construction material of iron or steel	$4,668,657	0.02%
6114	Other garments made up of knitted fabrics	$4,581,972	0.02%
9105	Other clocks	$4,568,077	0.02%
3209	Paints and varnishes, aqueous	$4,553,263	0.02%
9013	Liquid crystal devices	$4,500,364	0.02%
2839	Silicates; commercial alkali metal silicates	$4,484,848	0.02%
0803	Bananas and plantains	$4,478,304	0.02%
2936	Vitamins	$4,477,897	0.02%
6214	Shawls, scarves, etc, not knit	$4,471,558	0.02%
9024	Machines and appliances for testing the hardness, strength, compressibility, elasticity or other mechanical properties of materials	$4,396,259	0.02%
3902	Polymers of propylene or of other olefins, in primary forms	$4,366,394	0.02%
3507	Enzymes	$4,313,118	0.02%
5307	Yarn of jute or other textile bast fibers	$4,296,330	0.02%
8463	Other machine tools for working metal or cermets, without removal	$4,276,955	0.02%
2005	Homogenized vegetable preparations	$4,236,440	0.02%
8203	Files, rasps, pliers, pincers, tweezers, metal cutting shears, pipe cutter, and base metal parts thereof	$4,190,686	0.02%
5408	Woven fabrics of artificial filament yarn	$4,153,995	0.02%
4805	Other uncoated paper and paperboard	$4,149,165	0.02%
3802	Activated carbon	$4,124,283	0.02%

8506	Primary cells and primary batteries	$4,033,054	0.02%
3911	Petroleum resins, coumarone-indene resins, polyterpenes, polysulfides, polysulfones	$4,032,120	0.02%
8905	Floating or submersible drilling platforms	$4,026,354	0.02%
3305	Hair products	$4,001,521	0.02%
9017	Drafting tables and machines	$3,965,603	0.02%
7315	Chain and parts thereof, of iron or steel	$3,944,559	0.02%
3922	Baths, shower baths, sinks, washbasins, bidets, lavatory pans, seats and covers	$3,889,045	0.02%
7016	Glass paving blocks, slabs, bricks, squares, tiles or other molded products	$3,874,913	0.02%
2003	Mushrooms, prepared or preserved	$3,868,656	0.02%
8410	Hydraulic turbines, water wheels	$3,823,452	0.02%
2833	Sulfates; alums; peroxosulfates (persulfates)	$3,820,879	0.02%
2202	Waters flavored or sweetened	$3,771,814	0.02%
1512	Sunflower-seed or safflower oil, crude	$3,723,914	0.02%
8604	Railway or tramway maintenance or service vehicles	$3,720,307	0.02%
8215	Cutlery sets plated with precious metal	$3,704,531	0.02%
7324	Sanitary ware and parts of iron or steel	$3,701,813	0.02%
9610	Slates and boards, with writing or drawing surfaces	$3,684,533	0.02%
4002	Synthetic rubber	$3,653,297	0.02%
2804	Hydrogen, rare gases and other nonmetals	$3,651,717	0.02%
4823	Other paper, paperboard cut to size or shape	$3,632,112	0.02%
8436	Other agricultural, horticultural, forestry equipment; poultry incubators and brooders	$3,613,271	0.02%
0710	Frozen vegetables	$3,591,744	0.02%
6913	Statuettes and other ornamental ceramic articles	$3,576,693	0.02%
6212	Brassieres and parts thereof, not knit	$3,539,542	0.02%
8470	Calculating machines, cash registers	$3,531,423	0.02%
9613	Cigarette lighters	$3,510,600	0.02%
2933	Heterocyclic compounds with nitrogen hetero-atom(s) only	$3,489,515	0.02%
8904	Tugs and pusher craft	$3,458,332	0.02%
6303	Curtains drapes blinds valances, cotton, knit	$3,402,343	0.02%
3005	Wadding, gauze and bandages	$3,397,804	0.02%
4911	Other printed matter	$3,390,449	0.02%
7320	Springs of iron or steel	$3,362,279	0.02%
1905	Bread, pastry, cakes, biscuits and other baked goods	$3,349,896	0.02%
7202	Ferroalloys	$3,346,893	0.02%
6305	Sacks and bags, used for packing goods	$3,343,781	0.02%
7310	Tanks and similar containers, of iron or steel, not exceeding 300 liters	$3,332,493	0.02%
5513	Woven fabrics of < 85% synthetic staple fibers	$3,306,555	0.02%
8423	Weighing machinery	$3,282,633	0.02%
6702	Artificial flowers	$3,255,696	0.02%

6806	Slag wool, rock wool and similar mineral wools	$3,249,646	0.02%
7314	Cloth of iron or steel wire	$3,232,499	0.02%
6107	Men's undergarments	$3,224,473	0.02%
8204	Hand-operated spanners and wrenches	$3,213,871	0.02%
8453	Machinery for preparing, tanning or working hides, skins or leather	$3,186,942	0.02%
3707	Chemical preparations for photographic uses	$3,139,156	0.02%
8459	Machine tools for drilling, boring or milling by removing metal	$3,124,628	0.02%
5801	Woven pile fabrics	$3,100,537	0.02%
5503	Synthetic staple fibers	$3,095,318	0.02%
6209	Babies' garments, not knit	$3,085,381	0.02%
2916	Unsaturated acyclic monocarboxylic acids	$3,013,068	0.02%
8514	Industrial or laboratory electric furnaces	$3,001,067	0.02%
5804	Tulles and other net fabrics	$2,994,674	0.02%
5212	Other woven fabrics of cotton	$2,980,742	0.02%
9019	Mechano-therapy appliances	$2,931,389	0.02%
4821	Paper and paperboard labels	$2,885,087	0.02%
5514	Woven fabrics of < 85% synthetic staple fibers mixed mainly with cotton < 170 g/m2	$2,843,934	0.01%
7009	Glass mirrors	$2,771,883	0.01%
6101	Men's overcoats	$2,752,566	0.01%
7113	Jewelry of precious metal	$2,741,216	0.01%
8464	Machine tools for working stone	$2,722,264	0.01%
8457	Machining centers for working metal	$2,681,287	0.01%
3816	Refractory cements, mortars	$2,679,172	0.01%
7608	Aluminum tubes and pipes	$2,676,001	0.01%
1805	Cocoa powder, unsweetened	$2,658,030	0.01%
4203	Articles of apparel of leather	$2,640,473	0.01%
2208	Alcoholic preps for beverages	$2,637,576	0.01%
8448	Auxiliary machinery for use with knitting and textile machines	$2,631,528	0.01%
6601	Umbrellas	$2,628,401	0.01%
9025	Hydrometers and similar floating instruments, thermometers, pyrometers, barometers, hygrometers and psychrometers	$2,563,260	0.01%
9615	Combs, hair-slides etc of hard rubber or plastic	$2,532,961	0.01%
6117	Other clothing accessories, knitted or crocheted	$2,515,794	0.01%
3812	Prepared rubber accelerators	$2,487,119	0.01%
9010	Equipment for photographic laboratories	$2,484,197	0.01%
3301	Essential oils	$2,471,994	0.01%
7412	Copper tube or pipe fittings	$2,406,119	0.01%
6804	Stones for milling, grinding or pulping	$2,382,742	0.01%
8201	Hand tools base metal parts thereof spades, shovels, picks, forks and rakes; axes and similar hewing tools; pruners of any kind; scythes, sickles, hedge shears	$2,372,387	0.01%

6505	Hats, knitted or crocheted	$2,351,480	0.01%
6813	Friction material and articles thereof	$2,350,103	0.01%
8712	Bicycles	$2,348,560	0.01%
4820	Registers, account books, notebooks	$2,347,351	0.01%
1901	Malt extract	$2,345,718	0.01%
3913	Natural polymers	$2,307,910	0.01%
7301	Sheet piling of iron or steel	$2,306,642	0.01%
8212	Razors including safety razors, open blade razors	$2,273,298	0.01%
7419	Other articles of copper	$2,263,863	0.01%
3809	Finishing agents for dyeing	$2,263,583	0.01%
3701	Photographic plates	$2,257,094	0.01%
3215	Ink	$2,241,643	0.01%
8472	Other office machines	$2,238,359	0.01%
5208	Woven fabrics of cotton of > 85% weighing < 200 g/m2	$2,232,430	0.01%
3918	Floor coverings of plastics	$2,228,209	0.01%
0804	Dates, figs, pineapples, avocados, guavas and mangoes	$2,225,960	0.01%
9028	Gas, liquid or electricity supply or production meters	$2,214,394	0.01%
2505	Natural sands	$2,208,254	0.01%
2922	Oxygen-function amino-compounds	$2,184,792	0.01%
2935	Sulfonamides	$2,183,232	0.01%
7211	Hot box roll iron or non-alloy steel, flat, w 150-600mm, t >4mm, myp>35	$2,181,501	0.01%
8451	Machinery for washing, cleaning or drying fabrics	$2,174,276	0.01%
8527	Reception apparatus for radio broadcasting	$2,166,124	0.01%
0405	Butter	$2,164,229	0.01%
5512	Woven fabrics of > 85% synthetic staple fibers	$2,140,556	0.01%
8541	Diodes, transistors, semiconductor devices; photosensitive semiconductor devices, including photovoltaic cells	$2,140,423	0.01%
3405	Polishes and creams	$2,124,506	0.01%
8433	Harvesting or agricultural machinery	$2,105,184	0.01%
8715	Parts and accessories of motorcycles, bicycles or carriages	$2,090,715	0.01%
6205	Men's shirts, not knit	$2,068,630	0.01%
0802	Other nuts	$2,058,912	0.01%
2828	Hypochlorites; commercial calcium hypochlorite; chlorites; hypobromites	$2,052,914	0.01%
6811	Asbestos-cement or cellulose fiber-cement	$2,040,229	0.01%
2844	Radioactive chemical elements and radioactive isotopes	$2,037,979	0.01%
3208	Paints and varnishes, nonaqueous	$2,010,826	0.01%
2835	Phosphinates and phosphonates	$1,986,154	0.01%
5705	Other carpets and other textile floor coverings	$1,980,740	0.01%
1604	Prepared or preserved fish	$1,960,617	0.01%
8405	Producer gas or water gas generators	$1,960,046	0.01%
8432	Agricultural, forestry machinery for soil preparation	$1,954,526	0.01%

1602	Homogenized preparations of meat	$1,949,292	0.01%
0307	Molluscs	$1,935,193	0.01%
4013	Inner tubes of rubber	$1,930,314	0.01%
8202	Handsaws, and metal parts thereof	$1,927,743	0.01%
4809	Carbon paper	$1,924,044	0.01%
6304	Bedspreads, textile material, not elsewhere specified, knit or crochet	$1,913,692	0.01%
3601	Propellant powders	$1,911,516	0.01%
6111	Babies' garments and clothing accessories	$1,905,206	0.01%
8802	Aircraft, spacecraft & launch vehicles	$1,872,000	0.01%
2007	Jams, jellies	$1,855,552	0.01%
5205	Cotton yarn of > 85%	$1,844,224	0.01%
2915	Saturated acyclic monocarboxylic acids	$1,819,769	0.01%
8707	Vehicle Bodies	$1,816,798	0.01%
8513	Portable electric lamps designed to function by their own source of energy	$1,816,603	0.01%
2932	Heterocyclic compounds with oxygen hetero-atom(s) only	$1,815,828	0.01%
8454	Converters, ladles and casting machines used in metallurgy	$1,802,884	0.01%
2934	Nucleic acids and their salts	$1,792,581	0.01%
2004	Other vegetables, prepared or preserved	$1,792,508	0.01%
8416	Furnace burners for liquid fuel	$1,790,498	0.01%
8309	Stoppers, caps and lids	$1,769,210	0.01%
5907	Textile fabrics otherwise impregnated, coated or covered	$1,768,865	0.01%
1006	Rice	$1,765,879	0.01%
3905	Other vinyl polymers in primary forms	$1,764,114	0.01%
8609	Containers for carriage by one or more modes of transport	$1,753,178	0.01%
2517	Pebbles, gravel, broken & crushed stone for aggregate	$1,749,859	0.01%
8540	Thermionic, cold cathode or photocathode tubes	$1,729,151	0.01%
8445	Machines for preparing textile fibers	$1,720,552	0.01%
0404	Whey	$1,718,829	0.01%
4403	Wood in the rough	$1,707,215	0.01%
2940	Sugars, chemically pure, other than sucrose, lactose, maltose, glucose and fructose	$1,704,626	0.01%
9011	Compound optical microscopes	$1,698,564	0.01%
5703	Carpets, tufted	$1,693,824	0.01%
6207	Men's undergarments, not knit	$1,670,121	0.01%
6306	Tarpaulins, awnings and sunblinds	$1,630,262	0.01%
8468	Machinery and apparatus for soldering, brazing or welding, whether or not capable of cutting	$1,600,875	0.01%
8211	Sets of different knives, cutlery sets	$1,583,596	0.01%
5806	Narrow woven fabrics	$1,572,538	0.01%
6202	Womens overcoats, not knit	$1,569,127	0.01%
2703	Peat	$1,556,738	0.01%
9504	Articles for arcade, table or parlor games	$1,548,690	0.01%

1515	Linseed oil, crude	$1,538,965	0.01%
7115	Other articles of precious metals	$1,534,887	0.01%
6105	Men's shirts	$1,529,136	0.01%
7219	Flat-rolled products of stainless steel of a width > 600 mm	$1,524,087	0.01%
2821	Iron oxides and hydroxides	$1,509,171	0.01%
6210	Garments made of textile felts and nonwoven fabric	$1,486,356	0.01%
8545	Carbon electrodes or other articles of graphite or carbon used for electrical purposes	$1,470,315	0.01%
5702	Carpets, woven, not tufted or flocked, hand-woven rugs	$1,463,984	0.01%
2818	Artificial corundum	$1,463,560	0.01%
5401	Sewing thread of man-made filaments	$1,457,791	0.01%
8442	Machinery for making printing components	$1,452,895	0.01%
1206	Sunflower seeds	$1,437,710	0.01%
4417	Tools, broom handles, bodies etc of wood	$1,426,950	0.01%
9004	Spectacles, goggles, corrective, protective	$1,423,243	0.01%
5404	Synthetic monofilament, >67 dtex, thickness < 1mm	$1,418,779	0.01%
8713	Carriages for disabled persons	$1,418,287	0.01%
6401	Waterproof footwear	$1,415,544	0.01%
4902	Newspapers, journals and periodicals	$1,414,302	0.01%
4808	Paper and paperboard, corrugated	$1,411,621	0.01%
2530	Other mineral substances	$1,404,597	0.01%
5808	Braids in piece	$1,403,847	0.01%
8461	Machine tools for planing, shaping, slotting, gear cutting, or sawing	$1,391,891	0.01%
7003	Glass, cast or rolled	$1,390,482	0.01%
3406	Candles	$1,390,008	0.01%
2842	Other salts of inorganic acids or peroxoacids	$1,388,984	0.01%
8437	Machines for cleaning, sorting or grading seed; machinery used in the milling industry or for the working of cereals or dried leguminous vegetables	$1,355,926	0.01%
9029	Revolution counters; speedometers and tachometers	$1,347,231	0.01%
6909	Ceramic wares for laboratory uses; ceramic troughs used in agriculture; ceramic pots, jars and similar articles for packing of goods	$1,335,258	0.01%
5211	Woven fabrics of cotton of < 85% weighing > 200 g/m2	$1,331,380	0.01%
4421	Other articles of wood	$1,325,276	0.01%
3403	Lubricating products	$1,299,189	0.01%
0904	Pepper, whole	$1,298,618	0.01%
7220	Flat-rolled products of stainless steel of a width < 600 mm	$1,293,142	0.01%
8206	Tools of two or more types of hand tools, for retail sale	$1,288,245	0.01%
9001	Optical fibers	$1,274,072	0.01%
5607	Twine, cordage, ropes and cables, of jute, bast fibre	$1,273,510	0.01%
6808	Vegetable fiber used for panels, boards, tiles, blocks	$1,268,869	0.01%
5508	Sewing thread of man-made staple fibers	$1,253,652	0.01%

6810	Cement articles	$1,252,945	0.01%
8214	Other cutlery	$1,251,729	0.01%
2827	Chlorides, chloride oxides and chloride hydroxides; bromides and bromide oxides; iodides and iodide oxides	$1,201,994	0.01%
8213	Scissors, tailors/similar shears, blades thereof	$1,197,404	0.01%
2937	Hormones	$1,179,449	0.01%
6406	Parts of footwear	$1,179,079	0.01%
7317	Nails, tacks, staples and similar articles of iron or steel	$1,166,744	0.01%
2917	Polycarboxylic acids	$1,165,033	0.01%
7018	Glass beads	$1,158,856	0.01%
0806	Grapes	$1,154,301	0.01%
4104	Tanned hides and skins of bovine or equine animals	$1,152,412	0.01%
4813	Cigarette paper	$1,141,575	0.01%
2811	Other inorganic acids and other inorganic oxygen compounds of nonmetals	$1,139,556	0.01%
9609	Pencils, crayons, pencil leads, pastels, drawing charcoals or chalks	$1,116,643	0.01%
8306	Bells and gongs	$1,102,181	0.01%
9007	Cinematographic cameras and projectors	$1,095,312	0.01%
7106	Silver	$1,087,931	0.01%
3306	Dental hygiene products	$1,079,880	0.01%
7228	hollow drill bars and rods, of alloy or non-alloy steel	$1,068,096	0.01%
3813	Preparations and charges for fire-extinguishers	$1,046,239	0.01%
9612	Typewriter or similar ribbons	$1,044,397	0.01%
4415	Packing cases, boxes, crates, drums of wood	$1,039,511	0.01%
2501	Salt	$1,016,848	0.01%
2204	Wine of fresh grapes	$1,011,905	0.01%
8533	Electrical resistors	$1,004,338	0.01%
5209	Woven fabrics of cotton of < 85% weighing > 200 g/m2	$1,002,395	0.01%
2815	Sodium hydroxide; potassium hydroxide; peroxides of sodium or potassium	$1,001,625	0.01%
8303	Armored or reinforced safes, strong-boxes	$979,352	0.01%
4420	Wood marquetry, statuettes and other ornaments of wood	$966,208	0.01%
5608	Knotted netting of twine, cordage or rope	$959,063	0.01%
7413	Stranded wire, cables and similar articles of copper	$952,480	0.00%
2510	Natural calcium phosphates	$943,836	0.00%
9607	Slide fasteners and parts thereof	$931,792	0.00%
2308	Vegetable materials and waste	$923,423	0.00%
2909	Ethers	$909,486	0.00%
0204	Lamb meat	$906,882	0.00%
8903	Yachts	$900,377	0.00%
6206	Women's shirts, not knit	$889,079	0.00%
1008	Buckwheat	$883,346	0.00%

3104	Mineral or chemical fertilizers, potassic	$878,483	0.00%
2712	Petroleum jelly	$876,505	0.00%
6116	Gloves, mittens and mitts	$864,208	0.00%
8208	Knives and cutting blades for machines	$856,401	0.00%
9033	Parts and accessories for machines, appliances, instruments or apparatus	$854,086	0.00%
3404	Artificial and prepared waxes	$849,551	0.00%
3814	Organic composite solvents and thinners	$847,467	0.00%
5305	Coconut, abaca, ramie and other vegetable textile fibers	$845,085	0.00%
6815	Stone and other mineral articles	$834,477	0.00%
0306	Crustaceans	$828,729	0.00%
6914	Other ceramic articles	$826,522	0.00%
2606	Aluminium ores	$823,197	0.00%
2923	Quaternary ammonium salts and hydroxides	$820,500	0.00%
2309	Preparations of a kind used in animal feeding	$809,527	0.00%
9002	Lenses, prisms, mirrors and other optical elements	$793,547	0.00%
7104	Synthetic or semi-precious stones	$789,674	0.00%
7407	Copper bars, rods and profiles	$784,594	0.00%
8547	Insulating fittings for electrical machines, appliances or equipment	$768,762	0.00%
3916	Monofilament	$758,858	0.00%
4012	Retreaded or used pneumatic tires of rubber	$754,836	0.00%
7613	Aluminum containers for compressed or liquefied gas	$751,218	0.00%
2707	Oils and other products of the distillation of high temperature coal tar	$743,413	0.00%
7215	Other bars and rods of iron or nonalloy steel	$741,870	0.00%
8308	Clasps, frames with clasps, buckles, hooks, and the like of base metal used for clothing, footwear, awnings, handbags	$741,607	0.00%
5111	Woven fabrics of carded wool or carded fine animal hair	$741,297	0.00%
8305	Miscellaneous office goods	$740,970	0.00%
8709	Works trucks, self-propelled	$732,992	0.00%
7409	Copper plates, sheets and strip > 0.15 mm	$731,992	0.00%
2920	Esters of other inorganic acids of nonmetals	$731,852	0.00%
6102	Women's overcoats	$731,766	0.00%
5911	Textile fabric for card clothing, technical use	$719,551	0.00%
8460	Machine tools for finishing metal or cermets	$712,609	0.00%
8505	Electromagnets	$709,032	0.00%
4419	Tableware and kitchenware of wood	$704,346	0.00%
2508	Clays	$697,430	0.00%
9006	Photographic cameras	$693,464	0.00%
3213	Artists' colors	$692,878	0.00%
0910	Ginger	$677,457	0.00%
7403	Refined copper and copper alloys	$675,393	0.00%
7017	Laboratory, hygienic or pharmaceutical glassware	$671,625	0.00%

0712	Dried vegetables	$670,688	0.00%
5502	Artificial filament tow	$670,458	0.00%
2902	Cyclic hydrocarbons	$669,868	0.00%
9611	Date, sealing or numbering stamps and the like	$669,731	0.00%
7212	Flat rolled iron or non-alloy steel, width <600mm, plated with tin	$665,579	0.00%
3804	Residual lyes from wood pulp	$662,898	0.00%
3102	Mineral or chemical fertilizers, nitrogenous	$656,788	0.00%
4205	Other articles of leather	$653,596	0.00%
9003	Frames and mountings for spectacles, goggles or the like	$652,015	0.00%
2907	Phenols; phenol-alcohols	$648,099	0.00%
1521	Vegetable waxes not triglycerides	$627,968	0.00%
7222	Other bars and rods of stainless steel	$618,848	0.00%
9616	Scent sprayers and similar toilet sprayers	$609,504	0.00%
4803	Toilet etc household, sanitary stock	$601,407	0.00%
8439	Machinery for making pulp of cellulosic material or for making paper	$598,518	0.00%
9606	Buttons, press-fasteners, snap-fasteners and press-studs, button molds	$597,158	0.00%
0206	Edible offal of animals	$595,794	0.00%
1519	Stearic acid	$589,694	0.00%
6106	Women's shirts	$581,483	0.00%
0302	Fish, excluding fillets	$578,576	0.00%
2203	Beer	$575,772	0.00%
8210	Hand-operated appliances, food preparation, <10kg	$572,374	0.00%
0105	Fowls (< 185 grams)	$559,193	0.00%
2803	Carbon, nesoi	$556,977	0.00%
1804	Cocoa butter, fat, oil	$555,892	0.00%
9618	Mannequins	$552,791	0.00%
2832	Sulfites; thiosulfates	$550,900	0.00%
2921	Amine-function compounds	$546,003	0.00%
6805	Natural or artificial abrasive powder or grain	$534,298	0.00%
7410	Copper foil < 0.15 mm	$523,876	0.00%
8110	Antimony	$519,904	0.00%
4703	Chemical woodpulp, soda or sulfate, not dissolving grade	$517,549	0.00%
7313	Barbed wire of iron or steel	$505,982	0.00%
5704	Carpets of felt	$505,771	0.00%
8444	Machines to extrude, cut manmade textile fibres	$502,357	0.00%
6903	Other refractory ceramic goods	$502,318	0.00%
1210	Hop cones, powdered or pelleted	$496,971	0.00%
4408	Sheets for veneering for plywood	$495,455	0.00%
3212	Pigments, nonaqueous	$485,518	0.00%
8403	Central heating boilers	$480,727	0.00%
2840	Borates; peroxoborates	$472,316	0.00%

7319	Sewing needles, knitting needles and similar articles of iron or steel	$472,220	0.00%
6308	Needlecraft sets of woven fabric & yarn	$471,985	0.00%
8522	Parts and accessories for video or sound equipment	$471,779	0.00%
3501	Casein	$469,117	0.00%
6217	Clothing accessories not elsewhere specified, not knit	$462,358	0.00%
5105	Wool or animal hair, combed	$460,404	0.00%
2403	Cigarettes	$457,045	0.00%
4814	Wallpaper	$456,915	0.00%
8108	Titanium	$446,236	0.00%
8434	Milking and dairy machines	$442,624	0.00%
6216	Gloves, mittens and mitts	$441,893	0.00%
7316	Anchors, grapnels and parts thereof, of iron or steel	$440,717	0.00%
1904	Cereal foods	$439,479	0.00%
2101	Extracts of coffee, tea or maté	$438,790	0.00%
7020	Other articles of glass	$438,060	0.00%
5601	Wadding of textile materials	$436,197	0.00%
2930	Organo-sulfur compounds	$430,519	0.00%
8519	Sound recording apparatus	$422,168	0.00%
3207	Prepared pigments	$421,354	0.00%
9505	Festive, carnival or other entertainment articles	$419,763	0.00%
3602	Prepared explosives	$412,809	0.00%
2942	Other organic compounds	$411,118	0.00%
1208	Flours and meals of oil seeds	$411,027	0.00%
2711	Petroleum gases	$405,594	0.00%
5311	Woven fabrics of other vegetable textile fibers	$399,807	0.00%
2834	Nitrites; nitrates	$396,054	0.00%
3910	Silicones in primary forms	$395,689	0.00%
4015	Articles of apparel and clothing accessories of vulcanized rubber	$384,473	0.00%
7907	Other articles of zinc	$380,650	0.00%
5210	Woven fabrics of cotton of < 85% weighing < 200 g/m2	$380,112	0.00%
2849	Carbides	$377,726	0.00%
3810	Metal pickling preparations	$377,089	0.00%
0409	Honey	$376,783	0.00%
1207	Other oil seeds	$376,764	0.00%
1517	Margarine, not liquid	$365,205	0.00%
5901	Textile fabrics coated with gum or amylaceous	$363,527	0.00%
6905	Roofing tiles, chimney pots or other architectural ceramic ornaments	$361,046	0.00%
7801	Lead refined unwrought	$339,795	0.00%
8209	Tool plates/tips/etc, sintered metal carbide & cermet	$337,618	0.00%
9507	Fishing rods, fish hooks and other similar hunting or shooting equipment	$337,137	0.00%
7221	Bars and rods, stainless steel, hot-rolled	$333,492	0.00%

7904	Zinc bars, rods, profiles and wire	$333,086	0.00%
2831	Dithionites and sulfoxylates	$332,757	0.00%
5509	Yarn of synthetic staple fibers	$330,515	0.00%
1301	Lac	$329,725	0.00%
4807	Composite paper and paperboard	$326,412	0.00%
9016	Balances of a sensitivity of 50 milligram or better	$325,221	0.00%
2912	Aldehydes	$324,545	0.00%
8435	Presses, crushers used in the manufacture of wine, cider, fruit juices	$324,487	0.00%
8310	Sign plates, name plates, address plates and similar plates	$318,022	0.00%
4806	Vegetable parchment, greaseproof papers	$315,639	0.00%
0502	Bristles, hair of pigs, hogs or boars	$314,110	0.00%
8456	Machines for the removal of material by laser or other optic means	$313,855	0.00%
3407	Model and dental pastes and.waxes	$310,408	0.00%
7804	Lead foil of a thickness <2mm	$307,559	0.00%
2704	Coke etc of coal, lignite or peat, retort carbon	$307,063	0.00%
4602	Basketwork, wickerwork and other articles, made directly to shape from plaiting materials	$306,641	0.00%
1803	Cocoa paste not defatted	$301,386	0.00%
9101	Wrist watches and pocket watches in cases of precious metal	$300,715	0.00%
4414	Wooden frames for paintings, photographs, mirrors	$298,842	0.00%
5604	Rubber textiles	$292,859	0.00%
4704	Chemical woodpulp, sulfite, not dissolving grade	$292,129	0.00%
5909	Textile hosepiping and similar tubing	$286,382	0.00%
3001	Glands and other organs	$285,867	0.00%
4910	Calendars	$284,466	0.00%
7004	Glass, drawn or blown	$283,516	0.00%
8510	Shavers, hair clippers and hair-removing appliances	$280,126	0.00%
9508	Merry-go-rounds, boat-swings, shooting galleries and other fairground amusements	$280,022	0.00%
5910	Textile for transmission or conveyor belts	$274,845	0.00%
2837	Cyanides	$272,085	0.00%
5811	Quilted textile products in piece	$268,890	0.00%
7415	Nails, tacks, staples and similar articles of copper	$265,815	0.00%
3203	Coloring matter of vegetable or animal origin	$264,558	0.00%
8534	Electronic printed circuits	$264,546	0.00%
3914	Ion-exchangers based on natural and ethylene polymers	$263,685	0.00%
9008	Image projectors, other than cinematographic; photographic enlargers and reducers	$262,654	0.00%
2701	Coal; briquettes	$262,424	0.00%
6812	Asbestos fibres	$261,335	0.00%
8602	Other rail locomotives; locomotive tenders	$252,690	0.00%
3908	Polyamides in primary forms	$250,834	0.00%

3201	Tanning extracts of vegetable origin	$250,389	0.00%
3702	Photographic film in rolls	$246,534	0.00%
0909	Anise or badian seeds	$244,818	0.00%
1212	Locust beans, locust seeds	$243,990	0.00%
4003	Reclaimed rubber	$241,434	0.00%
1902	Pasta	$241,109	0.00%
7609	Aluminum tube or pipe fittings	$238,993	0.00%
2817	Zinc oxide and peroxide	$235,530	0.00%
7201	Pig iron	$232,484	0.00%
2516	Granite	$230,697	0.00%
4822	Bobbins, spools, cops of paper pulp	$230,642	0.00%
5112	Woven fabrics of combed wool or combed fine animal hair	$229,488	0.00%
2829	Chlorates and perchlorates; bromates and perbromates; iodates and periodates	$228,839	0.00%
5609	Articles of yarn strip, twine, cordage or rope, not elsewhere specified	$227,241	0.00%
6213	Handkerchiefs	$227,014	0.00%
0805	Citrus fruit	$223,447	0.00%
8446	Looms	$222,125	0.00%
2914	Ketones and quinones	$220,593	0.00%
5602	Felt	$220,289	0.00%
0809	Apricots	$220,142	0.00%
5605	Metallised yarn	$217,343	0.00%
2825	Hydrazine and hydroxylamine, inorganic salts	$216,651	0.00%
3210	Other paints and varnishes	$215,607	0.00%
3819	Hydraulic brake, transmission fluid <70% petroleum oi	$207,309	0.00%
3703	Photographic paper	$204,665	0.00%
1605	Crustaceans, molluscs and other aquatic invertebrates	$201,079	0.00%
3605	Matches	$198,539	0.00%
5204	Cotton sewing thread	$196,275	0.00%
5606	Gimp yarn	$193,616	0.00%
4007	Vulcanized rubber thread and cord	$193,516	0.00%
2621	Other slag and ash, including seaweed ash (kelp)	$191,736	0.00%
9106	Time of day recording apparatus and apparatus for measuring	$185,925	0.00%
3806	Rosin and resin acids	$184,696	0.00%
3202	Synthetic organic tanning substances	$180,218	0.00%
0101	Horses	$180,075	0.00%
2927	Diazo-, azo- or azoxy-compounds:	$179,867	0.00%
4201	Saddlery and harness for any animal	$177,394	0.00%
4503	Articles of natural cork	$177,050	0.00%
5906	Rubberized textile fabrics	$173,421	0.00%
0907	Cloves	$167,797	0.00%

4409	Wood continuously shaped along any of its edges	$167,637	0.00%
5802	Terry toweling and similar fabrics	$166,651	0.00%
4014	Hygienic or pharmaceutical articles of vulcanized rubber	$165,334	0.00%
9202	Other string musical instruments (for example, guitars, violins, harps)	$164,100	0.00%
6904	Ceramic building bricks	$162,212	0.00%
8304	Desk-top filing or card-index cabinets and parts thereof	$159,961	0.00%
2207	Ethyl alcohol > 80% by volume	$159,717	0.00%
7223	Wire of stainless steel	$159,369	0.00%
4017	Hard rubber	$159,071	0.00%
5403	Artificial filament yarn	$156,718	0.00%
0708	Legumes	$153,270	0.00%
7905	Zinc plates, sheets, strip and foil	$149,761	0.00%
2520	Gypsum	$148,310	0.00%
7229	Wire of other alloy steel	$147,842	0.00%
2906	Cyclic alcohols and their halogenated, sulfonated, nitrated or nitrosated derivatives	$145,317	0.00%
8001	Unwrought tin	$145,185	0.00%
2715	Bituminous mix, mastic from asphalt, bitumen/tar/pitc	$144,329	0.00%
2826	Fluorides; fluorosilicates, fluoroaluminates	$143,534	0.00%
2813	Sulfides of nonmetals	$143,350	0.00%
4006	Other forms of unvulcanized rubber	$141,078	0.00%
4905	Maps	$140,797	0.00%
5007	Woven fabrics of silk	$137,867	0.00%
8449	Machinery to manufacture or finish felt or nonwovens	$136,323	0.00%
1509	Olive oil, virgin	$135,341	0.00%
2006	Vegetables, fruits, nuts, fruit-peel, etc preserved	$134,084	0.00%
5506	Synthetic staple fibers, processed	$134,008	0.00%
2809	Diphosphorus pentaoxide; phosphoric acid; polyphosphoric acids	$129,733	0.00%
9208	Musicboxes, fairground organs, mechanical street organs and other musical instruments	$129,710	0.00%
9020	Other breathing appliances and gas masks	$125,592	0.00%
2209	Vinegars	$124,628	0.00%
6603	Parts of umbrellas or walking sticks	$119,385	0.00%
1104	Worked cereal groats	$119,219	0.00%
3820	Antifreezing preparations and deicing fluids	$117,718	0.00%
4816	Other carbon paper	$116,875	0.00%
4903	Children's picture, drawing or coloring books	$116,653	0.00%
2714	Bitumen and asphalt, natural	$115,558	0.00%
5207	Cotton yarn for retail sale	$114,548	0.00%
2823	Titanium oxides	$112,763	0.00%
0511	Animal products not elsewhere specified	$112,431	0.00%
2904	Sulfonated, nitrated or nitrosated derivatives of hydrocarbons	$111,512	0.00%

1211	Plants used in perfumery, in pharmacy or for insecticide	$111,143	0.00%
7418	Table, kitchen or other household articles of copper	$111,072	0.00%
8907	Other floating structures (for example, rafts, tanks, buoys and beacons)	$109,708	0.00%
7008	Multiple-walled insulating glass	$109,697	0.00%
9207	Musical instruments amplified electrically	$107,580	0.00%
7505	Nickel bars, rods, profiles and wire	$106,536	0.00%
2814	Ammonia	$106,419	0.00%
9605	Travel sets, toilet, sewing, shoe, clothes cleaning	$105,884	0.00%
2926	Nitrile-function compounds	$104,933	0.00%
1505	Wool grease, crude	$104,457	0.00%
8104	Magnesium	$101,836	0.00%
8420	Calendering or other rolling machines	$101,317	0.00%
9602	Worked vegetable or mineral carving material	$100,338	0.00%
3801	Artificial graphite	$99,386	0.00%
7014	Signaling glassware	$99,338	0.00%
7204	Ferrous waste and scrap	$98,857	0.00%
0801	Coconuts, Brazil nuts and cashew nuts	$98,849	0.00%
2925	Carboxyimide-function compounds	$98,797	0.00%
6309	Used clothes and textiles	$97,037	0.00%
7011	Glass envelopes	$97,010	0.00%
8478	Machinery for preparing or making up tobacco	$96,457	0.00%
3603	Safety or detonating fuses	$95,924	0.00%
4111	Composition leather	$93,285	0.00%
2615	Niobium (columbium), tantalum, vanadium or zirconium ores	$91,880	0.00%
5308	Yarn of other vegetable textile fibers	$90,692	0.00%
9005	Binoculars, monoculars, other optical telescopes, and mountings	$89,930	0.00%
6215	Ties, bow ties and cravats	$89,693	0.00%
8805	Aircraft launching gear	$88,436	0.00%
7806	Other articles of lead	$87,458	0.00%
6901	Bricks, blocks, tiles and other ceramic goods	$82,416	0.00%
1504	Fats and oils of fish or marine mammals	$82,151	0.00%
9205	Wind musical instruments	$81,718	0.00%
6504	Hats	$81,458	0.00%
8101	Tungsten (wolfram)	$80,925	0.00%
4812	Filter blocks of paper pulp	$80,566	0.00%
2614	Titanium ores	$80,496	0.00%
5406	Man-made filament yarn for retail sale	$80,463	0.00%
2807	Sulfuric acid; oleum	$78,582	0.00%
7015	Clock or watch glasses	$78,406	0.00%
4707	Recovered paper and paperboard	$78,204	0.00%
5201	Cotton raw	$77,764	0.00%

4908	Transfers (decalcomanias)	$77,611	0.00%
6814	Mica articles	$77,246	0.00%
2504	Natural graphite	$77,138	0.00%
2519	Natural magnesium carbonate	$76,632	0.00%
2919	Phosphoric esters and their salts	$74,873	0.00%
1401	Vegetable materials used primarily for plaiting	$74,142	0.00%
3503	Gelatin	$73,104	0.00%
9103	Clocks with watch movements	$72,878	0.00%
3821	Prepared culture media for development or maintenance of micro-organisms (including viruses and the like) or of plant, human or animal cells	$71,888	0.00%
7205	Powders, of pig iron, spiegeleisen, iron or steel	$71,328	0.00%
5006	Silk yarn for retail sale	$71,292	0.00%
6507	Headbands	$70,839	0.00%
9604	Hand sieves and hand riddles	$70,664	0.00%
9107	Time switches with clock or watch movement	$69,487	0.00%
4817	Letterstock	$68,189	0.00%
4906	Plans and drawings for architectural, engineering, industrial, commercial, topographical purposes	$66,546	0.00%
4406	Railway cross-ties of wood	$66,137	0.00%
2908	Halogenated, sulfonated, nitrated or nitrosated derivatives of phenols or phenol-alcohols	$66,020	0.00%
1520	Glycerol, crude	$64,712	0.00%
3604	Fireworks	$64,469	0.00%
2001	Vegetables, fruit, nuts preserved by vinegar	$64,303	0.00%
3705	Photographic plates and film, exposed and developed, not motion-picture film	$63,015	0.00%
9104	Instrument panel clocks and clocks of a similar type for vehicles, aircraft, spacecraft or vessels	$62,781	0.00%
2931	Other organo-inorganic compounds	$61,109	0.00%
5206	Cotton yarn of < 85%	$60,297	0.00%
4402	Wood charcoal	$60,088	0.00%
2620	Slag, ash and residues	$59,454	0.00%
5701	Carpets, knotted	$59,355	0.00%
8007	Other articles of tin	$59,328	0.00%
4413	Densified wood	$56,233	0.00%
2512	Siliceous fossil meals and earths	$55,800	0.00%
9209	Parts and accessories of musical instruments	$55,115	0.00%
6602	Walking sticks	$55,088	0.00%
4601	Plaits and products of plaiting materials	$53,571	0.00%
2805	Alkali or alkaline-earth metals; rare-earth metals, scandium and yttrium	$53,409	0.00%
2820	Manganese oxides	$53,194	0.00%
2525	Mica	$53,109	0.00%

2841	Salts of oxometallic or peroxometallic acids	$51,593	0.00%
6704	Wigs	$51,278	0.00%
4504	Agglomerated cork	$51,217	0.00%
0807	Melons	$50,361	0.00%
2847	Hydrogen peroxide	$50,326	0.00%
0811	Fruits and nuts frozen	$49,374	0.00%
2939	Vegetable alkaloids	$49,167	0.00%
7508	Other articles of nickel	$49,026	0.00%
9206	Percussion musical instruments	$48,297	0.00%
7006	Glass with edge workings or bent	$48,190	0.00%
4909	Printed or illustrated postcards	$47,695	0.00%
3706	Motion-picture film, exposed and developed	$47,518	0.00%
7002	Glass balls	$46,924	0.00%
6807	Asphalt	$46,894	0.00%
2938	Glycosides	$46,683	0.00%
2830	Sulfides; polysulfides	$46,484	0.00%
8105	Cobalt	$46,451	0.00%
0810	Other fresh fruit	$46,189	0.00%
2808	Sulfonitric acids	$45,933	0.00%
0711	Vegetables provisionally preserved	$45,677	0.00%
3504	Peptones	$44,944	0.00%
2806	Hydrogen chloride (Hydrochloric acid); chlorosulfuric acid	$44,336	0.00%
5807	Labels, badges and similar articles of textile materials	$43,105	0.00%
2511	Natural barium sulphate	$40,918	0.00%
2507	Kaolin	$39,825	0.00%
7507	Nickel tubes, pipes and tube or pipe fittings	$36,743	0.00%
2303	Starch residues	$36,670	0.00%
2529	Feldspar	$36,408	0.00%
2526	Natural steatite	$35,833	0.00%
2513	Pumice	$35,808	0.00%
7116	Articles of pearls	$34,962	0.00%
9201	Pianos	$33,059	0.00%
0906	Cinnamon, whole	$32,940	0.00%
9601	Worked ivory, bone, tortoise-shell, horn, antlers, coral, mother-of-pearl and other animal carving material	$32,422	0.00%
7406	Copper powders and flakes	$32,031	0.00%
2810	Oxides of boron; boric acids	$31,800	0.00%
2515	Marble and travertine	$31,477	0.00%
2910	Epoxides	$30,379	0.00%
1105	Potato flour or meal	$30,000	0.00%
2843	Colloidal precious metals; inorganic or organic compounds of precious metals	$29,411	0.00%

6906	Ceramic pipes, conduits, guttering and pipe fittings	$29,036	0.00%
0305	Fish flours, meals & pellets for human consumption	$27,712	0.00%
6803	Worked slate	$27,674	0.00%
5113	Woven fabrics of coarse animal hair or of horsehair	$27,281	0.00%
2302	Bran, sharps (middlings) and other residues	$27,000	0.00%
8003	Tin bars, rods, profiles and wire	$26,141	0.00%
2816	Hydroxide and peroxide of magnesium; oxides, hydroxides and peroxides, of strontium or barium	$25,815	0.00%
9012	Microscopes other than optical microscopes	$25,175	0.00%
0602	Live plants with roots	$24,592	0.00%
2801	Fluorine, chlorine, bromine and iodine	$24,478	0.00%
6113	Other garments, knitted or crocheted with impregnated plastics or rubber	$23,852	0.00%
7502	Nickel unwrought	$23,581	0.00%
4405	Wood wool	$22,781	0.00%
2851	Inorganic compounds, liquid or compressed air	$22,059	0.00%
9109	Clock movements, complete and assembled	$21,933	0.00%
0709	Other vegetables	$21,322	0.00%
9703	Original sculptures and statuary	$21,294	0.00%
5405	Artificial monofilament >67dtex t<1mm, strip, straws t<5mm	$21,144	0.00%
6310	Used or new rags textile scraps	$20,855	0.00%
4304	Artificial fur	$20,495	0.00%
0301	Ornamental fish, live	$20,395	0.00%
7001	Cullet and other scraps of glass	$19,821	0.00%
2824	Lead oxides	$19,811	0.00%
7226	Flat-rolled products of other alloy steel of a width < 600 mm	$19,412	0.00%
1103	Cereal groats, meal and pellets	$18,636	0.00%
0410	Edible products of animal origin	$18,500	0.00%
5310	Woven fabrics of jute or of other textile bast fibers	$18,040	0.00%
5902	Tire cord fabric of high tenacity yarn of nylon	$17,114	0.00%
5510	Yarn of artificial staple fibers	$17,039	0.00%
7227	Bars and rods, hot-rolled, in irregularly wound coils, of other alloy steel	$16,969	0.00%
2609	Tin ores	$16,793	0.00%
8706	Vehicle chassis fitted with engines	$16,331	0.00%
5809	Woven fabric incorporating metal threads	$15,657	0.00%
5511	Yarn of man-made staple fibers, for retail sale	$15,416	0.00%
5505	Waste of man-made fibers	$15,211	0.00%
2201	Waters natural	$14,570	0.00%
5501	Synthetic filament tow	$14,378	0.00%
8113	Cermets	$13,991	0.00%
5309	Woven fabrics of flax	$13,955	0.00%
1102	Cereal flours	$13,909	0.00%

9111	Watch cases and parts	$13,619	0.00%
1201	Soya beans	$13,616	0.00%
3915	Plastic waste, parings and scrap	$13,065	0.00%
9113	Watch straps	$12,940	0.00%
7114	Articles of goldsmiths' or silversmiths' wares	$12,531	0.00%
2819	Chromium oxides and hydroxides	$12,473	0.00%
4105	Tanned skins of sheep or lambs	$12,225	0.00%
2506	Quartz	$11,765	0.00%
9701	Paintings, drawings and pastels done by hand	$11,534	0.00%
8476	Automatic goods-vending machines	$11,039	0.00%
8548	Waste and scrap of batteries; used batteries	$10,983	0.00%
4501	Natural cork, raw	$10,919	0.00%
2402	Cigars	$10,842	0.00%
9114	Other clock or watch parts	$10,471	0.00%
5905	Textile wall coverings	$10,268	0.00%
2503	Sulphur	$9,704	0.00%
1204	Linseed	$9,573	0.00%
2709	Petroleum oils, crude	$9,239	0.00%
5303	Jute and other textile fibers	$8,869	0.00%
0504	Guts of animals except fish	$8,836	0.00%
7506	Nickel plates, sheets, strip and foil	$8,785	0.00%
4303	Articles of apparel of furskin	$8,415	0.00%
5507	Artificial staple fibers, processed	$7,854	0.00%
2509	Chalk	$7,014	0.00%
4004	Waste, parings and scrap of rubber	$6,955	0.00%
7110	Platinum	$6,895	0.00%
0706	Carrots, turnips and beets	$6,506	0.00%
2846	Compounds, inorganic or organic, of rare-earth metals	$6,376	0.00%
9614	Smoking pipes and cigar or cigarette holders	$6,343	0.00%
2901	Acyclic hydrocarbons	$6,285	0.00%
3805	Gum, wood or sulfate turpentine	$6,000	0.00%
8469	Typewriters other than printing machinery	$5,955	0.00%
2845	Isotopes not elsewhere specified	$5,300	0.00%
2705	Coal gas, water gas, not petroleum gases	$5,137	0.00%
4416	Casks, barrels, vats, tubs of wood	$5,042	0.00%
5203	Cotton, carded or combed	$4,596	0.00%
7218	Stainless steel in ingots or other primary forms	$4,481	0.00%
7504	Nickel powders and flakes	$4,411	0.00%
2205	Vermouth and other flavored wines	$4,227	0.00%
9108	Watch movements, complete and assembled	$4,158	0.00%
3704	Photographic plates, film, paper, exposed but not developed	$4,156	0.00%

7203	Ferrous products obtained by direct reduction of iron ore	$3,946	0.00%
7207	Semifinished products of iron or nonalloy steel	$3,932	0.00%
2928	Organic derivatives of hydrazine or of hydroxylamine:	$3,545	0.00%
8112	Other metals	$3,279	0.00%
2911	Acetals and hemiacetals	$3,154	0.00%
5805	Hand-woven tapestries	$3,148	0.00%
9307	Swords, cutlasses, bayonets, lances and similar arms	$2,706	0.00%
7224	Other alloy steel in primary form	$2,650	0.00%
0106	Live animals, except farm animals	$2,530	0.00%
9110	Complete watch or clock movements	$2,496	0.00%
4706	Pulps of fibers derived from recovered paper or paperboard	$2,395	0.00%
3502	Albumins (water soluble proteins)	$2,365	0.00%
1518	Processed animal, vegetable oils	$2,269	0.00%
2301	Flour or meal for animal feed	$2,215	0.00%
0210	Preserved meat	$2,161	0.00%
5306	Flax yarn	$2,116	0.00%
5908	Textile wicks	$1,980	0.00%
9705	Collections and collectors pieces	$1,848	0.00%
7402	Unrefined copper	$1,753	0.00%
0714	Manioc (cassava)	$1,736	0.00%
5504	Artificial staple fibers	$1,730	0.00%
4401	Fuel wood	$1,510	0.00%
6701	Skins and other parts of birds with their feathers or down	$1,441	0.00%
1107	Malt, not roasted	$1,325	0.00%
4108	Chamois leather	$1,325	0.00%
8111	Manganese	$1,325	0.00%
7611	Aluminium reservoirs, vats, tanks, etc	$1,229	0.00%
4907	Unused postage, revenue or similar stamps	$1,194	0.00%
5202	Cotton waste	$1,083	0.00%
3606	Ferrocerium and other pyrophoric alloys	$1,057	0.00%

Explore More Years »

ALGERIA IMPORT BY COUNTRIES

Abbrv	Name	Value	Percent
CHN	China	$4,524,838,075	23.62%
FRA	France	$3,698,623,158	19.30%
DEU	Germany	$2,182,203,762	11.39%
ITA	Italy	$1,910,406,505	9.97%
ARG	Argentina	$1,027,542,695	5.36%
BRA	Brazil	$862,783,981	4.50%
ESP	Spain	$723,413,393	3.78%

USA	United States	$604,029,367	3.15%
CAN	Canada	$325,740,108	1.70%
AUT	Austria	$297,897,552	1.55%
NGA	Nigeria	$243,753,287	1.27%
GBR	United Kingdom	$227,721,157	

BASIC TITLES FOR ALGERIA

title	ISBN
Algeria A "Spy" Guide - Strategic Information and Developments	1433000709
Algeria A Spy" Guide"	1438700636
Algeria Air Force Handbook	1433000717
Algeria Air Force Handbook	1438700644
Algeria Banking & Financial Market Handbook	1433000725
Algeria Banking & Financial Market Handbook	1438700652
Algeria Business and Investment Opportunities Yearbook	1433000733
Algeria Business and Investment Opportunities Yearbook	1438700660
Algeria Business and Investment Opportunities Yearbook Volume 1 Strategic Information and Opportunities	143877608X
Algeria Business and Investment Opportunities Yearbook Volume 2 Leading Export-Import, Business, Investment Opportunities and Projects	1577519868
Algeria Business Intelligence Report - Practical Information, Opportunities, Contcts	1433000741
Algeria Business Intelligence Report - Practical Information, Opportunities, Contcts	1438700679
Algeria Business Law Handbook - Strategic Information and Basic Laws	1438769210
Algeria Business Law Handbook - Strategic Information and Basic Laws	1438769210
Algeria Business Law Handbook - Strategic Information and Basic Laws	143300075X
Algeria Business Law Handbook - Strategic Information and Basic Laws	1438700687
Algeria Company Laws and Regulations Handbook	1433069342
Algeria Constitution and Citizenship Laws Handbook - Strategic Information and Basic Laws	1438778376
Algeria Country Study Guide - Strategic Information and Developments	1433000768
Algeria Country Study Guide - Strategic Information and Developments	1438700695
Algeria Country Study Guide - Strategic Information and Developments Volume 1 Strategic Information and Developments	1438773757
Algeria Customs, Trade Regulations and Procedures Handbook	1433000776
Algeria Customs, Trade Regulations and Procedures Handbook	1438700709
Algeria Diplomatic Handbook - Strategic Information and Developments	1433000784
Algeria Diplomatic Handbook - Strategic Information and Developments	1438700717
Algeria Ecology & Nature Protection Handbook	1433000792
Algeria Ecology & Nature Protection Handbook	1438700725
Algeria Ecology & Nature Protection Laws and Regulation Handbook	1433073137
Algeria Energy Policy, Laws and Regulation Handbook	1433070898
Algeria Energy Policy, Laws and Regulations Handbook	1438701292
Algeria Energy Policy, Laws and Regulations Handbook vol 2	1433000806

title	ISBN
Algeria Energy Sector Handbook	1433000814
Algeria Energy Sector Handbook	1438701306
Algeria Export-Import Trade and Business Directory	1433000822
Algeria Export-Import Trade and Business Directory	1438701314
Algeria Foreign Policy and Government Guide	1433000830
Algeria Foreign Policy and Government Guide	1438701322
Algeria Healthcare Sector Organization, Management and Payment Systems Handbook - Strategic Information, Programs and Regulations	9781433085789
Algeria Immigration Laws and Regulations Handbook - Strategic Information and Basic Laws	1438782020
Algeria Industrial and Business Directory	1433000849
Algeria Industrial and Business Directory	1438701330
Algeria Insolvency (Bankruptcy) Laws and Regulations Handbook - Strategic Information and Basic Laws	9781433085000
Algeria Internet and E-Commerce Investment and Business Guide - Strategic and Practical Information: Regulations and Opportunities	1433000857
Algeria Internet and E-Commerce Investment and Business Guide - Strategic and Practical Information: Regulations and Opportunities	1438701349
Algeria Investment and Business Guide - Strategic and Practical Information	1438766939
Algeria Investment and Business Guide - Strategic and Practical Information	1438766939
Algeria Investment and Business Guide - Strategic and Practical Information	1433000865
Algeria Investment and Business Guide - Strategic and Practical Information	1438701357
Algeria Investment and Business Guide Volume 2 Business, Investment Opportunities and Incentives	1577519086
Algeria Investment and Trade Laws and Regulations Handbook	1433075350
Algeria Labor Laws and Regulations Handbook - Strategic Information and Basic Laws	1438780222
Algeria Land Ownership and Agriculture Laws Handbook	1438758464
Algeria Mineral & Mining Sector Investment and Business Guide - Strategic and Practical Information	1433000873
Algeria Mineral & Mining Sector Investment and Business Guide - Strategic and Practical Information	1438701365
Algeria Mining Laws and Regulations Handbook	1433076896
Algeria Oil & Gas Sector Business & Investment Opportunities Yearbook	1433000881
Algeria Oil & Gas Sector Business & Investment Opportunities Yearbook	1438701373
Algeria Oil and Gas Exploration Laws and Regulation Handbook	1433078511
Algeria Privatization Programs and Regulations Handbook	143300089X
Algeria Privatization Programs and Regulations Handbook	1438701381
Algeria Recent Economic and Political Developments Yearbook	1433062011
Algeria Recent Economic and Political Developments Yearbook	1433062011
Algeria Recent Economic and Political Developments Yearbook	1433062011
Algeria Starting Business (Incorporating) in....Guide	1433064359
Algeria Taxation Laws and Regulations Handbook	143307916X
Algeria Telecom Laws and Regulations Handbook	1433081415
Algeria Telecommunication Industry Business Opportunities Handbook	1433000903

title	ISBN
Algeria Telecommunication Industry Business Opportunities Handbook	143870139X
Algeria Transportation Policy and Regulations Handbook	1433064367
Algeria: How to Invest, Start and Run Profitable Business in Algeria Guide - Practical Information, Opportunities, Contacts	9781433082726

BASIC TITLES FOR ALGERIA

IMPORTANT!
All publications are updated annually!
Please contact IBP, Inc. at ibpusa3@gmail.com for the latest ISBNs and additional information

TITLE
Algeria A "Spy" Guide - Strategic Information and Developments
Algeria A Spy" Guide"
Algeria Air Force Handbook
Algeria Air Force Handbook
Algeria Banking & Financial Market Handbook
Algeria Banking & Financial Market Handbook
Algeria Business and Investment Opportunities Yearbook
Algeria Business and Investment Opportunities Yearbook
Algeria Business and Investment Opportunities Yearbook Volume 1 Strategic Information and Opportunities
Algeria Business and Investment Opportunities Yearbook Volume 2 Leading Export-Import, Business, Investment Opportunities and Projects
Algeria Business Intelligence Report - Practical Information, Opportunities, Contacts
Algeria Business Intelligence Report - Practical Information, Opportunities, Contacts
Algeria Business Law Handbook - Strategic Information and Basic Laws
Algeria Business Law Handbook - Strategic Information and Basic Laws
Algeria Business Law Handbook - Strategic Information and Basic Laws
Algeria Business Law Handbook - Strategic Information and Basic Laws
Algeria Business Success Guide - Basic Practical Information and Contacts
Algeria Company Laws and Regulations Handbook
Algeria Company Laws and Regulations Handbook - Strategic Information and Basic Laws
Algeria Constitution and Citizenship Laws Handbook - Strategic Information and Basic Laws
Algeria Country Study Guide - Strategic Information and Developments
Algeria Country Study Guide - Strategic Information and Developments
Algeria Country Study Guide - Strategic Information and Developments Volume 1 Strategic Information and Developments
Algeria Criminal Laws, Regulations and Procedures Handbook - Strategic Information, Regulations, Procedures
Algeria Customs, Trade Regulations and Procedures Handbook
Algeria Customs, Trade Regulations and Procedures Handbook
Algeria Diplomatic Handbook - Strategic Information and Developments
Algeria Diplomatic Handbook - Strategic Information and Developments
Algeria Ecology & Nature Protection Handbook
Algeria Ecology & Nature Protection Handbook

TITLE
Algeria Ecology & Nature Protection Laws and Regulation Handbook
Algeria Electoral, Political Parties Laws and Regulations Handbook - Strategic Information, Regulations, Procedures
Algeria Energy Policy, Laws and Regulation Handbook
Algeria Energy Policy, Laws and Regulations Handbook
Algeria Energy Policy, Laws and Regulations Handbook vol 2
Algeria Energy Sector Handbook
Algeria Energy Sector Handbook
Algeria Export-Import Trade and Business Directory
Algeria Export-Import Trade and Business Directory
Algeria Fishing and Aquaculture Industry Handbook - Strategic Information, Regulations, Opportunities
Algeria Foreign Policy and Government Guide
Algeria Foreign Policy and Government Guide
Algeria Healthcare Sector Organization, Management and Payment Systems Handbook - Strategic Information, Programs and Regulations
Algeria Immigration Laws and Regulations Handbook - Strategic Information and Basic Laws
Algeria Industrial and Business Directory
Algeria Industrial and Business Directory
Algeria Insolvency (Bankruptcy) Laws and Regulations Handbook - Strategic Information and Basic Laws
Algeria Internet and E-Commerce Investment and Business Guide - Strategic and Practical Information: Regulations and Opportunities
Algeria Internet and E-Commerce Investment and Business Guide - Strategic and Practical Information: Regulations and Opportunities
Algeria Investment and Business Guide - Strategic and Practical Information
Algeria Investment and Business Guide - Strategic and Practical Information
Algeria Investment and Business Guide - Strategic and Practical Information
Algeria Investment and Business Guide - Strategic and Practical Information
Algeria Investment and Business Guide Volume 2 Business, Investment Opportunities and Incentives
Algeria Investment and Business Profile - Basic Information and Contacts for Succesful investment and Business Activity
Algeria Investment and Trade Laws and Regulations Handbook
Algeria Investment, Trade Strategy and Agreements Handbook - Strategic Information and Basic Agreements
Algeria Labor Laws and Regulations Handbook - Strategic Information and Basic Laws
Algeria Land Ownership and Agriculture Laws Handbook
Algeria Mineral & Mining Sector Investment and Business Guide - Strategic and Practical Information
Algeria Mineral & Mining Sector Investment and Business Guide - Strategic and Practical Information
Algeria Mining Laws and Regulations Handbook
Algeria Oil & Gas Sector Business & Investment Opportunities Yearbook
Algeria Oil & Gas Sector Business & Investment Opportunities Yearbook
Algeria Oil and Gas Exploration Laws and Regulation Handbook

TITLE
Algeria Privatization Programs and Regulations Handbook
Algeria Privatization Programs and Regulations Handbook
Algeria Recent Economic and Political Developments Yearbook
Algeria Recent Economic and Political Developments Yearbook
Algeria Recent Economic and Political Developments Yearbook
Algeria Starting Business (Incorporating) in....Guide
Algeria Tax Guide Volume 1 Strategic Information and Basic Regulations
Algeria Taxation Laws and Regulations Handbook
Algeria Telecom Laws and Regulations Handbook
Algeria Telecommunication Industry Business Opportunities Handbook
Algeria Telecommunication Industry Business Opportunities Handbook
Algeria Transportation Policy and Regulations Handbook
Algeria: How to Invest, Start and Run Profitable Business in Algeria Guide - Practical Information, Opportunities, Contacts

35.	Croatia Export-Import, Trade and Business Directory
36.	Cuba Export-Import, Trade and Business Directory
37.	Cyprus Export-Import, Trade and Business Directory
38.	Czech Republic Export-Import, Trade and Business Directory
39.	Denmark Export-Import, Trade and Business Directory
40.	Dominica Export-Import, Trade and Business Directory
41.	Dominican Republic Export-Import, Trade and Business Directory
42.	Dubai Export-Import, Trade and Business Directory
43.	Ecuador Export-Import, Trade and Business Directory
44.	Egypt Export-Import, Trade and Business Directory
45.	El Salvador Export-Import, Trade and Business Directory
46.	Equatorial Guinea Export-Import, Trade and Business Directory
47.	Estonia Export-Import, Trade and Business Directory
48.	Falkland Islands Export-Import, Trade and Business Directory
49.	Fiji Export-Import, Trade and Business Directory
50.	Finland Export-Import, Trade and Business Directory
51.	France Export-Import, Trade and Business Directory
52.	Georgia Export-Import, Trade and Business Directory
53.	Germany Export-Import, Trade and Business Directory
54.	Gibraltar Export-Import, Trade and Business Directory
55.	Greece Export-Import, Trade and Business Directory
56.	Grenada Export-Import, Trade and Business Directory
57.	Guam Investment & Business Guide
58.	Guatemala Export-Import, Trade and Business Directory
59.	Guernsey Export-Import, Trade and Business Directory
60.	Guyana Export-Import, Trade and Business Directory
61.	Haiti Export-Import, Trade and Business Directory
62.	Honduras Export-Import, Trade and Business Directory
63.	Hungary Export-Import, Trade and Business Directory
64.	Iceland Export-Import, Trade and Business Directory
65.	India Export-Import, Trade and Business Directory
66.	Indonesia Export-Import, Trade and Business Directory
67.	Iran Export-Import, Trade and Business Directory
68.	Iraq Export-Import, Trade and Business Directory
69.	Ireland Export-Import, Trade and Business Directory
70.	Israel Export-Import, Trade and Business Directory
71.	Italy Export-Import, Trade and Business Directory
72.	Jamaica Export-Import, Trade and Business Directory
73.	Japan Export-Import, Trade and Business Directory
74.	Jersey Export-Import, Trade and Business Directory
75.	Jordan Export-Import, Trade and Business Directory
76.	Kazakhstan Export-Import, Trade and Business Directory
77.	Kenya Export-Import, Trade and Business Directory
78.	Kiribati Export-Import, Trade and Business Directory

79. Korea, North Export-Import, Trade and Business Directory
80. Korea, South Export-Import, Trade and Business Directory
81. Kuwait Export-Import, Trade and Business Directory
82. Kyrgyzstan Export-Import, Trade and Business Directory
83. Laos Export-Import, Trade and Business Directory
84. Latvia Export-Import, Trade and Business Directory
85. Lebanon Export-Import, Trade and Business Directory
86. Libya Export-Import, Trade and Business Directory
87. Liechtenstein Export-Import, Trade and Business Directory
88. Lithuania Export-Import, Trade and Business Directory
89. Luxemburg Export-Import, Trade and Business Directory
90. Macao Export-Import, Trade and Business Directory
91. Macedonia, Republic Export-Import, Trade and Business Directory
92. Madagascar Export-Import, Trade and Business Directory
93. Malaysia Export-Import, Trade and Business Directory
94. Malta Export-Import, Trade and Business Directory
95. Man Export-Import, Trade and Business Directory
96. Mauritius Export-Import, Trade and Business Directory
97. Mauritius Export-Import, Trade and Business Directory
98. Mexico Export-Import, Trade and Business Directory
99. Micronesia Export-Import, Trade and Business Directory
100. Moldova Export-Import, Trade and Business Directory
101. Monaco Export-Import, Trade and Business Directory
102. Mongolia Export-Import, Trade and Business Directory
103. Morocco Export-Import, Trade and Business Directory
104. Myanmar Export-Import, Trade and Business Directory
105. Namibia Export-Import, Trade and Business Directory
106. Netherlands Export-Import, Trade and Business Directory
107. New Caledonia Export-Import, Trade and Business Directory
108. New Zealand Export-Import, Trade and Business Directory
109. Nicaragua Export-Import, Trade and Business Directory
110. Nigeria Export-Import, Trade and Business Directory
111. Northern Mariana Islands Export-Import, Trade and Business Directory
112. Norway Export-Import, Trade and Business Directory
113. Pakistan Export-Import, Trade and Business Directory
114. Panama Export-Import, Trade and Business Directory
115. Peru Export-Import, Trade and Business Directory
116. Philippines Export-Import, Trade and Business Directory
117. Poland Export-Import, Trade and Business Directory
118. Portugal Export-Import, Trade and Business Directory
119. Romania Export-Import, Trade and Business Directory
120. Russia Export-Import, Trade and Business Directory
121. Samoa (American) Investment & Business Guide
122. Samoa (Western) Export-Import, Trade and Business Directory

123. Saudi Arabia Export-Import, Trade and Business Directory
124. Scotland Export-Import, Trade and Business Directory
125. Singapore Export-Import, Trade and Business Directory
126. Slovakia Export-Import, Trade and Business Directory
127. Slovenia Export-Import, Trade and Business Directory
128. South Africa Export-Import, Trade and Business Directory
129. Spain Export-Import, Trade and Business Directory
130. Sri Lanka Export-Import, Trade and Business Directory
131. St. Helena Export-Import, Trade and Business Directory
132. Sudan Export-Import, Trade and Business Directory
133. Suriname Export-Import, Trade and Business Directory
134. Sweden Export-Import, Trade and Business Directory
135. Switzerland Export-Import, Trade and Business Directory
136. Syria Export Import & Business Directory
137. Taiwan Export-Import, Trade and Business Directory
138. Tajikistan Export-Import, Trade and Business Directory
139. Thailand Export-Import, Trade and Business Directory
140. Tunisia Export-Import, Trade and Business Directory
141. Turkey Export-Import, Trade and Business Directory
142. Turkmenistan Export-Import, Trade and Business Directory
143. Uganda Export-Import, Trade and Business Directory
144. Ukraine Export-Import, Trade and Business Directory
145. United Arab Emirates Export-Import, Trade and Business Directory
146. United Kingdom Export-Import, Trade and Business Directory
147. United States Export-Import, Trade and Business Directory
148. Uruguay Export-Import, Trade and Business Directory
149. US Export-Import, Trade and Business Directory
150. Uzbekistan Export-Import, Trade and Business Directory
151. Venezuela Export-Import, Trade and Business Directory
152. Vietnam Export-Import, Trade and Business Directory
153. Yugoslavia Export-Import, Trade and Business Directory

www.ingramcontent.com/pod-product-compliance
Lightning Source LLC
LaVergne TN
LVHW080026210926
848481LV00011B/3115